Of Sh  Pa

A Book

By Nick and Sue Fenn

For Maureen
who also loved being
part of the Service,
Sue

A wandering minstrel I –
A thing of shreds and patches,
Of ballads, songs and snatches,
And dreamy lullaby.

CONTENTS

INTRODUCTION

A British Ambassador to Ireland was once asked by the *Irish Times* whether he would write his memoirs after retirement. Alan Goodison replied, "In my experience diplomatic memoirs are either superficial or disloyal. I have no intention of being either." We agree. So this is not a diplomatic memoir.

Diplomacy is easy to caricature. We are thought to spend time wining and dining, or exploring exotic places at the taxpayer's expense. Or we engage in solemn negotiations in the chancelleries of the world on the great issues of peace and war, prosperity and poverty, tyranny and freedom. In our thirty-seven years in the service of the Crown, we have indeed done these things. But this book is not about that. It exploits no privileged access, reveals no secrets, betrays no confidence. It is not about the foibles of the good and the great.

Instead it has two themes. First, we try to present what fun diplomacy is – what people we meet, what places we go to, what bizarre circumstances we find ourselves in. It includes moments of high excitement and many little incidents along the way. It tries to build a picture of our experience by incremental anecdote, leaving the story to speak for itself.

Secondly, we try to paint a portrait of a marriage and a family, engaging with all this excitement and diversity, coping with the challenge and reward of a nomadic life, speaking foreign languages and living in foreign cultures. We have travelled together in the countries of our assignment. Sue has made a point of learning the language wherever we went. For us it has been a partnership from beginning to end. We have done it together. Our different perceptions have enriched us both. We hope they have enriched this book.

Others have had more exotic experiences. Any British traveller overseas may encounter termites, snakes and cockroaches – possibly earthquakes, kidnap and assassination. He may trek in Nepal, drive

1

across the Sahara, go white-water rafting in the Ganges. All will be found here. He will meet some characters who have passed that way: a widow who celebrated the death of her husband by buying a bus ticket from Victoria coach station to Bombay; a lady from Hampshire who swept the streets of Burma for the Japanese through the Second World War; an old man who lived in a garage in the sub-Sahara; an Englishman in Burma accused of murdering his wife. Perhaps you are in business wanting to sell aero-engines in China, cornflakes in Ireland, power distribution equipment in Burma, financial services in India – we were there, advising those who came before you. You will meet three royal princesses: in Pagan in 1961, at the Taj Mahal in 1992, in Ladakh in 1995. We have been privileged to witness some stirring events. If you happen to want an eyewitness report on the events here chronicled, you may find fuller and more authoritative accounts elsewhere, but you will also find them here.

When British Ministers engage in foreign policy, they need someone on the ground to prepare the way, to meet them at the airport and give them a home base in which to meet their colleagues, to counsel them in private and escort them in public, to see them off when they leave and to follow up their work when they have gone. This is what diplomats are for.

We have been fortunate to have lived this life, full of unexpected encounters and diverse experiences, some of it exotic, dangerous or squalid. Our book, like our home in Kent, harbours the bric-a-brac of diplomacy.

These fragments are gathered in this book. We try to tell it like it was. That is to say, we tell it as we remember it, which may not be quite the same thing. No two recollections are identical. At least we made this journey together, sharing our impressions and judgements as we went. So we have written this book together, testing each of our ageing memories against the other. Where we have disagreed we have negotiated in diplomatic style, matching draft with counter-draft until we reached a consensus text to which neither of us objects.

The fall-back position was to publish his and hers on facing pages and leave the reader to judge between us. It never came to that. We both stand by the outcome. It may lack some of Nick's more flamboyant flights of fancy, and some of Sue's patient chronological detail. Each chapter reports one posting. Each begins with a few paragraphs reflecting our early impressions of the country in order to render the subsequent yarns intelligible. The book concludes with a few fragmentary reflections on the diplomatic life we shared for thirty-seven years.

It does not pretend to be history. It is not even narrative. It recounts the memorable bits of a journey that we travelled together. We hope that it conveys something of the life of professional nomads. We hope that it is fun.

Susan and Nicholas Fenn
Applecroft, 2012

Chapter 1
Preparation 1959–60

The story begins in 1959. War and austerity, Churchill, Eden and Suez were all behind us. The Indian Empire was gone, but large parts of the atlas were still coloured pink. The Edwardian figure of Harold Macmillan was Prime Minister. "Life, dear boy, life itself." And, "You never had it so good."

In April 1959 a nervous young man climbed the stairs to the entrance to Burlington House. He was received by a tall gentleman in a frock coat with a clipboard in his hand. "Mr Fenn?" he said. "Come this way, sir." He conducted the candidate down a long corridor with statues of ancestors on either hand, and showed him into an enormous library. In the middle was a round table. Seated at one side were seven distinguished persons. On the other side was a single chair. This was the final interview.

The questions were led by Sir Laurence Helsby, Chief Civil Service Commissioner. For twenty minutes he asked questions to which there was no wrong answer, about childhood in London, wartime evacuation to Dartmoor, about school and university, National Service in the RAF, travel, sports and interests. He lulled the young man into a false sense of security. They had already decided to accept or reject him. This was a formality. He began to enjoy himself. Sir Laurence made to pass the questioning to his neighbour, then seemed to change his mind. "One last question, Mr Fenn. Can you give me a succinct analysis of the issues at stake in the politics of the Horn of Africa?" Panic. Cape Horn? No, wrong continent. South Africa? He launched into a discussion of the Cameroon which he had recently read about in *The Economist*. Too late he realised that this was the wrong side of the continent. "I am sorry, sir," he said, "the answer to your question is 'no'." Two of the panel had the grace to laugh. But not Sir Laurence.

"I see," he said. The young man knew that he had failed.

But he had not failed. A few days later he got a courteous letter from Sir Laurence, offering him an appointment in Her Majesty's Diplomatic Service. This meant that he could afford to get married. He hastened to send a telegram to inform his fiancée.

A scarlet-gowned student came flying down South Street and into the hushed rooms of St Andrews University Library. She was bursting with excitement and waving a small yellow telegram. Her quarry was deep in her files, final exams looming. By the time she had focused on the message scores of eyes were looking at her. She blushed as she read: *Third Secretary Fenn requests pleasure company Miss Susan Russell at altar in August.* These few words changed her whole future. She had been preparing not only for biochemistry exams but to be the wife of a Presbyterian minister. The telegram was beckoning her into the unknown world of the diplomatic service.

Gathering her books, she made her way to the post office and asked for a telegram form. After much thought she wrote: *Miss Susan Russell accepts with pleasure the kind invitation of Third Secretary Fenn and looks forward to meeting him at the altar in four months' time.* The clerk scrutinised the paper and slowly totted up the words. He whistled and stated the price. Then he smiled. "But I don't think you'll mind paying it." And so she had agreed to this new adventure.

Her family seemed to approve her choice, summed up in a telegram a few days later from her grandfather after a family reunion: *The young man makes a favourable impression!* It was not foreign travel that worried her. She had been born in Hong Kong and raised in South China until the Japanese chased the family out. With her brother she had spent most of the war years with a foster family

5

in America. The thought of living overseas was exciting. She would enjoy learning about other cultures. It was the diplomatic niceties which were daunting – protocol, placement, stuff like that. She knew that she would get it wrong. But if that was part of the marriage bargain she was deeply in love and it was a price worth paying.

Her fears were confirmed at her first meeting of the Diplomatic Wives Association; everyone else was wearing a hat. There was a small compromise at the next meeting in the shape of a big velvet bow on the back of her head. Most of the talks, however, were full of practical advice from Dr Medvei, Chief Medical Adviser to the Diplomatic Service, about coping with tropical heat, or from other luminaries on where to obtain summer clothing in the English winter. But one alarming talk to young brides confirmed the impression that diplomats were expected to be from the top drawer. A brave young woman asked a question about visiting cards (we had all been issued with boxes of them) and was reassured. "Don't worry, you use them abroad exactly as you do in England." Susan went home and wept. Catastrophe. Nick must get another job before she disgraced him.

But she did not insist and he did not get another job. In late August an eager young man walked down Whitehall, turned right into Downing Street – then still open to the public – and left under the Foreign Office arch. He was reporting for duty.

During the selection process he must have filled in a dozen forms, each of which asked whether he was married or single. He had truthfully ticked "single". They never asked whether he was engaged, which he had been from the outset. Now on his desk was another form asking the same question. Proudly he ticked "married" and within the hour was summoned by the Director of Personnel. The personnel department at that time was housed in Carlton House Terrace the other side of the park. The house had been the residence of the German Ambassador before the war. The instructions on how to work the lift were still written in German. The Ambassador's magnificent ballroom had been chopped into cubicles where Nick's new colleagues were beavering away on the personnel requirements of the embassy in Mexico and other mysterious matters. At the end of the corridor stood the carved gilt ballroom doors. You flung these open – and went into the loo. Nobody but Nick seemed to think this was funny. He found the way to the director's office.

Without looking up from his papers, the director asked, "Who is this woman?"

"You mean my wife, sir?"

"Of course I mean your wife. Come here, sit down and tell me about her." For ten minutes they discussed Susan. The young man grew anxious.

"Excuse me, sir," he said, "is there some objection to new entrants being married?"

The director stood up. He was a tall man. He looked down his long nose and remarked, "A wife, like a foreign language, is a normal professional requirement. Which brings me to the point. You speak no known language. Which-language-would-you-like-to-learn-we'd-like-you-to-learn-Burmese," – all in one word like that.

The young man paused. Then, greatly daring, "I'd like to learn Chinese – if I am being given a choice."

"You're not," he said. So that is how we came to learn Burmese. We have never regretted it.

Nick was sent for an academic year to the School of Oriental and African Studies in London to learn the rudiments of Burmese. He was lucky on two counts. First, he studied under the direction of a scholar, Professor Hla Pe, whose diffident manner concealed immense erudition. He directed the preparation of a monumental Burmese-English Dictionary which had been begun in 1926 by Professor Stewart: they were still halfway through the first letter of the Burmese alphabet. Nick's daily teacher was a young woman,

Anna Allott, who had recently visited Burma and had become skilled in its language and enthusiastic for its culture. Fortunately, her zeal as a teacher was combined with the patience of a saint. The third member of the department was a young Oxford graduate, John Okell, subsequently lecturer in Burmese at SOAS, whose job was to assist in the gathering of words for the dictionary. He specialised in musical terms since he was a flautist, and Hla Pe proclaimed himself tone deaf.

The second piece of luck was to begin in London rather than Rangoon. British scholars under the Raj had taught the Burmese that their grammar was akin to Latin. The language was still presented in Burma under this grotesque disguise. Hla Pe knew better. Burmese at SOAS was almost without grammar, its substantive words linked by a range of particles, its complex script beautiful and its five tones the stuff of music. The original language was simple, limited and monosyllabic, the language of the paddy field. Ideas were conveyed by words borrowed from Pali, the language of the Buddhist scriptures, which in turn derived from Sanskrit – an Indo-European language, polysyllabic and non-tonal. Technology borrowed English words distorted by transliteration. Nick once puzzled over four words in a translation, each of which he knew but which together made no sense: "Ein Zin Ha Wa". Only when he spoke the words aloud did they reveal the name of the then President of the United States. Nick never learned to speak Burmese well, but he learned to love it and to be fascinated by its culture – and perhaps to understand a little of the way people think when they think in Burmese.

Meanwhile, next door in the physics department of Birkbeck College, Susan was working for Professor John Bernal, Dr Aaron Klug and Dr Kenneth Holmes on the structure of viruses using X-ray studies of crystals. It was an inspiring atmosphere and very funny. Every morning as they paddled around the ground floor lab they asked each other whether anyone had remembered to buy a bucket. The water which cooled the X-ray machine was poured by hand through a hosepipe coiled round the main chamber. The water had nowhere to go but the floor. Famous physicists associated with the

8

nuclear bomb wandered in and out – Aldous Huxley, Linus Pauling and friends of Professor Bernal in the British Communist Party. At a bibulous dinner in 1950, Pablo Picasso had drawn a mural of two angels on Bernal's living room wall. Officially the young biochemist was employed as a computer assistant. The work involved taking lots of figures up the road to the building in Tavistock Street where a time slot had been booked on the university computer which was the size of a house. The numbers were fed in and the results spewed out. These then had to be plotted to reveal for the very first time the actual shape of the Tomato Mosaic Virus. (Years later, as we flew back into Rangoon in 1982, there was a small announcement in the official Burmese newspaper that Dr Aaron Klug had won the Nobel Prize for that work at Birkbeck. At the time of writing, he and Nick are both Honorary Fellows of Peterhouse, Cambridge.)

In this role, Susan was earning for a twenty-two-hour week almost twice Nick's salary as a junior public servant. She could have had a distinguished career in science. But when in due course Nick was posted to Mandalay, it did not occur to either of them that she should not give it all up and travel with him as the consort of the British vice-consul. There was not much work in biochemistry available in Mandalay.

A surprising exposure to diplomatic excitement came through the visit to London in April 1960 of Sue's American foster father, Joe Johnson. The Four-Power Summit in Paris had come to a disastrous end. An American spy plane had been shot down over Russia and Kruschev was triumphant with righteous indignation. The Americans agreed with their European allies to apologise at the opening of the next meeting before the Russians had time to protest. President de Gaulle in the chair was to have begun the session by saying, "I believe that President Eisenhower has something to say to us." Instead he said, "Does any delegation have a statement to make?" Kruschev jumped in and made such an intemperate attack on the US that Eisenhower had to withdraw and the conference collapsed. President de Gaulle had scuppered the event. We shall never know whether he did so on purpose. This eyewitness account was intoxicating stuff. It drew us into the real world of diplomacy and away from student protest and the Campaign for Nuclear Disarmament.

We were invited by Vernon and Ruth Donnison to drive with them to Burma. He had been the last Chief Secretary of the government of British Burma and they were making a sentimental journey "home". We longed to accept. But it would make us three months late for our first job in the service. We chose the conventional route by Bibby Line steam ship from Liverpool. As it turned out, we were late anyway because of a strike in Colombo Harbour. We could perfectly well have gone to Burma by car.

The SS *Leicestershire* bore us and all our worldly goods at leisurely pace through the Mediterranean Sea and the Suez Canal, as the temperatures rose and we got fatter and fatter. We took thirty-six almost identical photographs of the canal. It bore the scars of recent conflict and stranded ships wallowed in the lakes. In Port Sudan we went to church with handsome young men from Southern Sudan who were working temporarily in the docks. We delighted in their lusty singing, their crisp white shirts, blue shorts and long thin legs. Their bare feet gleamed as they knelt to receive communion. Outside in the streets Sue was shocked by the splashes of bright red, apparently from bloody spittle; the chewing of red betel nut is ubiquitous east of Suez.

Our fellow passengers included many expats returning to Burma from long leave in the UK. Home leave, or furlough, was only every three to five years and air travel exceptional. All were eager to teach us about our destination. One couple had a nasty two-year-old boy whose chief delight was throwing other children's toys into the sea and laughing at their tears. We would willingly have despatched him to fetch them back. Nick's teacher from SOAS, John Okell, was on board, going to Burma to look for musical terminology for the dictionary project. David and Charmaine Ince with their delightful two-year-old daughter Ghiselle were on their way to run the Mission to Seamen in Rangoon. David was a talented painter; the chapel and

10

Mission house were soon adorned with huge paintings of biblical scenes and of Charmaine. We later asked David to be godfather to our firstborn Robert, and Nick became godfather to their Peter.

The dock strike in Colombo enabled us to explore Ceylon (as it still was). We hired a car to take us to Kandy. We had to pump up its tyres in every garage on the way home. We were late for dinner with a senator. His clever and beautiful daughter had been on the boat with us, returning from post-graduate training in England. Nick was rendered speechless by a chilli. His alimentary tract has been a problem ever since, but he does like hot curries.

After a pause in Trincomalee to swing some cars ashore, the next stop would be Rangoon. One day a cry brought us to the rail to watch the blue sea change to muddy brown; the Irrawaddy river had come to meet us. Next morning we reached the mouth of the delta and the first glimpse of the land with which our love affair continues. At sunset we gazed in wonder at the golden Shwedagon pagoda.

Chapter 2
Burmese Apprenticeship
1960-63

Burma is richly endowed by nature. With tropical agriculture in the plains and temperate agriculture in the hills, anything which will grow anywhere in the world will grow somewhere in Burma. Its teak forests are legendary. Its waters teem with fish. It is self-sufficient in energy. It has large deposits of minerals. It boasts 85% of the world's jade, 85% of its rubies, and many other precious stones. It should be the richest nation in Asia. Instead it is the sixth poorest on earth.

This owes something to the incompetence and greed of its rulers over the last half century. It also owes something to the people and their religion. Buddhism teaches *karma* and reincarnation. One's lot in life is the sum product of actions in previous existences. There is nothing to be done about it except, by exceptional piety, to earn better luck next time round. This leads to acceptance of things which Western minds would find intolerable. It also leads to a capacity for contentment which Western minds must envy.

Economically self-sufficient, and encircled by the mountains and the sea, Burma is a natural loner in the world. The Burmese monarchy shared with China the notion that their throne was the centre of the universe and all foreigners equally barbarians. When the Chinese looked out over the parapet they could see that it was so. When the Burmese looked out over the parapet they saw China, and then India – two of the world's great civilisations. Then they saw the British. Their self-image did not correspond with reality. So it was better not to look over the parapet. The one feature of General Ne Win's revolution in 1962 which was popular was its xenophobia. Burma wanted nothing better than to be left alone.

Independence was won in the crucible of the Second World War. The national hero, General Aung San, used the Japanese to get rid of the British and then the British to get rid of the Japanese, earning himself the Churchillian rebuke "double-dyed traitor". Aung San was assassinated along with most of his Cabinet in 1947 and Burma came to independence under the pious and temporising leadership of U Nu. There were communist and separatist rebellions which in 1950 had clamoured at the gates of Rangoon. But the state had survived by patience, conciliation and compromise. In 1960 Burma was still an engagingly inefficient parliamentary democracy, its people poor but not malnourished, its politics unstable, its culture cherished and admired, its leader accepted amongst the councils of the Non-Aligned Movement. It was a happy country in which to begin.

The SS *Leicestershire* steamed up the Rangoon river and dropped anchor opposite the Strand Hotel. It was hot and humid. The great stupa of the Shwedagon Pagoda towered over the city. We first encountered the distinctive smell of Burma – drains and fish paste and frangipani flowers. Rangoon was strange and exotic – but also familiar. From the deck we could see the Union flag outside the British Embassy. It was a large building with more than 50 UK-based staff. (When Nick became Ambassador in 1982 he had a staff of eight. The present Ambassador has a staff of three.) In 1960, Sir Richard Allen had two counsellors overseeing eight colleagues in the political section, five in the commercial section, military, naval and air attaches and their staffs, with separate sections for consular affairs, information and administration. It is hard to remember what we all did.

A young colleague, Martin Morland – twenty-five years later Nick's successor as Ambassador in Rangoon – came on board to meet and brief us. He took us to the Strand Hotel where we were to stay until our car was unloaded so that we could drive north to Mandalay. A few days later the political counsellor, Dick Slater, took pity on us and invited us to stay with his rumbustious family. The children had a camp on the landing where we all assembled for a

13

conference before dinner. The password was "lollipops". The British service takes care of new arrivals.

Dick's wife Barbara took Nick aside at the beginning of a lunch party to ask him to look after one pretty young lady guest who did not speak English. He stammered through the conventional Burmese greetings. Everyone laughed. The lady was the daughter of the editor of the English language daily; her English was better than Nick's.

Before the *Leicestershire* sailed, the Ambassador went on board to lunch with the captain as convention required. Two years later his successor, Gordon Whitteridge, fulfilled the same customary obligation. As he left he noticed in the scuppers a cufflink box that looked very like his own. In due course his baggage crate was delivered to the residence. It was almost empty.

Mr Vice-Consul Fenton summoned Nick to coffee in his flat on the top floor of the embassy. We would be all right in Upper Burma, he opined, so long as we never ate anything that was not out of a tin. Mr Vice-Consul Fenton had never left Rangoon. Two days later we set off in our Morris 1000 Traveller Estate to drive the 450 miles north to Mandalay.

The road was full of potholes. At first it ran on a high embankment with paddy fields on either side. There was a lower track beside it for bullock carts to creak their slow progress from village to village. Wonderful old trees spread their wide branches to protect the traveller from the scorching sun. From time to time there were simple roofed platforms of wood and bamboo for travellers to rest in. There seemed to be very few people. But when we stopped to picnic we were surrounded by peasants who settled down to watch us. We ate our strange foreign food as quickly as possible and worked out a strategy to secure privacy after lunch.

Some of the village houses were on stilts with boats embedded in the dry mud. It must have looked different in the monsoon. At Pegu we made a quick visit to the pagoda – once clockwise round the bell-

14

like stupa – and then hurried on towards Toungoo. It took some time to find the bungalow of the public works department where we were to spend the night; three empty rooms and a verandah on stilts. We located nails from which to hang our mosquito nets and unpacked our bedding rolls with thin kapok mattresses and vestigial pillows. In the bathroom were three pots full of clean cold water, with shiny metal bowls for water pouring and plenty of holes in the floor. The latrine was at the far end of the compound. There was probably a caretaker but he did not appear. Mindful of Mr Vice-Consul Fenton, we ate for the last time out of tins. Later it became our routine when arriving in a new town in Burma to ask for the Chinese restaurant. We were often asked, "Red Chinese or White Chinese?" We would reply that politics did not matter. Which had the best food? It was usually red.

North of Toungoo the countryside became dustier. There were whitewashed stupas on every hilltop. The road surface had broken away at the edges so we had to play chicken with oncoming vehicles and hoot in frustration behind slow-moving traffic. Heavy lorries had a man at the back with an electric bell to tell the driver to pull over, but he was usually asleep so progress was slow. It is hard to hurry in Burma. The people were smiling and welcoming, often puzzled by Nick's rudimentary Burmese. All wore the national dress, the *longyi*, the Burmese version of the sarong. The women had flowers in their hair and *thanaka* paste on their cheeks which doubled as sunscreen and perfume. The traditional kiss is a sniff on the cheek. But it is bad manners to display emotion in public. Even thanks should be perfunctory because gratitude diminishes the merit earned by the giver. We had so much to learn.

The highway led into Mandalay past the airport and up to the walls of the moat around "the fort", once the palace of the last kings of Burma and in 1960 the headquarters of Burma army, Northern Command. On the corner of the main street was a banner proclaiming "Be kind to animals by not eating them".

We were to stay with John Slimming, British Information Officer in Upper Burma, and his tiny Malaysian Chinese wife, Lucy. They lived in a big house on Civil Lines off the south-east corner of the moat.

John was a character out of a novel, a chain-smoking, hard-drinking womaniser with a heart of gold. He had no time for the stray dogs which infested the city. He would be summoned to deal with a rabid dog since in theory no Buddhist would take a life under any circumstances. In the evenings he would report how many dogs he had hit as he drove like a maniac around his district. Once he got two at once – they were copulating. "Oh," said Lucy, "what a wonderful moment to die."

John once failed to recognise a Burmese colonel in his swimming trunks. The colonel commented bitterly, "I know, we Asians are all alike to you."

John replied at once, "I'm sorry, Colonel, but there is one I can tell from all the others – I don't think you've met my wife?"

The Commissioner-General for South East Asia came to open John's new British Library in Mandalay. In his speech he constantly referred to John as "Mr Slimmer". John in his reply could not resist comment. He was glad to note that having been slimming all his life he had finally become slimmer.

Back at the ranch Lucy and Sue were entertaining the aircrew, competing with them to empty a yard of ale in a single draught.

The convention was that when the temperature rose above 112 degrees Fahrenheit we would go out and play badminton in the sun because it was so marvellous when we stopped. Then we would lie on the marble floor and drink Bloody Marys. Unfortunately, Sue thought it was straight tomato juice and had to be put to bed. She slept for seventeen hours.

16

An unexpected visitor was a British lady of a certain age, Mrs Marjorie Alexander. She arrived alone by bus from Harpenden. Her reaction to her husband's death had been to go to Victoria coach station and buy a ticket to Bombay.

Two good friends of the Slimmings were a pair of UN leprologists. They were visiting every school in Mandalay to test for leprosy. The few who were infectious were removed. Others who tested positive were told they had a vitamin deficiency and put on a course of drugs supervised by the school. Andre Nousitou and Jacques Mallac believed that those children would be the last generation to suffer from this scourge. Look at it now.

Nick's real job was to learn the language. But he was also a "virtual vice-consul" with a big desk in the British Information Service office at which he sat for about an hour a week. Previous language students had stayed with a grand old scion of the Burmese royal house, Ma Ma Gyi Tokegale. We were lucky. We negotiated an arrangement with the University of Mandalay. We would teach spoken English two days a week and live in a house on the university estate.

We went to see the house. It was a concrete box surrounded by two feet of water with no access road and no boat. The university nightwatchman was squatting in it with his old mother. There were chickens in the bedroom and a sheep in the bathroom. We stayed for a week or two longer with John and Lucy Slimming.

The personnel services department of the Foreign Office wrote a snooty letter. An allowance was payable to officers newly arrived in post for the first six weeks only. Thereafter, they were expected to move into their own accommodation on a lower scale of allowance "except in very exceptional circumstances". Nick reported the condition of our house: the moat, the squatters, the chickens and the sheep. This was the situation, he concluded, but we were new to the service and could not say whether the circumstances were exceptional. The Office had the grace to reply. Not only was the allowance approved, but it would set a standard against which all subsequent applications would be judged.

We tackled for the first time the perennial problem of appointing servants. A nice young man named Aung Hla came to the Slimmings' house as a candidate cook under the beady eye of the butler, Rosario, as waggish a rogue as ever lived. For dessert Aung Hla offered evaporated milk, neat in brandy glasses. John quizzed Rosario, "What is this?"

Without a flicker, Rosario replied, "Independence Pudding, sir." Aung Hla did not get the job. He was appointed houseboy instead. He came from the Methodist Mission and had no experience of alcohol. Our first guests asked for gin and tonic and received a tumbler full of gin with a dash of tonic.

Everyone told us not to employ in the same household a Burman Buddhist houseboy and an Indian Catholic cook. We engaged Aung Hla because he was recommended by the local church. We employed Simon because his wife was the best teller of Burmese ghost stories that we had encountered.

One day there appeared in our kitchen a banded krait, so named because of the black and gold bands across its body. It is by reputation the most deadly snake in Burma – if you are bitten you die. But it does not attack humans intentionally – only if you step on it by mistake in the dark. And it lives on other snakes. So some Burmans keep them in their compound because then they know that they have only one snake to fear. The delicate question arose which of our two staff should deal with the banded krait. To Aung Hla it seemed obvious: as a Buddhist he was not permitted to kill; as a Catholic, Simon not only killed animals but ate them. Moreover, the kitchen was Simon's empire and the snake was in the kitchen. Simon took a different view, he was the senior servant, he had instructed Aung Hla to kill the snake and Aung Hla was guilty of insubordination. Eventually, Aung Hla lost his temper, seized a broom and slew the snake. Immediately, the Catholic rounded on the

Buddhist, pointed a quavering finger and declared, "Mr Buddha will be very angry with you."

Aung Hla was afraid. The next morning at breakfast he was nowhere to be seen. Simon said with a smirk that Mr Buddha was angry. Aung Hla was in bed with a temperature of 105. Sheer terror. At least that was Sue's diagnosis. She gave him aspirin. She sponged him until his temperature went down and sent him back to work. In an hour or so he was fine. She had saved his life. She might have killed him.

The two men never got on. A few weeks later Simon attacked Aung Hla with a kitchen knife and had to be sacked.

When we moved out to the university we unpacked our broken wedding presents which had arrived by bullock cart and settled into a new kind of life. Our job was to teach spoken English to classes of seventy – noisy eager youths at the back of the class and shy giggly girls at the front. We learned to teach from the rear. We asked the class to repeat "oily-wily, oily-wily". The chant came back "wily-wily, wily-wily". We wanted to learn Burmese from our students, so at the end of every lesson we invited them home. "No 29, University Estate – any time." Nobody came. Teachers are on a pedestal and you do not visit them at home. But as exam time drew near one bold spirit came to the door. We welcomed him in and explained the ground rules: half an hour English in exchange for half an hour Burmese. After that they came at breakfast, lunch and dinner.

There were anti-American demonstrations in Burma. The army had overrun the camp of some KMT remnants in the Shan hills and found weapons with American markings. Nick was in town when the mob came to our house. Sue was in bed with a tummy bug and was woken by the shouting. Aung Hla was sent to find out what was going on. He came back, fear mixed with amusement on his face. "They say they will burn down the house because you are Americans." What price the Atlantic Alliance?

19

"Please tell them that we are not Americans." Aung Hla came back with the message that since we were only friends of the Americans they would burn down the garage. That seemed to put the UK in its proper place. Again the message was sent. The garage was empty and belonged to the university. They moved off in search of other prey without discovering that in the house next door there lived a real American, an elderly professor of zoology and his wife. While he was teaching she had learned to play the Burmese harp.

At the end of term we had the unenviable task of examining the students in spoken English. We were all a bit on edge after the demonstrations. In 1960 a pass in spoken English was a necessary pre-requisite for a degree in any subject. Many students had learned English on paper for years but had little practice speaking it; the trick was to break down the barriers of shyness. One student was clearly terrified of Sue. After some prodding he revealed that he had been the leader of the riots. He believed that she was American and would therefore fail him. Mercifully, he spoke English quite well so she was able to pass him. Otherwise he would have been convinced that he had failed for political reasons.

The university nightwatchman who had been squatting in our house when we arrived now lived with his old mother in a little wooden hut on the other side of some scruffy wasteland. He showed no resentment at having been displaced. Indeed, he seemed to watch over us with fatherly care. One evening he asked Sue to visit his sick mother. Entering the hut, she looked around for some sign of life and realised that the heap of cloth in the corner hid a tiny, shivering old woman. It was winter and night temperatures had fallen to near zero. Warm blankets were provided and hot Horlicks every evening. When the cold spell was over the blankets were returned in perfect order.

A few days later we had guests for lunch. The watchman appeared at our door – a huge, shiny, fat man wearing nothing but a dhoti and a wide grin, carrying in his bare hands a pile of dripping raw meat. "A cow fell into a hole," he explained, "and had to be slaughtered, so I brought you some." A likely story! It was his way

20

of saying thank you for caring for his mother. The meat was probably illegal but impossible to refuse. (After the war the British administration had stopped the slaughter of cattle to build up the decimated herds. For religious reasons the Burmese Government had never repealed the law.)

John Okell came to live with us at the university. His hired jeep would not start on cold mornings, so the owner cycled three miles from the city just to coax it into life. John would go out each day to meet with local musicians by appointment to pursue his research into musical terms for the dictionary at SOAS. Most afternoons he would come back frustrated and out of his mind. The musicians were out, they were at a wedding or a funeral or visiting friends. John would race up to his room and slam the door. A few minutes later the house was filled with the soothing tones of his flute and we heaved a collective sigh of relief. Then he would come down wreathed in smiles and announce that he'd had a splendid day.

We had more minor stomach problems than usual. Sue suspected that the drinking water was not being boiled. Why should the servants bother if no one explained why it was necessary? A lesson in microbiology was required. She summoned the staff of three and, in a mixture of slow English and rudimentary Burmese, she tried to explain scientifically about germs, microbes, amoebae and other malign agents lurking in the water. Three blank faces stared back respectfully. She was making no impression. The cook's wife Margaret offered to interpret. In a torrent of words and gestures she described the evil work of these demons who could only be driven out by long boiling. Soon all three were promising to boil the water for hours. After the two men left Sue thanked Margaret for her assistance and asked what she had said. Margaret beamed in triumph. "I told them about the spirits of the water," she said. "They'll boil the water now. But as for us, we are Christians, we don't have to believe in germs, do we!"

We struck up a friendship with Ludu U Hla, the charming and cultivated editor of the local communist newspaper *Ludu – The*

21

People. He wrote a beautiful Burmese style, at once elegant and simple, so that even we could understand it. Nick took to reading the communist newspaper in preference to the pretentious journals recommended by his masters in Rangoon.

U Hla did us the honour of lunching with us one day, together with the professor of Burmese at the university and other pundits. To our astonishment he wrote about the occasion in his column the following day, amused to find a young Englishman who was trying to learn his language and whose wife served excellent Burmese food. With much travail, Nick composed a careful letter of thanks for his kindness. This too appeared in *Ludu* with tactful corrections. Thus, began a public correspondence which greatly improved Nick's use of Burmese idiom.

We went to stay with friends in Hong Kong for Christmas. On return Nick composed for *Ludu* an account of our visit, including the contrast between the wealth of the skyscraper culture and the poverty of the refugees from communism who lived in shacks clinging to the hillside. We were pleased with ourselves for getting into a communist newspaper, this implicit reference to the failure of Chinese communism. Unfortunately, this passage was translated in Rangoon and included in the Ambassador's weekly summary of the Burmese language press. This drew a formal rebuke. British officials did not attack colonialism in communist newspapers. The correspondence with U Hla was more circumspect thereafter.

On social occasions in Mandalay we made a point of wearing Burmese dress as a compliment to our hosts. We learned to eat with our fingers. One evening Nick proudly wore his new silk *longyi*, which unfortunately came undone at the waist while he was eating. At the end of the meal he had to rise and cross the room to wash his right hand in a bowl, frantically trying with his left hand to keep his *longyi* from falling around his feet. Our hosts were helpless with laughter.

We took every opportunity to travel in Upper Burma. With John and Lucy Slimming we paid our first visit to Pagan, the spectacular ancient capital of Burma. In those days there were no hotels in Pagan; travelling officials from foreign countries were permitted to stay in "circuit houses", handsome, decaying wooden bungalows built to serve British circuit judges on tour. This could be a mixed blessing. On this occasion we were thrown out of the Circuit House in the middle of the night by army officers.

The British Information Service in Mandalay used to show British films from the back of a Land Rover in isolated villages – films like Princess Margaret's wedding and the Asian Games. We would sit amongst the crowd and hear the shocked intake of breath when the swimmers took off their tracksuits. Before a show we would wander around the village to advertise it. We were invited into several homes to share their evening meal. It is the custom to cook extra rice, partly to feed monks but also in case a stranger should come by.

One of our most popular films was *Burma Victory*, a documentary about the British reinvasion of Burma at the end of the Second World War. John Slimming once showed this film in the village square in Homalin on the Upper Chindwin River, through which the British army had advanced. Some of the villagers appeared in the film. Most had never seen a film before. There were points in the film where the bushes parted and a Japanese scout looked out of the jungle. When the film was over the screen was full of arrow holes.

Nats are animist, pre-Buddhist spirits of the countryside who co-exist in many Burmese minds with the sophisticated teachings of Buddhism. There are thirty-seven great *Nats* with a secure place in Buddhist mythology. But there are also local *Nats* in many Burmese villages. A friend took us into the mountains north-east of Mandalay to see the spectacular feat of railway engineering at the Goteik Gorge. Near the road between Maymyo and Goteik there is a village which contains a British *Nat*. In 1942 the retreating British army had passed this way. One sergeant had been wounded and was left behind. The villagers tended his wounds and hid him from the

23

Japanese. In turn he had placed at their disposal his university degree in engineering, designing an irrigation system which enhanced the profitability of their fields. He also knew a thing or two about first aid. They loved him.

But eventually he was betrayed, taken out of the village and shot under a banyan tree. His spirit lives in that tree. There is a small shrine in his honour. His army webbing belt and gleaming cap badge hang in the shrine together with a wooden rifle. And each morning they bring him not rice but a steaming mug of NAAFI tea. He is the British *Nat*. At least that is the story we were told.

We drove north from Mandalay to the most famous *Nat* Festival in Upper Burma. We watched the dancers of all sexes allow their bodices to be stuffed with bank notes by drunken admirers. The sweet juice of a fresh pineapple still conjures up a vivid scene, with loud music from the *Nat* shrines, lepers lining the paths to beg, and young men licensed for the day to be cheeky to girls and foreigners.

We visited Taunggyi, capital of the Shan State, where Daw Mi Mi Khaing ran a school for the sons of Shan princes and wrote illuminating books on life in Burma. Her husband Sao Sai Mong was himself a prince and Chief Education Officer of the State. Between them they could have overawed us, but they just made us welcome, took us for a family picnic and inspired us to dig deep into Burmese culture.

We went to Bhamo on the Chinese border to visit the White Fathers, magnificent Irish missionaries who would go off for sixteen days at a time into the mountains and jungles, taking nothing and eating little so as not to burden the villagers. When they returned to the mother house we witnessed them stoking up for the next journey. Soup was followed by fish and chips, then roast chicken and all the trimmings, and then curry and rice, sweet pudding and fruit. And we were expected to keep up with them. Anyone from the British Embassy was welcome, provided we brought a bottle of Irish whisky

– and if we hadn't an Irish, then to be sure two bottles of Scotch would do.

We travelled downriver on the ferry from Bhamo. The cook expected us to have the same prodigious appetites. This was a beautiful slow drift from one village to the next, with pastoral scenes to delight the eye, sometimes stuck for a few hours on a sandbank. We would stop to pick up passengers in jolly confusion, diverse local manufactures spread out along the banks of the river. Sue appointed herself sanitary engineer for the cabin class loos since no one else seemed to be responsible. They functioned sweetly throughout the trip.

As the temperature rose there were more and more violent dust storms. The Old Testament was being read in the Methodist Church one Sunday evening. At the words "and smoke filled the temple" a whirlwind hit the building with deafening noise and stifling dust. The stuff got into our eyes, ears and noses, into our clothes and between the pages of our books. We swore it got into the butter wrapped up inside the fridge.

In the middle of the hot season is the Burmese New Year, the Water Festival. Historically, this was an annual opportunity to pay respect to elders by sprinkling scented water on them out of a silver bowl. By 1960 it was fire hoses in the streets. Everyone rushed madly about in jeeps or rickshaws, hurling water at everyone else. It lasted strictly from dawn until twelve noon, on three consecutive days. Everyone was drenched. But of course it did not matter because everyone was hot.

Three of our students invited us to visit them at home in April. They lived in Pakokku on the Chindwin, notoriously the hottest place in Burma in the hottest month of the year. No matter. We went.

They met us at the airport with long faces. The Methodist missionary had said that their homes were not good enough for us; we must stay at the manse. We established that they, for their part, still hoped that we would stay with them. So we left our luggage at their house and went to pay our respects to our compatriots. We accepted their kind offer of scrambled eggs, cucumber sandwiches and tea. We ate at one end of the living room while the students sat on hard chairs against the wall at the other end. We declined the hospitality of the manse.

Back with the students we belatedly recalled a session we'd had with them the previous week when they had asked us to describe to them a day in the life of an Englishman in Burma. Nick had mentioned a glass of whisky before dinner; and there in our bedroom was a bottle of whisky which must have cost them a month's income. We had also mentioned that in the morning we took a bath – not a splash at the well but total immersion. And behind their house they had built a bathroom in our honour. All the children in the village knew of this phenomenon. As soon as we emerged from the house with our towels they came running to peer through the slats to see if we really took all our clothes off. Fortunately, their parents soon shooed them off and we took our baths in privacy.

We had been given a lesson in hospitality, and shortly afterwards the Methodist missionary was posted to Cornwall.

On the wall of our dining room in Kent hangs a *paya-ka*. It is the front of a chest in which the scriptures used to be kept, crudely framed in teak with the nails sticking out. It is a Burmese strip cartoon, made in relief out of clay and plaster, sealed with lacquer and adorned with gold leaf. It depicts the Buddha as a prince going out in his chariot and encountering the old man, the sick man and the monk, which was the experience that converted him. Then we see him in his palace, saying goodbye to his sleeping wife, with his babe suckling at her breast. Then he mounts his horse and leaves through the palace gate accompanied by his faithful servant, Myin Swe Maung San. The spirits of the forest lift the hooves of the horse lest they should wake his wife. He canters off into history on the next panel. On the lid he would have been depicted sitting cross-legged

26

under the banyan tree in his moment of enlightenment. It is a priceless possession.

We found it in a pigsty. We were visiting a friend in Momeik, a village twenty miles south of Mandalay. He was a pig farmer. After an unsuccessful academic career at the University of Mandalay, he conned the Australian Government into giving him three Australian sows and one boar under the Colombo Plan. He was cross-breeding these animals with local pigs to his great financial advantage. The smell was memorable.

As we walked among the sties, he caught Nick with his head on one side examining a curious piece of wood which formed a part of one wall. "Oh, yes," he said, "that's rather interesting. It's a *paya-ka.* Would you like it?" We said we would. "OK, you can have it on two conditions. First, find another piece of wood to fill that hole, and second, take it to my aunt in Mandalay to have it restored." We did as we were told. And the *paya-ka* still hangs in our dining room.

One rewarding feature of the diplomatic service is the way it brings us into contact with compatriots all over the world who have been left behind by history. When we travelled in Upper Burma we took the opportunity to fulfil this ancient consular function. So we called on Mrs Childers in Kalaw in the Southern Shan State.

Mrs Childers was the widow of a British army officer who had died in Burma in 1926. She and her niece had been on the first plane which failed to get out of Myitkyina in 1942. Her niece had been killed beside her and she had been sent by the Japanese to sweep the streets. At the end of the war she had gone back to her cottage, replanted her garden and resumed her life.

The view was spectacular. The garden was "made in Hampshire". The door was opened by her Indian manservant, first engaged when he was a lion tamer for the Kaiser in the Berlin zoo in 1912. He said, "Mummy will be with you directly," and showed us into a drawing room dominated by an ancient wireless, permanently tuned to the

27

BBC World Service. Last month's issue of *Tatler* lay on the table. Mrs Childers served cucumber sandwiches and tea from a silver teapot. We talked about this and that. She disapproved almost equally of post-war Britain and post-independence Burma. She still spoke not a word of Burmese and actually told us that "if you are not understood in English you shout." But her heart was in Kalaw and she would live and die there. By the time we rose to leave we had enjoyed her company, but had concluded that this dinosaur did not have much to teach us.

In the hall she gave us a copy of Teilhard de Chardin's *Phenomenon of Man*, which had then been published about six weeks. She had read and enjoyed it in French. Would we like to borrow it? It was one of the seminal philosophical works of its generation. We had misjudged Mrs Childers.

Through the good offices of John Okell we were invited to stay for two months with a Burmese family in the small town of Amarapura, another former royal capital on the Irrawaddy river about ten miles south of Mandalay. U Nyunt was a weaver and employed a dozen people on piece rate. Sometimes when money was short the looms would go clackety clack all night. Daw Mya Thaung was a superb cook. The family spoke no English. U Nyunt was a master storyteller. In the evenings friends would drop in to persuade him to tell us a story. Once he had begun, the word would spread and other neighbours would gather. U Nyunt would play all the characters: the king, the young prince, the ogre and the damsel in distress. Each tale was told with such vigour, such gestures and facial expressions, that even foreigners could understand it. Later the group would fall to discussing the universe – politics, religion, local issues. All opinions were welcome including our stumbling contributions and the views of young children. All were heard with the same grave attention. No one was ever put down.

The arrangements were simple. All the family slept on the floor of the main room with separate mosquito nets for Grandma, Mother and Father, the four children and for us. There was little furniture so we lived out of our suitcase. Delicious meals were cooked in an area outside the weaving shed, mostly in the open air, and Sue learned the secrets of Burmese cookery, including its diversity and the novel idea that fish paste and chilli were not indispensable.

There was a big concrete water bunker beside the house but personal washing was at the village well, a hundred yards down the dusty lane. The drill goes like this. Set off wearing a *longyi* carrying another clean one as well as soap and towel. Draw water from the well in the communal bucket, throw water over your head and then soap all over through the cotton *longyi*. Rinse thoroughly. Next comes the tricky bit. Slip the dry *longyi* over the head and then wriggle modestly out of the wet one until you can tie the dry one in place. The local kids all come to watch. Wash the wet *longyi* and go home in triumph.

The first time we tried this U Nyunt rushed after us with extra towels. "One towel for your face," he hissed, "one for your body and a third for your feet." We had been about to disgrace him in public. Later he explained. It is important for British visitors to get the washing right because the British are believed to be a dirty race. A hygiene leaflet was circulated at the end of the war. Translated from austerity Britain it began "You should try to take a bath at least once a week". Burmese people shower at least twice a day, more often in the hot season.

The local *Nat* Festival was held after the monsoon rains when the swollen Irrawaddy had flooded most of the area around Amarapura. It went on for days. One auspicious day was chosen for the whole Nyunt household to join the crowds as the images from the local shrine were taken out into deep water to be washed. Hundreds of painted sampans jostled in the water with upturned tails like colourful ducks and bright eyes on the bows. Smaller boats were packed with goods for sale including fried snacks, offerings for the *Nats* and toys for children. Our boatman would not push off until every place was filled, so we waited until a group of high-spirited youths jumped in, rocking the boat alarmingly. They splashed us and

29

each other and began to lark about. Adult remonstrance made no difference, but when the youngest child screamed in terror the boys were instantly contrite. They wooed her with sweets and little presents. Only when she smiled did they settle down to enjoy the occasion. This respect for children is characteristic. It is a common sight to see a young man sitting with his *longyi* stretched between his knees reading while a baby sleeps in his lap.

The youngest child in the family, Myint Myint Aye, developed boils on her back and legs. Her parents consulted the *Nat* and came home with a black, tar-like paste to apply to the boils. The boils got worse and the child became feverish. We offered to take her to our knowledgeable and kindly doctor in Mandalay but they were afraid of offending the *Nat Gadaw,* the old lady who presided over the shrine. Sue made a careful note of the symptoms and drove into town to consult Dr Guha. He prescribed an antibiotic in a delicious chocolate syrup. To our great relief Myint Myint Aye was allowed to take it. She loved it and was soon back to her bright cheerful self and the skin lesions swiftly healed. We asked whether they would consult Dr Guha next time. The parents replied that there was no doubt that it was the *Nat* who had cured her. Their son, however, later studied medicine and became a renowned physician in Burma.

By the time we came to Amarapura, Sue had discovered that she was pregnant. What joy. But she had to get up in the night and make her way through the weaving shed to the latrine at the far end of the compound, where her torch lit up a multitude of shiny brown cockroaches and once or twice a snake. Nick consulted our host who understood immediately. He came back from the market brandishing a large bright yellow enamel chamber pot with a lid which was placed at the foot of Sue's sleeping mat. That night she woke as usual, crept out from under the mosquito net and perched herself on the pot. The noise which followed was like an alarm bell. It drew giggles from the children. When she got back to bed each member of the family in turn crept out to share the fun. In the morning we could hardly lift the potty to take it to the latrine.

We have the warmest memories of our friends in Amarapura. They were hospitable to a fault and keen to share their language and their culture with us – at some risk to themselves. Anti-Imperialist slogans were scrawled in the dust on our car parked outside, and U Nyunt himself was accused by a communist neighbour of being a running-dog. We taught the children of the school to sing "Old Macdonald had a Farm". The onomatopoeic animal noises were an instant success. In 2006 we went back to Amarapura. The school children came out to greet us. After many school generations the words had been lost in the mists of time. But they sang the chorus lustily: "Ee-aye-ee-aye-oh!" We found the house. Myint Myint Aye now runs the family business. She greeted us by name and brought out a photograph of us with the family forty-five years ago to prove it.

Sue, being pregnant, flew back to Mandalay alone after a visit to Rangoon. The co-pilot kept coming back and staring out of the porthole beside her. She asked whether she could help. "Yes," he said, "keep an eye on that engine. My instruments say it is on fire." Sue kept an eye and arrived safely in Mandalay.

When the Slimmings went on leave, the Fenns moved in to caretake their residence in the city. After living happily in the village for two months, air conditioning and running water seemed desirable. We turned on the shower but nothing happened. We turned on the pump for the water tower and got a shower underneath it – the tank was full of holes. The ceiling fans worked slowly, so we turned on the air conditioner and the meter burst into flames. Life in the village seemed suddenly superior.

We were to supervise the redecoration of the house which had been commissioned by the Slimmings before they left. The colours seemed gratuitously garish. Nick demanded to see the colour chart. Sure enough the colours chosen matched the numbers of the colour codes – but the Mandalay sun had faded the colours on the chart. We asked the painters to match the colours and ignore the numbers.

One hot afternoon a Land Rover drove into the compound with British number plates. Four young British soldiers climbed out, desperate for a cold beer. They had driven over the border from India, already a rare feat in those days, navigating on the basis of a pre-war map which showed a tarred road all the way. The border was now closed and the jungle had taken over the road. They had expected to change traveller's cheques at the border and to buy petrol on the way – perhaps even a night in a hotel. Instead they had hacked and winched their way to Mandalay and were now keen to press on to rejoin their regiment in Singapore. The explanation for their privilege was that the father of one of them had been at staff college with General Ne Win.

We drove back to Rangoon in high monsoon, ignorantly choosing the alternative route which ran close to the Irrawaddy. The tributary rivers had no bridges, but there were causeways marked by stakes. Of course the local children moved the markers. The trick, we learned, was to negotiate first the cost of passage, then we would be guided through the flood in joyous procession. At the fifth or sixth river Nick tired of this blackmail and waved away the eager young hands. He felt his way along the causeway until just yards from the southern shore one front wheel fell into the water. He accelerated and just managed to get the front wheels out of the water before the engine died. The children cheered happily and we went on our way.

At one point a bridge had been washed away. There was a detour through the paddy field. But two laden lorries had slipped off the track and blocked the route. Dozens of trucks and carts were lined up on each side waiting for something to happen. Their drivers were playing cards. We negotiated. One tin of fifty Senior Service cigarettes for each of the fifteen drivers. They carried our little car across the river.

The next river was more challenging. A group of armed insurgents of unspecified allegiance jumped out of the bamboo and demanded to see our passes. We offered our passports and waited anxiously while they studied them upside down. Nick's Burmese intrigued but did not impress them. But they understood *"Byitisha Thanyoun"* – British Embassy. Eventually they waved us on and we breathed again.

We had been allocated a house in Rangoon, 40 Prome Road. We arrived late, dumped our luggage, told the staff who came out to welcome us that they could have the evening off and went out to a Chinese restaurant. When we got home and switched on the light in our bedroom we could hardly see beyond our hands. The air was thick with flying termites. Half a dozen large rats were catching them, sitting up on their hind quarters and eating them. Nick set off after the rats with a tennis racket, swiped one into the open lavatory bowl and pulled the chain. Another ran down a hole in the floor and Sue pulled a piece of furniture over it. Liberal application of flit produced piles of dead ants and we fell wearily into bed.

The next day the embassy pest control officer pronounced the house unfit for human habitation. We moved into a more attractive house down the road. No 467 Prome Road had been designed to resemble a small French chateau by a Burmese architect who had never been to France. It boasted a circular tower and a large reception room two storeys high, with a shady terrace and a wooden tiled roof which leaked in the monsoon so that we had to scatter buckets all over the floor. The bedroom was air conditioned and as the monsoon began friends brought their violins, electric equipment and rare books for storage. We had to draw the line at a grand piano.

The landlady lived with her husband in the small house behind ours, a remarkable lady of great determination. She claimed to be the first woman of any nationality to have ridden from London to Edinburgh on a motorbike. She was cross with us when we installed electricity in the servants' quarters to diminish the fire risk from the open candles. She knew that she would have to follow suit. Ignorant foreigners!

A few nights after we moved in Sue was woken by a pain on her arm. She tiptoed to the bathroom to inspect and found neat tooth

33

marks. She woke Nick to complain. He ignored the travails of his wife and sat bolt upright pointing an indignant finger and shouting "that rat's eating my hairbrush!" Once again he gave chase with a tennis racket, pursuing the animal round and round the room while Sue sat on the bed helpless with laughter. When Nick began to flag, she opened the door to the back stairs and let it out. It was never seen again. We supposed it had come to inspect its new neighbours from the Agricultural and Rural Development Corporation next door.

The director general of the ARDC was a jolly, spherical gentleman named U Pooh. He became a friend.

In 1961 an Australian agronomist came to the Irrawaddy Delta where the best rice in the world grew in a kind of wild profusion. He brought to Burma the benefits of the Green Revolution – new strains of paddy, new techniques for irrigation and fertilisation. He taught them, quite literally, how two blades of rice could grow where one had grown before. The villagers were delighted and eagerly adopted all the new methods. Two years later he went back to the delta to see the results. He found that indeed they had doubled the yield, but instead of doubling the production they had halved the acreage, so that they got the same amount of rice for half the work; they valued leisure more than wealth. They were pleased to have more time to sit under the palm tree discussing the universe. They were very good at it.

U Pooh was equal to the challenge. He introduced Western cosmetics into the village store. The younger women quickly developed a taste for make-up. They had ways of their own to make their husbands increase the family income to pay for these expensive foreign products. Little by little the lost acreage came back into production. U Pooh's statistics pleased the government and the Green Revolution prevailed in the delta.

The winter in Burma is lovely. From November to March we enjoyed the best of an English summer day every day guaranteed. In March it begins to get hot. In April it is very hot. In May we begin to

34

doubt our survival. We pray for rain. Every afternoon great clouds build up with the humidity close to 100%. But it does not rain. When eventually the monsoon bursts, it rains every day from June until November.

The first time we witnessed this phenomenon Nick was driving home from the office in Rangoon. It began to rain, great scattered drops on the windscreen. Then suddenly the skies opened. Nick had to stop the car for three reasons. The wipers could not keep up with the rain. The road was filling up with water until it was seeping under the doors of the car. Thirdly, the water was full of naked children rejoicing in the water. There was nothing for it but to get out and join them. His suit was ruined.

Two students that we had known in Mandalay came to call from Rangoon University across the road. We thought this was just a courtesy. But they had an urgent and perplexing question. Would Nick please explain (in Burmese of course) what Father Christmas had to do with Jesus Christ.

Nick's job was to run the modest British aid programme in Burma established under the Colombo Plan. Dozens of young Burmese officials, doctors and technicians went to Britain to complete their education. A handful of British experts came to Burma to share their skills with their Burmese colleagues – experts in diverse disciplines: medicine, engineering, town planning, prawn culture, even the husbandry of elephants.

Nick also looked after the aid work in Burma for four other Commonwealth countries that were not separately represented in Rangoon – Canada, New Zealand, Malaysia and Singapore. Canada paid for Nick's services by providing him with an excellent Canadian PA who was perfectly capable of running the five-nation programme without his help. Canada ran a capital aid programme for which we unfairly got the credit – until a Canadian bridge under construction turned turtle. Mercifully the accident happened in the lunch hour and no one was hurt. But Nick was summoned to the Foreign Ministry

35

that afternoon to receive a demand that the Canadians should pay to build the bridge up again. Nick sought authority from the Canadian Ambassador in Kuala Lumpur who was cross-accredited in Rangoon to promise that the bridge would be rebuilt at Canadian expense. The Ambassador replied, "Authority not, repeat not, approved. Please procrastinate." They paid up in the end.

Now that Nick had a proper job, Sue had to find herself something to do. In those days the wife of a British diplomat was not allowed to take paid employment as supporting her husband was considered a full-time job in itself. Even a voluntary job required the Ambassador's permission (and he had to report to the Foreign Office if he considered it appropriate to agree). But Sue was determined not to become a bridge-playing spouse. She hankered after something that would use her scientific knowledge without contravening the rules of the service. She walked into the Medical College at the southern end of Prome Road and asked for the biochemistry department. Dr Myint Thein kindly let her conduct his research programme while he got on with teaching and running the department. It was the perfect solution. Sue found herself opening half-frozen frogs to implant little taps in their dorsal aorta, part of a programme to examine what changes affect the gamma globulin in blood. Burmese blood has uniquely high levels and Dr Myint Thein hoped to discover why. One afternoon she asked a tall young man passing through the lab to give her a hand. He was extremely helpful. She later discovered that he was the foremost eye surgeon in the country.

Sue also got roped in by the British Council to do some readings for the Burmese Broadcasting Service. Unfortunately, General Ne Win happened to hear a production of Shakespeare's *Julius Caesar* and took offence. It was said at the time that he disapproved of the assassination of emperors, or mistook remarks about Caesar's wife as a criticism of his own wife. More likely he just did not like foreigners dominating the domestic radio. So he banned them.

However, he did enjoy English plays. He was a patron of the Rangoon Amateur Dramatic Society and used to sit in the front row on first nights at the Mayo Marine Club on Strand Road. We were both keen members taking parts in Shaw's *Arms and the Man*, *Picnic* and other productions. Nick particularly enjoyed playing opposite the beautiful daughter of the senior civil servant in the Ministry for Foreign Affairs, while Sue, pregnant, became rounder and rounder.

The Indian nanny of a British colleague was to visit India while her employer was on leave. Sue helped her to accumulate the necessary dossier of papers. The queuing began early each morning. Everything stopped at regular intervals as food sellers brought bowls of steaming noodles to the tables of the clerks. Sue and Jayakarma went round and round the offices, day after day, until eventually all was ready. Sue offered to take her and her family to the docks. She had twelve passengers in our little car.

The Donnisons, who had invited us to drive with them to Burma, asked us to employ their former butler. U Ba took over our household. He soon discovered that we were not as grand as his former master. At the end of the month when we had his wages ready we were told that he had disappeared. We imagine that he was too proud to work at such a lowly level, but too embarrassed to explain why.

The Ambassador asked Sue to help the French Ambassador with his spoken English. She went to his residence for an hour or so in the afternoon just to chat. M Morel Franco had a good grasp of grammar and vocabulary but had never practised much and found the Anglophone diplomacy of Rangoon a bit of a challenge. At social functions he would seek Sue out just to get launched.

One afternoon they discussed race relations. His Excellency did not think he was a racist. He would not be at all upset if his son were to marry an African – "provided, of course, that she was of the nobility. But if he married a French commoner I would disinherit him".

Sue also made friends with the young wife of an Indonesian diplomat but was forbidden to visit her when the Indonesians burnt down the British Embassy in Djakarta. Repeated appeals against this ruling brought a one-off concession: Sue could call through the back door from a side street to congratulate her on the birth of her first baby. It was the first time that diplomatic events had impinged in this personal way and it hurt.

The social round was lively with lunches and dinners, occasional dances and the Four Animal Game, a simple form of gambling hinging on the throw of a dice marked with cock, snake, dragon and pig. We went to a Beetle drive at the residence given in support of the Burma-Britain Association. No one told us that the home team were not supposed to win. Nick won. He went up to receive his prize from the ambassadress – a teak cigarette box which we still possess. Lady Allen graciously presented the prize, and hissed through her smile, "A great intellectual achievement, you bastard."

Farewell parties for special colleagues were always a challenge. One close Australian friend was known for his cavalier attitude towards diplomatic convention. So we organised in his honour the most formal dinner we could devise – black tie, elaborate menu, a different wine with each course and – by borrowing staff – a waiter with white gloves behind each chair. John was with difficulty persuaded to wear black tie. The illiterate cook was tested on each course for weeks in advance and the menu was drawn in pictures on the kitchen wall. It worked. The evening was a great success. Inevitably the cook got drunk on the leftover wine. But we could not sack him, it was his triumph.

At a diplomatic dinner party Sue was puzzled by her British neighbour holding forth on matters Burmese in an utterly ignorant manner. Gently, she corrected him. That night she asked Nick why he had kicked her under the table. "That man was talking nonsense," said Nick, "but we have been in Burma for eight months and he has been here for eight years. We must defer to his experience – at least in public."

Princess Alexandra came to Burma in 1961, her first solo royal visit and our first experience of royal protocol. As the Burmese language officer of the embassy, Nick was attached to her party as "Equerry Extraordinary", which meant general dogsbody and interpreter in case of necessity. We took her to the great Shwedagon pagoda. The chairman of the pagoda trustees, in his best silk *longyi* and *kaung baung*, addressed Her Royal Highness in a language that Nick had never heard before in his life. He wished the stones would open under him. Then he dimly recalled from SOAS that Burma had a special royal language used only for kings – and since there had not been a king in Burma since 1885 this language had fallen into disuse. He explained to the chairman in Burmese that the princess was a very democratic princess and would not be at all offended if he spoke to her in everyday Burmese. He promised to interpret it into royal English. The chairman smiled and addressed Her Royal Highness thereafter in fluent English!

The rat pack was in attendance. The royal correspondent of the *Daily Express* asked our information officer, "Who's the boy?"

"You mean the interpreter?"

"Yes, could I call him a young attaché?"

"Well, yes, I suppose so."

"He's not married is he?"

"Yes, and his wife is expecting a baby." Without a word the journalist tore the page from his notebook and looked for other angles.

The princess took tea with the President of Burma, His Excellency U Win Maung. This fell some way short of a gastronomic

39

experience. It naturally included the Burmese delicacy pickled tea. Back in her sitting room she exclaimed, "My God, what one does eat for Queen and country!"

Alexandra's tour of Upper Burma was personally directed by General Ne Win, then still Chief of Army Staff under Prime Minister U Nu. We went to Taunggyi, capital of the Shan state, and to the Inle Lake where she transferred from a motorboat onto a royal barge to be drawn across the lake by a hundred leg-rowers. Her household were anxious that she should not be photographed at this point in case some disaster should befall. The Shan State information officer was asked to take the rat pack in another boat by a circuitous route so that they would arrive just too late to see the princess boarding the barge. He interpreted this request with too much zeal and the British press missed the entire afternoon – probably the most photogenic of the tour.

We went to Mandalay and thence by river steamer overnight down the Irrawaddy river to Pagan, twelfth century capital of Burma where 4000 pagodas crowd the river bank in a space four miles square. The programme for the boat trip said "Dinner – Black Tie". The General was clearly smitten with the beautiful young princess. Nick duly emerged from his cabin to find the princess in slacks with a tight-fitting sweater and the General in a purple flowered shirt. The Ambassador declared that Fenn was overdressed. But Fenn had packed no alternative. He took off his jacket and rolled up his sleeves. We danced all night. And in the morning we paid less attention to the pagodas of Pagan than they deserved.

The President of Burma gave a ball on Alexandra's last night in Burma. It was a romantic and memorable evening – the last such party at Government House. Sue's crinoline wedding dress was skilfully enlarged by seven inches.

Sadly, the consul's wife died in childbirth. Newly married but of a certain age, Daphne Dugdale had supposed her changed shape was due to being in the tropics. She was five months pregnant before the truth dawned and she was terrified. Throughout the next four months Dr. Lusk's chief concern was to reassure her that all would be well. She made him promise that she could have a caesarean if she couldn't bear the labour pains. In the event it should have been an uncomplicated birth but she insisted on the operation. So, in the simple, basic theatre of the Prome Road Nursing Home, a baby girl, healthy and beautiful, was safely delivered. But alas a complication following the operation required a blood transfusion for the mother and no matching blood could be found. Two BOAC pilots who always flew together were on their way in from Mingaladon airport, the only donors with rhesus negative blood of the necessary group which could be located. They arrived too late. The Ambassador sent for Nick and offered to fly Sue to Singapore for her confinement. Sue indignantly declined.

The Colombo Plan programme was negotiated with the Burmese authorities on the occasion of the annual visit of Chris Mandeville, scientific adviser of the Overseas Development Administration. In effect, he was Nick's boss in London. Chris proposed to visit Rangoon in mid February 1962. Nick asked if it could be brought forward to avoid the birth of our first child. The scientific adviser reorganised his entire Asian tour and came two weeks early at the end of January. The birth was two weeks early. Chris awoke on 28 January 1962 to find an empty house. We had decamped to the Prome Road Nursing Home on the lake shore a mile up the road. Our son was born that afternoon. The following day, as long planned, the two men flew north to visit current projects and look for new ones, including a visit to the remote and inaccessible Chin Hills. Nick boasted in Upper Burma that he had a baby son called Geoffrey. When he got back to the nursing home he found that Sue was calling him Timothy. The name had to be registered within ten days of birth and he was eight days old. We agreed a short list of alternatives and decided that we would both say our first choice aloud as soon as Nick arrived in the morning. We both said "Robert". In practice he was known as "Robin" for the first eight years of his life.

41

A few weeks later Sue and Robin were back in the nursing home for routine checks. At three o'clock in the morning on 2 March 1962, Sue woke to feed the baby. A low rumbling sound came through the open window. Tanks? She looked out. There was an army jeep under the porch and guns in the bushes. She went to the night nurse and told her there had been a revolution. Then the doorbell rang. Together the two women descended the stairway to find a dozen rifles poking through the security grille. The tiny nurse demanded what they were doing. They were after another patient, Sao Sai Long, known as "Shorty", Sawbwa of Kengtung, hereditary ruler of a principality in the eastern Shan states. Despite the guns, the nurse insisted that she was not permitted to release a patient without the doctor's authority. She unlocked the gate while she telephoned him – and discovered that the lines were dead. She went to wake Matron. Baby Robin and his mother confronted this group of excited and frustrated soldiers. They had already tried to arrest Shorty at his home and were running late. On an impulse, Sue invited the men to hold the baby. The guns were stacked against the wall and all attention focused on the smiling infant. Rob's first diplomatic triumph. Sue told them his Burmese name (Aung Kyaw) which was the name of the first student "martyr" in the Burmese fight for independence. He had climbed a tree to watch a demonstration and was killed accidentally by a warning shot over the crowd.

The atmosphere changed abruptly when Matron arrived. But the soldiers had to carry out their orders. Shorty was brought downstairs, borne aloft on Matron's instructions on a sedan chair like the Maharaja he was. Sue asked anxiously if there was anything she could do for him. He gave a regal wave. "No thank you, my dear, this is just one of those things." And he was borne off into the night. At nine o'clock his family came to the nursing home to settle the bill. (Twenty years later he told us that he had been correctly treated. His only suffering was to be locked up for seven years without charge or trial, and without knowing whether he would ever be released.)

When the telephones were restored, Sue phoned Nick at home. He was still asleep and wondered why she had disturbed him at this ungodly hour. But when he looked out of the window and saw the tanks he was all attention. He established that his wife and son were unhurt and rang the Ambassador. And that is how the British Embassy was the first embassy in Rangoon to report the Burmese revolution. Some foreigners who saw the tanks thought that a film was being made. We knew better!

Sue was a member of our Parochial Church Council. After church one Sunday there was an extraordinary meeting. A Burmese naval officer asked for their prayers. He had been ordered to take command of one of the foreign banks that were to be nationalised the following day. He confessed that he was hopeless with money and left the family finances in the care of his wife. But he had to obey orders. How soon did Sue share this confidential information with her diplomat husband?

Nick got hepatitis and turned bright yellow. Recuperation was notoriously slow. The family went up to the cool hill station at Taunggyi and stayed in an embassy bungalow. One night when it was quite dark the shutters of the living room slowly opened and a handsome young man stepped into the room. He introduced himself as a rebel Shan prince and asked the British Government to support his cause. Nick replied that Burma was a sovereign state. There was no way his government would interfere in its internal affairs. He feared that the house might be surrounded and did not know what would happen next. He need not have worried. Once the young prince had been convinced that his mission was futile he gravely presented Nick with a beautiful and businesslike sword stick, bowed and went out into the night the way he had come.

We went on local leave to the seaside resort of Ngapali on the Indian ocean. One morning Nick hired a tiny sail boat and set off alone in a stiff breeze. He disappeared behind an island just as the wind dropped. He was away so long that the American Ambassador, who was also on holiday, fed Sue fresh oysters. She has never liked them since. Nick sat for a while under the tropical sun. He began to burn. So he got into the sea and began to swim, pushing the boat.

Then he got under the boat to shield himself from the sun. He began to feel queer and feared sunstroke. So he took off his bathing trunks and put them on his head. When he got to the shore he forgot that he was naked and stumbled onto the beach. Instead of a loving welcome, Sue ordered him back into the sea until he was properly dressed.

One night we won a hideous plastic table lamp at a whist drive. We fell into bed laughing and fighting over it. In the morning Sue knew that our second child was on the way. Charlie was born in June 1963.

Our lovely old nanny, Naw Ohn Bwint, came to Sue one day. She liked working for us, she said, but she was too old to look after two babies. Could her friend come to help her? So fat nanny arrived. After a few weeks fat nanny confessed that she was too fat to work so could her niece do the work for her? This was Naw Lay Hsi, known as Lacey, who had worked for a friend of ours in Mandalay until she was knifed one night for teasing the nightwatchman once too often. By the time she came to us in Rangoon she had recovered from her ordeal but bore terrible scars. She was a happy and playful young woman. She looked after Robin while fat nanny and old nanny took care of little Charlie. It was a perfect arrangement.

Our house was on the main road from the docks. Streams of bright new tractors chugged past our gate, often gifts from East European countries. Robin loved to watch them. "Tratter" was his first English word. He learned four languages simultaneously. He spoke English with us, Karen with his nanny, Urdu with the cook, and Burmese was the only common language of the household. Not only that, but he knew which language he should use with whom – so that whom else would not understand him. One afternoon he was chatting with nanny in Burmese when Nick came into the room. He smiled wickedly and switched into Karen because what he was saying to Naw Ohn Bwint was private.

Immediately opposite our house in Rangoon was the university campus, so student demonstrations were also a part of our lives – much as they had been in St Andrews and Cambridge. Sue often pushed the pram round the hostels across the road. One morning we awoke to find ourselves standing beside the boys' cots, aware that the house was shaking and tiles falling. We thought it was an earthquake. In fact the army had blown up the students' union, using ten times the necessary quantity of explosives. Windows were broken for miles around. Not a sign was left of the low building in which the independence of Burma had been planned, nor indeed of the students who had been inside it.

We were to leave Burma in November. We prepared our farewell party for Guy Fawkes Night, with fireworks and a bonfire with a guy hanging from a gibbet. Nick had sacrificed his old RAF khaki drill uniform to dress the guy. We hung Chinese lanterns in the trees and set up food stalls around the garden to serve noodles and hamburgers, curries and pancakes – something for all tastes. The rector of the university was amongst the guests. He was horrified. "Nick," he said, "I know that is Guy Fawkes, but there are 200 students at the gate who think it's the General. For God's sake cut it down and burn it before there is a riot."

The Ambassador asked Nick to record before we left his valedictory impressions of Burma under Ne Win. Nick wrote frankly. Subsequently, the fifty year rule was amended so that confidential state papers could become public after thirty years – even if their authors were still in service. If that memorandum had been published while Nick was Ambassador in Rangoon, he would have been discredited. Why do we inflict such silly rules upon ourselves in the name of open government?

Chapter 3
Private Office 1963–67

Nick was astonished in 1963 to be invited to join the Private Office of the Secretary of State for Foreign Affairs. This is the fulcrum of the Foreign Office where politics, diplomacy and administration meet. In 1963 it was busy with a range of key issues: the Cold War, the Atlantic Alliance, the nuclear deterrent and the wisdom or otherwise of a Multi-Lateral Force; relations with the United States in the context of Vietnam; the British approach to the EEC; the movement of British interests out from east of Suez and into Europe; decolonisation in Africa; the succession to Harold Macmillan as leader of the Conservative Party and Prime Minister of the United Kingdom. It seemed bizarre to appoint to such an office a raw young diplomat with no experience of Whitehall or Westminster, whose only accomplishment was knowledge of the Burmese language. It still seems odd.

This was also, of course, our first home posting. We were not allowed the luxury of a voyage home by ship. The Office had discovered by then that it was cheaper to fly than to pay us for six weeks to do nothing. So we flew by Comet 4 into a foggy London in November 1963. Charlie was six months old and Robin not quite two. They had never worn clothes except a nappy. Robin thought it was quite fun dressing up in shirt and sweater and coat – but then he wanted to take them all off again. We were all jet-lagged. Robin woke at three in the morning and demanded to go for a walk. In vain did we explain that it was dark and cold and foggy and that he would not like it. He was adamant. So Nick got dressed. He opened the front door. Robin put his head down and charged out into the night and immediately came charging back. "Too cold, Daddy," he announced. Nevertheless, we went for a walk, Robin snuggling under his father's coat with his little triangular face peering anxiously into the fog.

We met a lady walking her dog. "Young man," she said imperiously, "what are you doing out here at this hour with that child?" How to explain to a stranger in the middle of the night about Burma and the Comet 4 and jet lag?

Nick replied irritably, "Madam, what are you doing out here at this hour with that dog?" He strode home clutching his son.

Robin lost his quadrilingual skills as soon as we came home. He would never speak of Naw Ohn Bwint. Sue's father was a psychiatrist. He told us that this mental block was serious. Robin thought that his beloved nanny had abandoned him and would be distrustful of others. We must make him speak of her. So for three weeks we said, "Poor nanny, how sad that we had to leave her behind in Burma. She will be grieving for Robin."

Then suddenly Robin burst into tears, sobbed for an hour, and thereafter spoke happily of nanny and the things they had done together. "Poor nanny. Sad to leave her behind."

We were lucky to find the perfect home for our small family, a new terraced house in a cul-de-sac in a friendly village within easy commuting distance of Charing Cross. Sue and the boys settled down to domesticity with the many similar families around them. There were always other children to play with in the sandpit or on the large wooden climbing frame on the grass. As far as the family were concerned, Nick could have been working in the city or any Whitehall department. He caught an early train each morning and returned after the children were asleep. In the course of time the boys joined the playgroup in the village hall, and when he reached the great age of five Robin attended the local primary school. The weekends were precious.

Once we had scraped together just enough to buy the house (£8,200, plus a little for carpets and curtains) money was rather tight. But Sue managed on £5 a week not only to buy enough food, pay the chemist's bills and petrol for the Hillman Imp, but paid ten shillings once a week for a kind lady to help in the house and look after the boys while she went into Orpington or Sevenoaks for major shopping. She got involved in the local amateur dramatics group and joined the Women's Institute. Invitations to grand occasions in London included her from time to time, but for the most part her life was bound by the daily routine of bringing up the boys and supporting Nick in his demanding job.

Summer holidays were spent camping on the West coast of Scotland. As we drove up through the industrial Midlands and northern cities we realised that we knew rather more about the life of Amarapura than we knew about Wigan, although we had been representing Wigan in Amarapura these past three years.

The rest of this Chapter is by Nick alone.

There were four of us. The Principal Private Secretary was a person of consequence in the Office and an intimate confidant of the boss. Nicko Henderson was a remarkable man. His dishevelled appearance belied his intellect and culture. He was later Ambassador to Poland, Germany, France and the United States. Tom Bridges was a consummate public servant, son of the former Cabinet Secretary, a future Ambassador in Italy and active member of the House of Lords. Norman Young kept the Minister's diary. Then there was me, responsible for the social life of the Secretary of State and for liaison with the departments of the office dealing with Asia.

Sir Alec Douglas-Home had gone across the road to No 10 before I arrived. My first boss was the great liberal Tory, R A Butler, author of the 1944 Education Act. It was a privilege to serve such an exalted personage. He had unrivalled experience of Whitehall having held every major office of state except one. But he was tired, and twice disappointed for No 10. His wife Molly was stridently resentful.

RAB betrayed vanity but not resentment. He thought that he would have made a better Prime Minister than Alec Douglas-Home but was never openly disloyal. "A good man, Alec," he used to say.

At the time I thought I knew the reason why RAB was not Prime Minister. He seemed incapable of making up his mind. During the year that I served him he took not a single significant decision on his own responsibility. Issues would emerge from the box with some masterly evasion scrawled across the bottom. They would be left to the Permanent Secretary, Sir Harold Caccia, or sent across the road to the Prime Minister, or brought to Cabinet. They could never be pinned on RAB.

Looking back, I think that this judgement says more about the impatience of youth than the wisdom of the boss. RAB's indecision was often the result of calculation: it was not in the interests of the UK, or of the government, or of the Office, or of RAB, that the question should reach a conclusion. So he invented a series of expedients to ensure that no conclusion was reached. Often he was right. Some decisions, if adequately postponed, simply go away. Life moves on. And RAB would be admired for finessing yet another tricky situation.

My first impression was his compassion. I found him one day shaking his head over the headlines in the evening paper. The Great Train Robber, Ronald Biggs, had been sentenced to forty years in prison. "Too long," said RAB. "No one can sustain such a sentence. It would be better to be hanged. I used to be Home Secretary, you know, I understand these things."

One of the fattest files in circulation was entitled "Decanting the Foreign Office". There was a controversial proposal to rebuild the great Victorian edifice. I was wholeheartedly in favour. Those who want to preserve the Foreign Office do not have to work in it. It might be razed to the ground or reconstructed inside its splendid façade. In either case the question was where should the FO go while building was in progress? Someone proposed that we should oust the

49

MOD from part of its ugly modern building across Whitehall. The Secretary of State for Defence, Peter Thorneycroft, had a counter-proposal. In a long minute to the Foreign Secretary he offered the FO instead a disused aerodrome outside London. The minute came out of RAB's box with the laconic comment "No reply".

Cyprus was a key question of the time. It was a complex issue of foreign policy so the FO led in Whitehall. But the island itself was the responsibility not of the Foreign Office but of the still separate Commonwealth Relations Office whose Secretary of State was Duncan Sandys. RAB and Sandys disliked each other and at the crucial time were barely on speaking terms. There was persistent disagreement on what to say to the Americans and at the United Nations. RAB held a long meeting in his office with advisers from both departments. Sandys refused to attend but no decision could be reached without his concurrence. Lord Carrington, then Minister without Portfolio, was despatched along the corridor to the Commonwealth Office to consult Sandys. Three times he went to and fro. Three times he reported dissent. Eventually he flung open the door and announced to the expectant meeting, "The tennis ball is back."

RAB received the Soviet Minister for Trade – a formal meeting with advisers on both sides. It was courting season for the pigeons which thronged the narrow balcony outside the window. The noise was deafening and embarrassing. I was instructed to "do something about those pigeons". I summoned the Office housekeeper who arrived with what looked like an enormous tube of toothpaste. He squeezed a liberal coating of a revolting substance onto the balustrade. The pigeons vanished.

A week later was the Trooping of the Colour on Horseguards Parade. The Foreign Secretary's balcony provides a privileged view of the ceremony. RAB and Molly invited distinguished guests in morning coats. RAB sat on the toothpaste. I was instructed to remove it. He would tolerate the pigeons.

RAB's indiscretion was legendary. The general election of 1964 was approaching. The Office was busy preparing briefs for an incoming administration, whether Conservative, Labour or Liberal. RAB became more and more gloomy. He took opportunities to corner each of his Private Secretaries alone and asked us which way we were going to vote. No other Minister could conceivably have asked such a question. One day I reported to him that the political editor of the *Daily Express* had asked for an interview. "I don't suppose that you are going to vote for us, are you?" he asked casually. I was astonished. I said that I thought that the country needed a change. "I expect you are right," said RAB. "Please tell George Gale that I will see him on the train to Warrington tonight." The front page of the *Daily Express* the next morning carried an electrifying article reporting what RAB was alleged to have said to Gale on the train. He had been taking private soundings. The Tories would lose the election. The Prime Minister was wrong about disarmament. Alec Douglas-Home found Ted Heath, then President of the Board of Trade, "a bit of a bore". When I reached the office that morning the telephone was already ringing. It was the President of the Board of Trade.

On election night we invited the ladies of the Private Office to dinner. We decorated the chimney piece with the election portraits of the three party leaders: Alec Home, Harold Wilson and Joe Grimmond. When the Tories lost a crucial seat and the pollsters began to predict a Labour victory, the picture of Sir Alec Douglas-Home detached itself from the brickwork and floated gently into the fire. Someone burst into tears. We brought out the whisky. Labour won with a majority of five.

My first impression of the incoming Labour administration was that they did not trust the civil service. We had after all loyally served their opponents for "thirteen wasted years". In fact much of the service welcomed the chance to draw a line under some of the past and make a new beginning.

Labour in opposition had nurtured idealistic ideas about foreign policy of which they were disabused in office. They liked the UN more than NATO. They hankered after unilateral nuclear disarmament. They believed in the notion of solidarity amongst Social Democratic governments in Europe. An early decision was to impose a surcharge on industrial imports from partner countries in the European Free Trade Association, without the prior consultation required by the Stockholm agreement. There was a howl of protest. The new Foreign Secretary, Patrick Gordon Walker, went to Copenhagen to defend the decision at a meeting of EFTA Ministers. He got no support. But, to my surprise, he asked for a meeting with only those Ministers who were from Social Democratic administrations, the delegations of Sweden, Denmark, Norway and half the delegation of Austria. He appealed to them in the name of Social Democratic solidarity. They drank his whisky. They were polite and sympathetic. They agreed not to be rude in the communiqué. But they insisted that the measure was illegal and had to be rescinded within six months.

Patrick Gordon Walker was the only Foreign Secretary of modern times who was a member of neither House of Parliament. He had lost his seat at Smethwick in the general election, defeated in an openly racist local campaign. The Tories were so embarrassed that they agreed not to challenge his appointment on condition that he fought a by-election at the earliest opportunity. Frank Sorenson, the popular sitting member for Leyton, was duly ennobled and a by-election declared.

At the beginning of 1965 we moved the Private Office to the green room in Leyton Town Hall and commuted from Whitehall with red boxes of official papers. Patrick Gordon Walker was a good Foreign Secretary but not a natural parliamentary candidate. He could not kiss babies. He would come out of the fog looking like a dejected bloodhound, unwind his long "Dr Who" scarf, sit down at the Mayor's table and share with us a bowl of spaghetti. He brightened as we consulted him about the problems of the world. Then he would sigh, get up, and go out into the fog.

One day Nicko Henderson came back from one of these excursions to Leyton and told us that our boss would lose the Leyton by-election. We were incredulous. We had assumed that Transport House would choose a constituency that Labour could not lose. But the people of Leyton thought otherwise. They resented being used at the government's convenience. There was a strong anti-carpetbagger vote. Gordon Walker lost and had to resign. Harold Wilson's majority was reduced to three. And Michael Stewart became Foreign Secretary.

This was an unexpected choice. Stewart had been Secretary of State for Education and before that Shadow Minister of Housing. He was not widely travelled. He worried that he did not speak French. He was to surprise us all.

Foreign Secretaries each have a personal seal to be used in signing treaties. I asked him what design he would like on his seal. He replied, "A tree, of course. Revelation, Chapter 22, verse 2." I scurried off in search of a Bible. It said "And the leaves of the tree are for the healing of the nations".

A few weeks later Michael Stewart was invited to speak at the Oxford teach-in on Vietnam – an all-day debate in the Oxford Union. We advised him not to go. The House would be packed against him. He would be shouted down. He listened quietly and then said, "You forget, I was President of that Union. I will go. Write me a speech." South East Asia department served up a perfectly respectable official draft which went into his box. It came out untouched. I asked whether he would like us to cancel his engagements for the rest of the day so that he could work on the speech. He said no. Then I knew he was sunk.

Henry Cabot Lodge had come over to speak for the Americans. When Michael Stewart arrived Cabot Lodge had lost control of the House. They were baying for blood. The new Foreign Secretary rose to address the Union – and the nation on television – in the most unpropitious circumstances we could have imagined. He began in his usual, modest, practical style: These teach-ins were useful. He looked forward to the day when they could be held in Moscow and Hanoi as well as in Harvard and Oxford. The communists had invaded South Vietnam. The Americans were ready for talks without preconditions. He outlined a possible basis for a settlement. He said nothing new. It was recognisably the official speech. But he spoke without a note, transforming the text as he went along, and speaking from the heart. Within a few minutes he had the House eating out of his hand. They could see that for Michael Stewart the Vietnam War was not about the strategic balance of power or the domino theory, it was about peasants dying in paddy fields. He sat down to applause and answered hostile questions firmly and fluently for three quarters of an hour.

Sir Winston Churchill died and the world descended on London for his state funeral. Michael Stewart received his new colleagues from around the world at twenty minute intervals throughout that terrible weekend. Briefs were confined to one page of A4. We had one minute with the boss before each meeting to give him three points to make. He delivered these points with such skill that each of his visitors left with the impression that the new Foreign Secretary had made a special study of his country. The Queen entertained at Buckingham Palace the representatives of Commonwealth countries. The Secretary of State gave a lunch for other heads of delegation at Lancaster House. Moise Tshombe came from the Congo. His splendid silver star fell off his jacket on the steps and I had to pin it on again. Tshombe will make another appearance later in our story.

At home Sue and the boys watched the funeral on television. When the coffin was loaded onto the state barge, Susan shed a tear. Robin came across the room and climbed on her knee. "Never mind, Mummy, when you are dead we'll put you in a box like that."

Michael Stewart went to Djakarta – the first visit by a British Minister since confrontation. I travelled from the airport in the last car with the protocol officer. As we approached the centre of the city he became visibly agitated. "Mr Fenn," he said, "I have to show you the saddest sight in Indonesia. It is the British Embassy." The skeleton of the embassy building stood stark against the dying sun.

One job of the Junior Private Secretary on these visits was to attend to the dress of the Secretary of State. That night Michael Stewart attended the official Indonesian dinner in his carpet slippers. My fault.

President Frei of Chile paid a state visit to Britain. The Foreign Secretary was to give him a dinner. In the light of the long tradition of naval co-operation between the two countries, it was decided to give the dinner in the Painted Hall at the Royal Naval College, Greenwich. It fell to me to negotiate with the Admiral President of the college, who wanted to dominate the evening on his own patch. I had to insist that the Secretary of State and not the Admiral would sit in the State Chair. In exchange I conceded that the Admiral could nominate one third of the 276 guests. He nominated seventeen senior naval officers and seventy-five junior officers of the Women's Royal Naval Service. I took the seating plan home for the weekend and we had 276 little named and colour coded cards all over my study floor. Every time we did the plan it ended with rows of wrens at the bottom of the table. So we forgot about protocol and promoted the wrens. Everyone was happy. On the night, however, there was an unexpected three-line whip and almost all the Members of Parliament had to withdraw from the dinner. The seating plan had to be done all over again as the guests were arriving. The programme provided for the President to return to London by barge. But it was raining. I could not consult the Foreign Secretary in the middle of dinner. I cancelled the barge and laid on cars. The President was disappointed and Michael Stewart was dismayed. It was not my finest hour.

The government wished to give independence to British Guiana. The problem was that two thirds of its territory was claimed by Venezuela. We could not responsibly launch Guiana into sovereign independence with a territorial claim of that magnitude hanging over it. We had to persuade the government of Venezuela to abandon the claim or to agree to some mechanism for putting it on ice. The Foreign Secretary went to Geneva for a week to conduct bilateral negotiations with his Venezuelan colleague, Dr Irribarren. There were twelve people in the room. Dr Irribarren spoke for an hour in the style of an orator addressing a public meeting. Michael Stewart responded, rationally and quietly, for ten minutes. Then they adjourned for lunch. The same pattern was repeated morning and afternoon for three days. On the fourth morning my colleague who was with him noticed that the Secretary of State was taking careful notes as the Foreign Minister was speaking. He leaned forward eagerly. Was Stewart planning some subtle initiative to break the log-jam? Michael Stewart was translating his official briefs into Greek sonnets.

On 11 August 1966, HMG devalued the pound. The decision was taken at night by the Prime Minister and the Chancellor of the Exchequer. They did not consult George Brown, First Secretary of State for Economic Affairs, who could not immediately be found. George was furious. There was a row. Harold Wilson decided that George Brown and Michael Stewart should swap jobs. So on 12 August, when all self-respecting mandarins were on holiday, there arrived as Foreign Secretary one of the most remarkable men ever to have held that office. The Permanent Under Secretary, Sir Paul Gore-Booth, was in a caravan in France. The Principal Private Secretary, by then Murray MacLehose, later Governor of Hong Kong, was in his Scottish fastness. It fell to me to receive the new master on the steps of the Foreign Office on a Saturday morning. I showed him his office. He did not like it. For decades a portrait of King George III had hung over the mantelpiece. George Brown declared that the King was the least successful of his predecessors. "Bring me Palmerston." I spent the rest of the weekend scouring Whitehall for a picture of Palmerston.

George had arranged a holiday for the following three weeks in a villa on the cliffs above Kinsale in County Cork, lent to him by Jack Lynch, then the Irish Taoiseach. So twice a week I commuted by Aer

Lingus from Heathrow to Cork bearing the first offerings of the Foreign Office to its new master. Everything was wrong. The approach to the EEC was "pusillanimous". The policy on South East Asia was "insensitive". The approach to China, where the embassy in Peking was about to become a victim of the Cultural Revolution, was insufficiently robust. On the top of one box was a handwritten note from the PUS, hastily recalled from France, enclosing a telegram from the Consul General in Shanghai. The mob was at the gates. They had told the luckless consul that the royal coat of arms was an affront to Chinese dignity. If he did not take it down he would be roasted alive. He would be grateful for instructions. Paul's note informed the Secretary of State that he had instructed the Consul General to remove the coat of arms. George was furious. He told me to get the PUS on the telephone. I had never used an Irish telephone before and it took a little time, the Secretary of State pacing up and down. When at last I got through he seized the phone. "Paul," he bellowed, "you and I are both Irishmen. We don't haul down the Union flag anywhere, ever." Paul Gore-Booth countermanded his earlier telegram to Shanghai. The new instructions arrived too late to preserve the coat of arms and fry the Consul General.

George Brown was an enthusiastic European. He commissioned a full review of policy towards the EEC. Sir Con O'Neil prepared a comprehensive assessment which recommended that we should launch a new application to join the Union but predicted failure. That word was not in the Foreign Secretary's lexicon. He read the submission with mounting anger and eventually leapt to his feet and hit me with the file. No malice. Just frustration. I went for a walk along the cliffs. When I got back, George was contrite. I did not report this incident at the time, even to Murray MacLehose.

George Brown's handwriting was even worse than RAB's. He wrote in red ink all over the text of submissions which did not find favour. He used language that was deemed inappropriate to the public service. I became expert in excising this scrawl and replacing it with a short Private Secretary Minute "The Secretary of State was displeased with this submission".

57

George was a workaholic. He would come home from a dinner and work his way through his box. He expected his staff to keep the same hours. One Saturday night I got home after midnight, ate dinner and fell asleep. The telephone rang. Sue went downstairs to answer it. The night telephonist at the office said that the Secretary of State would like to speak to Mr Fenn. Sue gave the poor man a piece of her mind. "Does that man understand how impossible he is? Nick has been slaving away all day, a Saturday, when he should have been playing with his children. It is now after midnight. He is fast asleep. But hold on, I will wake him up, though it is totally unreasonable!"

Sleepily I took the call. "Nick," said the Secretary of State with unaccustomed meekness, "it's George. I am so sorry to trouble you…" He had heard every word. After that Sue had George Brown eating out of her hand.

He was an Anglo-Catholic. As he said himself, he needed the confessional. He once asked me whether I was a Christian. I replied that I had been brought up a Presbyterian but was now an Anglican. "Presbyterian!" he exclaimed, "that's not Christian. There is not much comfort in that."

George was to go to Moscow to solve the Vietnam War with his friend Gromyko. I had to tell him in the morning that he could not go because Moscow airport was fogbound. So, for the second time, he hit me. No malice. Just frustration. He was not about to be prevented from fulfilling his destiny by a little matter of fog. We went. We had breakfast with the Ambassador in Copenhagen and took off for Moscow in an aircraft of the Queen's Flight. Three times the Squadron Leader pilot tried to land at Moscow and three times he was told by air traffic control to overshoot. We were diverted to Leningrad. I suppose that the local authorities had about twenty minutes notice of the arrival of their distinguished guest. At Leningrad it was snowing but there was no fog. As we taxied to the remotest corner of the airfield, twelve long Zim limousines drove onto the tarmac and stony-faced gentlemen got out and stood to attention in the snow. George came down the steps, shook hands with each of them and got into the first car. Then the PUS, the Under Secretary, and so on. There were twelve cars and thirteen members of the delegation of which I was the junior. The last car sped off into the night leaving me in the snow on Leningrad Airport with thirteen boxes of British state secrets. The Soviet security people thought I was the funniest thing they had ever seen. We took the overnight train to Moscow and arrived for the talks unshaven, frozen stiff and without breakfast. It was my first visit behind the Iron Curtain.

We were in Paris. George got bored with a reception and tried to come home early. The Ambassador's car was not there. He took what he thought was a taxi. It was a French police car. When the Ambassador got home there was a blazing row. I tried to intervene but Murray MacLehose told me to go to bed. In the morning he said that it was his job to remonstrate with George Brown, not mine. The service owes Murray a greater debt than it ever knew. George used to call him "my gloomy Scot". As we left Paris, the Ambassador gave me a bottle of superb brandy. "To say thank you," he said. "You need it more than I do."

George Brown had the reputation of being a heavy drinker. This is not quite fair. He was one of those unfortunate people whose judgement is affected by one sherry. He did indeed behave uncouthly on social occasions. It is true that he once asked the Papal Nuncio to dance, mistaking him for a lady in a red dress. It became one of our functions to ensure that the Secretary of State took no major decisions after lunch. When I left the Private Office he gave me a photograph of himself – as was the custom – on which he had written, "Thank you for ten and a half exciting months: some time you must tell me about them".

I remember him as a figure out of a Greek tragedy – a great man with a fatal flaw. Having more to forgive than most of my colleagues, I claim the right to be fundamentally pro-George. He was an instinctive politician, whose decisions were taken by untutored intuition. Difficult for Mandarins, but often right, and always

59

courageous. I forgive him for two reasons. First, the Foreign Office is the kind of institution which needs occasionally to be picked up and shaken. Since the departure of Ernie Bevin we had had a series of chiefs who were rather like us. George was different. He shook us rigid. And did us a power of good. Second, on the fundamental question facing British foreign policy at the time – namely out from east of Suez and into Europe, he was 100% right – and only he could have picked up Harold Wilson and thrust him into Europe. We should honour his memory.

I shall always be grateful for four years in the Private Office under four such different Secretaries of State. A Private Secretary has a privileged role well above his station. He sees the papers, takes the record at meetings, gets to know the senior figures in the Office and the government, he sees foreign statesmen in action. He interprets the Minister to his department and the department to the Minister. He learns to have a foot in both camps and to be loyal to both masters. He wields disproportionate power. He tenders advice to the Minister every day, not in his own name but on behalf of the responsible officials. He needs to know their minds. He often has to speak in the name of the Secretary of State and must know his master so well that he does not have to ask before he does so. A good Private Secretary oils the wheels of state, ensuring that the Minister always knows what his officials recommend and officials always know what the Minister has decided. These two of course are not always the same. When the Minister overrules official advice it is the duty of the Private Secretary to uphold that decision, sometimes in the face of officials far his senior. Junior Private Secretaries need to unlearn the trappings of power as soon as they leave the Private Office.

We were posted to Algiers. I was sent alone to Tours on the Loire in central France, to "hone" my French. They speak "Oxford French" in Tours. I stayed in a mini-chateau just north of the river as a paying guest along with two beautiful Spanish girls and a German au pair. Our host was a Gaullist. He had an excellent cellar. He taught correspondence courses in fourteen languages. I wondered whether his other languages were as bad as his English.

President de Gaulle paid a state visit to Canada and delivered his famous toast at a state banquet in Quebec, "*vive Quebec libre*". Even my host, M Janelle, thought the old man had gone a bit far this time and for two or three days amity ruled in the household. Then de Gaulle came home early, because the Canadians very properly threw him out. He addressed the French nation on television – a caricature of himself with his piercing eyes and Gallic shrug. I thought it was funny. But Janelle fell on his knees before the television set demanding pardon of the master for having doubted him. We had a problem. That evening Janelle got out his finest claret. He rose unsteadily to his feet, looked me in the eye, lifted his glass and said "*vive Quebec libre*". What does a British diplomat do then? I did want that claret. I rose to my feet, looked him in the eye, raised my glass and said "*vive Quebec*". There was silence for a moment. Then, very slowly, Janelle extended his arm and we clinked glasses. Every evening thereafter for the next six weeks we went through that absurd ritual before drinking his best wines. My French improved rapidly.

A few days after my arrival, Mme Janelle was taken off in a green van and certified insane. M Janelle was kind enough to say that this had been building up for some time and it had nothing to do with my arrival. But what was he to do? Neither he nor the au pair could cook. Would my wife mind coming out for the rest of the summer to run the chateau? Susan arrived with the two little boys. The children slept in drawers. For four weeks Sue did the marketing, catering and cooking and we lived very well. In the end Janelle gave me a bill for board and lodging for all four of us!

I was abruptly summoned back to London for a personal meeting with the Secretary of State. Moise Tshombe, former President of the Congo, had been hijacked over the Mediterranean by a mad Belgian and taken to Algiers. The aircraft and the pilots were British. The Algerians assumed, wrongly, that it was a British plot. George

61

Brown demanded the immediate release of the pilots and their plane. The more fuss he made the more certain did the Algerians become that this was indeed a plot. Ministers do not jump up and down for *pilots*. George mobilised Marshal Tito. He mobilised the Pope. In desperation he mobilised Fenn. I was known to have been his Private Secretary and I was in any case going to Algiers. So I was to be his special emissary, entrusted with a letter in George's inimitable and illegible hand to be delivered personally to the President of Algeria, Houari Boumedienne. I knew just enough about diplomacy to realise that this was an utterly unrealistic scenario. George interrupted a meeting with his Minister of State for Disarmament, Lord Chalfont, to give me his personal instructions. Alun Chalfont looked on with a discreet grin while George delivered his tirade. I demurred, but George would brook no argument. I was to leave that evening.

We crossed France in a train with the letter burning a hole in my pocket. While we were asleep the Algerians, for their own reasons, released the pilots. I think George went to his grave believing that I did it!

Chapter 4
Algeria 1967–69

In 1967 Algeria had been independent for five years and was still recovering from the bloodiest colonial war in history. The Battle for Algiers, inflamed by the doctrines of Jean-Paul Sartre, had shocked the world by its ferocity. We felt a sharp edge to the hostility – quite different from the easy-going tolerance of Burma. Algerians complained that France had bequeathed them a "colonial agriculture"; splendid vineyards produced fine wines which Muslims could not drink. They sought to play a leading role in the counsels of the Third World, the Organisation of African Unity (OAU), the Arab League, the United Nations, the Group of Seventy-Seven, always stridently anti-Imperialist.

Strictly speaking, Algeria had never been a proper colony, it had been a part of metropolitan France for a hundred years. Even their anti-French slogans were shouted in French. Algerian Arabic is the patois of the Mahgreb. When President Boumedienne addressed his people on television – as he sometimes did for hours at a time – they had to go to the French language newspaper in the morning to find out what he had said. Houari Boumedienne had been educated in Cairo and spoke classical Arabic – a language which Algerians called "Egyptian".

In 1965 the antagonism against Europe and the West became specifically anti-British. Ian Smith, Prime Minister of the British colony of Rhodesia, made a Unilateral Declaration of Independence designed to preserve white minority rule. The OAU decided that all member states should break diplomatic relations with the UK. Together, with four others, Algeria actually did so. The British Ambassador, Sir Tom Bromley, was expelled. British interests in Algeria were placed under the protection of the Swiss Government.

63

The embassy became the British Interests Section of the Swiss Embassy. We kept our own office and communications with London, but our boss was the Swiss Ambassador who had to be kept informed of all matters of importance. Britain was in the doghouse. Algerian officials took every opportunity to rub our noses in it. We were in good company. For different (Middle Eastern) reasons the Algerians broke relations also with the United States and the Federal Republic of Germany, who also chose Switzerland as their protecting power. Four separate diplomatic offices in Algiers flew the Swiss flag. It was nicknamed *"L'Empire Suisse"*.

It was a hostile and unpleasant environment in which to live and work. An angry mob set out to burn the British Consulate. They made a mistake and attacked the offices of the British Council whose representative Bill McAlpine was lucky to escape with his life. The Algerian Minister for Tourism came for his regular English lesson the next day and was indignant to find the office closed.

There were consolations. Algiers is a fascinating city with its blend of Arabic, Berber and French culture, its mosques and markets and the curve of its natural harbour. Algeria is a beautiful country. There were unspoiled beaches along the Mediterranean coast and flourishing farms in the narrow coastal strip. The peaks of the Atlas mountains towered over the plains. Beyond the mountains lay the magic and menace of the great Sahara Desert. In spite of the professional problems we felt elated at the prospect.

Nick gave George Brown's personal letter to the Head of the British Interests Section, Simon Dawbarn. It was never mentioned again. A few months later Simon was posted to Athens and Nick became Head of Section.

We had read in the post-report about the crumbling Villa Gardner, formerly a home for retired British nannies and merchant seamen, which was to be our home for the next few years. We read in the British newspapers that our predecessors, the Kay family, had been thrown into the street in a wave of anti-British sentiment, and the

64

doors sealed against them. Fortunately this "little misunderstanding" was sorted out before we arrived. A small house at the bottom of our garden was still occupied by an Algerian family. Electricity for the whole compound was delivered through their meter. As long as we continued to pay the entire bill they did not bother us.

We were happy to put up with dark, gloomy rooms and mushrooms growing on the thick walls, rightly guessing that the house would be beautifully cool in summer. The big garden sloping down the hillside had geraniums and bougainvillea, a tall whispering palm tree and an orange tree just right for a treehouse. The shady terrace with a magnificent view of the bay had a tinkling fountain and colourful Moorish tiles decorating the windows and alcoves – it was a house with character.

We inherited a remarkable maid, Zorah, who ran the house with energy and enthusiasm, was a marvellous cook and was never put out by unexpected guests. British residents from the desert used to stay with us whenever they came to Algiers. Zorah always made them welcome whatever else was going on.

She had very few teeth. We offered to pay any dental bills, if she'd like to get them sorted out. (Former French employers, *Pieds Noirs,* had started treatment for her, pulling out most of her teeth, and then fled to France during the Battle for Algiers.) We took her to the embassy's recommended dentist. Months later, when she was comfortable with beautiful new dentures, we asked for the bill. The dentist who had seen her often and had exchanged stories of the independence struggle refused to charge anything. He told us it was a privilege to help a woman of such courage and integrity. We agreed.

She was a devout Muslim, arriving every morning wrapped in her white *burka* with a little white face mask trimmed with lace. She kept Ramadan but had views about those who kept it too strictly, allowing eager children to fast like an adult. She knew of cases where children had died as a result. She was adamant that the daily fast must be broken with soup first, then tea or water, and only later,

65

after about half an hour, more food – not straight into a feast of rich food as most families did. She made a superb *coq au vin* and would share it with us because the alcohol had all boiled off. She willingly cooked pork for us but would not eat it herself in any form. At big parties we always carefully labelled any food containing pork. Confident government officials would remove the label and wear it in their buttonhole while cheerfully consuming everything – including alcohol.

We loved Zorah dearly and she cared for us like a mother. Whenever we had a fever or a tummy upset she had a miraculous *tisane* to cure it, usually made from something in the garden. And she was eager to share her culture with us. Few Algerians invited foreigners into their homes. But Zorah invited Sue to a circumcision party in her block of flats where she met lots of Zohra's friends and neighbours. Two boys who had been circumcised were like little princes in white knee-length tunics, fussed over by everyone and enjoying being the centre of attention. Most of the women kept their boy babies quiet by masturbating them. There were of course no men present.

Zorah took Sue and our nanny to a "Turkish bath". It was an ancient building in the Kasbah. Having stripped off the three women joined the main group of naked bathers in the biggest hall. Most of the others were lolling around the steam source, or being rubbed by attendants. They were fat young brides preparing for marriage. All body hair was removed by rubbing with pumice and a green scouring powder. Weight loss was a bonus.

Up on the hill above the city neighbours shared our rambling complex of buildings, a British businessman Peter Jolly and his wife Joan, a French dentist and family, two retired spinster nurses, and the Haden family, British missionaries from the south who had retreated to Algiers during the troubles and were awaiting instructions. They had children the same age as ours and all five attended the International School where Mrs. Haden taught. Sue's first encounter with Peter and Joan was to confess that she had smashed into their car in the communal underground garage. Coming into it from brilliant sunlight, she did not see another car parked inside and ran straight into it. Not a good start. One day Mrs. Haden developed a horrible cold and came home early from school. Sue took her round "a swig" of hot water containing lemon juice, honey, cinnamon essence, soluble aspirin and a slug of whisky. When asked for the recipe of this amazing "cure" Sue did not mention the whisky, knowing the Hadens were teetotallers, and in any case could not obtain whisky.

The frequency of diplomatic evening engagements made it necessary for us to engage a nanny for the boys. We found a lively lass from Sidcup in Kent called Beverley. She nearly passed out when we had our inoculations together and she confessed that the sight of blood made her faint. One evening in Algiers as we were getting ready to go out to a diplomatic function, she knocked gently on our door and asked us to come with her. "It's not as bad as it looks," she said leading us into the bathroom. Five year old Charlie appeared to be sitting in a bath of blood, a bit shocked but hardly whimpering. "He slipped on the soap," Beverley explained as we lifted him up to be dried. At the hospital they assured us he had been a brave boy as they put seven stitches across the back of his small head. Once he had settled down in his own bed to sleep we rushed off late to a diplomatic function. A Scandinavian Ambassador scolded us for our late appearance, reminding us how "junior" we were. He apologised when we explained. A few weeks later the same man kindly invited us to his home for dinner. This time it was Robert who had to be taken to hospital after falling from our fountain. He was posing as Eros above the water and slipped. When Nick phoned to explain that we would be late, our host asked faintly how many sons we had.

Often when we got home from an evening on duty Beverley would still be reading to the boys who were fast asleep beside her. She loved their books having had none she could remember when she was their age. One terrible night she did not return from a party. She had gone out with a group of young people, mostly Algerians,

67

that she did not know very well. We phoned around but found no leads. At first light she phoned and asked Nick to come and pick her up. As she walked through the front door, bruised and scratched, her hair dishevelled, her clothes torn, she grinned and said, "It's not as bad as it looks. He didn't get me." Slowly the tale of kidnap and attempted rape came out – with a huge black eye to prove it – but she kept her sense of humour, talked it out, and was soon able to continue life as normal. But she once flew at Sue in a rage for saying she was enjoying life in Algeria. "No foreigner likes it!"

One of our first dinner parties at the Villa Gardner came to grief. The guest of honour was a Lebanese journalist working for Reuters. His American wife was heavily pregnant. As she took her place at the table her chair disintegrated beneath her. Anxiously, Nick lifted her to her feet and with a chivalrous flourish offered her his own chair. The back came away in his hand. Sue swore that we would entertain no more until we had new dining room furniture. Given the uncertain state of Anglo-Algerian relations, the Ministry of Public Building and Works was not enthusiastic. We borrowed the dining room chairs from the Ambassador's vacant residence. Fortunately, our chairs arrived just before the new Ambassador.

One of our first trips into the interior was to visit the Save the Children Fund team at a desert town called Messaad, about 300 miles south of Algiers. They allowed us and our two boys to sleep on the roof of the hospital. Waking at dawn we witnessed the whole world "catch fire" in the crimson sunrise. The staff had many problems not encountered elsewhere. A beautiful child was recovering from meningitis but they feared she would live; her brain had been damaged and the local staff told them that a beautiful girl with mental problems would only be used as a prostitute. Then the doctor decided to resign because the government would not back his TB eradication programme. In Nigeria, where he had worked before, nomads who did not finish the course of medication knew they stood to lose all government benefits. In Algeria people gave up treatment as soon as they felt better, thus establishing a strain of TB which could not be treated. Before he left however, the doctor took home at his own expense a small boy who had destroyed his food pipe by drinking bleach he thought was lemonade. The Algerians accepted that he would have to live the rest of his life in hospital where they fed him artificially. In England the oesophagus was replaced and the boy returned to his own village having acquired a taste for fish and chips.

The SCF midwife took Sue on her rounds and into the family homes to check the mothers and babies. In one large compound the proud father, aged seventy plus, was seated in a place of honour receiving a stream of well-wishers. In the corner of the courtyard we found a very young girl, his fifteenth wife, and her newborn twin boys. She was wearing her only dress, caked in blood and mud, covered in flies, ignored by the household. SCF had provided a cardboard box with a square of mosquito netting for the crib and a generous supply of Horlicks to nourish the mother. The circumstances were so miserable Sue was surprised and delighted to hear months later that mother and twins were flourishing.

One of those SCF nurses had a miraculous escape. Driving a Land Rover on the main road she must have hit sand on the tarmac. She regained consciousness to find her head in the hands of a young French doctor who happened to see the accident. He was a consultant who specialised in injuries to the neck. He held her head in the lifesaving position till someone else turned up and was able to call help. He oversaw the hospital treatment, still himself holding the broken neck safely. When Sue visited her in the hospital in Algiers she was all plastered up. Three months later she was back at work in Messaad.

Visitors from Britain had a good time. There are beaches for picnicking, Roman ruins to explore, the Atlas mountains and Sahara Desert. A Cambridge underwater archaeology team invited us to join them for a picnic dinner under the olive trees in the ruins of Tipasa, west of Algiers. Unfortunately, Nick was late home and drove off like a madman in the wrong direction. He would not admit he was lost until he drove into a field of cabbages. Under a full moon Sue gently reminded him it was their wedding anniversary. The students forgave him because this last day of their exploration had been a triumph. They had located the harbour walls of the ancient city's port in the last section of coast to be explored.

A visit by Sue's parents coincided with an uprising by part of the army against the government. The air force was sent to destroy a column of tanks approaching Algiers. But the instruction to diplomats to stay at home got lost for a month. Leaving the children at home with Beverley, we were able to drive a complete circle south of the Atlas mountains without being stopped. At a roadblock at Ouargla, 400 miles south, we could truthfully say that we were on our way back to Algiers. But the police produced lengthy forms for everyone to fill in. Well, not quite everyone. Sue and her mother did not count – they were only women – so sat smugly in the back of the car while the two "people" filled in the place and date of birth of their grandfathers.

We enjoyed the ruins of Timgad in warm sunshine. Small boys hawked Roman coins picked up in the dust. Quarrelsome families of storks on the hotel chimney pots kept us awake all night. The honeymoon suite had a bath the size of a modest swimming pool, but no water even to flush the loo. The best Roman ruins are at Djemila which means "beautiful", and they are. There was an enchanting hotel built round a cool courtyard with tinkling fountain and a huge vine to shade the dining tables. We could not help noticing that the modern plumbing was more primitive than the elaborate system in the ancient city. We sat sunning ourselves on comfortable loo seats in the public baths trying to imagine the conversations retired Roman legionaries would have had there.

Next time we set out for a picnic at Tipasa, just along the coast, we were stopped by a roadblock informing us that foreigners were not allowed to leave the city – the instruction issued a month earlier had just reached them. Sure enough the ban lasted another month.

With Nick's brother Barnaby we went camel riding on a visit to Wendy Campbell-Purdie, the "Woman against the Desert" at Bou Saada. Her heroic planting of trees had enabled her to harvest her first crop of barley. She was passionate about the micro-climate which trees can produce, and the urgent imperative to keep goats under control – an eco-missionary before her time. Alas, she also loved the bottle, and this and her loneliness were in the end her downfall. But not before she had made converts, even in Algeria, and some of her trees are still battling to keep the desert at bay. When we took another friend to visit her she generously laid on a *meschui* dinner – a whole young lamb cooked slowly on a spit with herb stuffing and spicy oil to baste it. It was served whole on a low table with the bleak head almost in our animal-loving friend's lap. The senior lady is invited to eat the eyes. The senior gentleman gets the testicles. With small sharp knives we hacked off delicious hunks of crisp meat eaten with freshly baked bread and Algerian wine, a feast indeed.

Near Biskra and the fabulous canyon, Balcons de Roufi – birthplace of the Algerian struggle for independence – are the ruins of a village called Baniane. A French doctor and his wife who were visiting the area learned of an appalling massacre of the inhabitants during the war and made up his mind to help the people. In the midst of the ruins they rebuilt the simple houses using local materials in such a way that they could be used as a hotel, provide jobs and income. We parked our car in the oasis under the palm trees and a young man appeared to carry our luggage up the steep pathway into the village. Our mud built room had minimal furniture made from palm trees. The floor mat and bedding were in vibrant colours. All, including the showers, were spotlessly clean. Dinner on a flat roof under the stars was delicious French cuisine using locally grown vegetables. The quiet and the brilliance of the stars overhead fixed this as one of our most memorable evenings in Algeria.

Home life was full of incident. A stray cat produced a litter of kittens in our cellar. Our French neighbours gave us a tortoise with a Union flag painted on the shell. Sue nearly ran over President

71

Boumedienne when he climbed out of a car almost under her wheels – that *would* have been a diplomatic incident! Shopping involved taking our own empty bottles for any liquids such as oil, wine or milk. Driving round town had an unexpected hazard. Men with mental problems were believed to be victims of French torture and were therefore heroes to be cherished. The traffic would suddenly stop for a deranged man standing, sitting or dancing in the middle of the road. Someone would gently lead him out of danger and the cars moved on.

We frequently joined the queues at the El Biar bakery to buy a special thick pizza as soon as it came out of the oven. Buying grapes one day Sue was offered a few to taste. Too late she became aware of envious eyes watching her. It was Ramadan and she was savouring forbidden fruit. Down by the old mosque in the old city was a row of fantastic fish restaurants where all the fish were laid out on marble slabs for the patrons to choose their meal. We became addicted to the local fish soup. We never discovered why one establishment was crowded for a few weeks and then another got all the custom. They seemed to take it in turns.

As in Burma, so in Algeria, we would carry a consular brief when we travelled outside the capital. In the oasis town of Biskra we called on an elderly Englishman who drew a minuscule pension through the embassy. He had been the proprietor of a substantial date farm in French Algeria. Rightly suspecting that foreigners would not be allowed to own such establishments after independence, he legally adopted an Algerian son and gave him the entire property. The Algerian family now lived in the big house and ran the farm. The old man was permitted to live alone in the garage. He did not complain.

We dined with an Algerian friend in his charming old villa in Blida, the city he represented in the assembly. He proudly told us that at the last election his agent had come an hour after polling began to congratulate him on winning – with 101% of the vote.

He had lived many years in New York before independence representing the Algerian liberation movement at the UN. He and his colleagues had very little money and there came a time when they were hungry and desperate. They pooled their remaining dimes and he set off to the Lower West side of Manhattan to gamble. He was remarkably successful. In the early morning he began to walk home. As he crossed Times Square a stranger asked him for a light. He produced his lighter and started to cross the street. A sudden fear made him feel in his pocket. No wallet. He raced after the man, pinned him to the wall, searched his pockets, removed the wallet and sent him fleeing down the street. When he got back to his companions he reported his triumphant mission, ending with his encounter in Times Square. He dived into his pocket and with a flourish produced... the stranger's wallet! His own, with all his winnings, was still deep inside his coat.

We always assumed that our phones were tapped. One day it was proved. Sue was trying to organise a family picnic with American friends. When they were cut off she stood for a moment, phone in hand, wondering whether to phone back at once or wait a few minutes. Then the entire conversation was played back to her. Someone had pressed the wrong button. The same thing happened years later in Peking. It taught us what trivia one talks in most telephone conversations.

We saw quite a lot of our American and European colleagues. A Spanish diplomat took us to a nightclub to see belly dancing and was amused that Nick soon fell fast asleep.

We travelled with German and Dutch friends across the desert to the Tassili mountains in the south-east to explore the ancient rock paintings there. The preparatory meetings included a Spanish couple until she found she was pregnant again. We spent a lot of time discussing family planning. Several friends were mixed Catholic/Protestant marriages, trying to accommodate the contradictory teaching of two strands of Christian faith.

Planning the trip was fun. The Dutch wanted a big breakfast, the Germans a big lunch, and we preferred a big dinner in the evening when there would be time to prepare and enjoy it. In the event, of course, we had three big meals a day all across the Sahara. In the mountains one of the hired donkeys carried nothing but wine.

On the first day out of Algiers one Land Rover turned back with clutch problems. The other vehicle stopped at a big oil town, In Amenas, for a thorough mechanical check before plunging off road and into dune land. We learned never to stop for the night after dark. We woke one morning to find that our campsite was in the middle of a dry river bed. A flash flood overnight would have washed us away. We threatened not to travel with the Dutch again because they were too clean – always washing in precious water. We were embarrassed on the way home when we met a posh French expedition, fashionably dressed and equipped with modern communications. We were scruffy, unshaven and with little more than basic camping gear and boxes of loo paper.

Our Algerian driver had never been into the Sahara before. He seemed to be muttering a prayer: *C'est mon pays, c'est vraiment mon pays?* – Is this really my country? We had to change a wheel in a sandstorm and the whole Land Rover, fully laden, fell off a jury-rigged "jack" balanced precariously on stones. The driver damaged his hand. We also hit a typical desert hazard. In the middle of the day there are no shadows to warn of holes in the sand. The leading Land Rover plunged into a deep hole at full tilt. From the following car it looked as if they had hit a mine. Sand flew in all directions as the car rose several feet in the air. We counted the people climbing out. No one was hurt but the front axle was bent. Miraculously the car managed to drive, slowly, the remaining miles to Djanet, the oasis from which we climbed into the mountains to see the rock paintings. By this time we were three days late. As we drove into town a rescue party was setting out to find us. We had complied with the Algerian rule that when driving in the desert one must report to police stations with an estimate of journey times. The rule had worked.

Also arriving were two motor bikes bearing mad Scotsmen, Ian Wilson and Martin Cruickshank, en route to Chad. Ian was preparing a PhD thesis at Reading University on crescent-shaped sand dunes and had advertised for a biker who could navigate with a sextant. We all stayed at the simple hotel while we prepared for our onward journeys. The cyclists were navigating with a school atlas with the whole of Africa on one page. We discovered that they did not have enough petrol to get them to the next town. We gave them twenty litres in a jerrycan but the only way they could carry it was to jettison twenty litres of water. They solved the problem by burying Martin's kilt in the sand and preparing a pirate's map to help them to find it on the way back. "The third rock from the left", it read. "Knock three times and ask for Abdullah". We did not seriously expect to see them again, but we invited them to dinner in Algiers on 13 December. They turned up at exactly the appointed time.

A former Mayor of Djanet, an Italian named Oswaldo, took us all under his wing. He still seemed to run everything from the garage to the bread supply. He had driven 500 miles to In Amenas to get French bread for a visiting Libyan military delegation. On his way home he had bagged an "illegal" gazelle and he sent round a leg to our hotel. Fortunately, our equipment included a pressure cooker. Oswaldo had three beautiful daughters. We wonder what became of them.

We hired a Tuareg guide to lead us to the paintings, making sure that one of the donkey men could translate from Tamachek into Arabic, while another translated from Arabic into French. Up on the plateau we moved camp every two days and were able to see many of the paintings, 3,000–5,000 years old. It was astonishing to observe lively artistic records of animals and people long gone. The paintings record their cultural evolution, from primitive religious icons through hunting scenes to great herds of buffalo, gracious court dances and elaborate hairstyles. One entire wall was covered in cattle; a cow could not survive for a week in that desert today. Then about three thousand years ago the standard of painting declines and the camel appears. You can "see" the desert advancing on these people.

75

We got home to Algiers after two weeks in the desert. Robert hurled himself into his father's arms and declared, "Daddy, Daddy, Daddy, Charles has got chicken pox, and oh, Daddy, you've *almost* got a beard." Nick shaved.

While Nick was away in the UK for his brother's funeral, Sue took the family for a trip to visit the western resort town of Bougie. She should not have gone without permission from the Foreign Ministry. The authority was repeatedly promised but never arrived. They were busy with an OAU Heads of Government meeting. So Sue went anyway with the two boys, Beverley, and a visiting friend from England. They had a marvellous weekend on the beach, probably doing too much swimming because Sue was sick all night and there was no running water in the hotel after ten at night. Next morning, as they were about to set off home, Beverley took the car to fill it with petrol. She returned with a police escort. The family had to go to the police station, angry, frightened and Sue feeling ill. When the officer in charge started to question them, Sue decided she could either burst into tears and play the weak woman, or assume a calm pose of righteous indignation and argue – and stretch her French. The police complaint was not the lack of permission to travel, but that Beverley had called the policeman "un béte". After about twenty minutes, while a curious crowd gathered outside the station, Sue managed to convince the police that the party was innocent of all charges, and that Beverley was owed an apology for the fright they had given her, which in turn had made her uncharacteristically rude to the policeman. The poor man was ordered to come in and apologise. Then we were all seen on our way, swearing undying friendship with the police and the Algerian people, and that we would come again soon to visit Bougie bringing Nick. The two small boys found the episode rather bewildering.

On a trip with the children round the western desert we took our new nanny, Elaine. Our first campsite was one of the most beautiful we ever discovered. Just over the top of the Atlas mountains, south of Mascara, there was a silver birch grove carpeted with wild flowers on the edge of a canyon with magnificent views south across the valley to the desert beyond. It was idyllic and we started to set up camp. Within minutes people began to arrive from nowhere and settle down to watch. There was no suggestion that they objected to us so we smiled and carried on. We cooked a meal, set the chairs and table and made up the beds inside the big frame tent. As we sat down to eat, a grave patriarchal figure stepped forward and addressed us in perfect French. He apologised for their rudeness. He hoped we would excuse them because they found us so astonishing. In a few minutes, he said, we had constructed before their very eyes a fully equipped house offering more comfort than they had ever seen. But he assured us we were welcome and that they would now leave us. We would not be disturbed. And so it proved. He clapped his hands and the audience disappeared. But we had to get up before dawn in order to have a little privacy as we knew the children would return as early as possible to watch us.

Next evening we camped on the western edge of the "Grand Erg Occidental" not far from Colomb Bechar (as it was still called). On the third night a sandstorm forced us to stop early and in the swirling dust we knew little of our surroundings. By morning light we discovered we were perched on the edge of a cliff above the town of Beni Abbes. The boys scared Sue by jumping off the cliff when she could not see that the sand below was piled up almost to the top. Far below us a camel fair was taking place and the noise was deafening. On that trip Elaine introduced us to reading aloud as a way to pass the time. For hundreds of miles there is nothing to see out of the window. We got through scores of books in this way.

When we stopped the car beyond Timimoun to explore a fort and the ancient irrigation system, an old man detached himself from a group of walkers and sat himself in our car. We had not a word in common but his instructions were clear. We were to drive him along the road to his village. When we got there he just got out and walked off. It was too dark to drive much further so we found a spot overlooking his home. As we got ready for bed we heard giggles. Nick switched on the headlights of the car and the gaggle of kids fled screaming into the darkness. Surprisingly, we had a completely peaceful night.

Halfway round the great circle of the erg we met our German friends and made a superb camp together in the middle of some massive dunes. While the adults cooked supper the children played happily, the youngest crawling slowly up and up the massive pile of sand following a beetle. When at last all seven children were asleep we sat a long time round a little fire under a canopy of brilliant stars, watching satellites move slowly overhead. Hours later, as we all slept, a fierce sandstorm struck. It flattened one tent and the children scrambled in to share our big frame tent. As the storm whirled around us we anchored the tent by piling sand as high as we could around the outside using plastic trays as shovels. Next morning the sand-laden wind still raging. We shared breakfast including hand-painted Easter eggs. A solitary camel came to seek refuge from the wind. He lay down with just his head inside our tent, calmly watching us eat, as the sandstorm continued to blast our camp. Sadly, that was the end of that expedition. There was no sign of the wind abating and everything was full of the fine apricot-coloured talc of the region.

On the main road just below the embassy there was a little whitewashed church. This had been the "English Church" in Algiers but had been closed at the time of the troubles. At first we went each Sunday to the Eglise Reformee, a French Protestant church well established in Algeria. We discovered however that there were quite a number of Christians who were not comfortable worshipping in French or Arabic. We conceived the idea of reopening the little building, not as an Anglican Church, but as a church for those of all Protestant denominations who would prefer to worship in the English language.

The Anglican Archbishop in Jerusalem was not enthusiastic but he did not forbid it. We formed a church council. Each of us in turn was responsible for arranging the service on a particular Sunday. We lassoed passing clergy. We had Anglicans, Presbyterians,

Methodists, Baptists, Mormons and others. If we could not find an ordained minister, we did it ourselves. Of course the service varied from Sunday to Sunday, but we built up a congregation. The curious thing was that within a few months we began to develop our own liturgy, which owed something to the *Book of Common Prayer* but much else besides. By the time we left Algeria, this was a flourishing little community.

We picnicked in the sand dunes beside the sea. We were not intending to spy but we observed a young Algerian with a lady shrouded in Muslim *burka* walking hand in hand along the shore. They looked this way and that. Believing herself to be unobserved, she shed her *burka* to reveal a stunning figure and tiny bikini. For ten minutes they frolicked together in the waves. Then she came out, resumed her uniform and went back to their car. Possibly an Algerian official with a French wife?

British girls sometimes fell in love with Algerian men at British universities and married without understanding the culture of Algeria. They would resent their subjection to their husbands – and even more to their mothers-in-law. Sometimes they were beaten. Occasionally they would run away and come by night to the house of the British consul, battered and abused. The consul's wife would always take them in, bathe their wounds and give them a meal and a bed. The consul would issue a temporary passport and take them to the airport in the morning to catch the first plane out of Algerian jurisdiction. This was a contravention of Algerian and international law. Was it wrong?

The Seychelles was still a British colony. The Chief Minister, James Mancham, came to Algeria to attend a meeting of the Organisation of African Unity. He was expected to make a stirring anti-British speech. Instead he paid graceful tribute to the generosity and integrity of British administration and the reluctance with which the territory was proceeding towards independence. He was invited to leave the country. He came to dinner with us on the way to the

79

airport and asked Nick to call at the conference centre the following day to collect his laundry.

An African Commonwealth representative berated Nick for British policies in Africa. The Ghanaian *Charge d'Affaires* rebuked him: "you cannot talk to this man like that – he's your father."

One consequence of the colonisation of Africa is the division of the continent into Anglophone and Francophone regions. European diplomats were used to acting informally as interpreters. Nick once found himself in this situation with two colleagues whom he did not know – the First Secretary from the embassy of Senegal and a pretty young lady from Ghana. About five minutes into the conversation he discovered to his chagrin that they were husband and wife. He apologised for his impertinence. But they were amused and we became friends. When we left Algeria some months later we had the pleasure of passing on to them a range of baby equipment, including a large old-fashioned pram, which the boys no longer needed.

The Soviet Union invaded Czechoslovakia in 1968. The Algerian media covered the Prague Spring exclusively from Soviet press releases. The brave young Czech *Charge d'Affaires* circulated a formal diplomatic note to other missions in Algiers declaring that his government had never invited the Soviet tanks into Czechoslovakia. On a social occasion, Nick was able to thank him for his courage. The next day he was recalled by his government and never seen again.

Nick's main job was to conduct with the Algerians two sets of parallel negotiations:

• in the *souk* in disguise with a Special Counsellor from the presidency, for the release of the "Tshombe aircraft" an HS125, call sign Golf Alpha Sierra November Uniform – GASNU.

• in the Foreign Ministry in collar and tie for the resumption of diplomatic relations between the UK and Algeria.

There was an unspoken agreement that these objectives must be achieved simultaneously. The British Government could not accept the resumption of relations while a British aircraft was held illegally. The Algerian Government would not release the aircraft without the resumption of relations. For the British the release of the aircraft was in practice a precondition. For the Algerians it must appear as the natural consequence of the improvement in relations. Both governments however insisted that the two negotiations were entirely separate. They were parallel and simultaneous, but also unrelated to each other. Hence the absurd disguise.

One day Nick was summoned to the Foreign Ministry to receive the "instructions" of the Algerian Government. He was to arrange for a personal representative of the Foreign Secretary (by now again Michael Stewart) to arrive in Algeria at noon the following day to finalise both sets of negotiations. Nick swallowed – and promised best efforts. As good luck would have it, the Iraqis chose that moment to break diplomatic relations with Britain and expel our experienced Ambassador, Sir Richard Beaumont, from Baghdad. He was diverted to Algiers and arrived at five minutes after noon. Nick's stock in Algiers rose. Sir Richard was received with elaborate deference – and "incarcerated" for a week in a government guest house in the hills above the city. He was a courteous man, but even his patience began to wear thin after the third day of unexplained detention.

Eventually we learned the truth. Abdelazziz Bouteflika, then Foreign Minister of Algeria (and now its President), had had his tonsils out. Would we please be patient for a little longer? We went on excursions along the coast and into the Atlas mountains. Eventually Bouteflika received us in the military hospital. Sir Richard expected to hear the Minister's views on Anglo-Algerian relations, perhaps even some apology for the outrageous way he had been treated. Bouteflika said that his doctors had forbidden him to speak, so he preferred to listen. Beaumont rose to the occasion and delivered a little speech. Her Majesty's Government sought to maintain cordial relations with all nations. He quoted Sir Winston Churchill: "the purpose of diplomatic relations is not to confer a compliment but to secure a convenience." We and the Algerians might not agree on all subjects, but it was useful to be in touch with each other. We attached importance to our relations with Algeria. The break was not of our making. We would be happy to repair it. Naturally we would expect the release of the aircraft in that context. He would be interested to hear the Minister's views on how we should proceed. The Minister who was forbidden to speak then spoke without drawing breath for forty minutes. He enlarged upon the three-fold destiny of Algeria – Arab, African and Mediterranean (of which last group the United Kingdom seemed to be an honorary member). It was breathtaking stuff – but it did not answer Dick Beaumont's question.

As they left, Nick asked the Director of European Affairs in the Foreign Ministry whether we had resumed relations. He said, "yes, tomorrow at noon." And the aircraft? "Ten days' time."

Sir Richard and Nick discussed the situation. Should we trust the Algerians? Why had the Foreign Minister not told us himself that he would like to resume relations tomorrow and seek our concurrence? Nick telephoned the director. Would he be correct to report to London that the Algerian Government proposed to resume diplomatic relations at noon the next day and undertook to release GASNU by a named date ten days later. Mr Mahrouf said "yes" and rang off. Nick so reported, both to the Foreign Office in London and to the Swiss Ambassador. Sir Richard Beaumont caught the last plane home that night.

In the morning Nick briefed the staff. He explained to the telephonist that, from twelve noon onwards, he should stop answering the telephone *"Service des Interets Britanniques, Ambassade de Suisse"*. Instead he should say *"Ambassade de Grande Bretagne"*. The first caller after twelve noon was Susan (who is partly Scottish). With a flourish he said *"Ambassade d'Angleterre"*. Sue gave him a piece of her mind on the subject of

82

British identities, and he came into Nick's office on his knees to apologise.

From the terrace of the Villa Gardner one could see the roof of the office just down the hill. The consul wrestled with the flagpole and, on the stroke of noon, broke out the Union flag. Alas, it had been in storage for too long and was full of holes. It had to be taken down and replaced with the spare flag which was much too small.

We had invited the British staff for beer and sandwiches to celebrate. By chance we had a house guest that week, the British writer and journalist Judith Listowel. We'd had to keep the negotiations secret from her. But Sue encouraged her out onto the terrace where she watched these unedifying proceedings with mounting incredulity. She joined us for our little party. The next day she reported the raising of the Union Jack on African soil, and tactfully did not mention the holes.

A week later two British pilots arrived to fly GASNU home. Nick took them to the secret airbase where the hijacked plane had landed eighteen months before. He was not supposed to know even of the existence of the base. But the guard snapped smartly to attention and the British flag flew incongruously down the serried ranks of MIGs. There at the very end was the toy aeroplane which had been the focus of so much diplomatic angst. The pilots sought air traffic control clearance for take-off. This was refused. The aircraft could not be permitted to take off because it had never arrived. The impasse could only be resolved by the Director General of Civil Aviation, whose office was at the international airport the other side of town. We drove across the city. Same impasse. Eventually Nick's contact from the President's office telephoned the Interior Minister Ahmed Mehdigri and secured his reluctant authority. Back to the military base. Too late. The aircraft had been in mothballs for too long. The pilots would not fly at night.

The following morning all went well. When Nick got back to the office he telegraphed London "GASNU left Algerian soil at 06.30

83

GMT. *Laus Deo "*. The response was a manuscript note from the Permanent Under Secretary reproaching him for using Latin in official communications.

By accident, Nick at the age of thirty-one was *Charge d'Affaires* in a territory half the size of Western Europe. We became the mascots of the diplomatic corps. By the same token the resumption of relations brought a new Ambassador to Algiers, Sir Martin Le Quesne. It was a relief and a delight to welcome him. But Nick became redundant and our stay in Algeria was truncated.

In preparation for his new boss, Nick looked through the drawers of the Ambassador's desk. He found a copy of a manuscript despatch from the British Consul General in the mid-nineteenth century. It was a compilation of all that the consul had been able to find out about his predecessors. It transpired that the first British consul in Algiers had arrived in 1620, some years before the first French consul. Another holder of the office had been kidnapped by the Algerian authorities and hewn in pieces before the Dey. His successor was naturally reluctant to disembark from his ship. Nick thought it better not to leave this document in the new Ambassador's desk. He sent it to London.

A decision was needed about our National Day celebration – the Queen's birthday party. The Foreign Ministry could not confirm that the new Ambassador would present his credentials before the due date, so we were asked to organise it. The first problem was a dearth of alcohol. All diplomats were limited to a very small ration of imported alcohol. The British divided the allowance between the whole Embassy staff – a few bottles each. We mostly drank the local wine, but on a National Day guests would expect to be offered something a little more distinctive. For a National Day there was a special allowance and we quickly put in an order for spirits and such goodies as smoked salmon and "caviar". But then, in May 1968, there was a national strike in France and our order got stuck in Marseilles. With French banks closed the French Embassy ran out of money and we and other allies were able to give them a temporary

84

bridging loan. So they could hardly ignore our plea for alcohol for the QBP. The French lent champagne and the Americans whisky.

Given our status as mascots, we decided we could give a different QBP. It was the time of "Carnaby Street", "I'm backing Britain" T-shirts, and Union flags on everything, so we ordered lots from the UK. Then we engaged the university jazz band, hired hundreds of coloured lights for the residence garden and invited hundreds of people. The weather was sure to be balmy, dry and not yet too hot.

On the morning of the party we woke to torrential rain. At lunchtime we stood on the Ambassador's terrace in tears as our coloured lights slowly filled with water. All our hopes of a spectacular re-entry to the social life of the capital seemed to have floated away in the unseasonal deluge. By noon it was obvious the party had to be indoors. The entire embassy staff turned out to shift furniture. The wives were already preparing food in the residence kitchens. As we welcomed our guests at six thirty we knew that all our efforts had come to naught. But at eleven o'clock almost everyone was dancing and at midnight a delegation from the staff begged us to wind the party up! A certain flop had finished up as one of the best parties we ever gave.

On 1 May 1969 the Algerian radio informed us that the UK was "the only so-called developed country which did not have a holiday for the workers on May Day". On that note we packed our family into our overstuffed estate car and drove off towards Morocco and our new post in New York.

Saharan postscript
Twenty years later, while we were serving in Ireland, our son Robert, by then a First Secretary in the FCO, was posted to Lagos. Casually over breakfast in Dublin Sue said, "Let's go to Lagos for Christmas."
Nick was reading the *Irish Times*.

"What a good idea," he said.

"Let's drive," pursued Sue.

"What a good... I beg your pardon." Either Sue had taken leave of her senses or she had a hazy idea of geography. But she was absolutely serious. So of course we went. We bought a reconditioned, desert-modified, long wheel-based Land Rover called Bertie. We had all the kit: a large French frame tent with four inflatable mattresses, gas cooker, heater and light, stores for ten days, 140 litres of petrol on the roof and 140 litres of water in the back, an emergency engineering box, a sand ladder and spade and a large scale map. The party consisted of the two of us and our two younger children, Charles aged twenty-six and Julia nearly sixteen.

We left in November 1989. As we journeyed south we followed on the short wave radio the dramatic collapse of the Soviet Empire in Eastern Europe. We drove across France to Marseilles and took the ferry to Algiers. We ran into a violent Mediterranean storm. Almost everyone was seasick. But the captain insisted that his lieutenant should show us over the ship. In particular he wanted to show off his new diesel engine. Of all the places on earth, that engine room was where we least wanted to be. At this point the lieutenant discovered that our plan was to drive to Lagos via Tamanrasset. At 9,000 feet in the Hoggar Mountains above Tamanrasset there was a hermitage called Assekrem. Two French priests had said Mass there every day for thirty years. We planned to join them on Christmas morning. "Oh," exclaimed the lieutenant, "one of those hermits is my uncle. Would you please take him his Christmas present?" So then we *had* to go to Assekrem.

We spent a night at the embassy in Algiers and set off over the high Atlas and down across the tundra of the sub-Sahara to Laghouat, to the ancient desert town of Ghardaia and on across the sand dunes to the oasis of El Golea. We had two punctures, which was tiresome because we had only two spares. In order to change a wheel we had to unload the Land Rover. We got quite good at it. We concluded that the vehicle was overloaded. We moved the petrol cans to the forward end of the roof so that the weight was better distributed. Nick poured eighty litres of good Kentish water into the desert sand. It almost broke his heart. But we had no more punctures.

From El Golea the track led across the Plateau du Tademait, one hundred kilometres of flat black rock. There was an incongruous sign saying "Parking". We could have parked anywhere. Another incongruous sign said "Café 2 kilometres". We did not believe it. But there it was, a small concrete building with a diesel generator which sold cold beer and excellent *cous-cous*. One wall was whitewashed for graffiti. A message said in English, "From Fred to all his friends in Blackburn: what are you doing here?" Another in French said simply "*Ou est la mer?*"

At the oasis of In Salah we met an Australian who was riding from Capetown to London on a pedal bicycle. He had suffered so many punctures that he could no longer repair his tyres. He had ordered new ones, but they had not yet arrived and he had been camping in In Salah for six weeks. We asked what we could do to help him. He asked for Vegemite. We only had Marmite, which he graciously acknowledged was the next best thing.

South of In Salah lies the real Sahara, great rolling sand dunes, outcrops of rock in bizarre shapes, sometimes a dry river bed. The track was variable, sometimes quite good, sometimes rocky, sometimes barely discernible. We used the compass. We would choose our campsite for the night about four o'clock, erect the tent, inflate the mattresses, set up the gas, get supper on to cook, and then settle down to our first whisky of the evening as the sun set behind the sand dunes – outrageously romantic.

From time to time there would appear on the horizon a small figure waving. A child from a nomadic family was begging water. It was a rule of the desert that no such request should ever be refused. So we would stop and funnel a few litres of water into his plastic can. The child would smile and wave and set off into the desert all alone; he knew exactly where he was and where he was going.

Sue had secretly brought Christmas with her. On the morning of 25 December we had tiny stockings, a six-inch high Christmas tree adorned the dashboard and for dinner we had turkey and all the trimmings with an excellent French wine.

We turned off the piste to climb the mountain track to Assekrem. About twenty kilometres from the route (where in case of accident we would have been quickly found) the engine suddenly died. Charlie who was driving exclaimed, "My God, I wish it was a puncture." So we knew we were in trouble. The engine was too hot to touch. We opened the bonnet and sat in the shade of the car pretending that we had always planned to picnic in this ghastly place. We had three university degrees between us but none of us was an engineer and the repair kit was really for show. We thought it might be an obstruction in the fuel line – but the petrol flowed freely. Nor was there any clogging of the air filter. So, as we had feared, it must be electrics. No spark. We changed the plugs. Still no spark. Nick was planning to walk back to the main track to seek help when Charlie suddenly asked, "Dad, do you think this wire should be joined on to something?" We found its terminal and the car started like a bird. But we had wasted three hours. We were driving up that dreadful mountain road long after dark, one of us walking in front with a torch to ensure that we avoided cliffs and boulders. We arrived very late at Assekrem.

At dawn we climbed on foot the last 600 feet to the hermitage – a little stone-built chapel perched high on the mountains with its lunar landscape all around. We were welcomed with courtesy. We sat on the floor. When it came to communion we were invited forward. We explained that we were "*croyants mais non pas Catholiques*". The priest replied in English, "Do you think that matters here?" It is the only time that we have made our communion at a Catholic Mass. We presented the lieutenant's gift and were rewarded with a cup of Nescafe. *Vaut le voyage.*

So to Tamanrasset, the last substantial town in Algeria, 600 kilometres from the border. We checked into a simple hotel and repacked Bertie from the bottom up. After some discussion we engaged the services of a Malian guide. Just before the frontier was the last great obstacle – Laouni – dubbed by foreigners the "Looney Dune"; no road, no track, just wave upon wave of soft sand for miles and miles strewn with immense boulders. Four-wheel drive strongly recommended. The dunes were littered with the charred remains of burnt out cars that had failed to make the passage. Young Europeans – mostly Germans, Austrians and French – made their living by driving Mercedes cars across the Sahara. They could not be sold in Algeria but fetched a fortune if they got to Ivory Coast. About one third made the grade. If they got irretrievably stuck they had to be set alight and photographed burning to prove to the authorities that they had not been illegally sold on the Algerian market. Hence the rusty skeletons that littered the Looney Dune. We pulled out two cars that were stuck in the sand.

We reached the Algerian frontier town of Ain Guezzam – a one-camel town if ever there was one – a store with no stores, a petrol station with no petrol and no one about in the street. Our guide urged us to drive on. We knew that the border post closed between noon and three o'clock for siesta. We were going to be late. We drove faster and faster and arrived in a swirl of sand and dust at ten minutes to twelve. The frontier police were efficient and courteous and demanded beer. Nick presented our passports to customs at three minutes to twelve. The guichet was slammed shut in his face. So we had lunch. A strange assortment of vehicles assembled for immigration and customs control: two or three Mercedes, a big truck, a handful of Land Cruisers and jeeps and an Italian honeymoon couple in a small Fiat. We wondered how they had got through the dune and whether they could possibly reach Nigeria.

Fourteen kilometres to the south lay the Niger frontier post of Assemaka where we had to unload the Land Rover for customs inspection. In Niger the landscape changed. We turned east and drove for a day and a half across flat featureless desert, looking for the slag heaps of the French uranium mine at Arlit. We lunched in a restaurant to celebrate. The meat was tough. Our French neighbour pronounced *"C'est du Zebre"*.

From Arlit there was a road south to Agadez, a large oasis town with a famous mosque with a tall spiked mud spire. After days under canvas we decided to check into the *Hotel de l'Air*, converted from the palace of the former Sultan. It was a mistake. The "hotel" was a cold, dirty, primitive hostel with no creature comforts and surly service. The rudimentary shower flowed into stinking drains.

Niger has a law. Foreigners must have their passport stamped at every police station. Fortunately there are not many police stations. But there is one at Agadez. Nick set off alone with the four passports. It was further than he had expected and it was dusk when he arrived. He made his first mistake. The police corporal on duty was asleep. You do not wake up police corporals in Agadez. Grumpily the corporal looked at the passports.

He spoke perfect French. "You are trying to deceive me", he said. Nick protested, but the corporal persisted. "You are pretending to be an Ambassador. Real Ambassadors come in Mercedes – at least our Ambassadors do."

Nick could see his point. He had twelve days growth of beard and a shaggy old anorak. And he had come on foot. "I do not have the honour to be accredited to your great country," he ventured, "but I am an Ambassador."

"Where are you Ambassador?"

Nick made his second mistake. "I am Ambassador in Ireland."

"Where's that?" There was a Mercator projection of the world on the wall. Nick pointed to Ireland on the map, but the corporal was not convinced. "That's part of England."

"You tell that to the Irish." There ensued a preposterous discussion of Anglo-Irish relations in French in the middle of the Sahara desert.

Finally the corporal came clean. "I know why you have not come in your car," he said, "it is so that you cannot give me my present."

Nick made his third mistake. He decided to lose his temper. "I am an official of my government and you are an official of your government. If I had said to you what you had just said to me I would be sacked."

"Monsieur l'Ambassadeur," said the corporal smoothly, conceding the point for the first time, "the essence of diplomacy is interpretation between one culture and another."

"Yes," said Nick cautiously.

"Monsieur l'Ambassadeur, you are talking about corruption. I am talking about how much pleasure it would give you to give me a present."

He got a tape of Greek music and we got our passports stamped.

It was by now quite dark. On his way home Nick crossed the night market (a thousand miles from the sea in an entirely Francophone environment). A very black lady with very few clothes nudged him in the ribs and said in English, "Hello, sailor." It made his day.

We had agreed to meet Rob on the Nigerian side of the frontier between Zinder and Kano. We set off early from Zinder, heading west and then south to the main crossing point marked on our map at Magaria between Sassoumbouroum and Zango. After about half an hour Julia asked to look at the map, and then said quietly, "Dad, you are going the wrong way. Rob said the crossing was at Kongola." We studied the map. Nick was less than convinced but Julia insisted. We

91

turned round, went back to Zinder, suffered another series of police checks and set off south to Kongola. The crossing was tedious and long. We emerged on the Nigerian side an hour late. No Rob. The tension in the car was palpable. It was essential that Julia's intervention should be justified. For half an hour we drove in total silence. Then suddenly there they were, two diplomatic Land Rovers with Rob, his fiancée, his Dutch colleague and five friends. There was an explosion of relief and happiness.

The rest of the journey was less eventful. The Yankari Game Reserve with no game but magnificent hot springs and a warden who supported Manchester United. The new capital city of Abuja then consisted of a complex system of motorways, a magnificent mosque and the Hilton Hotel where a waiter spilled a colourful cocktail over Julia's only clean shirt. There was some anxiety about security when the three vehicles got separated on the motorway in the approach to Lagos. We had covered 4,567 miles from London to Lagos in twenty-one days.

A week later, Nick had to fly home to stand to attention for the Irish Presidency of the European Union. Julia had to go back to school. So Sue and Charlie drove back with two of Rob's friends.

The rest of this chapter is by Sue alone.

The journey north through Nigeria was a frightening experience. We had been told in Lagos that we should not attempt it without an escort; law and order had broken down and no one was to be trusted, least of all anyone in uniform. But we had to get home. We took turns to read aloud a very funny novel, "The Case of the Beiderbecke Tapes" and kept alert for trouble. We were flagged down by a group in ill-assorted uniforms who demanded that we pay road tax. It was only a few pounds so we paid and hurried on.

Our map was rather out of date but we knew we had to reach Sokoto before dark and we saw no signs to it. We were just about to turn back to the safety of Ilorin when Charlie asked for the compass.

We were driving due east instead of north, and to our amazement soon arrived at the city of Kaduna – by a route not marked on our map. We checked into the Durbar Hotel and slept soundly. On arrival, and again on checking out next morning, we had to complete a full inventory of our two rooms, despite paying a deposit of 400 naira per room. Every light bulb and waste bin, sheet and curtain had to be counted. How sad. Before leaving town we visited every bank trying to change our excess nairas, until a kindly bank manager took pity on us and admitted that not a single bank in town had any foreign currency

The crossing into Niger was marred by a sinister "Special Branch" policeman who threatened to lock me up. After we had got through all the other officialdom, he took me into an empty hut where he kept me standing in silence for about ten minutes, just playing with our four passports. Eventually I asked if there was something wrong with our passports.

"No," he said, "I'm just thinking about locking you up."

"Why would you do that?"

"Do you know who I am?"

"Well, not precisely, but you're an official of your government."

"Yes. I'm Special Branch."

"So how can I help you?"

"If I locked you up, your government would be informed and then there would be discussions between your government and mine, and, after a long time, you would probably be set free."

"But why would you want to do that?"

I thought he was having fun at my expense because he was bored. Eventually he let me go. The boys looked scared when I emerged and asked anxiously what had been going on behind closed doors. I told them. They said I should have realised he wanted money, a thought which had never crossed my mind.

The Hotel de L'Air at Agadez gave us a warm welcome back. The whole town was in a state of shock the day after the Paris-Dakar rally had crashed through. Charlie and I had a ground floor room which stank. The smell seemed to be coming up the plughole of the shower from some unimaginable horror below. A glass of water standing on the hole solved the problem.

On the road out of Agadez we were stopped by our "favourite policeman". He was barely recognisable in the blowing sand of the "harmatan", well wrapped in a massive touareg turban and veil. But his voice I knew, especially when he asked where was "le Vieux" – and for sweets for his children.

Later that same day we passed a long camel train going north. A man dropped down from the saddle and ran across the sand to us. He looked old and ill, but spoke no French. I gave him a dose of soluble aspirin and a few to take later. I hoped he did not take them all at once.

Beyond Arlit, where we picked up a guide, we found a beautiful campsite in some unspoiled primrose-coloured dunes. A fearless gerbil joined us for dinner. Not a sound could be heard under the star-spangled sky. The boys slept without a tent.

In the middle of the next night in the Algerian desert a line of army trucks thundered past very close to our tent and one jeep stopped to ask for cigarettes. The boys played the soldiers along casually and they moved off without seeing me. They probably meant no harm but we felt intimidated just by their inquisitive and assured manner.

On a flat open stretch of sand next morning we became aware of a score of bright lights approaching along the horizon. When they converged on our Land Rover we found ourselves surrounded by excited Italian motorcyclists who had lost four of their number. Later we diverted to tell three bikers to hurry on and catch them up.

In the government hotel in the beautiful oasis town of Timimoun we nearly got lynched by a group of tourists; the hotel had no water – not even for the coffee machine – and in we walked carrying twenty litres each. The hotel at Tarit was even more delightful – the perfect place to study the prehistoric rock carvings on a nearby cliff, and to bid farewell to the Great Erg and its magnificent dunes.

At the crossing into Morocco at Beni Ouif I got into a muddle about our money and the officials, who hated having to deal with a mere woman, were suspicious. Every crossing is stressful because one feels like a criminal, despite being totally innocent of wrongdoing. But we got through in about an hour and sped off north through Morocco feeling a sense of homecoming as we approached Europe ("Europe" in this context was the Spanish enclave of Melilla). At the frontier I handed the policeman our four passports smiling broadly. "British?" he asked and I nodded. Without looking at them he handed them back saying, "Welcome to Spain," and waved us on. We cheered so loudly I feared he might suspect that we had "pulled a fast one" so we quickly sobered up.

Neil and Guy were in a hurry to get back to work so we stayed in hotels most of the return journey. This enabled us to drive further in the dark, where roads were reliable, and to depart more quickly in the morning without having to dismantle a camp. Yet, being geologists, they had stopped again and again to gather rock samples. These were to raise eyebrows at the UK customs. The channel crossing was rough. The ferry had to wait for a couple of hours outside Dover before being allowed to dock. We sat in the restaurant, at a table which was tipping many degrees from horizontal, finalising the accounts.

95

As we drove off the boat home in England we were immediately signalled into a customs bay for a thorough search. It looked like a tip-off. My confidence that we had nothing to hide, together with our pride in the adventure behind us, must have annoyed the men on duty. They gave us the most thorough search of the whole six-week trip. We had perfected an unpacking routine for every border crossing and were happy to show off how speedily we could do it. The large groundsheet spread behind the Land Rover soon had neat piles of all we possessed, stacked ready for an orderly repack. They opened everything. The knife Neil had bought in Agadez was more than three inches long and Special Branch were summoned. We were solemnly warned that if there was a knifing reported in the region of Birkbeck College (where Neil was a lecturer) they would come straight to his address. We could not take it seriously and that annoyed the officials even more. We were euphoric and they were cross, unable to relate to us innocents abroad. Our arrival in England was more stressful than any of the frontier crossings in Africa.

In total the return journey was more expensive, even though we crossed from Melilla to Malaga instead of Algiers to Marseilles. But we had another cause for euphoria. The outbound journey had taken three weeks, we got back in sixteen days – by a route which was 500 miles longer!

Chapter 5
UN New York 1969-72

The United Nations in 1969 had already disappointed the high hopes of the founding fathers and was widely regarded as an ineffective talking shop. Nevertheless, it expressed as no other organisation on earth the aspirations of mankind. If it did not exist it would have to be invented. Almost all serious problems came to the UN eventually – usually too late for effective diplomacy. And every major statesman in the world visited the UN building sooner or later. It was a marvellous place for a young diplomat learning his trade.

The dominant issues were the Middle East, development, Southern Africa including Rhodesia and apartheid, and the rhetoric of anti-colonialism. Specific issues which arose in our time included the celebration of the twenty-fifth anniversary of the UN, and the representation of China.

The most important issue of all – the Cold War – did not appear on the agenda but affected everything that happened. The organisation was split and often paralysed by East-West antagonism, the balance of terror and the vetoes of the five Permanent Members of the Security Council. And this was as it should be. The UN was divided because the world was divided. Only if it reflected the realities of global power could the UN seek realistic solutions.

The Secretary General was U Thant, a Burmese diplomat. He was no fiery idealist like Dag Hammarskjold, but a soft-spoken, shrewd and gentle man whose heart was in the right place on every issue but who had little influence on the major powers. The Foreign Office had suggested to Nick when he was appointed to New York that it would be useful for him to address the Secretary General in his own language. In practice he was able to wish him good morning in the

97

corridor on perhaps three occasions. Sue had more opportunity as she attended Spanish lessons on the thirty-ninth floor of the UN building where U Thant had his office.

Nick's job was "First Secretary, Public Affairs", in effect press secretary to the Minister of State and Permanent Representative, Lord Caradon. His business was to promote British policy on UN questions to the international press corps. The formal instrument for this was a brief daily on-the-record press conference at the UN building at twelve fifteen each morning, following the UN spokesman at twelve noon and followed by the United States at twelve thirty. The facility was available equally to all delegations. For some reason only the British and the Americans took advantage of it. Most of the real work was done in private meetings with key journalists to ensure that they understood the British point of view on issues that arose at the UN.

We arrived by ship on the SS *United States*, sailing past the Statue of Liberty at dawn, when Manhattan looks dreamy and magical in the soft pastel colours of sunrise. It is a good way to arrive anywhere, but this was the last time we were allowed to travel to post by ship – too expensive. For a diplomat and his family the sea crossing provided a priceless period of limbo, between the frantic activity of packing up one home and making a new one, between preparation for a new assignment and beginning a new job. With hindsight we did not do enough preparation for New York. For Burma and Algeria, which we had not known at all, we had studied the language and culture, history and geography, religion and politics. We felt we knew New York from American colleagues, from films and literature. We did not need to lay in provisions – except for Marmite and TCP. But the city seemed more foreign than we had expected. (Not many weeks later Nick incautiously confessed during a news conference at the UN that New York felt more foreign to him than Paris. An American journalist from Los Angeles quipped that he felt the same way. New York was more foreign than Paris!)

98

We arrived just before Charlie's sixth Birthday and Joe Johnson (Sue's wartime foster father) came to the Beverley Hotel for a birthday tea party. We had been temporarily lodged in a very small apartment with tiny kitchenette, one twin room and a sofa-bed in the sitting area for us parents. So we jumped at the opportunity of moving into a large apartment on the tenth floor of 35, East 84th Street when it was vacated by a departing colleague. It had many grand features which awed us, especially the acres of mirrors and glittering chandeliers in the eau-de-nil master bedroom. It also had a gigantic walk-in wardrobe – the biggest we had ever seen and were not likely to fill. The boys had a good big room too. But the only bedroom available for Nick's cousin, Rosemary Arnott, who was to arrive soon to help look after the boys (and another child on the way which never made it to full term) was a tiny servant's quarter off the kitchen. The other problem only emerged at night: scores of enormous cockroaches. The pest control officer eventually gave up the struggle saying the whole building was infested. On one pointless visit he caught Sue cleaning the outside of her windows and warned her in colourful terms that it was against the law except on the ground floor.

We shipped to New York the car we had bought for Algeria – a Ford Cortina Estate. We collected it from the docks, driving on side lights in the lighted streets, as we would at home. We made our first acquaintance with the New York Police Department. The officer kicked the car with his boots and shouted, "Git yer lights on." We kept it in the underground garage of the apartment block next door, where it was immediately dubbed "the li'l green English Ford". We would telephone when we wanted it, ask for "the li'l green Ford" and walk round to collect it. It was always waiting for us. Three weeks before Christmas a card was stuck under the windscreen wipers wishing us a Merry Christmas "from the boys at the garage". We thought that was mighty civil. The effect was only slightly spoiled by an identical card one week later. "Merry Christmas from the boys at the garage – Second Notice". They got a case of Paddy Whisky. Indeed, we wrapped a second case of whisky to distribute amongst the staff of the apartment block. The little car had the last laugh.

99

When we took it to Canada for Christmas in temperatures twenty degrees below zero centigrade we discovered that ours was the only car without a block heater plugged into the wall. Ours was also the only car that would start in the morning.

We began to explore the city. First across the street to the wonderful Metropolitan Museum looking for the art of the Native Americans. "No, ma'am, all the Red Indian stuff is in the Natural History Museum across Central Park." So we got to explore the park as well, later on bikes, and in the winter on ice skates. The ice-rink at the southern end was posh with piped music – Viennese waltzes. The one in the north – next to Harlem – had all the excitement, energy and enthusiasm of the black community, and tall athletic youths, eager to teach two little blond boys with cute foreign accents.

One snowy day Rosemary returned with her charges in great distress – she had dropped a family ring on the footpath and had failed to find it in the snow. About three months later on a glorious spring walk together she said, "It's about here I lost my ring."

"Is that it?" asked Sue, and picked it up! (More than twenty years later, when Robert was working for UKMIS as a young diplomat, he had his wedding reception in Central Park and was rowed across the lake in a gondola with his bride.)

We visited different churches hoping to find one in which we all felt at home. Nick being brought up Presbyterian/Quaker/ Methodist/United Reformed, and Sue High Anglican/Church of Scotland/Brethren, we were Catholic in our churchmanship. In the end we joined the Brick Presbyterian Church in Park Avenue partly because it was the closest. The Sunday school was excellent, the regular Sunday worship intellectually challenging, the liturgy familiar if rather "higher" than expected and the congregation welcoming. We threw ourselves into the life of the church and made many friends.

Shopping had its own hazards for a newcomer. It was not explained that the price on an item was not what actually had to be paid for it. To the listed price had to be added city and state taxes so Sue was frequently caught offering too little cash for purchases. Once, early on, Sue picked up a number of things and presented them at the check-out. The cashier kept shouting, "How big is your bill?"

Sue kept saying, "I'm sorry, I haven't added it up yet." Impasse. A kindly bystander explained that "bill" did not mean "invoice", but currency note. The till was short of change. If Sue presented a note of large denomination the cashier would have to go away and get more cash. (Within a couple of years it was almost impossible to pay for anything with cash. Only credit cards were acceptable.)

This first summer American colleagues from Algiers lent us their summer cottage on a lake in Vermont. It was a magical escape from the heat. The people were welcoming and generous. We paddled round the shore calling on the neighbours and sharing meals. Every family kept food scraps to feed a communal pig which was given to a poor family at the end of the season. In the boys' bedroom Sue found a couple of drawers full of *Penthouse* and other "adult" magazines. She gathered them up to throw out, telling the boys they were rubbish. On her way to the bins she realised she had condemned the magazines without ever having opened one. This was not right. So she sat on the back doorstep turning the pages to make good her education. But the boys were standing just behind her. Did they believe her explanation of what she was doing and why?

We took the children to Grand Cayman to recover from the General Assembly. The beach hotel had a swimming pool cut out of the coral reef with a channel to the open sea with myriad tropical fish. We could start swimming in the pool and then snorkel out straight into fairyland. We flew back to New York after changing planes at Miami. Nick put his hand into the pocket of his mackintosh and pulled out a Cuban passport – the possession of which was illegal in the United States. At some point he must have picked up the wrong coat. He sent the offending document to the Czechoslovak

Embassy in Washington who looked after Cuban interests. It was never acknowledged.

Another holiday took us to visit Sue's brother Martin and his family in California. We visited the painted desert in Arizona. The telephone number of our motel was "Dinosaur City 1". We noticed from the map that our route took us through a place called Two Guns. The radio announced at that moment, "The City of Two Guns is no more." A few minutes later we reached Two Guns which was a crossroads with a petrol station. The petrol station had burnt down. We told the boys that we could go to the bottom of the Grand Canyon on mules. But a notice declared that all tourists taking that route must either be manifestly between the ages of twelve and eighty, or have a doctor's certificate to prove that appearances were deceptive. We hired a light aircraft instead and spent a breathtaking hour playing amongst the towers and gorges of that stupendous place. Years later Rob became a resident clerk in the Foreign Office. His first case was a young couple who had died in an aircraft accident in the Grand Canyon.

In Algiers we had been negotiating to buy a small yacht for Mediterranean sailing. When we were abruptly transferred to the UN we assumed that sailing in New York was a rich man's sport. We could never afford to keep a boat. But we discovered that most of our colleagues had a share in a country cottage of some kind, known affectionately as a "shack", in order to keep sane in the New York summer. Eighteen months rent of one of these cottages was enough to buy the yacht. So we had it delivered, a twenty-one foot plastic bathtub called a "Vivacity", with twin keels, four small berths, two small sails, a compass and a Seagull outboard motor. We called her *Djemila* after the spectacular Roman ruins in the Algerian desert. The inflatable tender was named *Timimoun* after another oasis town. We joined the Huguenot Yacht Club just across the state border in Massachusetts. It was a forty-minute drive from our apartment. We sailed outbound on Saturday and inbound on Sunday – and if the world had gone to war on a Saturday evening we would not have known.

102

The north shore of Long Island is studded with beautiful little harbours. For convenience we registered *Djemila* in Felixstowe and flew the red ensign. When we put into port after a vigorous sail, passers-by would ask kindly, "Did you have a rough crossing?" as if a tiny vessel like ours could conceivably have navigated the wild Atlantic. We would modestly acknowledge that the crossing had had its moments. Then Rob and Charles would put their small faces out of the fo'c'sle hatch, drawing the exclamation, "You brought the kids!"

We were not quite up to the smart standards of the Huguenot Yacht Club. *Djemila* could not compete with the big yachts. The outboard had no reverse gear so we had to sail onto our moorings which caused consternation among the neighbours.

When the time came to leave New York we sold the boat for most of what we paid for it and went for a nostalgic last sail. As we ghosted up the channel to the club at sunset on a dying wind, we were frankly paying more attention to each other than to the navigation and went gently aground on a flat rock on a falling tide. Nick took a sounding with the boathook and ordered the mate overboard. Sue jumped and disappeared. Gallantly Nick jumped in to rescue her. Between us we pushed *Djemila* off the rock before she stuck fast, the sail filled and she moved away. Charlie put his head out of the cabin and called anxiously, "What do I do now?" We swam for it, and were never found out in this disgraceful piece of seamanship.

The apartment continued to "bug us" so we moved to Park Avenue number 1175 – a very grand address. The departing colleagues took the key with them to the airport by mistake. By the time we got access all our plants had died of cold in the removal van. The flat was on the thirteenth floor – cheaper than other floors. It was light and spacious and spotlessly clean – no sign or smell of cockroaches. Every month a lugubrious man appeared at the back door. "It's the exterminator, ma'am," and sprayed all around the pipes and drains.

Sue used to get told off by building staff, especially the maintenance man, Eddie, for opening the back door without first checking who was there. Several of the staff became good friends and would do anything for the boys, see them safely across the street to go and play at a friend's house, or mend their bicycles. One morning Wes, the Jamaican lift operator, greeted Sue with unexpected accuracy. "Happy Birthday, Mrs Fenn. How old are you?" Slightly taken aback Sue said that she was thirty-five. "Ha," exclaimed Wes, "the Good Book gives us three score years and ten. It's downhill all the way from here!"

The only serious incident in this home was a flood. The fifteenth floor penthouse had a Japanese garden. Delinquent children who lived there decided to see how many of the pebbles on the roof could be pushed down the drains. It was a walled garden so when it rained the roof became a swimming pool. Sue sitting at her dressing table two floors down became aware that the Venetian blind behind the mirror had become a waterfall. She rushed upstairs to find the landlady and her cheerful Scottish housekeeper trying to catch a torrent of water funnelling through the ceiling with a plastic dustbin. We quickly formed a chain of buckets to empty into the nearest bath. The flood eventually reached the tenth floor. Pushing into the walls was like prodding a saturated sponge, the water oozed out. The smell lasted all year. Personally we suffered no damage at all and refused to sue our landlady, despite her pleas. She wanted the biggest case possible against her tenants. HMG never sues and carries its own insurance.

One brilliant feature of this apartment was the "sexy shower", a tiled cubicle with powerful jets of water squirting from six positions at the sides as well, as a shower head the size of a dinner plate. No problem getting the boys to wash.

The boys had left their school in Algiers before Easter and American schools did not reopen till Labour Day, a five-month gap. So lessons were started at home with materials brought from the UK. At lunch the boys would solemnly report to their mother (Sue) things that their teacher (Sue) had taught them. In the end they both got places at Daltons, an excellent school just round the corner. Some of the other parents resented the ease with which our boys had gained entrance to a highly prestigious school on the strength of a happy interview which Robin and Charles had thoroughly enjoyed.

Three curious memories of Daltons stay with Sue. One is how extraordinarily beautiful the teachers were. She was not accustomed to think of teachers as glamorous. Another was the wicked waste of food at lunchtime. Each pupil was given a tray at his desk with every imaginable sort of food on it, a cooked hot meal, a salad, a dessert, fresh fruit, a yogurt, a fruit drink, milk, potato chips, a roll or bagel – far more than any one child could possibly eat. After about half an hour the tray was collected and almost everything on it swept into the trash can. Thirdly, our boys' enthusiasm for reading, which had an unusual genesis; at break time the choice was to play in the street or read in the library. Unfortunately, the numerous dogs of the Upper East Side had always used the street before them, so they chose the library.

The headmaster made it clear that any child found with drugs would be expelled. When this rule was enforced it appeared that the parents of the offending children had powerful friends on the school board. All parents were invited to a meeting at the school to discuss the ruling. The head was threatened with instant dismissal. Nick and Sue attended and were soon witnessing a noisy, heated debate in which physical force was threatened and fists raised. The parents, all wealthy, all from the professions or the world of arts and media, were raging on both sides of the argument. The chairman almost lost control. We were mesmerised. Then a lawyer stood up to ask a question and none of these "liberal" combatants could be seen to interrupt him – because he was black. Moreover he was brilliant, and soon had the seething angry crowd silent and disciplined. So a rational debate continued. The vote supported the headmaster. The "too liberal" parents left the premises in high dudgeon and for good.

Our boys made friends among their classmates and they visited each other's homes after school. Robin and Charles learned to control their envy now that they were the "poor" children, and to accept that Santa Claus would not be likely to bring them a huge mini rocket which could do everything but fly. Their friends learned that the British not only speak differently but sit down together for meals. The visiting kids were told not to raid the fridge when they felt hungry, but to wait till called to table and to join in the conversation with the adults. What was worse they were asked to stay at the table until everyone had finished. Our boys were learning too – mostly the language. When asked where his brother was, Robin replied, "I think he's in the 'barthroom' because he needed to go to the 'be'throom'."

The boys also discovered they had relations "Stateside of the pond". Joe Johnson, who had graced Charlie's sixth birthday party at the hotel, lived in Princeton and we were soon all invited to visit him and Kitty there. One visit coincided with the Apollo moon landing and their cruel parents insisted on waking the boys to watch the event on television. They can barely remember it. We also visited Anne (Sue's foster sister) and Herb Stone and their daughters Kitty and Peggy. They lived just across the Hudson River in a leafy suburb, Englewood, a short drive away. Both Sue and Nick had Canadian first cousins on both sides of their families, so many happy gatherings in Montreal and Ontario were arranged summer and winter.

The drive to Montreal normally took eight hours. One snowy winter it took fifty-six hours – following the snowplough. The morning news was dominated by the arrival of heavy snowfalls so we went back to bed. Later we stood at the windows peering into the totally white scene. What could we have for lunch with all the shops shut? Sue had wrapped the substantial remains of yesterday's Christmas turkey in "saran-wrap" and placed it in the freezing

106

outside garbage bin overnight. As she tried to remove it from the bin she was aware of two small boys beside her shaking their little blond heads. No way were they going to eat out of the trash can, even if it was clean and safe. So we prepared for a long journey. We had sleeping bags in the car and several thermoses of hot drinks and lots of food. The drive became an adventure. The first day we got all of ninety miles – to Kingston, New York. On the second day Nick assured the family that we would be all right if we got to the border as the Canadians understood about snow. We got to the border. It was closed. Only Canadian citizens were admitted. Nick made clear what he thought of this demonstration of Commonwealth solidarity, but we had to stay in New York State and find a motel, hurriedly opened for the crisis. We got into Canada on the third morning. The US authorities did not want to bother stamping our passports. But we knew that if we left without the stamp we would not be readmitted to the United States. So we insisted.

Another year the famous Easter Parade – which we dressed up for of course – was cancelled because of snow.

St. Patrick's Day Parade was something else. The Irish took over the city and drunks staggered out of bars all day. We were warned we must wear something green if we ventured onto the streets, which in places were literally spattered with blood. Many New York policemen were of Irish descent and had the day off to celebrate. The IRA began to dominate the parades all over America, particularly in New York, and "The Troubles" in Northern Ireland spilled over into our daily lives. There were bomb threats and phone calls to our apartment full of hate and chilling threats. All mail, even bouquets of flowers, had to be suspect. This was a foretaste of similar unpleasantness fifteen years later at the embassy in Dublin.

On the day we arrived in New York the UK Mission had been mourning the death of a young Australian security guard. He had given a bottle party the previous evening. Three young thugs had followed some of his guests to the party and demanded admission. He said that they would be welcome if they brought a bottle as all the other guests had done. So they shot him dead on his own doorstep. These were violent days in the city. British kids had been knocked off their bikes and robbed while cycling in public parks, women had been mugged and had their purses stolen, and a British flautist had been hit so hard on his mouth he would never play again.

The New York police advised the public to give up their money quickly – no heroics please. "Always carry $15 cash – enough for a heroin fix." So naturally the job for the muggers became easier. Sue thought this would only encourage robbery and vowed she would not give in that easily.

At noon one Saturday on her way to the supermarket she was stopped in the street by an agitated young woman. She gazed in disbelief at the gun pressing into her stomach. A glimmer of hope appeared. A tall man rounded the corner with bags of dry-cleaning over his broad shoulders. Sue stopped him and asked for help. "Give her what she wants," he spat out, and ran. Sue produced her wallet. She tried to persuade the girl to share what little money she had in it, and expressed sorrow that she should be in such trouble. But in the end she had to hand over the wallet. She then suggested they have coffee together, to talk. But now she had nothing to pay for a coffee, so she invited the girl into the apartment. Surprisingly, she agreed.

They went into the back entrance and up in the elevator. On the way the girl had second thoughts: "You are leading me into a police trap."

"You are free to go anytime." She did not turn back. Inside the kitchen Sue asked for the gun to be placed in her coat pocket which she hung on the back of the door. Sitting at the kitchen table over several cups of coffee and cigarettes, Maria poured out her story. Yes, she had been on heroin so her baby had been taken away. She was now on methadone and could only get her baby back if she went to the hospital with a long list of things which they said the baby would need. But she had no money. She had sold all her clothes for food. Sue took her into her walk-in wardrobe and offered her anything she liked – they were about the same size. Maria looked carefully and then said firmly that she did not like Sue's style. Rosemary had been playing with Charles in his bedroom. She came to check anxiously if everything was all right and accepted Sue's assurances with some reluctance. Sitting down again for another cup of coffee Maria handed back all Sue's money. It lay between them on the table while the whole unhappy story poured out. It could have been true, it was certainly enough to make them weep together. Then Sue decided that the cash – enough for the family's weekend shopping – should be divided equally, and that half was an unsolicited gift for Maria. They parted at a bus stop on Lexington Avenue with hugs and tears.

Nick was alarmed when told of Sue's audacious behaviour, certain the woman had been "casing the joint" and that we would soon be burgled. But even though Sue wrote and sent Christmas and Easter cards to the address left by Maria, nothing was ever heard of her again.

One evening, a week or so later, Sue told Nick that she had to pop out to the local "deli" for some milk. He asked her to wait while he finished something so he could come with her. She waited. She asked again and waited again. In the end she said she had to go at once or the deli would be closed. She went out. The deli closed in her face as she arrived. So she set off to walk several blocks to the next one. She thought she sensed someone behind her. Just after midnight the streets were empty but she was being followed. She darted down a side street trying to throw them off. It did not work. She walked more quickly. Could she reach the shop soon enough? As she crossed a street she could see the man out of the corner of her eye. He was in shadow but she was now certain he was after her. She decided to run for it. He caught up with her and grabbed her shoulder bag. Just before she screamed she realised it was Nick. The wretched man had, he said, been trying to teach her a lesson. As she sobbed into his shoulder she just had it in her heart to forgive him. And, in New York, she never again went out alone after midnight.

109

One day in our local supermarket Sue stopped to help a young black mother pick up a pile of tin cans which her toddler had knocked over. A passing white woman poured a terrifying stream of abuse onto the pair of them leaving them both bewildered.

Yet another incident dramatised the tensions of daily life. Sue was coming up on an escalator in Grand Central Station when her shoulder bag accidentally swung forward, brushing the legs of a middle-aged woman on the step above. Immediately Sue began to apologise. The woman exploded and screamed that she was being mugged. It was an extraordinary performance. The more Sue tried to explain and calm her the more hysterical the "victim" became. It was frightening and embarrassing. A well-spoken, well-dressed young man, an Afro-American, stopped to help. This only made the woman scream and shout more, saying it was a conspiracy against her. In the end there was nothing to do but walk away.

New York provided the catalyst for a crucial family decision. Daltons was Robin's third school in a third continent with new teachers, new friends and different spelling. He was only seven. When the senior school moved across town to a different campus, we decided to discuss with the children the possibility of boarding school in England. They would have to commute alone, but they would at least receive a coherent education. It was a hard decision but all of us agreed it made sense – at least academically. At the end of our summer holiday in England we took Robin to The Downs School, near Malvern, which Nick had loved twenty-five years earlier. Robin reverted to his given name, Robert. His first letter home said, "I'm very homesick, but don't worry, by the time this letter reaches you I'll be all right" – we seemed that far away. A year later Charles joined him.

Sue looked for something useful to do when the boys were in school. Getting a job was still discouraged by the diplomatic service. Finding that the first language of New York is Spanish, with more Spanish language newspapers than English ones, she joined a class at the UN – on the thirty-ninth floor of the Secretariat. Occasionally she

110

was able to greet the Secretary General, U Thant in his own language. She also joined a French conversation group to keep up what she had acquired in Algeria. They met in each other's homes and formed close friendships often across political divides. A Czech friend in the group said she understood why so many New Yorkers had to visit a psychiatrist regularly. "They always smile and tell us how wonderful everything is, their kids are perfect, they all have excellent health and no money worries. No worries at all. But real life is not like that. So they have to go to someone who is paid to listen to how awful the kids are, how the husband's job isn't going well, etc, etc."

Impressed by the number of violent incidents she had witnessed, Sue decided to take up judo for self-defence at the YWCA. One participant told the group she had already experienced harassment by a group of young thugs in a supermarket; they had driven her menacingly into an aisle cul-de-sac late one night. She vividly described how she turned on them with what she hoped was a professional-looking stance and grunted loudly. It was enough to send the bullies screaming away.

Being a regular visitor to the "Y", Sue got roped into a programme for young Chinese girls brought up within the protective walls of Chinatown. The idea was to introduce them to the big city around them before they set out to look for a job. We took them to shops, museums and restaurants – which were not Chinese – and Sue took them round the public areas of the UN building. On one visit a child was in great distress when she found her purse missing. She knew she would never find it and her parents would never let her out again. At the lost property office she at first refused to fill in the necessary form describing her missing purse and contents. But once she had signed it her purse was handed over with a smile. She was speechless with joy and astonishment. She had discovered what many who work there experience every day: the UN Headquarters complex is not New York. What is more, the UN Post Office is much more efficient than the American one and the staff much more helpful.

111

Sue felt at home in the UN buildings, sometimes meeting Nick in the Delegates' Lounge, before lunching with a colleague or attending debates in the public gallery. The boys were treated to lunch in the Delegates Dining Room every school holiday. They always chose the most adventurous item on the menu, frogs' legs, caviar or bird's nest soup. The lounge was a fantastic place to meet people from all over the world. On entering it paid to study the delegates carefully to avoid being "caught out" by someone not seen for five or ten years. It just took a moment's thought to dredge up the name and surprise them with a cheery greeting.

Along the wide carpeted corridor delegates would stride up and down in deep thought, conversation or argument. Unwittingly they so charged up the carpet that carelessly placing a hand on metal resulted in a painful shock. As soon as the central heating took over from the air conditioning in the autumn, UN staff would cover metal doors handles and railings with rubber insulation.

With the wife of the Indian Ambassador, Sue attended every one of the Heads of State and Governments' speeches during the session to celebrate the twenty-fifth anniversary in 1970. Others were there of course, but the two of them agreed they were the only ones to make it to every one of these highly charged speeches. There were more interesting debates in the Security Council Chamber. Nick was often summoned by his pager when we were out sailing in Long Island Sound. We never once finished a club yacht race.

There was a lively organisation within the UN community to support the spouses – still mostly wives. It grew out of concern for the many young women who were plucked out of their families, friends and cultures to accompany their husbands when they were posted to the UN. Quite a few spoke no English and had never left their homes before. One woman became so desperate she pushed her three children before her out of her high apartment building. Concerned colleagues formed the UN Women's Association. From this small initiative the group quickly became a huge social organisation which had frequently to renew its roots as it lost touch with those who really needed it. Nations took it in turn to lay on an afternoon's entertainment. With nearly a hundred countries involved the turn did not come often, so when it did we felt we had to pull out all the stops. Lady Caradon, looking well ahead to the British party, asked every British wife to grow cress so we could serve cress sandwiches. We had two bathrooms green with it. On the day we hosted a fashion show and the British wives took turns to help the emaciated models effect their quick changes behind the scenes.

It was through the UN Association that we joined a weekend skiing in upstate New York. Charlie was a natural. Nick was not. Charlie also came with us to spend a splendid weekend with an American journalist's family beside the Charles River in Massachusetts. It was in mid winter and we were exhilarated by ice skating for miles along the river, blown along by the wind. We stopped from time to time to talk to fishermen with their lines down through holes in the thick ice. The Greenway family had recently returned from an assignment in Vietnam, bringing a Vietnamese "nanny" with them. She had been asked by immigration on arrival how long she intended to stay. Looking down at her three young charges she replied, "Until the last of the girls is married." This wonderful woman had adopted the whole family and managed them all.

Once a week Sue joined a team in a church hall to teach spoken English to new immigrants. It was not for complete novices but to encourage those who had some English but were too shy to use it – not unlike Sue's attempts to teach the French Ambassador in Rangoon. The pupils could not be more mixed in age, origin, and educational background. Some surprising stories unfolded. A young man from Eastern Europe, recently arrived, declared that America was all that he disliked and feared. Then why did he come? To preserve his sanity. He had been manager of a medium-sized factory which made batteries. Every battery was sent to the Soviet Union in "War Reparations" – in 1968. All the workers hated the Soviet Union and did their best to sabotage the batteries. Quality control was a nightmare. Yet that is what he was paid for. He needed to be able to take pride in his work and to do it well. In the end he knew he would have a breakdown if he could not find work which he could do to the best of his ability. So with much difficulty he made his way to the United States. It seemed a strange reason for leaving one's family and homeland. He now enjoyed his work and was grateful to the people of America for welcoming him. But he hated the ethos: no criticism of success and no sympathy for failure. He missed his country terribly and would return if there were a regime change.

Sue worked regularly for a programme based in Mount Sinai Hospital. The idea was to give the most deprived children a "Headstart" through play. In the children's waiting room the only games freely available were "educational". The children, mostly of Puerta Rican origin, were beautifully dressed and well fed, and their parents brought them regularly to the clinics because they cared. But there was very little communication between the children and the adults. When the kids were about to go home we invited the parents to take home whatever game the child had shown most interest in. They could borrow it till the next visit. If they wanted to exchange it for a different game they could come back at any time. But our rules stipulated that the parents could only play with the children for five minutes a day. With a second toy they could play ten minutes a day – no more. After a few visits the parents were begging to be allowed to play a little longer. No one had ever told them that playing with their children was a parental responsibility. No one had told them it was fun. After a few months the changes in the relationship between the children and parent was staggering. We on the programme would guess which were "our" families just by how they talked to each other. One morning, when Sue was alone in the hospital playroom, a young man came in and asked if he could watch and play with the children. After about an hour he asked who was running the programme. Sue explained that the director was away in Washington pleading for more funds. He said that he was involved in a similar "Headstart" programme in another district of New York and had noticed that some families had much better communication between the parents and children. On investigation he found they had all been in our programme. He was so impressed he would like to help. Could he give us a cheque? Sue thanked him but did not read it properly till after he had left. It was for $10,000 and signed David Rockerfeller.

Sue attended a meeting for volunteers. The hospital presented a number of badges, which was nice, and the head of volunteers gave a talk about how wonderful (yes) and unique (no) the service was. Volunteering, she said, was unknown outside the United States. Controlling herself till a quiet moment afterwards, Sue told this lady that people did voluntary work like this all over the world. She seemed astonished.

When the troubled Apollo 13 space mission was returning to earth, Sue happened to be at Mount Sinai Hospital. Televisions everywhere were broadcasting the chilling, nail-biting story. Were we about to witness three brave men burnt up before our horrified gaze? Many had predicted disaster because it was number thirteen. As the moment of re-entry into the earth's atmosphere arrived people all over the hospital were among the millions watching with bated breath. When the first voice reached us from that dot in the Pacific Ocean wild cheers were followed by a truly heart-warming show of concerned humanity. Everyone hugged everyone else whether patient or doctor, cleaner or visitor. Tears flowed in relief and for one glorious moment we were as one in the family of mankind.

Diplomats by international convention are provided with free parking spaces in diplomatic cities. It is also the convention that diplomats are not punished for contravening the law of their host country. The reason for this is that they are agents of their own governments and must not be subjected to pressure by their hosts. They pay income tax for example to their own government, not in the country where they live. British diplomats however are disciplined by their own government if they break local law and diplomatic immunity is often waived. Some other governments are less scrupulous. One morning Nick drove to work in the United Kingdom Mission to the United Nations on Third Avenue. As he approached the reserved parking spaces an American car pulled up in the last vacant spot. Nick got out and politely reminded the driver that these spaces were reserved for diplomats. He was told rather less politely where to go. "You diplomats can park anywhere without being fined." Nick tried to explain that if he got a parking ticket he would be in much worse trouble than just a fine. This cut no ice. He parked at a meter, went to his office and reported the offending vehicle. Within a few minutes it had been towed away by the New York Police Department.

The British Mission was a frequent target for demonstrations – anti-colonial, pro-Israel, pro-development, pro-IRA. We never ceased to wonder at the strength of the Irish lobby or the naivety of peace-loving Americans who for a generation were conned into supporting the most violent terrorists on earth. Often the only way to get in and out of the building was to join the demonstration on the outside and peel off when it reached the revolving door. Nick showed the technique to our new Ambassador, Fred Warner, and was horrified the next day to look out of his window and see the Ambassador cheerfully parading around behind a placard which read "Brits out of Ireland" while press photographers photographed the demonstration. Nick was fearful that some enterprising editor would recognise the Ambassador and publish the picture. Fortunately, Ambassador Warner's face was not yet known in New York and the picture was never published. It was only a matter of time before the Irish Government sought to mobilise the United Nations itself in support of its cause in Northern Ireland. Bloody Sunday provided the opportunity. Foreign Minister Paddy Hillery came to New York to lobby for a Security Council Resolution condemning the United Kingdom. He was well received in the United States but less well at the UN. His proposal was a flagrant interference in the domestic affairs of a member state and other members had good reason not to set a precedent. Many had minority problems of their own. To the French we whispered "Bretons", to the Spanish "Basques", even to the Americans "blacks". Crude, no doubt, but effective. Paddy Hillery did not press the matter.

From Lord Caradon we learnt many things – how to combine rigorous defence of British interests with a compassionate understanding of the concerns of suffering humanity; how to defuse a tense meeting with the judicious use of humour and comic verse; how to be liked and respected in a bitterly divided environment. The United Kingdom punched above its weight at the UN under his humane and skilful leadership.

There were too many parties at the UN and every nation felt that it had to celebrate its National Day and other occasions besides. Permanent Representatives were often invited to two or three receptions an evening with a dinner to follow. Hugh Caradon would always accept these invitations and would always attend. The trick, he once explained to us, was to do something memorable as you arrive such as kiss the wrong wife, shake hands vigorously with the representative of a hostile power, or even drop a glass. That way the host would remember that you had attended. Then you could do a quick circuit of the company smiling beneficently, make an unobtrusive escape through the back door and move on swiftly to the next reception. Lord Caradon reckoned to be able to attend three parties in half an hour in such a way that each host would believe that he had been there all evening. So far as we know he was never caught.

Lady Caradon was a power in her own right in the British delegation and in diplomatic New York. New York cabbies are famous. Once on her way home from the airport Sylvia Caradon's driver was lamenting the prohibitive cost of his forthcoming hernia operation. Sylvia asked gently whether there was not a case for a National Health Service as in Britain. "Lady," said the cabbie, "are you a socialist?"

"Yes," replied Sylvia, "my husband is a minister in the Labour Government in London." The cabbie pulled off the motorway.

"Lady," he said, "get out of my cab. I don't have socialists in my cab." Lady Caradon was abandoned on the Through Way – and dined out on the story for weeks.

The job was about the press and the media. Nick spent the morning in the office, finding out what was going on and clearing his lines with senior colleagues, on key issues with Lord Caradon himself. The afternoon was at the UN building, either in the Security Council or simply walking the press floor. Sometimes he had urgent messages to convey and cases to commend. Often he was simply seeing and being seen, finding out what were the issues that were bothering journalists and floating British notions on the questions of the day. The press conferences were always "on-the-record", and everything said could be quoted and attributed. Conversations on the press floor in journalists' offices or in bars and restaurants were "unattributable"; they could be ascribed to "a diplomatic source", hopefully a "usually reliable source" but never identified as British.

The relationship between a government press officer and a journalist is ambivalent. Their interests are never identical. But they are in each other's pockets. A spokesman who misleads the press will not be trusted again. A journalist who betrays a confidence will not receive another. Whether they like it or not, they are colleagues in the business, new every morning, of rendering government intelligible to its citizens. Nick learned to discriminate and the frankness with which he spoke reflected his degree of trust for his interlocutor. After a few months he began to show to trusted journalists bootleg copies of secret telegrams so that they would understand the issues which faced the British Government. Then they would discuss how this information could be reflected in public. He was never betrayed. Ten years later, as Head of News Department in London, he tried to re-establish the same relationship but found it impossible. Journalists would no longer undertake to protect a confidence. So they were told rather less. So they dug harder. There was a descending spiral of reticence and resentment (Chapter 9).

118

The New York experience led to some lifelong friendships: Bob Estabrook of the *Washington Post*, Richard Hottelet of CBS News, Donald Grant of *St Louis Post-Dispatch* and Geoffrey Myers of the *Daily Telegraph*.

One vehicle for publicising British activity at the UN was to release Lord Caradon's public engagements. At a press conference one day Nick was explaining what his master had been doing "in the interstices" of these engagements. The UN correspondent of Associated Press asked how to spell "interstices". Nick obliged. "G A P S," he said. This exchange was published in the "Peterborough" column of the *Daily Telegraph*.

A particular friend was the press officer of the Argentine Mission who rejoiced in the name of Billy McGough. It may be thought ironic in view of later events, but in those days the British and Argentine Governments were agreed that their dispute over the Falkland Islands/Malvinas was a matter for bilateral consultation, not for public debate at the UN. The anti-colonial committee of the General Assembly, known as the Committee of Twenty-Four, tried each year to schedule a debate, and each year the British and Argentine Missions were instructed to resist this. It became an annual ceremony. Billy and Nick would meet for an excellent lunch, then repair to the press floor and solemnly march in step the length of the floor to place their identical press releases on the racks in precise synchronisation. Cheap theatre perhaps but it made its point.

Nick had another spat with the Committee of Twenty-Four when it put forward a draft resolution proposing instant independence for the island of Pitcairn, which then had a population of eighty-six. He prepared a spoof press release from the newly independent government of Pitcairn announcing that all eighty-six islanders had been appointed to the Cabinet, including a one year old child. He left copies of this document on the press floor (without the crest of the British delegation) and refused to speculate about its authorship.

119

The United States appointed as an Ambassador to the United Nations for the General Assembly Shirley Temple Black, well known as a child film star, who was then seeking to make a name for herself as a political figure in California. She wrote an article in the *San Francisco Examiner* which was so impenetrably full of jargon as to be literally unintelligible. Nick sent a copy to his US colleague asking for a translation. Nick Bush replied that he did not understand it either. He would be glad to oblige if we would first indicate in which recognised language the original article was written.

The issue which commanded the greatest flow of words, then as now, was the Middle East. The crucial document at that time was Security Council Resolution 242, tabled by Lord Caradon and passed unanimously on 22 November 1967 after the Six Day War. It enshrined the key bargain: territory for peace – Israeli agreement to withdraw against Arab agreement to make peace. This was expressed in Operative Paragraph 1 in the following terms: *withdrawal of Israeli armed forces from territories occupied in the recent conflict* and *acknowledgement of the sovereignty, territorial integrity and political independence of every state in the area and their right to live in peace within secure and recognised boundaries free from threats or acts of force.* The phrase withdrawal "from territories occupied in the recent conflict" did not in English determine which territories. But in French the resolution reads *"des territoires"* which would naturally be translated "from the territories" (ie all of them). Both Hugh Caradon and George Brown claimed to have negotiated this constructive ambiguity with Soviet Foreign Minister Gromyko as they stood at adjacent urinals in the gentleman's toilet. We never could establish which claim was correct.

The Middle East remains one of the most explosive issues in the world, composed as it is of two colossal historic injustices – the injustice done to the Jewish people, first by the Romans and then by generations of Europeans culminating in the horrors of the Nazi gas chambers, and the injustice done to the Palestinian people, not least by Britain in the Balfour declaration of 1917 in supposing that the Jewish question could be solved at the expense of Palestinians. It is a

120

tragedy for the Middle East, and indeed for the United Nations, that steady Soviet support for the Arabs and steady United States support for Israel prevented the parliament of mankind from making any significant contribution to a peaceful settlement.

Much harm was done to the Palestinian cause at this time by the Popular Front for the Liberation of Palestine. They provoked international consternation by a spectacular series of hijacks of commercial airliners to a remote airstrip in the Jordanian desert. One such hijack was a scheduled British Airways flight carrying children on their way back to boarding school. The pressures on Edward Heath's new government were overwhelming. The PFPL had the good sense to release the women and children but a number of men were held hostage against the release of Palestinians in detention, including one of the hijackers, Leila Khaled, then held in Ealing Police Station. In the end Britain released Leila Khaled as part of a package deal which secured the release of the hostages. We thought then, and think still, that this was a mistake. Britain had enjoyed an enviable reputation for inflexibility in the face of blackmail. British travellers had been the safer for it. Now suddenly we became a soft touch; it was worthwhile to kidnap British citizens. It took us a decade to regain our tough reputation with some help from the Germans at the Munich Olympics. As for the PFPL, their terrorism was born of frustration at the inability of the international community to meet their grievances. But their media triumph was short-lived. The fame they sought turned to notoriety. They were not trusted again.

The Chinese seat at the UN, including the Security Council, was still held by the Nationalist Chinese Government which since 1949 had controlled only the island of Taiwan. The obvious solution was for Peking to be given the Chinese seat, including permanent membership of the Security Council, while Taiwan was admitted to the UN as a member state in its own right. But neither China would accept this "two-China solution". The only thing they agreed about was that there was only one China of which both claimed to be the legitimate government. So the most populous nation on earth was

121

excluded from the councils of the United Nations, while a veto was wielded by an offshore island. Each year the case for change grew stronger. Each year both Chinas refused to compromise. Each year member states had to vote. Each year the vote for Peking grew. There was a clear simple majority for giving the seat to Peking. But there was a complication. The substantive vote was regularly preceded by a procedural resolution to determine whether or not the seating of a quarter of the human race was or was not "an important question". If it was it would require a two-thirds majority to change the status quo. So those who wanted change had to pretend that the question was not important so that it could be carried by a simple majority.

The United Kingdom had recognised Peking in January 1950. This was the origin of the quotation from Winston Churchill which Sir Richard Beaumont had quoted to Abdelazziz Bouteflika in the military hospital in Algiers: "The purpose of diplomatic relations is not to confer a compliment but to secure a convenience," (Chapter 4). British policy has always been pragmatic. We recognise governments, not because we love them but because we accept that in practice they control the national territory, and it is therefore useful to be able to do business with them. Accordingly, we regularly voted for the seating of Peking. But we also voted for the proposition that this was an important question, both to please the Americans and because the question was manifestly important. At the General Assembly in 1971 we changed our position on the "important question", voting through gritted teeth for a self-evident absurdity on the ground that the exclusion of China was an even greater absurdity.

The British Mission began to receive hate mail from Americans who felt betrayed by the allies they had saved in the Second World War. It was hard for an Englishman to understand the passion of Americans on this subject. For them China was not the "Far East" but the "Near West". American endeavour in China, political, military, commercial, missionary, was very great. Chiang Kai-shek was a wartime ally and remained a key partner in United States policy in Asia. It was a matter not of practicality but of loyalty. They

122

denounced British treachery. Nick replied to every letter, patiently explaining that the exclusion of one quarter of mankind was absurd and damaging to the United Nations because it did not correspond to the real world, that British policy was based not on morals but on pragmatism, and that we had reversed our position on the "important question" because it had become an obstacle to sensible reform; he quoted Winston Churchill who was still a hero in the United States. This line cut little ice in the fevered atmosphere. Many correspondents wrote a second time to complain that if British policy was not based on morals then it should be. How could the United States remain allied to such turncoats?

The British switch on the procedural resolution began to influence others. It seemed for the first time that the change might be made. Representations were made in the capitals of the waverers. It was one of the rare debates at the UN where the outcome was in doubt until the final vote. By good fortune, Sue was present to witness the excitement. She had come to the UN to hear a speech by Maurice Schumann because she had been told that he spoke the most beautiful French. She found herself in a crowded General Assembly for the China debate. When the voting began the atmosphere was like a horse race with punters leaping around, much shouting and gesticulating, and as each vote was recorded on the overhead screens the odds were recalculated again and again. The experts knew which votes were critical and about halfway through the procedure there was a great cry of triumph. The "important question" was defeated by three votes. Before the substantive vote, the experienced representative of Taiwan made a dignified speech. He and his delegation left the chamber for ever. The seating of communist China was then formally carried by a substantial majority. A little bit of history had been made. The Permanent Representative of the United States who had led the campaign against this outcome was one George Bush. It was an act of genius subsequently to appoint him as the American Representative in Peking (Chapter 7).

Lord Caradon was not only Permanent Representative, he was also a political appointee and a Minister, a member of a famous political family. The four sons of Isaac Foot were Michael, later leader of the Labour Party; Dingle, then Solicitor General; John, a leading West Country solicitor; and Hugh Caradon who as Sir Hugh Foot had been the last colonial Governor of Kenya and Cyprus. As the British General Election drew near the question arose what would happen to Lord Caradon if Labour lost power in London. On public occasions Caradon's answer was always the same. He would explain "the tribal customs of the English" in order to make clear that his family name was Foot. Then he would refer his audience to Psalm 121 verse 3: "He will not suffer thy foot to be moved".

But moved he was. Labour lost the election by a narrow margin and Edward Heath became Prime Minister. We were in mid-air over the Atlantic on our way home on leave. We were greeted by our brother-in-law at Dublin Airport with the news that Nick had a new boss. Sir Alec Douglas-Home had been appointed Foreign Secretary, Lord Caradon had already left New York and his successor had been announced – Sir Colin Crowe, a career diplomat. We returned for our last six months at the UN covering the General Assembly of 1971. At Nick's first press conference on return he was asked how British policy at the UN would be affected by this change in London. He acknowledged that there had been a general election in his country since he had last addressed the press corps. He spoke for a new government and a new Permanent Representative. He therefore would not accept, as a commentary on anything he was about to say, a quotation from anything he may have said before. Everyone laughed and the issue was defused.

In the New Year we were recalled to take up an unexpected appointment in London.

Chapter 6
Science and Technology
1972-75

Since Nick had a degree in mediaeval history from the University of Cambridge, he was perhaps a natural choice to be Assistant Head of Science and Technology Department in the Foreign and Commonwealth Office, responsible for the peaceful uses of atomic energy, the administration of the Non-Proliferation Treaty (NPT) and other mysterious matters. He was scared. His predecessor had been a nuclear physicist by training and there would need to be a change of style. During his first week he went to meetings in Whitehall and emerged without a notion what had been discussed, let alone decided. Then someone lent him a small book called *Penguin Atoms*. In the back there was a two-page glossary which he learned by heart. Whitehall began to be intelligible.

Initially the job was about the diplomatic aspects of civil nuclear power generation, representation on nuclear matters at the European Economic Community in Brussels and the International Atomic Energy Agency in Vienna, the negotiation of safeguards under the NPT and of arrangements for continuing trade in small quantities of nuclear material, the management of the tripartite collaboration with Germany and the Netherlands for the enrichment of nuclear material by centrifuge, and fending off Irish anxieties about Sellafield. The issues were complex and highly political, but limited. Science and Technology Department was regarded in the Office as a technical backwater. Petroleum was handled by a separate Oil Department.

Then disaster struck in the form of the first international energy crisis of 1972–73. The Organisation of Petroleum Exporting Countries (OPEC) and its Middle Eastern sister the Organisation of

125

Arab Petroleum Exporting Countries (OAPEC) began to turn down the tap for political reasons, and to discriminate between their customers, withholding oil supplies from certain importing nations, notably Israel, the United States and (quaintly) the Netherlands. The technical backwater became the fulcrum for the economic interests of the Western world, for relations with the Middle East, for the viability of British oil companies overseas and for solidarity with our American allies and our European partners. The FCO moved swiftly to merge STD with Oil Department to create the first Energy Department in Whitehall. Nick was promoted counsellor and found himself deputy to the new Head of Energy Department, Jock Taylor. Life became more exciting.

These stirring events had been stimulated by the Yom Kippur War. We had been on holiday in Italy with Nick's parents. With his father Nick climbed the Leaning Tower of Pisa. We admired the famous racecourse at Sienna and the paintings in Florence. Mother was slowly losing her sight. She had spent a year meticulously researching the field and had a list of fourteen famous pictures which she was determined to see before it was too late. She saw them all and made a beautiful scrapbook to record our tour. Throughout the holiday Nick's attention was divided. World events were focusing on his little patch in the Foreign Office. His life would be very different when he got home. But he was not there to help his colleagues under pressure or to influence the outcome.

For the last year of our posting in New York we had let our little terraced house near Orpington. We had some nasty shocks when we returned. The woman of the house had been struggling through a nervous breakdown and chain-smoked her way through every day. The internal paintwork looked white near the floor, but went through various shades of brown to mahogany near the ceiling. A fridge full of food had been switched off for a month. The larder was also full of rotting food and leftovers. The curtains when we tried to close them stuck together as with sticky paste. The pretty quarry tiles around the fireplace had been painted bright glossy red. Unpaid bills accumulated. To add to our welcome there was a miners' strike, with electricity off for hours even before the three-day week began. One night Nick and Sue found themselves on their stomachs on the hearth scraping off the red paint by candlelight. They gave up the task in giggles. When the boys came home for the Easter holidays the house shrank. It had been a happy home for eight years but we had clearly grown out of it. This was 1972 when "gazumping" entered our vocabulary and houses disappeared from the agents' lists before they could be surveyed. By September, after several heartbreaks over lovely houses which met our criteria, we decided to try auction. Sue's parents were moving too, from the family home in Redhill into the Rectory at Bentley in Hampshire – a tied house. So to keep a stake in the housing market they offered to buy the little house in Halstead. Nick's father offered to provide a bridging loan if we found a house at auction, because we knew we would have to write a cheque immediately for 10% of the auction price and there was precious little in the bank.

Nick had to go to Mexico for a conference in September. When the boys were back at school Sue started some serious house-hunting. She discovered during her searches that there was a neglected area of Kent in the middle of a triangle formed by Maidstone in the north, Tonbridge in the west and Ashford in the east. Sometimes called "The Sink of Kent" because of regular flooding, this plot in the Garden of England had been written off by relevant council departments as far as development was concerned. The water table was too high. Most of the available property was too expensive but one oast house looked possible. The conversion was incomplete, so we could add our own finishing touches. It had a tiny garden, so Nick visited the farmer next door to negotiate a price for a corner of his adjacent orchard, if, but only if, we were successful at auction. The farmer had no interest in selling, but Nick took a bottle of whisky to encourage the discussion and in the morning he could not remember what he had agreed to. Nick took the afternoon off and we joined the excitement of the auction rooms in the Star Hotel in Maidstone. We agreed our absolutely maximum bid. Every time Nick took his pipe out of his mouth the auctioneer added a thousand pounds. When we reached our top price there was silence. It was the owner's reserve price and we were the only (innocent) bidders. We moved on 13 November and have lived here happily ever since.

At Christmas we gave the boys a dog ("a nice wee cross" to quote the vet). Heidi quickly became a member of the family and together we explored the open country around our new home. With her in charge we were happy for the boys to roam and play outside all day. The two boys at the farm became good friends and they spent time in each other's houses or building forts at the dump from discarded hay bales.

Julia made her appearance in January 1974. Sue joined the local babysitting circle and was able to get out to village activities even when Nick was away. She joined the WI making new friends and taking part in the varied events, including going as a local representative to the annual meeting in the Albert Hall. As a member of the Marden Theatre Group she took part in several productions and even persuaded Nick to play the corpse in *Murder at the Vicarage* because the part did not need rehearsals. He was word perfect from the outset. Julia came to rehearsals in her carrycot. The enlarged family revelled in the fresh air and freedom of living in a quiet country backwater.

Summer holidays were spent on the west coast of Scotland in an old school house on Loch Hourn, and with friends in their croft further north between Lochinver and Cape Wrath.

Apart from occasional diplomatic functions in London our family life was normal and ordinary, no different from that of our friends – except that we used Burmese to talk privately when the boys mastered too much French.

The energy crisis provoked fuel rationing, opportunistic strikes by miners and train drivers, social unrest in the United Kingdom and other countries and a dramatic change of lifestyle. Nick was suddenly detached from the family. Commuting became a nightmare. Trains barely ran. The roads were jammed with angry commuters from five o'clock in the morning until eight o'clock at night. Nick would drive to Beckenham to collect his new boss and together they would inch their way into London. A forty-five minute journey took three hours each way. Any driver with spare seats would always pick up hitch-hikers. On one occasion we picked up two taciturn women who got out in Camberwell. When we got to the office we found that they had slashed the back seat of Jock's car and left a note which read "to two scabs, from two miners' wives". We were more cautious thereafter. Camp beds were issued in the office. Only front line departments were allowed to burn electricity. At dusk Nick's office would suddenly fill up with very senior colleagues.

The international situation was no better. Oil rationing struck at the heart of partnership between consumer nations. There were calls to share what oil there was in defiance of the Arab boycott of the US and the Netherlands. The French were reluctant. A letter to *The Times* read:

Sharing oil to help the Dutch
Does not seem to please us much.
But playing fair was Britain's wont
If Pompidou or Pompidon't.

The maddening thing was that oil sharing was already happening under the radar by informal arrangement between oil companies privately approved by governments. But we could not acknowledge this lest it should provoke retaliation by the suppliers and leave us all with less oil to share.

The International Energy Agency was invented as a club for oil importers to balance (or confront) OPEC. There was endless argument on the policy appropriate for nations which were at the same time powerful and helpless. In parallel the North-South Dialogue sought to identify common interests between producers and consumers of oil and between givers and receivers of aid. It was heady stuff – crucial and prolonged negotiations amongst officials of

129

disparate governments whose common interest was that they were all short of sleep.

Meanwhile "routine" work continued at the International Atomic Energy Agency (IAEA) in Vienna to follow up and implement the Non-Proliferation Treaty. The treaty required safeguards on nuclear material traded between nations. It seemed absurd to mobilise the expensive paraphernalia of international safeguards on trade in negligible quantities like the luminous hands on a watch. But how to define negligible? The question was fraught with difficulties – security, political, commercial. A Committee of the IAEA laboured for three years under the chairmanship of a charming Swiss professor Claude Zangger. In the end it agreed on a "Trigger List", which identified the quantities and qualities of nuclear material which trigger safeguards. Professor Zangger gave a dinner for delegates in his home village in the Alps to celebrate this small victory for common sense. He made a speech comparing his committee to a Swiss cheese: *on commence avec les troues:* you begin with the holes. Someone else contributed a limerick based on the legal tag: *de minimis non curat lex:* the law does not concern itself with trifles:

There once was a lawyer named Rex
With diminutive organs of sex.
Had up for exposure
He made this disclosure:
De minimis non curat lex.

Ministers at this time were wrestling with the choice of nuclear reactor to replace the first generation of nuclear power stations and improve the security of Britain's energy supply. Some Ministers disliked nuclear power on safety or moral grounds. This objection became more difficult to sustain when the energy crisis brutally exposed our dependence on OPEC oil. The British nuclear industry wanted to build more Advanced Gas-Cooled Reactors (AGRs) which were designed and built in Britain. Most other countries with nuclear power industries had opted for one of the two American designs – Light Water Reactors (LWRs) or Pressurised Water Reactors

130

(PWRs). We advised Foreign Office Ministers that splendid isolation was not a sensible posture in this field. On foreign policy grounds we recommended the LWR. They chose the AGR, essentially for nationalistic-industrial reasons. When Nick got home that night Sue had been listening to *Question Time*. The consensus had been that Ministers had been nobbled by their civil servants into taking the wrong decision. The Minister on the programme knew perfectly well that this was the opposite of the truth but he chose not to say so. Sue knew the truth too, and had steam coming out of her ears. Nick was past caring. He had done his best. It was for politicians to decide and to carry the can.

We knew we were due for an overseas posting in 1975. Nick was asked informally whether we would be interested in Cairo. We got excited about the pyramids. Then abruptly the post was filled by a candidate much better qualified than Nick. Would we like to go to China instead? We got excited about the Forbidden City and the Great Wall.

We asked for the Peking post-report. Amongst other caveats was that dogs were not a good idea. The accommodation was a flat in the diplomatic compound, the Chinese were frightened of dogs and ate strays. We all looked at Heidi with alarm. Happily we found a home for her in Marden. She was later handed on to a retired shepherd and when we came home on leave we decided there was no point in visiting her. If she recognised us that would only upset us all since we could not take her back to Peking. The trauma was such that we vowed never to have a dog again.

But we did need to find a nanny for baby Julia and put the usual notice in *The Lady*. China was still in the throes of the Cultural Revolution and no one seemed very keen to accompany us. Then the office sent us a letter from a young Scotswoman who was so keen to see the People's Republic for herself she had taught herself Chinese. As a trial run for all concerned Anne Newell came on holiday with us in the West Country. Nick's parents joined the party and commented that Julia would learn to speak with good clear consonants. She had reached the age of eighteen months and was already a great chatterbox.

We got our documents in order and inoculations up to date. Sue did an enormous shop – dry goods for six of us for a year. "Boots" were suspicious of the large orders for aspirin and the like. Once they had understood that we were really going to China they were very helpful. And three years later most of the Alka Seltzer came back unopened.

On 5 June 1975 the journey began with a visit to Marden Memorial Hall to vote in the Referendum on British entry into the European Economic Community. This was not only because we wanted to cast our vote; we feared that the pro-European Chinese might ask us whether we had done so. Duty done, we made for Heathrow and the long flight to Hong Kong. The plane was a Boeing 747 in which the upstairs cabin was transformed pro tem into a nursery. Nick, Sue and new nanny Anne took it in turns to look after baby Julia. She seemed the model baby, quietly sleeping most of the way. But she had to be woken for the descent into Hong Kong and understandably she screamed for the next couple of hours. This did not phase the Governor's ADC who had come to meet us. He eased us out of the plane, down the steps and into the Rolls Royce which was waiting for us on the tarmac. The Governor had been Nick's boss in the Private Office ten years earlier and he and his wife kindly invited us to stay with them in Government House. Only Julia failed to be impressed by the Gurkha guards saluting smartly and the gracious mansion overlooking the harbour. Murray and Squeak (sic) apologised for demoting us to the Duke of Edinburgh's suite – the Queen's roof was leaking! Anne and baby Julia were whisked away to their apartment while we explored ours – they discovered the swimming pool first.

We found we each had dressing rooms and bathrooms, one single bed as well as a vast double bedroom and a spacious sitting room, all elegantly furnished. Our luggage was still on its way from the airport so we had a quick tidy up and tiptoed down to tea. Sir Murray and

132

Lady Maclehose soon made us feel at home and explained the programme arranged for us during the days before we crossed into China and caught the flight to Peking.

When we returned to our rooms our luggage had been unpacked for us and put where our personal servants, valet and maid, thought it should go. But most of it was missing. And all the silly little useful things which Sue had pushed in at the last moment were set out accusingly on the shelves; a row of wooden clothes pegs stood to attention on one shelf, on another the Marmite and stock cubes were marshalled with the oven cleaning pads.

Warm baths had been drawn for us and clothes laid out which the staff had chosen as more or less adequate for the evening. The rest had been sent off to be laundered, dry-cleaned or mended. All this gently implied criticism might have made us inwardly shrink but we got the giggles instead. Like going through the Narnian wardrobe we were in a new world and were enjoying it. We just lived the moment and tried to fulfil the role allocated to us. At dinner the Governor's piper played for the four of us while marching round and round the table. The same piper woke us next morning, playing a little further away. After breakfast Nick went off to numerous meetings as part of his briefing for Peking, and Sue was taken shopping. Some elegant coffee cups were purchased and colourful cushions for the Peking flat. Everyone we met was kind and helpful, so the grandness of the lifestyle seemed less extraordinary. One could if necessary get used to it.

We were invited to Happy Valley Racecourse to lunch with our hosts in the Governor's spacious box. We hailed a taxi downtown. At first the driver refused to take us. His whole family had been ruined by gambling on the horses at Happy Valley. It was an evil place, he said. He relented only when Nick explained that we were only going for lunch. But we got the full lecture on the iniquities of gambling all the way there. Our fellow guests were wealthy Chinese. When they compared their losses at blackjack the previous evening we understood what our taxi driver was worried about. The sums were in four or five figures. Later we were taken on a mini cruise on the Governor's yacht to be shown the islands and where some of the problems were. Nick was taken in a helicopter over the New Territories to see where the refugees were infiltrating. Anne said very little but Julia settled happily into the new routine. Other sightseeing in the colony was similar to the visit we had made from Rangoon in 1960, though the slums were less evident and the people more prosperous.

We were driven to the crossing point. Behind us lay the colour and vitality of free Hong Kong. Ahead of us the masses of the people in identical Mao suits and uniform haircuts. In China one never travels alone. We were soon swept up by the appointed guides who saw us safely onto the train to the airport. It was hot and humid and while we waited for the plane for Peking, baby Julia slept. Sue fanned her while gazing with a thousand different emotions at this new country, the land of her birth, so foreign, so uniform, so colourless. A steep learning curve had begun.

Chapter 7
China: 1975-77

China is an extraordinary country. It is immense with vast tracts of mountain and desert, great rivers and teeming millions – one quarter of the human race. It has a great and distinctive civilisation. For two thousand years the throne in Peking was the centre of the universe and all foreigners equally were barbarians. Such is the power of this ancient culture that by the time you have lived there for three years you begin to believe it.

Mao Tse-tung had dominated China since the communist revolution of 1949. Mao was a visionary and a tyrant, believed to be responsible for the deaths of seventy million people. In 1958 the "Great Leap Forward" systematically sacrificed agriculture and food for industrial development and exports, provoking the "Great Famine" in which some thirty-eight million people died from starvation. At a party conference in 1962, President Liu Shao-chi voiced the views of many party leaders in bravely denouncing the Great Leap as a Great Disaster, forcing Mao to draw back from the extremes of his fanaticism. There followed the Sino-Soviet dispute, the great purge of his political enemies and the Cultural Revolution which sought to replace traditional Chinese culture with "Marxism-Leninism-Mao-Tse-tung-Thought" and to take revenge on the moderate leadership of Liu Shao-chi and Chou En-lai. In 1975 Mao was in his dotage but China was still governed in his name and none dared challenge him in public.

This was by far the most foreign place in which we lived and worked; exotic culture, fascinating language, doctrinaire socialism, unpredictable dictatorship, climate of fear. Its policies, both at home and abroad, were a mass of dogmatic contradictions uttered by the Great Helmsman himself, administered by a suave and plausible

135

bureaucracy who had inherited the mantle of the Imperial mandarinate. China was hostile to the UK because of Hong Kong – then still a successful British colony and a thorn in the side of Chinese communism. The British Embassy in Peking had been sacked and burned by a Chinese mob in 1966. On the other hand, the European Union was cultivated by China because it was neither Russia nor America. On the principle that your enemy's enemy is your friend, China sought good relations with Europe as a counterweight to Brezhnev's Soviet Union.

Peking is the most expert British Embassy in the world. Nick was the Ambassador's deputy – and the only one of the ten senior members of staff who was not a specialist Sinologist. The Ambassador, Sir Edward Youde, was a diplomat of vast Chinese experience who came nearer than most foreigners to understanding Mao's China – the intrigues and subterfuges, the suffering and endurance, the pride and the penury of China. He used to say that Nick's job was to remind him that the rest of the world existed, and to make wise remarks at office meetings like "Remember the Soviet Union". Under Teddy Youde the embassy acquired a reputation in London for being alarmist. Our telegrams were laced with reports and forebodings of disaster. Thirty years later when we read about these times in scholarly books we find that we did not know a tithe of it. We were accused of exaggeration, but things in China were ten times worse than we said they were.

Six weeks after our arrival, Teddy Youde went on leave and Nick became *Charge d'Affaires*, technically responsible for British relations with a quarter of the human race. Two weeks later there burst upon the world an utterly opaque and very Chinese crisis – the Water Margin Campaign. *The Water Margin* was a fourteenth century Chinese novel, popularly supposed to be one of Mao's favourite books. It told of a Chinese Robin Hood, an outlaw who robbed the rich and gave to the poor, but in the end integrated his band of rebels into the Imperial army. In July 1975 there appeared on an inside page of *The People's Daily* a review criticising this arcane work as if it had been published yesterday. In the English translation

136

this literary debate coined a new word: "capitulationism". All China watchers in Peking agreed that this was significant, but they did not agree on what it meant. Was Mao depicted as Robin Hood or as the Emperor? Was it the rebellion or the peace that was under attack? Was the article the work of Mao's cronies or his enemies? Nick clearly had to say something to London – but what? He gathered his expert colleagues to brainstorm the phenomenon for two hours and sent them away to draft a telegram. They argued among themselves for the rest of the day and submitted an inconclusive draft that was nineteen pages long. Nick took it home, abridged it to two and a half pages, added an innocent layman's opinion and sent it off. London's reaction was a private note from the Permanent Under Secretary reproaching Nick for verbosity. The analysis was no doubt useful to specialists but was far too long for general distribution. A lesson hard learned. He should have seen the original! It transpired in the end that the campaign was orchestrated by Mao himself to attack Prime Minister Chou En-Lai and other senior colleagues who had criticised the excesses of the Cultural Revolution. They were guilty, it seemed, of "capitulationism".

That summer the Diplomatic Services Bureau (DSB), monopoly suppliers of Chinese staff to the diplomatic corps, circulated to all embassies a draft contract to govern the employment of Chinese citizens in diplomatic missions. It contained several pages on the obligations of employers, and a single paragraph on the obligations of employees, who were required to work to the best of their ability. About half the missions in Peking signed the document without serious thought. The Chinese controlled these matters anyway and the text of the document would make no practical difference. But it was clear to Nick that the FCO would never countenance a document of this kind. He declined to sign and sought to rally other EU representatives to support his stand. Preoccupied with his early duties in China and the responsibilities of *Charge d'Affaires*, he put it out of his mind. Then he paid his first call on the director of the DSB. The director pushed a copy of the draft across his desk. He observed that it was very hot in Peking in August. No doubt Mrs Fenn would like to have some help in the flat. Alas, the DSB would be unable to provide any staff to missions which refused to sign, above all those who encouraged other missions in their intransigence. It was indeed very hot and Sue was indeed in trouble. But we could not yield to blackmail. We contrived to negotiate with the Chinese People's Insurance Company, a policy which precisely matched the obligations of the employer in the DSB's monstrous contract and persuaded Personnel Services Department of the FCO to pay the modest premium. Then we could sign. Over time this arrangement became standard practice amongst embassies in China.

As a kind of backhanded compliment, the DSB assigned to the British Counsellor the best cook in Peking, Lao Wu, who had learned his trade at the French Embassy. We also had an excellent "Ahyi" or maid (literally "Auntie". She was responsible for all the household duties except cooking and looking after Julia). Like all the others they had to leave their work from time to time to attend political lectures, but they stayed with us till the end of our posting. We also had the same Mandarin teacher, Mrs. Deng, twice a week. She was a strong, caring person. We suspected that she had been brought up a Christian; when asked she readily explained to Ayhi about Easter eggs and angels – and then was embarrassed when she realised that we had been listening.

The iniquities of the DSB were a running theme of diplomatic life in China. Domestic staff would be removed without warning at inconvenient moments, just when the cook had learned the kids' favourite meals or how to prepare the employer's national dish. One colleague had her children's nanny taken away and given to another family in the same compound. Her children were devastated to see "their nanny" playing in the park with other strange children. An Egyptian colleague had her cook removed just as her own country's President, on an official visit, was driving in from the airport. The wife of the Netherlands' Ambassador wanted to serve some blinis with the excellent local caviar. She mixed the batter herself. Sadly the cook did not understand that the batter needed cooking and the yellow liquid was presented as a pool for the fish eggs to swim in. It was usually possible to hire extra staff for a reception but they might

138

be straight from the commune and have no idea what a gin and tonic was. Poor kids! Hoping for three waiters to arrive to help at a reception, we spotted three young lads skulking outside our entrance and sent Lao Wu down to investigate. He brought them up and showed them the bathroom where they could change. They locked themselves in until the party was over.

At one of the first diplomatic dinners we attended, the antics of the staff reduced our hostess to tears. It was more like the Mad Hatter's Tea Party as plates arrived or disappeared at bewildering speed, sometimes with food, sometimes empty. Everyone except our hostess declared this was quite normal and we vowed never to take official entertaining too seriously. The alternative strategy, adopted by our own Ambassador, was to teach a couple of simple meals to the cook, eat them day after day until they were passable and then serve one or the other to invited guests. The results were delicious but it became a bit of a joke. "You dined at the British Residence? Did you have the fish or the chicken menu?" How blessed we were with dear Lao Wu.

Mrs Deng once gave us a stern lecture when we left little Julia for too long in the care of Nanny Anne while we went on tour. She said Anne was too depressed to be left in charge. In truth, Julia had developed bronchitis and then asthma. We had kept in touch all the time by phone and knew the embassy (RAF) nurse, Joyce, was looking after Julia's health. Anne had expected Mao's China to be a Utopia, a classless society. She found instead that the pay gap between workers and party cadres was not only much bigger than in the West, but that they were kept apart physically by special schools and shops as well as housing. They were driven around in big cars with closed curtains shutting off all sight of the bosses from the pedalling masses. To keep the masses from mixing with foreigners, even from the likes of enthusiastic Anne (who had taught herself Mandarin at home), she found local people were pushed out of eating places as soon as she walked in. It was sad to see her idealism destroyed so quickly and we feared a nervous breakdown. By the end of the year she had pulled through her despair and went back to Scotland to train as a teacher.

While on leave in the summer of 1976 we put an advertisement in *The Lady* for a new nanny to come back to China with us. It appeared two days after the news of the horrific earthquake in Tangshan, yet we got seventy-nine applications for the post. Although we had explained that the nanny would have to share a bedroom with two-year old Julia during school holidays (when the boys would be home too), more than half the replies told us they were single parents and would have to bring their child too. Others disqualified themselves because they were under the minimum twenty-one years we had stipulated. We got the list down to six or eight and invited them to come and spend a day with us in Kent. Tina was nearly last on the list. When we took her back to the station to catch her train she turned to us and sweetly begged us to choose her. Charlie stated firmly that we did not need to see any more candidates. We had all been smitten.

And so it was that she and several of her family gathered at Heathrow in September for the Swissair flight to Peking. Nick had been recalled early and Sue had never had to make the travel arrangements on her own before. A tannoy announcement informed us that the Peking plane was waiting for us. The three girls, Tina, Julia and Sue ran for the gate. In rushing us through no one spotted that we had failed to get Tina a visa. At Bombay we were given landing cards to fill in and discovered our appalling mistake. We kept our counsel until well on our way.

The stewardess was philosophical. "You may have to come on with us to Shanghai while the embassy sorts it out." Tina suggested that a short stay in a Chinese prison would be an interesting experience. In the end events took over. The landing at Peking Airport was so bad that everything breakable finished up in a pile in the aisles, awash with gin and expensive perfume. The Chinese officials who came on board to check the passengers before allowing us out had to climb over the debris. In so far as they glanced at us it was to smile at Julia who was intrigued by all the excitement.

The three girls trooped into the terminal building. They could see Nick on the viewing gallery overhead. Sue shouted that there might be a delay because Tina did not have a visa. Nick thought she was joking. Eventually he found them sitting demurely in the immigration hall. He had found a Chinese-speaking colleague, Roger Garside, who had also been meeting someone. After a lot of discussion the perplexed officials released Tina into the custody of the embassy against the promise to get the essential document the very next day. Who says their bureaucracy was unbending? So far as we know, Tina is still the only foreign resident of Peking ever to be admitted without a visa.

Tina proved to be an amazing asset. As a nanny for Julia she was unflappable, imaginative and caring. Julia used to describe in vivid detail the wonderful voyages she had been on with Tina – to Fiji and other exotic places. She became a good friend not only to our family but to the rest of the foreign community. Nick used to ask what was wrong with all the young men because she was not married – though she got several proposals, including one at Peking Railway Station on the day we left. We called her "Our Mary Poppins" and everyone knew why. (She did of course find Mr. Right after returning to Cornwall.)

The diplomatic compound had armed guards at every entrance – to keep us in and the Chinese people out, so we lived with the absurdity that only residents were allowed to come and go. Even fire engines had to get passes from the Foreign Ministry – a process which, they said, would take about a week and was of limited value if a house was burning down. One small block of flats where only British staff lived had a fire in the rubbish chute and we had to put it out ourselves. When the Australian residence caught fire the firemen refused to drive into the compound so the Ambassador himself climbed into the cab and drove the engine in. Then the firemen reluctantly manned the hoses.

141

Our compound consisted of several four-storey blocks of flats built by the Russians in the 1950s when relations between the two communist giants had been good. They were planned for diplomats and had useful devices built in. We soon discovered the secret drawers in the skirting boards and the tops of wooden doors. Although we were "swept" from time to time, we lived with the assumption that all our conversations could be overheard. Knowing that the most useful information to an enemy is gossip about individual's weaknesses and problems – money, alcohol, affairs, etc. – one learned never to gossip about such things, even in bed. When Nick had information of a sensitive nature to share he would come into the flat and turn on all the devices we owned which made a noise, radios, tape recorders, record players and switch them on facing each other in the sitting room. Within this circle of sound he would quickly tell what needed to be said. It happened rarely but reminded us that walls do have ears. The phones were of course tapped. Sue once again had the weird experience of having a conversation played back before she had finished it.

Following the "incident" when the embassy had been sacked in 1966, the British had been allowed to supply their own paint and employ their own painters. We had distinctive bright red doors and some of us sported a pair of traditional stone lions to guard it. Other less fortunate diplomats had to accept whatever the Chinese decided for them. Or they could pay for a choice of colour and then pay again when they left China to have the walls returned to whatever garish colour had first been applied. So much of life was determined by our Chinese hosts and so little was left to individual discretion. Even shopping was simplified to one Friendship Store. Soon after we arrived the centre passed a decree forbidding the sale in any province of anything that was not grown or produced there. Overnight bananas disappeared. We wrote almost daily in the "Suggestions Book" "Please can we have some bananas?" Every time an official crossed the hall from the counter where we had been observed and tore the page out of the book. Nothing happened. When we went south we bought huge quantities but the train was so hot the bananas were

142

black by the time we got back to Peking. In the fish department we chose a big carp swimming in a tank. The assistant would knock it on the head and you took it home. Once it jumped off our kitchen table an hour after it had been "killed". Meat bought by the kilo was just one amorphous lump of beef, lamb or pork. Chicken was pretty reliable. There was plenty of caviar. One kind of a cheese, like Edam but with a pale purple rind, was provided to meet the weird taste of foreigners. Upstairs there were luxurious cashmere scarves and sweaters, padded coats and some furniture. Underwear and T-shirts were available in the Alf Garnett style but no women's clothes. There were displays of dress and furniture fabrics and expensive bright silks in primary colours. These were unrationed whereas we had to obtain coupons to buy cotton. The tailoring department was quite good at copying clothes but to Anne's amazement there were absolutely no ready-made clothes except the padded coats.

Downtown were the Commission Shops where people could bring unneeded porcelain, scrolls, antiques and bric-a-brac to sell. The men and women on duty in these shops were immensely knowledgeable and happily discoursed on the qualities of what was displayed. They rarely seemed to sell anything – the prices were too high for most foreigners. Sue got close to buying a beautiful dish but was embarrassed to find the price on the ticket applied to the wooden stand only. After saving up she bought one delightful scroll of children playing with a ball by a contemporary artist, Chen Lin Zai. It carried that essential wax seal which authorised export.

In the centre of Peking stands the Forbidden City, ancient palace of the Emperors, now familiar through tourism and television, but in 1975 still little known outside China. It is a stupendous place. Pavilions and palaces, audience chambers and private apartments, lie scattered amongst formal courtyards and shady gardens – a worthy site for the centre of the universe. And next door, west of the Forbidden City, was the real Forbidden City, Zhong Nan Hai where Chairman Mao Tse-tung was waiting for death.

143

In the grounds of the nearby Temple of the Earth, Commonwealth embassies played an annual cricket tournament attracting a crowd of curious onlookers. The game seemed so bizarre to our Chinese friends that they drew closer and closer to see what was going on, until eventually they were fielding at silly mid-off. A Chinese-speaking fielder would have to show them the hard ball and appeal to them to keep their distance in the interests of safety. This worked for a few overs but had frequently to be repeated. We took to playing with a tennis ball for fear of a diplomatic incident. The only other way to disperse a gawping crowd was to get out a camera.

For 2,000 years the Great Wall of China has protected the Empire from the barbarians to the north. It remains stupendous, winding its way among the hills, and was freely accessible. Chinese tourists and foreigners mingled as we climbed the steep steps. Just off the road to the Great Wall were the Ming Tombs where the tombs of thirteen Ming Emperors, each enclosed in a high stone wall, were scattered along the "valley of the kings". This valley seemed to be accepted by the Chinese authorities as a playground for foreigners, and it was possible to take a brisk walk without interference. Some of the tombs were in quite good repair – although neglected by the authorities – and different foreign nationalities "adopted" specific tombs, the British tomb, the French tomb, the American tomb and so on. We would arrange to meet other families for a picnic at the British tomb and get quite miffed if colleagues from other embassies were in occupation of "our" tomb.

The great lake at the Summer Palace, west of the city, would freeze solid in winter. We rigged a makeshift sail on the children's sledge so that they could go spanking from one end to the other, so long as Daddy towed the sledge back upwind. By tradition the British Consul General entertained the entire British community in China to Mrs Beaton's Hot Rum Punch on the ice on Boxing Day. This custom was less onerous than it sounds since in our day the community was only about one hundred strong. We adjourned afterwards to lunch together in the Pavilion for Listening to Orioles.

144

On a picnic at the Summer Palace, little Julia discovered during a game of hide and seek that if she hid her face in her hands she was not truly hidden. If she could see us, then we could see her. Without warning she jumped over a wall. It was eighteen inches high on her side and fifteen feet on the other. There was a single cry and then silence. We looked down on the inert body of our beloved daughter, spreadeagled on the paving stones. It seemed to take an age to climb down to her. She was breathing and conscious, protected by the thick padded coat, hood and scarf. On the drive to the Capital Hospital, which was used to treating foreigners, Tina, skilled in first aid, made sure she stayed awake. Within half an hour the three foremost specialists in China attended her. It was the first day of Chinese New Year – as if in London we had sought treatment on Good Friday or Christmas Eve. It would not have happened on the NHS. They had state of the art machines which indicated no internal bleeding. They asked permission to use Chinese medicine as well as Western. We were past caring what they used. Within a week Julia was home and frisking about as if nothing had happened. It had been concussion and seems to have had no ill effect. We are very grateful to those Chinese physicians.

We were grateful again when Sue got pneumonia following a bad dose of flu. A small group of enthusiastic thespians had rehearsed one of Noel Coward's one act plays, *Hands Across the Sea*, and were offering it as after-dinner entertainment to colleagues who had the space in their flats. After we were committed Sue got flu and should have gone to bed. But one of the cast was on the point of leaving Peking and so we would have had to cancel altogether. Sue insisted that "The show must go on". One night she was onstage with a temperature of 103F and naturally got an even worse dose. When it would not get better the nurse took Sue down to the hospital. The Chinese doctor said that there was nothing wrong. The British nurse demanded a fluoroscope. Pneumonia was clear for all to see. The doctor went into panic mode and tried to admit Sue to intensive care. The nurse promised to visit Sue at home twice a day for three weeks to administer antibiotic injections. After that an amazing herbal concoction looking like garbage but tasting like honey did the trick.

But the air of the city was so polluted that most of the foreign community, and so far as we could tell many of the Chinese, suffered bronchial problems in the winter. In the flat, air-conditioners in the summer and humidifiers in the winter were in constant use. A weekly job was to wash the filters in these machines and the oily black filth which darkened the water was instructive. Between cold dry winter and hot humid summer the Peking spring was beautiful till the sand-laden winds blew in from the north-east. Then face masks became essential.

Some Chinese customs were unaffected by the Cultural Revolution. At dawn and dusk old men would take their canaries for a walk in their cages. Others would practice Tai Chi under the trees. A small café in the temple park served excellent Jao Tse – savoury dumplings filled with minced meat and herbs.

Communism had not dimmed the Chinese enthusiasm for good food. Formal banquets in the Great Hall of the People were particularly good. Party cadres and foreign visitors had a range of excellent restaurants to choose from. A favourite dish was Peking Duck – cooked in the oven with the carcase full of water so that it steamed inside as it roasted outside. Three restaurants offered this speciality, known to foreigners as the "Big Duck", the "Little Duck" and the "Sick Duck" near the hospital. At the end of each school holidays we would take the embassy children to share Mongolian hotpot before their long flight home to school. This would be followed by sticky apple fritters, a dessert which was guaranteed to make a great deal of mess with hairs of fine sugar caramel spread across the table. (The cooks loved to decorate desserts with this confection dubbed "Harold Caccia's hair" after a distinguished British diplomat who had the misfortune to lose all his hair while serving in Peking.)

There were seven million bicycles in Peking. They commuted in reverse, flowing in a great tide out of the city in the mornings to the factories in the suburbs, and returning in the evenings to their homes in the lanes and alleys of the ancient city. On a social occasion Nick sat next to the Mayor of Peking. By way of conversation Nick observed that the Chinese Highway Code provided for bicycles to carry lights. How did it come about that the only bicycles to carry lights were the bicycles which belonged to foreigners? The Mayor thought for a moment and then replied, "Mr Counsellor is quite correct. The Highway Code does provide for bicycles to carry lights. But, you see, the masses decided otherwise." This seemed to be the perfect Maoist answer. Most foreign residents in Peking soon took to the bicycle and we bought ourselves a pair of good solid workhorses. The place is so flat and there were so few cars that it was safe for children. Our boys would set off on their bikes to explore the city on their own. If they had an accident bystanders would immediately cart them off to the hospital and inform the embassy. There were no other imaginable dangers. The boys had more freedom in Peking than in New York.

Within the diplomatic compounds it made sense to use a bicycle even to attend National Day receptions. We first met Barbara and George Bush as we parked our respective bikes. One African Ambassador had his national flag attached to the handlebars and would arrive at diplomatic functions sitting on the bicycle seat with his First Secretary standing up on the pedals.

As was our custom in a new posting we set out on our first Sunday to attend church. The Chinese Government had reluctantly allowed two churches to reopen during the Cultural Revolution, one of the two Catholic cathedrals and a small chapel which used to belong to the YMCA and now declared itself part of the Three Self Movement. About eight elderly Chinese, who spoke no English, were allowed to attend and supervise the service. It seemed to follow the pattern of a familiar Anglican or Methodist Communion service, and the congregation were invited to come up to the front to receive the sacraments, standing in a semicircle in front of the table. One time a Chinese guide who had brought some foreigners came up to scrutinise our faces as we accepted the bread and wine – an odd experience. The foreigners who attended regularly included George

147

Bush Senior with his family, several African Ambassadors, Filipinos and some of the foreign students attending Peking University. They spoke Chinese and were able to exchange a few words with the Chinese congregation, informing them that foreigners also met in their homes for Bible study and prayer during the week. In return they learned that the Chinese Christians had only one page at a time of the Bible for each family. This had to be circulated on a regular rota. When we took Roman Catholic visitors to the cathedral joining a small group of Catholic Chinese licensed to attend Mass, we were as at home in the liturgy as our visitors because it was still in Latin.

On Easter morning a large group of foreign Christians picnicked together in the ruins of the old Summer Palace. One could easily imagine what a beautiful place it had been before the plundering European troops destroyed it not many decades before.

From these contacts we knew that there were sixteen Christians in China – eight Catholics and eight Protestants. We subsequently learned that there were three million in our time and thirty million now.

It has been said that actors are frustrated diplomats and diplomats frustrated actors. British missions abroad are well known for their amateur shows in posts where there is little local cultural entertainment. The famous Peking Opera had been banned as decadent, and the films, circuses and ballets approved by the regime were few and far between and less than stimulating. So there were some remarkable British pantomimes involving the visiting children as well as many of the staff. Tickets available to the foreign community sold like hot cakes and every night the "Amenity Hall" was crowded to the doors.

One year we thought that Sino-British relations had improved enough for us to invite the Chinese staff of the embassy to the dress rehearsal of *Jack and the Beanstalk*. It was a challenge for the actors against a stream of animated interpretation, but the gusts of laughter were compensation enough. The Dame's huge balloon boobs needed

148

no explanation and when they burst the cheers were deafening. But next morning the Chinese "shop steward" asked to see Nick officially. It was not to say thank you. He looked solemn and declined a seat.

"That giant," he said.

"Yes?"

"He was a bad element."

"Yes, he ate babies."

"If he was a bad element, why was he the only one in Chinese dress?"

Nick swallowed and gave the true explanation. "Because he was a small man pretending to be a big man – and because you have such wonderful Chinese padded coats in the market..." No joy.

"Please arrange a different costume tonight."

A non-Chinese costume was devised. And never again were the Chinese staff invited to our shows.

Blithe Spirit, Hands Across the Sea and *Dick Whittington* were well supported. So it was nothing out of the ordinary that many of the Diplomatic Corps were watching *Murder at the Vicarage* when news filtered out that the "Gang of Four" had been arrested (See below). Nick was on stage with most of the rest of Chancery. Sue was in charge of make-up. It was surreal. As an actor came off stage Sue pushed them to a telephone whispering how many minutes they had before going on stage again. The exhausted actors switched from their part in the drama to their diplomatic duties and back again as the incredible news was unfolding. When the story broke to the rest of the world there were accusations from some members of the diplomatic community that the theatrical show was a cunning ruse by the British to let them get the story out first.

We were sometimes asked to organise events with a Commonwealth connection. A traditional British garden fete was held in the residence garden to celebrate the Queen's jubilee in June 1977 and raise money for a Commonwealth charity. The British Embassy staff arranged lucky dips and raffles, races for the children and the usual competitions like "Guess the Weight of a Cake", hoop-la and coconut shies. There were cream teas and homemade jam for sale and Sue made hundreds of yards of red, white and blue bunting to hang from tree to tree. It used up all her cotton coupons.

There was a party at Christmas time for Commonwealth children. Nepalese and Afghan diplomats insisted that they were members of the Commonwealth. Their children were invited. The afternoon began with games for the youngest, musical bumps and pass the parcel, followed by more difficult games and competitions. Very small prizes were awarded and control was maintained by judicious use of a loud whistle. After fish and chips served in newspaper there was a disco. We covered the walls of the Amenities Hall with sheets of white card and issued every guest with a felt tip pen as they arrived. The graffiti which appeared over the evening were amazing, cartoons, funny poems and jokes. We kept the card for years as a reminder of those kids.

Another group we got to know was the British students at Peking and Shanghai Universities. If one of them had to be hospitalised Sue tried to visit. On one such visit to the students' hospital near Peking University she was accosted by eager young people in several European languages all asking the same question: When is Beethoven's Birthday? There was a rumour that on that day the Chinese radio would broadcast music by Beethoven who had just been revealed to be a favourite composer of Marx and Engels. Sure enough, on his birthday, music by Beethoven was played all day.

One of the students received a parcel from her mother. It had been opened by the authorities. They denied touching it. Then how come half her mother's letter arrived in one package and the other half several days later?

There were several hundred students from non-communist countries. They wanted to travel within China during their holidays. The Chinese Government insisted they must travel first class and stay at first-class hotels. They could not afford it. In any case it was anathema to students to use "soft class" as the Chinese called it. So they organised a sit-down strike in the main travel centre in downtown Peking. It lasted three days while harassed officials argued and cajoled them. And in the end by being stubborn and polite the students won.

One dreadful day Nick had to inform a British tourist that her husband had died. She had arrived the night before with a group of Friends of the British Museum at the beginning of a two-week visit to China. Her husband, Professor Hamilton-Fairlie, a leading authority on cancer, had gone separately on a lecture tour in Australia. Returning to his home in Hampstead he noticed something odd under a neighbour's car. It blew up and killed him instantly – the work of the IRA.

When Nick broke the news to his widow he explained that the embassy had booked her onto the night flight home to London, but she would need to get through that day. Sue offered to look after her and she opted to do as much sightseeing as could be fitted in. So between meals in our flat and bouts of weeping the two of them raced through all the main sights. Mrs. Hamilton-Fairlie had just bought a Polaroid camera – brand new technology. She visited the Summer Palace, Forbidden City and Temple of Heaven, photographing the people she saw and giving them their photographs. The happy amazement of the old women and the children as they watched the pictures of themselves develop before their eyes went a long way towards comforting that unhappy lady. She begged to be protected from the media circus which would greet her at London Airport. HMG did what they could and she undertook to give a press conference soon. True to her promise she submitted to this ordeal with her children not long after they had been reunited. Some lady.

Foreign diplomats were not allowed to travel outside Peking without permission from the Foreign Ministry. Green lines on the road marked the limit and soldiers with machine guns kept watch from their sentry boxes. But Eastern China was beginning to be accessible and we jumped at every opportunity.

We stayed in government hotels – we had no choice – and were escorted by charming English-speaking guides from the moment we stepped off the train. It was a service. It was also surveillance. One young guide let slip his frustration that he was not allowed to go to university because he was "already too well educated" – he might become elitist. He commented with reference to current politics that our hotel was "on the water margin". On another occasion we offered sympathy to our guide for the devastating earthquake which had struck southern China. She denied that there had been such an earthquake – until the following morning when she clamoured to be told how we knew. We had of course heard it on the BBC World Service.

We often travelled by train. It was comfortable with excellent food, hot tea in porcelain mugs and chilled local beer. We got to see parts of China that we could not usually reach. Our train once stopped on an embankment. We observed a political gathering in a village square. Bored peasants listened to a local party official harangue them on the slogans of the hour. In a culvert nearby a couple were making love, oblivious of the rest of the world. Humanity survives politics.

Everything was on a huge scale, the bridges over the great rivers, the mile upon mile of paddy fields, the enormous factories and hundreds of bicycles. And everywhere we had to carry with us in cash all the money we might need. There was no other way to pay.

152

We had a small suitcase filled with notes which we left in the compartment when we went to the restaurant car. China was really safe for foreigners in those days; we never locked our flat or car or bedroom door even in hotels. Sue would leave her bag on the shop counter while examining a tablecloth or mousetrap, never worrying that it would not be there when she made up her mind what to buy. The only things we ever lost were pocket-sized Chinese objects like cloisonné ashtrays from our crated baggage when we returned to the UK.

Shanghai was as impressive as we had expected. We cringed at the sign on the famous bund: "Dogs and Chinese not admitted". The Mayor of Shanghai told us that there was no crime in his city. "Mr Mayor," exclaimed Nick, "that is marvellous – a city of twelve million people and no crime?"

The Mayor looked embarrassed. He consulted his colleagues. Then he said, "Last year, one rape and two stolen bicycles." We visited a tea garden and factory in the countryside outside the city and were treated to fragrant cups of jasmine tea. In a carpet factory we were told we could not buy anything because they sent all their work to Harrods.

We took a boat trip down the Shanghai River to see the vast expanse of the Yangtse. It smelled like the sea but there were no gulls. There had been programmes to destroy birds because they competed for grain with the people. We saw a young man knocked off his bicycle and instinctively moved to help. The guide stopped us saying, "It doesn't matter, he's only Chinese."

In Nanking the streets are lined with plane trees. The sacred way to the tomb of Emperor Hong Wu is lined with stone animals like the approach to the Ming Tombs. The vast memorial tomb of Sun Yat-sen stands on a hill top with a panoramic view of the countryside. The city of Suzhou provides a living introduction to the ancient art of Chinese gardens.

We visited the birthplace of Chairman Mao at Shao Shan near Changsha. It was not a hovel as we had imagined but a spacious farmhouse. The crowds moved around it with awe as if in a church. The bedroom where he was born was roped off as in a stately home in England. They showed us the pond where he swam and the fields he once ploughed. It should have been an idyllic childhood.

Nearby is the tomb of the Han princess, about two thousand years before Mao. It has been skilfully excavated and the contents displayed in a dedicated museum. On the ground floor, neatly laid out were the sarcophagus and coffins, layer upon layer like a Russian doll. All the artefacts buried with it were on show; silks and lacquer utensils, food and personal items. We were shown a film of the opening of the tomb when, after carefully penetrating layers of charcoal and clay, the coffin was revealed perfect and undisturbed after two millennia. The camera roamed round the faces of the archaeologists as the wonder dawned. In the basement museum the inhabitant of this perfect tomb is laid out in a sort of operating theatre. As we gazed down on the body of this tiny woman, we wondered what sort of powerful person she must have been two thousand years ago to have such a tomb. All her organs forensically studied and laid out around her were labelled in Latin – which made it easier for us. The illnesses she had suffered from in life were listed and what she had eaten for her last meal.

At one large commune in central China we watched a thousand peasants with wheelbarrows cheerfully moving a mountain from one field to another. Their bleak homes were furnished with solid beds called kangs with fireplaces underneath for wintertime. The Barefoot Doctor programme was explained to us. Young people with rudimentary training administered primary care based on traditional medicines, herbal remedies, acupuncture, oil massages, often effective and much cheaper than Western medicine. Life on these collectives was not easy or comfortable but there was pride and dignity and a certain mutual care not found amongst the poor in most developing countries.

In Yenan we learned about the Long March from the south in 1935. The yellow loess canyons became the headquarters of the young Communist Party of China. Buildings carved out of the cliffs once housed the revolutionaries and their numerous committees and political organisations. In one we noticed for the first time a group photo from which a comrade, who had since fallen from favour, had been airbrushed. We stayed in a prison-like hotel and ate sorgum porridge for breakfast. We then had the worst flight ever, over the hills in an unpressurised, high-winged, twin-engine plane. The air hostesses donned pretty frilly aprons to serve us with boiled sweets, but their faces never softened as we ascended with a deafening roar through the clouds. The passenger seats were like old-fashioned deckchairs, the metal backs loosely hinged. There were no seatbelts so we held on grimly. The pain grew excruciating. Surely our eardrums would burst. Long after we bounced down onto the runway our ears ached and for about three hours we were deaf. Never travel without earplugs.

Xian more than made up for the flight. It is not a beautiful city but bursting with interest and history. First the Forest of Steles – one inscribed with the Classic of Filial Piety, another with the oldest map of China and a third recording the arrival of a Nestorian priest, and the foundation of a Christian chapel in 781. Nick enquired about the damage to the top of the Great Goose Pagoda. "Oh, that was the earthquake," replied the guide. There had been an earthquake in Peking a few weeks earlier, but this one had struck in the year 647. Little Goose Pagoda was dated 684. From the top one could see the southern edge of the Tang dynasty town for about two miles; it was three times the size of modern Xian. Then, as now, the mandarins kept detailed records of everyone and everything. We went to look at the outside of the Emperor Qin Shi Huang Di's gigantic tomb. The terracotta army had not yet been uncovered but our guides were hopeful that excavations would begin soon.

The tourist hotel in Luoyang was reputed to be the largest in China, built by the Russians during the early days of Sino-Soviet friendship. The dining room was like a railway station. The only

155

other guests were European diplomats like us, trying to get off the beaten track. The draw for tourists was the great caves with mammoth Buddha statues and religious carvings.

Bai Dai He is a seaside resort in north-east China, where the Great Wall meets the sea. Accommodation was made available in dormitories for foreign diplomats who wanted to escape the heat of summer in Peking. There was no mixing with the local population even on the beach. We were instructed to swim only within the netted area which would protect us from sharks. The Chinese swam outside the nets, apparently they could take their chance. Big sign boards in Chinese and English told us what we could and could not do. For example we were not to board a boat to sail across the sea. Our sons aged twelve and thirteen were good swimmers and in no time were diving over the rope across the end of the netted area, daring the sharks to follow. Early next morning we observed more nets being fixed across the seaward opening. The Peoples' army who were dotted around in sentry boxes – to keep us safe – certainly kept an eye on us.

Nick took the boys to Da Tong north-west of the capital, close to the Soviet border. They visited a factory which produced China's massive steam engines. One engine had just reached the end of the production line and was getting up steam for the first time. Robert and Charlie were invited to open the throttle and make it move. They visited a special cake factory. After the usual "short introduction", the boys were asked to open a wardrobe door to reveal a narrow staircase descending into the bowels of the earth. The entire factory had been replicated underground "in case the enemy should invade". Nick was not the first to see the weakness of this strategy. The air underground was circulated by a pump driven by an internal combustion engine on the surface. All the invader would have to do was to put a potato up the exhaust pipe.

Occasionally there would be a jolly group of overseas Chinese lured back to their origins and feted by the Party. These Westernised middle-aged men and women, laden with modern camera equipment,

156

were encouraged to share their expertise during their visit. Often they would come back again to advise and keep their cousins abreast of commercial and scientific advances which had been lost during the Cultural Revolution. It was a clever idea of someone's and probably went some way to keep China from falling too far behind the rest of the world. Mao in his drive to destroy class and elitism had removed all competition. No exams in which one might shine above his peers, and in factories no competition to produce either quality or profit. It was an Alice-in-Wonderland world.

We made one visit to Ulan Bator, capital of Mongolia. It was minus 37 degrees centigrade. It had been minus 57 degrees the previous week. Four Russian experts had driven out onto the steppe. They had been discovered frozen to death as they peered into the engine of their jeep. Before we left Peking, Sue went to the big department store in Wang Fu Jing to buy padded coats large enough to wear over our sheepskin ones. We travelled in an elegant compartment. Plush red seats made into comfortable bunks at night, the walls were panelled in mahogany and the wide washbasin had a special opening in the waste pipe for pouring boiling water down to unblock the ice. A splendid samovar at the end of the corridor produced boiling water night and day. At the frontier railway station we all had to disembark while the wheels were changed for a different gauge – and again on the way back. We played Scrabble in the waiting room during the two-hour wait, attracting a crowd of friendly spectators. The Gobi Desert went on and on with only one diversion – a Soviet airfield where MIGs were taking off and landing as we chugged past. We stayed in the residence which occupied a quarter of the long embassy block. Chancery was beneath the Ambassador's flat and the other half of the building housed the rest of the UK staff, couples both of whom worked in the office.

There were four and a half embassies in Mongolia. The Russian Embassy was huge and everywhere we saw signs of its "colonial" occupation. India, Japan and the UK had small missions. His Excellency the Ambassador of France chose to spend the winter months in Paris. Our embassy was quite busy since it acted for the

Americans, some Europeans and most of the Commonwealth. We were told that it actually made a profit from the fees earned as "protecting power" – a little like the Swiss in Algiers in 1968. The back garden was filled with greenhouses where in the summer months between June and September everyone industriously produced vegetables for the freezers. The only vegetables in the shops were cabbages brought by train from Moscow. The Mongolians seemed to live entirely on mares' milk and cheese and a little meat, bread and rice. No fruit or vegetables.

Our hosts Miles and Anne Ponsonby gave us a wonderful time. We visited the heroic Soviet sights, a tank which had valiantly struggled all the way from Moscow to Berlin, a huge war memorial to Soviet dead, none of whom had died in or for Mongolia, and of course Stalin himself in the central square. Every year the diplomatic corps had to parade at the war memorial to honour the Soviet dead in ceremonies orchestrated entirely by the Soviets. It made us wonder whether we had been as insensitive as this in our former colonies. When Anne Ponsonby had mentioned to the wife of the President of Mongolia that she planned to learn the Mongolian language, the reply was immediate. "Why bother? We all speak Russian here."

At the top of the town was an ancient Buddhist temple. We stood in the snow as a few faithful old folk turned the prayer wheels and burned incense in a huge bronze "cauldron". The Summer Palace looked totally Chinese, the Winter Palace totally Russian. The city itself consisted of a Russian built central square with the "Mares' Milk" hotel (nicknamed because of the smell), the Friendship Store and big ugly administrative buildings surrounded by a sea of yurt tents. These prefabs of wooden floors and wool walls were attractive, mobile and fairly warm. But we learned that few babies born in the winter months survived. The cheerful cook at the residence told Sue she had had thirteen children and none had survived.

We had bright sunshine every day. The air outside shimmered magically because all the water in the air had frozen. Eyelashes froze together, eyebrows grew icicles and everyone pulled out a big

158

handkerchief on entering a building because the melt began at once and the mopping up too. It was comical to observe. And the cold had to be taken seriously. One of the Queen's Messengers, who brought up the diplomatic bag from Peking every fortnight, foolishly crossed the courtyard without putting on his coat. Pneumonia followed.

Pneumonia is indeed the great killer in this poor country and the life expectancy was then the lowest in the world. Our embassy's efforts to help were frustrated by the Soviets. We were shown cases of drugs for pneumonia which they were prevented from donating to the Mongolian government. The instructions on the packages had been translated into Mongolian as well as Russian, but one hurdle after another was placed in the way.

A feature of our lives in China was the colony of Hong Kong. It existed on Chinese sufferance partly because the fresh water supply came from China. The authorities had only to turn the tap off to bring the colony to its knees. But it was not as simple as that. It was a colony not by conquest but by treaty, and the Chinese were scrupulous about honouring the letter of their agreements. The treaty provided that the island of Hong Kong and Stonecutter's Island were British in perpetuity – but the islands were unsustainable without the New Territories which were British by lease expiring in 1997. A great deal of anxiety and work was expended on how to deal with the historical accident of this date. It cast its shadow ahead because Hong Kong lived by business confidence – and confidence would inevitably erode as the date approached, unless the future could be established by agreement with the Government of China. In a paradoxical way this gave Britain and China a common interest in the stability and prosperity of Hong Kong. In due course Geoffrey Howe's agreement with China on Hong Kong exploited this common interest. But this was another day's work.

Meanwhile the Governor in Hong Kong and the British Ambassador in Peking were the custodians of the colony and its mysterious future. These two very senior figures had institutionally divergent priorities. Governor MacLehose was concerned above all to sustain the peace, prosperity and viability of the territory. China was important as it affected these things. Ambassador Youde was responsible for wider British interests in China. Hong Kong was important as one of these interests. Consultation between them was an ongoing process and not always smooth. The counsellor in Peking and the Political Adviser in Hong Kong became heavily involved. Nick was often in Hong Kong.

There was no direct air link. Travellers from Peking took the internal Chinese airline to Guang Zhou and stayed in the Friendship Hotel. In the morning they took the train to the border town of Shum Chun where we had first entered China, a showcase marble palace with its famous banner "We have friends all over the world". Then they carried their own luggage across a little wooden bridge over the waterway that marked the border; sometimes there were bodies floating in the water – unsuccessful fugitives from the blessings of communism. Then there were three signs one behind the other. The first said "Do Not Spit". The second said "Drink Coca Cola". Only the third said "Welcome to Hong Kong". Nobody else seemed to find this funny. The Union flag flew from a black wooden hut which housed immigration and customs officials at the border post of Lo Wu – in marked contrast to the grandeur of Shum Chun. Then on by toy train to Kow Loon, the bright lights and busyness, the harbour ferry to Hong Kong Island and a car to Government House. This journey between two worlds was always a culture shock. Even a British official felt a country cousin in this capital of capitalism.

One regular traveller to Hong Kong was Ambassador Akwei, the charming and sophisticated representative of Ghana who, among other things, was a regular tennis partner of George Bush. At the Friendship Hotel in Guang Zhou he was required to pay for his room in advance – because he was black. When he discovered that Asian and European colleagues were settling their accounts on departure in the usual way, he decided to make a stand. He tells the story. At registration he declined to pay, grabbed his room key, dashed off down the corridor and locked himself in his room. Increasingly senior members of the hotel staff knocked on his door demanding

160

payment. Finally, the manager declared that if he would not open the door he would batter it down. Very well, thought Akwei, if they think I am a savage I shall behave like a savage. He took off all his clothes. When the Chinese carpenter broke into the room he leapt naked from his bed screaming like a dervish. The staff fled from the room. Ambassador Akwei paid on departure in future.

Our two sons, by now aged thirteen and eleven, were commuting to boarding school in England. There was no direct air link between London and Peking. We were reluctant to subject them to the rigours of the journey via Hong Kong. So the approved route was via Zurich and on by Swissair, or to Paris and on by Air France. But the short-haul flight from Heathrow to make a connection elsewhere in Europe was vulnerable to disruption by winter weather. On one occasion their flight to Zurich was cancelled through fog. The daughter of the Ambassador, some years their senior, was travelling with them and talked them onto a flight to Tokyo on the ground that it was vaguely in the right direction. They were met by the Ambassador's Rolls Royce, spent the night at the residence and were taken back in the morning to catch the daily flight to Peking. There was a traffic jam on the airport road and they were going to miss the flight. The Ambassador's driver, ever resourceful, flagged down a traffic cop going in the other direction. Under police escort, siren wailing, the children whizzed up the wrong carriageway and straight onto the tarmac where the aircraft was waiting. That evening at a reception in Peking we overheard a European colleague speculating about a mysterious VIP delegation from Tokyo who had kept the morning flight waiting and arrived with a police escort in a Rolls Royce. What were the Japanese up to? We knew better.

Then Iran Air advertised a weekly direct flight London–Teheran–Peking and we thought our problem had been solved. Rob and Charlie flew to Teheran. Three children from another British family had been booked via Tehran the previous week with strict instructions to stay on the aircraft during the stopover. They did as they were told. The aircraft was towed into the hanger. It was not a direct flight at all. The connecting flight had already departed and the next flight to Peking was the following week. Eventually airport staff came upon the children and took them off to the Iran Air Hotel in town where they went to sleep on a sofa in reception. They were eventually rescued by the British Embassy who gave them a whale of a time in Iran. Rather late in the day we heard of this experience and desperately telegraphed Teheran to solicit their assistance. They responded nobly. The two little boys having been abandoned with their suitcases on the tarmac were rescued by a young member of the Teheran Embassy and caught the Peking flight by the skin of their teeth, together with their three friends who had been in Iran for a week.

Robert and Charles – and Julia in her time – became seasoned travellers, confident and even blasé. By way of cautionary tale we told them the story of the schoolchildren hijacked to the Jordanian desert (Chapter 5). Having just lived through these disjointed journeys via Teheran and Tokyo, Robert complained, "Why does nothing exciting ever happen to us?"

The education of children is always a problem for professional nomads. We took the view from the beginning that our children were entitled to a coherent education and that in the circumstances that meant boarding school in England. The alternative was a different school every few years, with different friends and different teachers, in a different language and a different education system. The children acquiesced. Mercifully they thrived at boarding school. Some colleagues were less fortunate. Others believed in principle that their children should profit from the diversity of culture and should go to school wherever the family was sent. A colleague in China held this belief. He sent his eleven year old daughter to a Chinese school. She learned fluent Chinese in double quick time and seemed to enjoy the experience. Then one day she came home asking, "Daddy, was it Jesus Christ or Mao Tse-tung who died for our sins?" He realised that a certain cultural confusion was setting in.

It was not only children who posed a problem. It was also ageing parents. Sue's parents had themselves lived in China and accepted readily enough that we were abroad on duty. But to Nick's parents Peking seemed not just the other side of the world but the other side of the moon. They were in their late seventies and felt that their only surviving son should have been nearby to look after them. Nick's mother was almost blind. The issue was dramatised in September 2006 shortly after the death of Mao Tse-tung when the embassy was working flat out. Two successive diplomatic bags from London to Peking were delayed, so three arrived simultaneously. They contained three letters to Nick from his mother. The first informed him that his father had gone blind overnight with macular degeneration and asked whether he could come home to help. The second was carefully understanding about the delay and hoped for an early reply. The third asked whether he cared. Nick was on the telephone within minutes. His mother said that the immediate crisis was over. There was nothing he could do. Given the circumstances in China he did not go home.

The same wayward bag contained a summons for Nick to appear in Maidstone Crown Court the following day on a charge of non-payment of income tax. This was the first intimation that there was a problem. Nick sent a telegram to Welfare Section at the FCO asking them to explain to the court that he could not physically get back in time, and to invite the Inland Revenue to explain the problem. The Revenue refused. They had information that he had failed to declare income. It was up to him to identify his misdemeanour and submit payment. Nick sat up late three nights running, trawling through his financial papers in vain. He had with him in China only the papers for the previous three years. He confessed failure. The Revenue told him to go back earlier. It transpired that he would have found the mistake if he had brought to China papers for another six weeks. We had bought a house in 1972. In the course of the transaction we had had a large sum of money in a savings account for a few weeks and had earned the princely sum of £72 interest which Nick had forgotten all about. He was penitent about his oversight but dismayed that his colleagues in the Revenue should have persecuted him at long distance at such a time. They never seemed like colleagues again.

163

Our diaries for these three years remind us of our daily lives. We had Chinese lessons twice a week. There was a meeting of senior embassy staff every morning to report developments, each in our separate fields. The Ambassador took this meeting himself once a week. On other days Nick was in the chair. Much effort was expended on co-ordination of the European community in China; political counsellors met every week and cultural counsellors once a month. Beyond the EC, the diplomatic consultation was usually bilateral; calls and lunches with colleagues from the United States, Canada, Australia, New Zealand, Japan, India, Pakistan, Sri Lanka, the Soviet Union and many others. Routine bilateral consultation with the Chinese authorities often fell to Nick; discussion for example of Hong Kong, the cultural exchange programme, United Nations matters, consular issues, the arrangements for bilateral visits. The Queen's Messengers came to Peking once a week and had to be looked after before they set off by train for Ulan Bator. British visitors included Ministers, senior Members of Parliament, opposition spokesmen, FCO and other officials, colleagues from Hong Kong, the Royal College of Defence Studies, also the Royal Society, the National Farmers Union, the Lord Provost of Glasgow, the Coventry Chamber of Commerce, Shorts Brothers, Rolls Royce and Shell, Friends of the Tate and National Galleries, British Vice-Chancellors, writers, academics and English language teachers, and delegations of Molecular Biologists, Agricultural Engineers, Geo-physicists, Remote Sensors, Geo-morphologists, Biological controllers, the Ideal Home Exhibition. On the sporting side we had weightlifters and a forlorn table tennis team.

Four of these visitors are worth separate mention.

Anthony Crosland paid an official visit to China as Secretary of State in May 1976 at a time of particular interest in Chinese affairs. He had only just been appointed and gamely took on this visit arranged for his predecessor although he was already ill and died a few months later. He and his wife Susan were genuine socialists, eager to see the transformation which communism had wrought in China, and disappointed by what they found. Mrs Crosland was sceptical about the luxury in which she supposed that diplomats worked, and impressed by the Spartan conditions of diplomatic life in Peking. Sue gave a lunch for her to meet some of the wives. On discovering they were all unemployed she asked what we would choose to do. She learnt that all had at least third level qualifications and most had professional lives in the UK. She considered this an appalling waste. She was horrified to discover that diplomatic wives were not allowed to take paid employment in most countries. When she got home she set about trying to reform this feature of our lives.

Margaret Thatcher came as Leader of the Opposition in April 1977. Her daughter Carol was terrified of China. Mrs Thatcher was businesslike. She made no concessions to Easter which fell during her visit. Sue was asked to deliver a message to Mrs Thatcher in her state guest house on Easter morning. "Good morning, Mrs Thatcher," she said, "Happy Easter."

"Oh, is it Easter? Well, what do you want?" Sue delivered her message. Without another word Mrs Thatcher attacked her boiled egg. She was not favourably impressed by the heroic spitting of Vice Premier Deng Xiao-ping. We took her to the Great Wall of China. Edward Heath had climbed the wall on his recent visit. Mrs Thatcher's first question was "How far did Ted get?" She got further. The Chinese assessment of foreign leaders was always intriguing. Edward Heath was a friend of China because he had championed British accession to the European Economic Community. Margaret Thatcher was a friend because of her strident antagonism to the Soviet Union. (Sue was detailed to look after Carol Thatcher who was appalled by all she saw. Even the drive in from the airport was spooky; very few cars, lots of identical bicycles and at night almost no light. In order to read, people squatted in the pools of light beneath the few street lights. Everyone dressed alike and there seemed to be no colour anywhere. The roadside trees were grown as a crop in uniform straight lines between the road surface and the dreary blocks of workers' flats.)

Sir Kenneth Keith, Chairman of Rolls Royce, came to sign a massive contract, negotiated over the previous three years, for the sale to China of the RB211 aero engine. He expected to stay for two days. But the Chinese reopened small points in the agreement and quibbled over the translation for a week. They knew perfectly well that Sir Kenneth had other pressing business to attend to, and that once he was in Peking he could not afford to leave without signing the contract. By this simple tactic they wrung out of Rolls Royce concessions which the company had resisted throughout the negotiations.

A delegation of British acupuncturists came as guests of the Chinese medical authorities. The reception we gave for them and their Chinese hosts was a curiosity. In Peking, the home of acupuncture, the British visitors eagerly pressed the claims of the technique as a cure for many ills. The Chinese were puzzled. For them acupuncture was a part of mainstream treatment, the handmaiden both of traditional Chinese remedies and of modern Western medicine. They smiled inscrutably while vivid stories were told of miraculous cures. They plainly regarded their visitors as cranks.

China received a series of state visits, mostly to consolidate its influence in the Third World. The centrepiece of these visits was a grand banquet in the Great Hall of the People in Tiananmen Square. The visiting President and his entourage would be entertained by very senior Chinese representatives, sometimes Premier Chou En-lai himself. All the one hundred Ambassadors in Peking would also be invited, as our French colleague put it "pour faire la tapisserie – to provide a background tapestry". If Ambassadors were not available their deputies were expected to attend. The food was good. Chinese Emperors had served 101 courses. communist China served twelve, each of them succulent.

Speeches would be exchanged. Texts would be issued to the diplomatic corps and to the press in Chinese, in the language of the guest and also in English. At this stage in the Sino-Soviet dispute, the

166

Soviet and other Eastern bloc representatives would walk out in protest when the Chinese host pronounced certain trigger words. Western representatives would amuse themselves by speed reading the text to predict when the Russians would walk out. On one occasion the Soviet Ambassador was on leave and the senior East European present was the Ambassador of Bulgaria. The Chinese host pronounced the word "hegemony" and paused for the walkout. The Bulgarian did not budge. The Soviet *Charge* became agitated. Western diplomats began to mutter about a split in the Eastern bloc. Eventually, the delinquent Ambassador woke up and made for the door, his blushing colleagues in his wake.

The exchange of speeches would normally take about half an hour. One evening the President of Sao Tome e Principe, who spoke for 65,000 people, harangued the representatives of a quarter of the human race in Spanish for three hours. The Director of Protocol took out a newspaper and ostentatiously read it.

Formal Chinese speeches would end with the toast "gam-bei", meaning literally "reverse your glass". This was rendered in the English text as "bottoms up!" which seemed faintly inappropriate for a state banquet. One day in honour of International Women's Day the ladies of the diplomatic corps were invited to the Great Hall by the senior lady in China, Soong Ching-ling, the ninety year old widow of Sun Yat-sen. The conclusion of her speech was translated into English as "Ladies Bottoms Up". The phrase "bottoms up!" was thereafter omitted from the English text.

The year 1976 was in the Chinese calendar "The Year of the Dragon". In Chinese mythology, this is the year in which dynasties change.

It began in January with the death of Premier Chou En-lai – and all China wept (including our cook who wept into the soup and had to be sent home). Chou remains a controversial figure and has been harshly criticised for his complicity in the Cultural Revolution. Nick thought of Mao as a kind of Philosopher King, a ruthless tyrant with his head in the clouds, who was prepared to break and break and break again – to break even the Communist Party of China itself – in pursuit of his vision of a China that had truly stood up. By contrast Chou was the consummate administrator and diplomat, a peacemaker, willing to accept compromise which fell short of outright victory, always one step behind Mao and never challenging for the leadership, but unobtrusively sticking China together again as Mao broke it in pieces. He was a kind of hero. It would have been better for China if Mao had died first so that Chou could preside over the transition. But it was not to be. Whatever the merits of this simplistic version, there is no doubt that Chou was hugely popular in China. It was widely believed that he had been persecuted by Mao and that he had stood up for the interests of the long-suffering people. His death provoked an outpouring of public grief. A million people lined the streets of the capital to pay their last respects as the hearse moved from the hospital to the crematorium. Chairman Mao boycotted the memorial service.

Then in February came the second fall of Deng Xiao-ping, Deputy Prime Minister, protagonist for moderation and for policies that would improve living standards, the real architect of the reaction against the Cultural Revolution. Mao lost no time after Chou's death in sacking Deng and denouncing him by name. Deng was put under house arrest. Overnight there mysteriously appeared, hanging in the trees around Tiananmen Square, a number of little bottles. Deng was a tiny man. His second name Xiao-ping can mean "little bottle". He was moved to a place of detention away from his home. But he was a popular figure and there was an obvious difficulty about what to do with him. The fattest file in the British Embassy was renamed "The Dung Disposal Problem".

The closest ally of Chou and Deng was Marshal Yeh Jian-ying, Army Chief of Staff, who wanted the army to defend China from its enemies not to involve itself in politics and internal repression. Yeh was also suspended and removed from his command on the spurious grounds that he was ill. He held court in his home in the army

168

compound in the Western Hills, biding his time until the chairman should die.

Also in February, the disgraced former President of the United States, Richard Nixon, came to Peking at Mao's personal invitation to take private farewell and to speak about the tragic ending of great men. Nixon's first visit in 1972 had been less than cordial, but it had marked a breakthrough in China's international relations. His second visit seemed to baffle him as much as it embarrassed future President George Bush at the US Liaison Office.

In April China celebrated the Festival of Ancestors when traditionally Chinese families sweep the graves of their forebears as a token of respect. Chou En-lai's ashes had been scattered over China from an aeroplane to prevent them becoming a focus of disaffection. The people were nevertheless determined to honour him. Crowds swarmed into Tiananmen Square carrying countless wreaths adorned with seditious poems praising and mourning Chou, attacking Mao's absence from the memorial service, and criticising the policies which had inflicted so much suffering on the people. The criticism became bolder with each passing day. After three days the great portrait of Mao Tse-tung on the Gate of Heavenly Peace stared out over a forest of wreaths dedicated to another man. Too much. Overnight the square was cleared and when the people came with more wreaths in the morning they were turned back by the militia. Enraged, they overturned and burnt a police jeep within a stone's throw of Mao's house. This was perhaps the first expression of public opinion in China since 1949. Nick and his two small sons sat on a stone lion and watched it happen. When Charles went home to prep school he wrote an essay on what he had done in the holidays. It began "I watched history in the making..."

To replace Chou En-lai as Prime Minister, Mao had appointed a middle ranking official named Hua Kuo-feng, who had been Head of the Secret Police but was not known nationally, let alone internationally. He was dubbed by the diplomatic corps Hua Kuo-who? In May there appeared overnight in every Chinese city a copy

169

of an oil painting depicting the fresh-faced young Hua paying court to Mao Tse-tung. Mao is giving him a scroll on which was written in Chinese characters "With you in charge, I am at ease". Hua was never formally designated as Mao's successor during his lifetime, but the painting made his appointment a foregone conclusion. He must be the only person ever to attain supreme public office on the basis of an oil painting.

June saw the death at the age of ninety of Marshal Zhu Deh, veteran of the Long March, the most senior surviving army leader, still widely respected. He had quarrelled with Mao repeatedly since the 1920s but had been living in retirement and his death provoked no great public reaction.

Disaster struck China in July. An earthquake measuring 8.2 on the Richter scale struck the mining city of Tang Shan, a hundred miles north-east of Peking. Many of the men were underground. They did not stand a chance. Others, asleep in bed, were hurled against the ceiling and killed. The city was about the size of Nottingham. A quarter of a million people died and the Chinese said not a word. Every embassy in Peking went to the Foreign Ministry to offer sympathy and help. All offers were courteously declined, this was a Chinese problem which would be solved in a Chinese way. A year later we passed through Tang Shan by train. The city looked like Dresden at the end of the Second World War. Survivors lived in white tents in neat squares around the suburbs. Two great steam engines, which must have been at the station when the earthquake struck, still lay beside the track – a mass of twisted metal like a broken toy. We marvelled at the power of nature and the stoicism of the survivors. Life went on, even in Tang Shan.

We were formally advised by the Chinese authorities not to enter our embassy building nor to live in blocks of flats more than four storeys high because of the risk of aftershocks. For some weeks the embassy was run from the tennis court. Families from high-rise buildings camped in the recreation hall. It was difficult to maintain diplomatic courtesies in such circumstances. HMG in their wisdom

170

chose this moment to resume diplomatic relations with Democratic Kampuchea (the Cambodia of Pol Pot). Peking was the only capital in which both governments were represented, so Peking was instructed to exchange the instruments of recognition. Unfortunately, the *Charge d'Affaires* forgot. His Excellency the Ambassador of Democratic Kampuchea arrived at the British Embassy at the appointed time in his formal Chinese Mao suit. The embassy received him initially in bathing trunks.

During these excitements, the family Fenn was on leave on the west coast of Scotland in a cottage which is three miles from the road, nineteen miles from a telephone and forty-two miles from a shop. It was a favourite retreat. The FCO insisted that officers on holiday should leave contact details with their departments in London. Our arrangement was that the office should send a telegram to the farm at the head of the loch, on the understanding that we would enquire from time to time whether there was a message. One sunny afternoon Nick rowed up the loch to receive a consignment of supplies which had been delivered by the postman. He loaded the stores into the boat and walked up to the farm. Was there a message? Why yes, there was a wee telegram. Now where would I have been after putting the wee telegram? Please come in and have a wee dram while I look for it. Aye here it is, behind the clock. Nick sipped his whisky and opened the telegram. It instructed him to telephone the office immediately, dated three days ago. He got in the car, drove the nineteen miles and telephoned the office. "Oh, it's you."

"Yes, of course it's me. You asked me to telephone."

"Well we had intended to recall you to Peking, but it's too late now." The system worked perfectly!

In due course, however, Nick was indeed recalled and had to leave Sue to engage a new nanny for Julia (Tina – see above), relet the house, procure a host of items which we had learned to need in China and to join him in Peking when the boys went back to school. All in a day's work for a diplomatic wife.

171

There were aftershocks in Peking. By this time we were back in our own flat. One evening we felt a strong tremor and saw the ceiling lights swinging. Nick was at his desk and Tina and Sue were in the same room designing the costumes for the embassy pantomime. As the solid walls began to ripple and a dull roar rose from below ground, we hastened to stand in adjacent doorways. If the building collapsed we would have a greater chance of survival there. Meanwhile, embassy staff gathered in the recreation hall with their small suitcases of essential possessions and bedded down for the night. By morning it was safe to go home.

Our Italian colleague had an engaging habit of talking very fast in English, French and Italian simultaneously, emphasising his points with dramatic gestures using all four limbs (our children called him The Machine Gun). He had imported into China on his arrival a pair of priceless Ming vases which stood on a bureau at one end of his long living room on the eleventh floor. He was at the other end when the earthquake struck. To his horror he saw the vases begin to sway. He set off to rescue them, but the floor was buckling like a tidal wave. As he fell he cannoned into the bureau. The vases fell and Franco caught one of them in each arm. They were unharmed. So was he. But he told the story with high drama, again and again.

By the grace of God the earthquake had struck in the summer. We wondered uneasily what we would have done if it had been ten degrees below zero centigrade. Nick asked London for Arctic tenting. It transpired that the army stockpiled Arctic tenting in Hong Kong. It came up by train within a week. Why did the British army need Arctic tenting in Hong Kong?

We asked for volunteers to repair and insulate some outbuildings in the embassy compound so that they could be used as refuges in case of need. Everybody turned out on a Saturday morning. The standard of decoration left something to be desired, but flagging morale was strengthened by this common enterprise.

172

Soon we had other things to worry about than earthquakes. On 9 September Mao Tse-tung died. The news was released overnight 9–10 September. All China held its breath. Everyone knew that there was a titanic power struggle behind the scenes. Moderate leaders like Deng Xiao-ping and Marshal Yeh Jian-ying wanted pragmatic policies to raise living standards and break with the ideological legacy of Mao. The radicals, whose titular leader was Mao's widow, Jiang Qing, wanted to perpetuate the Cultural Revolution in order to cling to power. Madame Mao and her three henchmen had been dubbed by Mao himself the "Gang of Four". The other three were Zhang Chun-qiao, a wily old party apparatchik known as "The Cobra", Yao Wen-yuan, the media chief, and the young chairman of the party in Shanghai, Wang Hong-wen. Acting Party Chairman Hua Kuo-feng and his immediate colleagues stood undecided in the middle. Dutiful demonstrations passed our flat every day, professing their sorrow at the passing of the most cordially hated leader in the world. The diplomatic corps attended Mao's funeral and filed past his coffin, murmuring insincere condolences to the Chief of Protocol.

Exactly one month later, at two thirty in the morning on 10 October, we were awoken by a demonstration of a different kind; drums and cymbals, laughing and leaping, with huge banners proclaiming "Da dao si ren bang – Down with the Gang of Four". At a tense meeting of the Central Committee the moderates had narrowly won. The radicals had withdrawn to their stronghold in Shanghai and made the mistake of trying to raise a popular revolt which was half-hearted and easily put down by the army. The Gang of Four were under arrest.

On Christmas Day 1976, Hua Kuo-feng stood on the Gate of Heavenly Peace where Mao had stood in 1949 to proclaim the communist revolution, symbolically claiming the succession. The speech he made might have been written by Deng Xiao-ping and probably was. It was a moderate manifesto. The wheel full circle. The Year of the Dragon had begun with the death of the key moderate leader Chou En-lai, had seen the radicals riding high during the summer under Mao's enfeebled patronage, and now after

173

his death ended with the total triumph of the moderates. A quarter of the human race marched off in a new direction. This was political theatre of a high order. We had been paid to sit in the front row of the stalls to watch the pageant and try to make sense of it. We were conscious of the privilege.

A year later on 14 September 1977, Mao's Mausoleum was inaugurated in Tiananmen Square. Once more the diplomatic corps filed past the coffin of the now embalmed corpse. Curiously, Mao Tse-tung looked a year older.

That summer we visited the southern city of Guelin. The scenery is just like Chinese paintings. Limestone hills rise straight from river level. Twisted pines cling to the slopes. Wisps of cloud linger near the summit. The river winds through the hills. Local fishermen use cormorants to catch the fish and a rope ladder arrangement along the shore helps them move against the flow of water on their return. Villages tucked between the rock cliffs tumble to the water's edge. Children raced towards the boat to watch us pull in to land. Back in town Sue went to the tourist shop in the hotel looking for a gift to take to Hong Kong. She had an exquisite jade teacup in her hand when a young woman ran into the room, pigtails flying. From the excited gabble one name was repeated over and over, "Deng Xiao-ping, Deng Xiao-ping." Carefully putting down the cup, Sue ran to the lift and returned to the bedroom on the tenth floor. She grabbed the radio. Sure enough, a BBC News bulletin was just announcing that the pragmatic Deng Xiao-ping had been returned to power. We were invited to watch an old patriotic film after dinner. As we sat in a darkened hall trying to concentrate on the heroes and heroines of the story we were distracted by shouting outside. Soon there was a procession assembling and, when at last the film was over, we went out into the street to witness the exuberance and joy of a people who sensed that the Cultural Revolution was drawing to a close.

Deng's return began to make a difference. A few months later, Nick visited a ceramics factory in Nanchang. It was like many others we had seen. Rows of workers in white overalls sat at slow conveyor belts making cheap white china. But at the end of the factory floor was a low platform on which sat an old man dressed as an Imperial Mandarin. As each new batch of china came off the conveyor belt it was laid before him with an air almost of reverence. He examined each plate in turn and placed them on a separate pile. Every now and again he would throw a plate dismissively over his shoulder so that behind him there was a growing heap of broken china. "Who is that?" Nick asked in astonishment.

"He's Quality Control," they said. "He's back."

Each year Nick negotiated with the Director of Cultural Relations in the Chinese Foreign Ministry a bilateral agreement which governed our cultural exchanges for the following twelve months. In recent years this agreement had provided for fifteen Chinese students to study in British universities while fifteen British students studied at the Universities of Peking and Shanghai. We thought that we detected a cultural thaw following the Year of the Dragon. Greatly daring, Nick proposed in his draft for 1977 to double both numbers to thirty. The director's face fell. "I see that Mr Counsellor proposes to double the number of students next year," he said. "Is this your government's last word? We were thinking of one thousand."

We knew that we were to leave China at the end of 1977. The Chinese had a gracious custom of giving to departing diplomats who had not caused them offence a farewell gift in the form of permission to travel to some part of China that was usually off limits. The departing Danish Ambassador, for example, had been allowed to go to Tibet. Susan was born in Hong Kong and lived the first two years of her life in Pakhoi in South China (now Beihai) where her father had been a missionary doctor working amongst lepers. Nick called on other business on the Deputy Director of Protocol. He mentioned as he took his leave that sadly he would be leaving China in three months. At once Mr Liu suggested a valedictory tour and asked where Nick would like to go. Nick rehearsed his wife's early history and asked whether a visit to Pakhoi might be possible. There was no place in China where she would rather go than the place of her

175

childhood where she could visit her sister's grave. We knew it was a long shot. Pakhoi was now a Chinese naval base fifty miles from the Vietnam border and Sino-Vietnamese relations were very bad. Mr Liu looked worried, but he promised to consult his colleagues and see what might be possible.

Two weeks later at the Afghan National Day Mr Liu lay in wait. As Nick stepped from the French windows into the Ambassador's garden he seized him by the hand and took him behind the bushes. He was distressed. He had already referred the matter to the responsible comrade in the department concerned. He was very sorry to say that it would not be possible for reasons of military security over which he had no control. Nick fenced for a few minutes, stressing Sue's feeling for her dead sister, which in Chinese terms amounted to a family obligation. But this only increased Mr Liu's distress without changing the decision. Nick knew that he was wasting his time. Perhaps we could go to the Guelin Gorge instead? Mr Liu cheered up. That would certainly be possible. Then suddenly the mask slipped. Mr Liu took both of Nick's hands in both his own. "Would you do something for me, Mr Fenn? Please tell your wife when you are alone, and please tell her that… I understand how she feels." Mr Liu dissolved in tears and disappeared into the bushes. Nick felt a heel. He had ruthlessly exploited a Chinese cultural imperative for selfish reasons. Sue would certainly have liked to visit Pakhoi – but she did not feel about it as she would have felt if she had been Chinese. We went to Guelin instead – and it was very beautiful.

We left China in November. For the first and only time in our diplomatic service we left post without knowing where we were to be posted. We were told to despatch our heavy baggage to London.

We went out through Hong Kong as we had arrived in 1975, and had our last intensive discussions about the future of the colony with the Governor and his staff. Ten years later this future was resolved under Deng Xiao-ping's creative slogan "one nation, two systems". Our boss in Peking, Sir Edward Youde, ironically succeeded Sir

Murray MacLehose as Governor and worked as hard as anyone to secure the future of the colony. Geoffrey Howe's Hong Kong agreement laid down the basis of a Special Economic Zone within the People's Republic but under separate and different administration. Chris Patten, the last British Governor, tried to improve on that agreement to secure more democracy for the people of Hong Kong. Sir Percy Craddock, who as Ambassador in Peking had negotiated the agreement, publicly attacked the serving Governor for putting the achievement at risk. Democracy was not the Chinese way. Governor Patten left Hong Kong on time in 1997 – and Chinese Hong Kong has been a great success.

Postscript – 2001

In 2001 we at last got to visit Tibet. The Royal Society for Asian Affairs organised a tour in the footsteps of Sir Francis Younghusband, founder of the society, who famously fought his way from Calcutta to Lhasa in 1904. Like other foreign visitors we were impressed by its towering mountains, extreme poverty, extravagant religion – and by the reality of Chinese rule. Tibet is occupied territory and the Tibetans are a subject race. Some features of this are obvious to the traveller; military presence, mutual antipathy, the imposition of the Chinese language, mutually agreed apartheid, with the Chinese at one end of town in new concrete boxes and the Tibetans at the other end in old stone houses. The place feels like a colony – like Soviet Mongolia or British Hong Kong.

Chinese will is absolute that "Tibet is part of China". There is no discernible prospect that this will be internationally contested. Most living Tibetans know no other way of life and know very little of the outside world. It does them no kindness to offer them unrealistic expectations of external intervention. The future of Tibet depends upon the internal dynamics of China – upon the struggle between capitalist economics and totalitarian politics.

Tibet has consistently asked the outside world to leave her alone. This request has been consistently denied – by China, by Russia, by Britain, certainly by Sir Francis Younghusband. In modern terms it

177

was we, the tourists, who were "trespassers on the roof of the world". We came home sharing some of the pride of Sir Francis at his stupendous achievement – and some of the shame that he came to feel for intruding upon Tibet's distinctive culture.

We returned from Lhasa via Peking and were awestruck by the changes in the quarter century since we left. Peking looks like Hong Kong – high-rise buildings, four-lane highways, neon lights, restaurants serving Chinese and foreigners together, massage parlours, insistent traders on the streets, Kentucky Fried Chicken on Tiananmen Square, Macdonalds at the Legation Railway Station, a chairlift up the Great Wall of China! We were absurdly indignant. Our guide acknowledged the problem of the poor in Peking; medical care, social security, unemployment. It must be good for China that such questions can be asked. But the Forbidden City is reassuringly unchanged – the heart of a great empire still.

Eric and Kay Fenn on board SS Leicestershire to see us off to Burma
September 1960.

On the road to Mandalay September 1960.

Our heavy baggage arrives in Mandalay 1960.

U Nyunt's family.

Four brothers enter a monastery, Mandalay 1960.

Robin scrutinises his new mother Jan.1962.

Boys with Zorha, Beverley(R) and friends, Algiers 1967.

185

Early morning for Robin and Charlie in the Atlas 1968.

The young crew on Djemila off Long Island 1969.

At a Security Council Meeting in 1969.

Too young to walk into Grand Canyon so fly.

The bridge to cross from Hong Kong to PRC 1976.

Three boys dressed for coal mine in Datung 1976.

Tributes to Chou En Lai Spring 1976.

Firecrackers for fall of Gang of Four,October 1976.

Painting of Mao with Hua Kuo Feng Oct. 1976.

Julia admires local children in Peking 1976.

Nick and Julia have Great Wall to themselves 1976.

Nick sailing on Inya Lake, Rangoon.

House party in Rangoon for Monty's 85th.

Circuit House Bedroom on Tour in Burma.

Joining in Water Festival, Rangoon 1984.

March 2nd 1984 with Monty, Shorty and Twee.

Visiting Suu Kyi January 2011.

Inspecting Irish Lighthouses 1980s.

Kissing the Blarney Stone.

Mid Sahara in shade of our Landrover 1989.

Another tree to plant in India.

At a Sikh gathering to honour Manmohan Singh in Delhi.

One of several meetings with Dalai Lama in India and Ireland.

Serious talk with George Bush Snr. and USA Ambassador in Delhi.

Learning about Street Children in Andra Pradesh.

Official call on H.M. King of Bhutan 1992.

Three Excellencies to honour Nalini.

Visit to Jodhpur with Judy and Douglas Hurd.

Breakfast, Delhi Residence with visiting family at Christmas.

Enjoying Craft Museum with John Major in Delhi 1995.

H.E. calls on Collector of Bangaram.

On duty together with Sonya Gandhi in Delhi 1995.

H.R.H. Diana on official visit Dehli February 1992.

Tribute to Fallen Kohima 1994.

Staff of Residence Christmas 1995.

A reluctant farewell to India and the Service 19.2.96.

Being dragged from BHC compound.

Her most loyal servant after 37 years.

Chapter 8
Royal College of Defence Studies 1978

When we got home to London our posting notice was waiting for us. Nick was to spend the calendar year 1978 as a student at the Royal College of Defence Studies. We lived at home at Applecroft and Nick commuted to London to attend the course.

Most of this chapter is by Nick alone. It reflects the College as it was in 1978. It has changed a good deal since.

The RCDS is the premier British Defence College. Colonels and Brigadiers go there to learn how to be Generals, how to think in political and strategic terms rather than tactical and technical. The College is at Seaford House, standing elegantly at the south-east corner of Belgrave Square. Two thirds of the students are from the armed services, but they generously invite one third civilians to stimulate non-military thinking. In those days (alas, no longer) there were always three counsellors from the FCO. My two FCO colleagues were Nigel Broomfield, later Ambassador to the GDR and to Germany, and Andrew Palmer, later Ambassador to Cuba and to the Holy See. Two thirds of the students are British, but one third are from overseas, predominantly from NATO and the Commonwealth, to stimulate international thinking. In 1978 there were students from twenty-five countries, from USA, Canada, Australia and New Zealand, from Belgium, France, Germany, Greece, Portugal, Spain and Turkey, from India, Pakistan, Ghana, Guyana, Kenya, Malaysia and Nigeria, and also from Egypt, Iran, Israel, Japan and Saudi Arabia. For twelve months we lived and worked together, hearing the same lectures, commenting from our very different experience, arguing over lunch or dinner, sometimes long into the night.

It was a professional sabbatical year. The programme set the tone. The first item was "1–15 January: New Year Holiday". The last item was "15–31 December: Christmas Holiday". The lecturers were distinguished military figures, diplomats, academics, or politicians of national, sometimes international, renown. The level of discussion was high. We began with the strategic doctrine of NATO, nuclear deterrence and other military matters. We looked in turn at the superpowers, at strategy, at economics, at management, at contemporary society, at subversion and revolutionary conflict, at science and technology and the defence of Europe. Before the end we were discussing the economic and social issues of the UK, the European Union, NATO and the UN, the political problems of the world's hotspots and whether the United Kingdom was worth defending anyway.

In the course of the year we made visits in small groups to different parts of the UK. Nick's group visited Wales with a briefing by the Welsh Office in Cardiff, discussion of Welsh nationalism and nuclear weapons with students, the closure of coal mines with miners in the valleys, the difficulties of agriculture and the Common Agricultural Policy with farmers in Snowdonia. We visited the Dinorwig Hydro-Electric scheme, a magic power station inside a mountain in North Wales which pumps water up using excess power overnight and releases it in a rush to meet peak demand the following day.

We made visits to each of the three services. We took turns to helm a frigate. I was able to pilot an aeroplane for the first time since I left the University Air Squadron in 1959. A New Zealand navy captain was the only man to stand a Chieftain tank on its gun. We visited army, navy and air commands, the Police College at Bramshill and the Headquarters of NATO and the European Union.

In the autumn we spent a month on overseas tour. Nick visited Africa which he scarcely knew at all. We looked at the very different French colonial inheritance in Ivory Coast, at the devastation of oil wealth in Nigeria, at the travails of democracy (and the spectacular wildlife) in Kenya, and the division of Sudan between north and south, Arab and African, Muslim and Christian. On the way home we went to see the pyramids in Egypt and the chaotic profusion of the National Museum in Cairo.

We each wrote a thesis. Nick chose to write on international terrorism – perhaps prophetically given our future involvement in Ireland and India. In 1978 this meant principally the hijacking of aircraft and the kidnapping of diplomats and other public figures. He concluded loftily that "the present writer would welcome a public statement by Her Majesty's Government that they would never, in any circumstances, pay any price, bend any policy, or release any prisoner, to buy freedom or immunity for their servants. Certainly – from the safety of his study in Kent on a summer afternoon – he hopes that HMG will never make any such concession for him".

Perhaps the most important part of the year at RCDS lay not in the lectures or seminars or theses, but in the friendships we formed across wide international barriers and in what we learned from each other. The company included for example brigadiers from Israel and from Egypt who had commanded tank formations against each other in the Sinai Desert. After dinner they could sometimes be persuaded, towards the end of the course when the barriers were reduced by familiarity and respect, to use the salt and pepper to represent tank formations and to demonstrate to each other and to us how their battles had been lost and won. The same could be said of our colleagues from India and Pakistan who had faced each other across the inhospitable Siachen glacier in the high Himalaya. Brigadier Roddy Rodrigues subsequently became Chief of Staff of the Indian army while we were in India, and later Governor of Punjab. When the lectures seemed dull or interminable we remembered that they dealt with different aspects of real wars fought by real people who had become our friends. Our understanding was illuminated by the experience of our colleagues.

The year 1978 was a pause for reflection in lives that were becoming increasingly frenetic. It was marked by a leisurely

226

commute from Marden to Charing Cross and a walk across St James's Park to Belgrave Square. We expected the pace of life to quicken as Nick's studies came to an end. But at the end of the year nothing happened. Nick was summoned to the FCO and told to embark upon "a period of intensive preparation for an unidentified assignment". This was Foreign Office speak. Nick had been nominated to become Head of News Department and Foreign Office spokesman, an appointment which involves also being Press Secretary to the Secretary of State and naturally requires his personal approval. But Dr David Owen had sensibly declined to make any appointment because he knew that Labour would lose the next general election.

So Nick was in limbo. He attended courses in economics and in television presentation. He was invited to write the scenario for a terrorism exercise in Whitehall. This meant writing the first half of a novel, getting HMG into the most awkward possible tangle, and leaving the experts to unravel it. Nick invented the hijack to Kuwait of an airliner with an implausible passenger list, including a trusted adviser of the President of the United States, a beautiful Holywood film star, an Indian millionaire, a British Ambassador and the commander of an African guerrilla movement. The preparation involved a secret visit to Cyprus for consultation with the British High Commissioner and the Commander of British Forces in the Sovereign Base Areas which were to deputise for Kuwait in the story. It was fun to write. By the time the exercise was run Nick was already in post. But he was not allowed to participate because he knew too much of the background.

As election night approached in May 1979 we had guests from the United States. Sue's foster sister Anne Stone and her husband, Herb, and her foster brother, Bill Johnson, were arriving overnight. On the morning after the election, having been up watching the results almost all night, we welcomed the party at the little flat in Pont Street. Bill sensibly fell into a comfortable bed while the rest of us walked across the park to watch Mrs.Thatcher arrive for the first time at Number 10. We heard her recite the prayer of St.Francis of Assisi to the astonished journalists and eager crowd:

Lord make me an instrument of your peace.
Where there is hatred, let me sow love,
Where there is injury, pardon,
Where there is doubt, faith,
Where there is despair, hope,
Where there is darkness, light,
Where there is sadness, joy.

Downing Street was still open to the public. A large group of people from all walks of life had gathered to witness the dawn of the Thatcher era.

Two days later Nick was summoned to call on the new Secretary of State. An extraordinary new appointment was about to begin.

Chapter 9
News Department 1979-82

In the spring of 1979 Britain and its government stood on the brink of disaster. James Callaghan had contrived by compromise to sustain the management of the country and to keep alive some flickering flame of Labour aspirations. Trade Unions harried him from the left. The Tories, under radical new leadership, harried him from the right. The economy was in desperate straits. In the spring the government collapsed, the Conservatives won by a landslide, and Margaret Thatcher came to Downing Street with that incongruous quotation from St Francis of Assisi.

Her Foreign Secretary was Lord Carrington. He had won the Military Cross in the Grenadier Guards during the war, was first appointed a Minister by Sir Winston Churchill in 1951, had served as High Commissioner in Australia while we had been at university, and had led for the Conservatives in the House of Lords since 1964. Behind his effortless aristocratic manner he hid a razor-sharp intelligence, a ruthless pursuit of his objectives and a deep human compassion. Foreigners often underestimated this patrician toff which enabled him to run rings round them.

Nick was duly summoned and presented to the new boss. "Oh, it's you," he said. "That's all right then." Perhaps he recognised the Junior Private Secretary to RAB in 1964. It seemed for a moment that the interview was at an end. Almost as an afterthought he told Nick to sit down and tell him how he would approach the job. Nick had had six months to think about this question. He made a little speech. He would offer him loyalty and obedience. He would try to do it his way. He would not tell lies to the press because he would be found out and discredited. He would look for forms of words which served the national interest while preserving the integrity of the

Foreign Secretary. He would try to establish with journalists a relationship of confidence as he had done in New York ten years earlier. In return he asked for Lord Carrington's trust and the trust of his senior officials. He hoped that the Secretary of State would put up with his presence at meetings so that he could understand his mind and his policies in order to project them. He would offer him feedback on the press, telling him not only what they were writing but what they were thinking... The Secretary of State had heard enough platitudes. "That's all fine," he said. "Now let's see how we get on. Come and see me for five minutes at eight forty every morning. You won't find the press so easy as they were ten years ago."

He was of course quite right. Nick went down the great marble staircase past the famous picture of Britannia Nutrix to meet his colleagues and take charge of his new department.

The Head of News Department plays a unique role in the Foreign Office. He is first a Head of Department responsible to his Under Secretary and his staff for the administration of the work. News Department is a collegiate enterprise. Each desk officer shadows a number of other departments, prepares draft lines to take on issues within his parish and delivers these lines to the press. He will be the first port of call for an enquiring journalist. The Head of News Department is, secondly, the Foreign Office spokesman, responsible to the Permanent Under Secretary for the co-ordination of the entire output and the relationship with the media. He attends, and often conducts, the daily press conference and briefs senior journalists and editors. Thirdly, he is Press Secretary to the Secretary of State, responsible directly to the Minister for ensuring that what the department says in public reflects not only the view of the Office but also the mind of its master. He arranges interviews and press conferences for Foreign Office Ministers. He travels with the Secretary of State and manages his public relations while on tour.

The day begins with intake. He must read the British press and be aware of press comment in the major organs of other countries. He calls briefly on the Secretary of State to take his mind on thorny current issues and to warn him of unexpected booby traps. He reads the telegrams from posts abroad which give a snapshot of the state of the world that morning. He attends the Permanent Under Secretary's morning meeting at which senior officials discuss the situation and decide on the broad line of action for the day. Armed with all this diverse information, he holds his own meeting of the department to finalise the lines to take. What are the key foreign policy issues which the Secretary of State would like to see publicly clarified? What initiatives should be highlighted? What does the FCO hope to read in the press the next morning? What does it fear to read? How should it reply to awkward questions that are likely to arise? Then at twelve fifteen the news conference begins the daily output. Often he will lunch with a journalist or a colleague. If foreign issues are discussed in Parliament the Head of News Department will attend, particularly if the Secretary of State is to speak. In the early evening he will hold an unattributable briefing for groups of senior journalists – the "trusties" from the major papers, radio and television diplomatic correspondents, sometimes the popular press or foreign correspondents accredited in London. As the stories begin to clarify in the course of the day, he spends a good deal of time on the telephone dealing with the particular lines which individual diplomatic correspondents may be taking. Before he goes home he ensures that the departmental duty officer is fully up to speed and knows where he can be contacted if necessary.

Lord Carrington was an early riser. His wish to meet Nick every morning at eight forty posed a problem. In order to get there in time from Marden he would have to catch a train before the papers were available in the village. It became clear that he would have to have a *pied 'a terre* in town. A colleague kindly lent us his comfortable flat in Pont Street. When he needed to have it back Nick took digs in Vincent Square. Both were within easy walking distance of Whitehall. Weekend commuting is a barbarous lifestyle, the one serious disadvantage of the job.

Life in Kent for Sue and the children was much the same as for any small family whose breadwinner appears at weekends needing to catch up on sleep. Julia now aged five joined first the village pre-school play group and then the excellent primary school. The boys continued to enjoy boarding at Kingswood in Bath and Sue got stuck into community activities. Nick was away so much Sue tried offering Bed and Breakfast – strictly for foreign visitors only. She gave it up because the Revenue office interfered too much. Probably trying to help they kept insisting she work out her costs in detail and charge more. But she wasn't in it for the money. She wanted, believe this or not, to give her guests from foreign parts travelling on restricted budgets a specially good time and a good impression of Britain. So then she changed to taking in student midwives, attached for three months to the village midwife. As lodgers these were delightful guests and taught Sue a lot about the NHS.

As usual the family went to the West coast of Scotland for the summer break, using the motor-rail for the London–Inverness section of the journey. It was magic to go to sleep in London and wake up in the Highlands ready for a huge breakfast at the station hotel in Inverness. Runival, the croft on Loch Hourn never failed to enchant.

During term time when the boys were away at school, Sue sometimes attended social events in London but she kept in touch with the Service mostly by joining the committee of the Diplomatic Service Wives Association. Her brief, which she had to develop from scratch, was "Medical and Welfare". There was very little support for wives and families at the time compared to current norms. We focused on the families of officers declared "persona non grata" or those evacuated from war zones or natural disasters. But so many letters came in from distressed individuals that the job of a professional welfare officer became an obvious necessity. Some of the sad letters, say from new young mums, blamed the office for all their ills. Sue was sufficiently in touch with similar families in Kent to know the problems were the same at home. The real difference was the lack of support overseas to replace family, friends, the welfare state and the helpful charities we can turn to in Britain when things go wrong. Soon great steps were taken by the office to put in place a better support system for families overseas. Often the barrier for families was being surrounded by a strange language. Encouragement for spouses to study the local language began about this time too. The system for calculating what is a "Hardship Post" was radically revised. There had to be one subjective element in order to explain why Tripoli with its wonderful climate, excellent medical facilities only a short distance from home was the most unpopular posting, whereas Rangoon with its awful climate, repressive regime, long distance from home and terrible hospitals was often in demand. A new "Gadaffi factor" was added to the calculation.

Two unconnected changes motivated Sue to get politically active outside the service. Diplomatic spouses were no longer barred from joining UK political parties. Clearly serving diplomats should not openly support one party over another. But the wives were now "allowed" actually to join parties. This new "freedom" coincided with the birth of the Social Democratic Party and, judging by the comments of her colleagues, most of them joined the SDP of Shirley Williams, Bill Rogers, David Owen and Roy Jenkins. There was great excitement at the grass roots and small groups met all over the country to "thrash out" the policies of this new political movement. Even in the tiny hamlet of Chainhurst a new group, which included a dentist and a farm labourer, seriously undertook to advise "the centre" on education, health, pensions and employment. Sadly, their first election coincided with the beginning of the Falklands War. Canvassers were told again and again at cottage doors and council flats, "Well I would have voted for you but now we're at war I must vote for the government." Nick was away so much he did not realise that instead of displaying posters and car stickers for all three major parties, as was our custom, Sue only put up ones for the SDP. Unluckily a salesman came to the house offering aerial photographs of Applecroft. The lone poster was clearly visible.

The rest of this chapter is by Nick alone

A few weeks into the job I invited the diplomatic correspondents of the major papers to a drink one evening to get acquainted. I described the relationship I had enjoyed with their colleagues at the United Nations. We were in each other's pockets. If I told them a lie I would not again be believed. If they betrayed a confidence they would not again be trusted. I hoped that I could share a lot of confidence so that they would understand the issues that Ministers faced and the decisions that they took – and then we would discuss how much of all this could be reported. We were colleagues in the enterprise, new every morning, of rendering government intelligible to its citizens. They turned me down flat. They and I were not on the same side. They could not run the risk of being seen as Foreign Office poodles. It was for me to decide how much I would tell them. They had other ways to find out what I chose to withhold. If I talked to them on an unattributable basis, they would respect that constraint and I would not be directly quoted. But they must be free to write anything I chose to tell them. I said that in that case I would tell them rather little. It was not a good start. As the boss had warned me, the relationship between government and press had changed over ten years.

In the event all this was quickly overtaken by the first major diplomatic business of the new administration. Lord Carrington came to the Foreign Office determined to resolve the running sore of Rhodesia which had been like an albatross around the neck of British diplomacy for most of my working life, not least in Algeria (Chapter 4). Ian Smith had declared UDI in 1965. David Owen had travelled relentlessly in Africa in the search for a negotiated solution, but successive British Governments had failed either to restore legality or to bring the rebels to heel. Two competing liberation movements sought to destroy the white government by armed insurrection. Joshua Nkomo's (predominantly Matabele) Zimbabwe African People's Union mounted raids from safe haven in Zambia. Robert Mugabe's (predominantly Shona) Zimbabwe African National Union occupied territory in the east and promoted uprisings from safe haven in Mozambique. But the illegal white government controlled the armed forces. Neither side could defeat the other. Casualties mounted. International opinion was overwhelmingly with the liberation movements. Britain was held responsible for tolerating illegality and racism. But it was neither militarily nor politically feasible for any British Government to resolve the problem by force.

Lord Carrington's plan was deceptively simple. He would ignore both Ian Smith's illegal declaration of independence and the rebellion of the liberation movements. He would pretend that Rhodesia was a British colony like any other approaching independence. He would convene a constitutional conference at Lancaster House, ostensibly just like the conferences that had preceded independence for many other colonies. He would invite all the parties. He would build upon the common interest they had acquired over the years in stopping the bloodshed and securing internationally recognised legal independence under black majority rule, but with appropriate safeguards for the white minority. It was a gigantic confidence trick. If it failed we would be no worse off. It might even work.

The stage was set. The delegations were invited for September 1979. A Press Centre was established at Little St James's – off Green Park and just across the road from Lancaster House. I handed over the day-to-day management of News Department to my deputy, Nick Elam, and moved my office across the park. I was to be full-time spokesman of the conference, and at the same time spokesman for its chairman, Lord Carrington, and for the British delegation. The Press Officers of the other delegations were also provided with offices at the Press Centre with all facilities including closed-circuit television so that each of us could observe what the others were saying. To discourage grandstanding the press were excluded from the conference itself. But I was to give an on-the-record account immediately after each plenary session. My colleagues from the Patriotic Front (ZANU and ZAPU in tactical alliance) and for Bishop Muzorewa's Government of Zimbabwe-Rhodesia were invited to challenge and correct my version of events. Only once did they do

235

so. About halfway through the conference the ZAPU spokesman fiercely attacked me for omitting a proposal that had been tabled that morning by Mr Nkomo. He was absolutely right. I had turned over two pages in my notes and overlooked Mr Nkomo's intervention. I at once took the stage, apologised, expounded the Nkomo proposal and invited his spokesman to comment. He had nothing more to say. The tension dissolved in laughter.

This on-the-record pantomime was a straightforward exercise in diplomatic reporting. I tried to tell it like it was. Later in the day there was a press conference at which more partisan points could be made. In the evening I would conduct unattributable briefings for the British press and sometimes also for others. The headlines in the day's papers were relevant to the conference diplomacy. It was surprisingly easy to lead the press to reflect the mood most favourable to the success of the conference. This is where it was essential to have a press spokesman who is trusted to be part of the team. So long as I knew what my colleagues were trying to achieve on any one day, so long as I had the opportunity to feed into these tactical decisions the likely effect that would be produced in the media, so long could I usually produce the public reaction required by the interests of diplomacy. There was always good coverage. We were the only show in town.

There were parliamentary considerations. The Shadow Minister for Information, Chris Smith, tabled a question complaining that policy was being announced by faceless officials at Lancaster House which should properly be declared in this House. It seemed to me that in constitutional terms Mr Smith had a point. I made a submission to the Secretary of State offering to stand down and suggesting that Mr Richard Luce MP, then a Foreign Office Minister and a member of the British delegation, might properly take my place. The submission came back with a robust rejoinder in red ink: "Balls. C". I was encouraged to continue.

The conference divided its complex business into three phases, on the understanding that nothing was agreed until all had been agreed.

We first addressed the constitution for an independent Zimbabwe; parliamentary democracy with a figurehead president and a Prime Minister responsible to Parliament; independent judiciary, human rights and free press; majority rule with safeguards for the minority including twenty reserved seats in an assembly of one hundred for the first ten years. Then we turned to the interim arrangements for the governance of the country until free and fair elections could be held; the anachronistic reaffirmation of British colonial authority in Africa; the administration under the direction of a British Governor with British supervision of the elections. Finally, the most sensitive matter of all was the ceasefire; the guerrillas to surrender their weapons and assemble in designated areas under British command, and the Rhodesian armed forces to return to barracks. All these were astonishing proposals. Each phase in turn was debated in formal plenary session. The delegations were predictably miles apart. Then Lord Carrington would conduct secret negotiations with each delegation in private to press them towards the centre ground. The most significant of these private sessions were always the meetings with Bishop Muzorewa and Ian Smith. Carrington pressed them ruthlessly to acquiesce in something which just might avoid the breakdown of the conference. Having extracted his pound of flesh from the whites, he then added a little zest of his own and tabled the result as the chairman's "compromise proposals" on a take-it-or-leave-it basis. The draft was made public at the same time. These were exciting days. The press prophesied disaster. All delegations protested. All acquiesced. Chapter by patient chapter, the fairy tale was written.

Lord Carrington had certain advantages. He subordinated other objectives to this one – and as a Minister in the House of Lords he was better able to do this than a Minister in the Commons would have been. We mobilised diplomatic pressure on the parties through their friends, calling in favours and urging the cause of peace in African capitals through the Commonwealth, the Americans, the European Union and, in the case of Ian Smith, South Africa. He was able to capitalise on the one thing the parties had in common – weariness with civil war and the shared belief that this was the last

237

chance saloon. The proposals were horrific – but the alternative was always worse. Finally, Carrington had one advantage over David Owen which was never publicly acknowledged. For a Tory Foreign Secretary the ultimate weapon was to cut his losses, settle with Smith, legislate independence for Rhodesia under its present constitution and take the resulting international flak. A large part of the Conservative Party wanted and expected this to happen. The Prime Minister would have been relieved. In the middle of the conference the Secretary of State had to address his party conference in Blackpool and found them baying for precisely this outcome. They did not know how they were strengthening his hand. After the Blackpool conference I was authorised to start talking about the British Government's determination to secure "a first-class solution", thus implicitly acknowledging the possibility of a second-class outcome.

When the Patriotic Front was finally brought to accept the interim arrangements, Joshua Nkomo acquiesced with graceful humour. "OK, you send us your Governor with his cocked hat, and we will provide him with a white horse."

The most difficult moment was the tabling of the chairman's proposals on the ceasefire. To the Patriotic Front they looked like surrender and the assembly areas looked like concentration camps. My ZANU colleague, Eddison Zvobgo, waxed passionate on the subject. The proposals were "fathered by Mrs Thatcher in concubinage with Satan Botha". I commented on-the-record that I found his sexual imagery a trifle confusing.

Late that night the ceasefire was agreed in principle and the entire agreement was put together for final approval and signature. Ian Smith went home in a huff. Lord Carrington took the bold decision to initiate the British interim administration of Rhodesia before the agreement had been signed. On 17 December Lord Soames flew to Salisbury with a handful of senior advisers and took up residence in Government House. I had to pretend that this piece of effrontery was

238

a pragmatic provision to ensure a flying start when formal agreement was reached.

In London we began to relax. I went home midweek to attend a dinner party in the village. I had a telephone call as I ate my duck. The General commanding the Commonwealth Monitoring Force was a warrior rather than a diplomat. He had misspoken at a press conference in Harare. Lord Soames wanted a press spokesman who knew the diplomatic background. I was to fly to Harare the following morning "on loan for a month".

On Christmas Day Lady Soames gathered her husband's staff round the Governor's table for turkey and trimmings. Another telephone call. It was Lord Carrington wishing Lord Soames a happy Christmas. What did Christopher want for Christmas? He wanted Fenn.

All this was personally most unwelcome. It meant abandoning the family for three months, reneging on my promise to Susan that we would spend Christmas together when the conference was over and celebrate Rob's eighteenth birthday as a family. It meant three months living alone in the Monomatapa Hotel. I was the spokesman for the government of a country of which I knew nothing. At my first press conference I was asked an indignant question about the state of the roads in Bulawayo and had to ask "Where's Bulawayo?" In reality of course my job was to project the implementation of the Lancaster House agreement – to help to make the fairy tale come true.

Step by step it did indeed come true. British subalterns stood to attention under palm trees and Marxist guerrillas came out of the jungle, stacked their rifles against the tree and meekly went to their appointed assembly areas. The Rhodesian armed forces were confined to barracks. The ceasefire held. British Election monitors fanned out over the country to supervise the arrangements for the freest and fairest elections that Zimbabwe has ever known. The politicians began to campaign with large public meetings which were

239

miraculously peaceful. We found it hard to believe. The press found it even harder.

For most of this interim period we did not need a political heavyweight as Governor. The Deputy Governor, Sir Anthony Duff, could perfectly well have done the job. Soames paced up and down the immaculate gardens of Government House like a caged lion. He wanted to be out assuring the people that the elections would indeed be free and fair. For security reasons he could not act like a democratic politician – or even like a constitutional monarch. But when we came to the end game a political heavyweight was precisely what we needed.

One morning there was bad news; intelligence reports that Mugabe was cheating. He had indeed assembled his guerrillas as to about two thirds. The remaining one third had returned to their villages, hidden their rifles and were intimidating the people. Some of us were incredulous. Mugabe was going to win anyway and had no need to cheat. Why should he put his future power at risk in this foolhardy manner? But the evidence was strong. The Governor was formally advised to send for Mugabe, confront him with the evidence and disqualify him from the elections. If Christopher Soames had acted on this advice the whole enterprise would have been destroyed and the civil war resumed.

We summoned Mugabe. He said he would come with twelve armed men. We said the Governor wished to see him alone. He came. He was ushered in. The interview was expected to last five minutes, ten at most. It lasted three quarters of an hour. Then these two very different men came out into the hall arm in arm. We shall never know what personal chemistry may have been responsible. But Mugabe was not disqualified and the elections proceeded. British policemen in their incongruous helmets stood beside the polling booths as guarantors of fair play. The results came in. The whites had won their twenty reserved seats. Joshua Nkomo, who thought of himself as the father of African nationalism in Zimbabwe, received precisely his tribal entitlement of twenty seats. Mugabe won fifty-

240

seven. Muzorewa won three. It would have been hard to imagine a more decisive outcome. The armed forces had contemplated a *coup d'etat* in the event of a close finish. They may have been discouraged by the overwhelming result. There was no coup. Soames sent for Mugabe and invited him to form a government. Mugabe invited Soames to be the first titular President of free Zimbabwe. Wisely, Soames declined. Mugabe appointed The Rev Canaan Banana.

The press regarded all this with mounting incredulity. By the end there were 1,002 journalists from almost every nation on earth accredited at the Press Centre in central Harare. It would have been sad if the figure had been 998! Almost all of them expected failure and most wanted it – success never makes good copy. I faced huge daily press conferences with dozens of television cameras, and difficult evening briefings with the British journalists to try to sustain their confidence in the integrity of the enterprise.

One issue caused particular difficulty. The South African Government had deployed troops across Beit Bridge into Zimbabwean territory, presumably to protect the bridge from sabotage. A British journalist discovered they were there and asked whether the Governor had authorised their presence. Had Lord Soames stopped beating his wife? I stalled and sought urgent instructions. For a week I had to fend off nightly questions. Eventually, the Governor did indeed authorise their presence so that I could say that he had done so. I spent a whole day devising a detailed line to take. I wanted the statement to be made in response to a question so that it would not look too contrived. As ill luck would have it, there was some other major issue that evening and I forgot all about it. Just as I was adjourning the press conference after the regulation forty-five minutes, the diplomatic correspondent of BBC Television, one John Humphrys, said, "Nick, I don't suppose that there is anything new to say about Beit Bridge?" God bless Humphrys.

"Well, yes, John," I said, desperately fishing for the brief, "as a matter of fact there is." The exchanges went on for another forty-five

241

minutes while they tried to trap me into admitting that the South African troops had entered illegally and were not welcome. It was the longest press conference I ever conducted.

There was a lull in the story in early 1980 after the establishment of the interim administration and the ceasefire and before the elections. I was allowed to escape for two weeks holiday with my family in England. My absence was noticed after a week and a leading South African paper, *The Courier of Pretoria*, ran a front page story: "Where is Fenn?" They speculated that I had gone underground to influence the elections or had had a row with the Governor and been sacked. It did not occur to the writer that I might be asleep at home in Kent.

The Rhodesia saga ran for a full six months from Lancaster House to independence day. The settlement was a diplomatic triumph for Lord Carrington. We had stopped a bloody civil war that neither side could win and launched a new nation into sovereign independence. We had established conditions that could have led to racial harmony and prosperity. Diplomats should never count chickens. Look at the story of Zimbabwe since then. Look at it now.

After the high excitement of Zimbabwe, I was looking forward to a less stressful time in my regular job in London. Certain events stick in the mind not because they were typical of News Department but because they were unusual. In a few weeks we were back on the front pages with an incident of very different stamp.

The BBC wanted to show a film called *Death of a Princess* which purported to show that a princess of the Saudi royal house had been assassinated by her family because she had been caught in an illicit sexual relationship outside marriage. In British eyes this was a sad little story. In Saudi eyes it was an outrageous calumny, an attack on the King's family by an official organ of the British Government. They threatened dire consequences if the film was shown – consequences for oil supplies, contracts, jobs, for the stability of the Middle East. Ministers hesitated. From where I sat it was a straightforward issue of the freedom of the media. HMG could not possibly censor the BBC. We should explain to the Saudi Ambassador that HMG was not responsible for the editorial content of the BBC and leave it at that. My colleagues in Middle East Department took a different view. The consequences for the British economy and for policy in the Middle East were so serious that we should make a major effort to prevent the film from being screened. Sir Ian Gilmour, who as Lord Privy Seal was Lord Carrington's deputy and a former newspaper editor himself, telephoned his friends in the BBC who were polite but unmoved. The programme was postponed for a week but eventually screened. The consequences were less than dire.

Another Saudi complication arose over the sad death of a British nurse, Helen Smith, who fell from the balcony of her flat in Riyadh. On the face of it this was the tragic aftermath of a boozy party in a country where alcohol was illegal. But Helen's father, a retired policeman, flew to Riyadh and laboured for many months to prove that his daughter was murdered. The press constantly sought to elicit a "Foreign Office View" on a subject on which the Foreign Office quite properly had no view. It was thirty years before Mr Smith would allow his daughter's body to be buried.

One day the entire staff of the small British Embassy in El Salvador mysteriously disappeared, leaving a note pinned to the locked door saying that the embassy was temporarily closed and they would be back soon. It reminded me of The House at Pooh Corner, "Wol out. Bakson". In fact of course they had taken refuge in a safe house in response to an immediate threat to their security – but we could not say so without putting their lives and our relations with El Salvador at risk. I was told to explain that the closure of the embassy was a temporary administrative measure, that the Ambassador and his staff were on holiday and would be back in business shortly. Nobody believed me. Every morning for a week I explained at the PUS's morning meeting that this line was not plausible and could not be sustained. Every morning I was told to shut up and get on with the job. In the end I was authorised to arrange for a confidential press briefing by a senior colleague who told trusted correspondents enough of the background to sustain the story for a few more days. Then, mercifully, the embassy reopened and the story went away.

A junior colleague in the FCO alas committed suicide by jumping out of a high window. A journalist got wind of the story and telephoned for confirmation. The difficulty was that the wife of the deceased had gone shopping and could not immediately be traced. It was a cardinal rule that we never said anything in such circumstances until the next of kin had been informed. I briefed all my colleagues in the department and stood in the newsroom while the same journalist rang each of them in turn, trying to persuade someone to confirm his story. I returned his call. I described his recent conduct as unprofessional. He thought he had a story. I had told him that we had nothing to say on the subject. I now undertook that if and when we did have anything to say, he would be the first to hear, on condition that he stopped telephoning my colleagues. Three hours later he got his scoop. He never got another out of me.

The *Daily Mail* and the *Daily Express* still had full-time diplomatic correspondents who were among our most regular clients. The rest of the popular press ignored anything beyond the White Cliffs of Dover so did not normally trouble us. But one morning the *Daily Star* splashed across its front page a damaging and entirely fictitious report on one of our most sensitive subjects. I took the unusual step of telephoning the editor personally to remonstrate. "Your front page," I said, "it's not true."

"I know."

"Then why did you print it? You did not even take the trouble to check with us first. I am always willing to advise..."

"Mr Fenn," he interrupted, "you have not understood. I am not in the information business. I am in the entertainment business." I did not know quite what to say next.

On another occasion one of the most responsible of the popular journals carried an uncharacteristically distorted report on a current issue. I invited their Diplomatic Editor to discuss it. He readily acknowledged that the report was in crucial respects wrong and the headline was mendacious. Why in that case had he allowed it to appear under his name? He invited me to read the article again, starting from paragraph four. It was a professional and accurate report, but rather dull. He explained that the headline and the first three paragraphs had been added by a sub-editor. If he had insisted on removing them, the whole article would have been spiked. "Would you prefer readers of my paper to have no window on the world at all?" The answer to that question was "yes", but I understood his concern.

We had a public service strike. All Heads of Department were instructed to report to Personnel Department the names of any officers who were absent from duty. I regarded this instruction as offensive and intrusive but had no choice but to comply. I called the department together. I told them that for my part I regarded a public service strike as a contradiction in terms. We ran a public service. If all of them stayed away I would run News Department single-handed on that day. But I knew that I was paid more than they were and that some junior salaries were a disgrace. If colleagues chose to join the strike I would have to report them as instructed, but I would do all I could to shield them from the consequences. No one stayed away.

One evening I was running for my train up Whitehall. My way was barred by an enormous man carrying a placard: "No popery". The big man explained that for the first time since the reformation a Roman Catholic was to preach in Westminster Abbey and all good Christians should turn out to resist "the scarlet woman". I said that I preferred to catch my train. It was my first encounter with The Rev Dr Ian Paisley.

The relationship between the Foreign Secretary and the Prime Minister is always a key to effective foreign policy. Peter Carrington was a leading moderate in Mrs Thatcher's radical Cabinet, what the

245

Prime Minister called "a wet". He was not afraid to stand up to her, but even he had to choose his ground with care, and he had little appetite for the kind of trench warfare which was sometimes necessary to carry moderation in that context. He won over Rhodesia and was always careful to present it as Mrs Thatcher's triumph. The battleground was usually Europe. Lord Carrington had been convinced of the need for European unity since as a young Major he had stood in the ruins of Cologne and seen what devastation was caused when the nations of Europe went to war. Margaret Thatcher was famously Euro-sceptic. She disliked foreigners. She disliked the Foreign Office because it was professionally inclined to see the other fellow's point of view. She disliked Lord Carrington's willingness to look for reasonable compromise rather than victory.

This uneasy relationship was reflected in the enforced partnership between the Prime Minister's Press Secretary and the Foreign Office spokesman. Bernard Ingham was a tough, bluff Yorkshireman who spoke his mind trenchantly and had little time for the bromide which was my stock in trade. Early on we lunched together and agreed that we would each stick to our last – and that if our principals fell out we would still keep in touch. For the most part we operated in different fields, he with the political correspondents and the parliamentary lobby, I with the diplomatic correspondents, foreign editors and the representatives in London of overseas papers. But when foreign policy became an issue in domestic political terms we had to work hard to maintain a colleaguely partnership. He was happy enough to let me lead on Rhodesia – but Europe was different.

For the most part it was an advantage to have a Foreign Secretary in the Lords. Unlike his predecessor, he did not have to nurse a marginal constituency in Devonport. He was free to attend to the demands of the job whenever they arose. He was much better able to travel abroad. But just occasionally there were problems. Lord Carrington persuaded the EU Council of Ministers to impose retrospective sanctions on Iran. As soon as we got home we knew that it would not stick. Douglas Hurd, Minister of State, met him in the corridor and implored him to reverse the decision which would never be approved in the House of Commons. To general embarrassment he had to send messages to other EU Foreign Ministers explaining that the UK would not be able to implement the decision which he himself had urged. I do not believe that a House of Commons Minister would have made this mistake.

In the course of my three years with Lord Carrington, I accompanied him on visits to eighty-one countries. I felt I knew the inside of every Hilton Hotel in the world.

The Prime Minister of Malaysia launched a bitter attack on Britain and announced his policy of "buy British last". Lord Carrington flew to Kuala Lumpur to confront this threat to British commercial interests. Dr Mahatir had sixteen charges against us. Carrington had a good brief which he deployed in masterly fashion, rebutting each charge in turn and in detail. At the end of the meeting it was clear that we were not guilty as charged. But there was another indictment which was not on the charge sheet: we had taken Malaysia for granted. Guilty, my Lord.

Lord Carrington took up the cause of the Vietnamese Boat People, refugees from Vietnam who had been living for years in boats in Hong Kong harbour. While we were there I called on the Director of Information of the Hong Kong Government, John Slimming, who had been my boss in Mandalay in 1960 (Chapter 2). He had thrown himself heart and soul into a crusade to bring the plight of the boat people to international attention. He campaigned night and day. He still chain-smoked. He looked dreadful. When we got home I told Sue that John sent his love. I thought he was working himself to death for the Vietnamese refugees. When I got to the office there was a telegram to report that he had dropped dead at his desk.

We went to Moscow. Andrei Gromyko was still Foreign Minister, still pretending that he did not speak English. He gave us lunch in a dacha in the hills above Moscow. In his speech Lord Carrington acknowledged that he had been Foreign Minister of his country for seventeen months. His host had been Foreign Minister for seventeen years. Gromyko interrupted in English. "My Lord," he said – which was already something, coming from the Soviet Union – "it is quality not quantity that counts."

At a G7 meeting in Venice an American journalist was importunate for a short television interview against the backdrop of the Grand Canal. It proved difficult to find the right spot or the right time. In the end we rigged an armchair in a tree with a stunning background and a large umbrella overhead to keep off the rain. Lord Carrington climbed uncomplainingly into the tree and conducted the interview with aplomb. Nothing more was said of the matter and it never happened again.

The Prime Minister and the Foreign Secretary travelled together for meetings of the European council. Bernard Ingham and I were in tow, performing our careful double act of soft cop/hard cop. After the first day of a European Council the Union is always in crisis. The Heads of State and Government go off to their state banquet leaving their staffs to wait anxiously for their return. About half past ten Mrs Thatcher would come back to the residence of the Ambassador. She would accept a strong whisky soda, settle into a chair and in six or seven concise sentences outline the issue and invite views. First, of course, the Foreign Secretary, the PUS, the Permanent Representative to the European Union, the Ambassador to the host country. It was said of Mrs Thatcher that she never listened, never consulted. Quite wrong. On these embattled evenings she wanted to know everyone's views. Hey, you Nick, hiding behind the sofa, what do you think? The discussion would go on late into the night. At last the Prime Minister's husband Dennis would get up and say, "Margaret, it's time to go to bed." Thank God for Dennis. We went to sleep. We were back at eight o'clock. We felt as though we had just crossed the Atlantic. The Prime Minister had already had her hair done and was looking elegant and composed. Then in another six or seven sentences she would announce the solution with perfect, sometimes painful, clarity. If anyone then said, "But, Prime Minister…" it was too late. You should have said that last night. The

248

issue had been round and round in that computer mind and emerged in the morning as fully formed policy. I did not always agree with her decisions but I always knew what they were. By eight thirty in the morning the British delegation was fanning out knowing exactly what we were trying to achieve, while the Italians were still in bed. It was a significant national advantage.

On Friday 2 April Argentina invaded the Falkland Islands. The Governor's last telegram did not get through and for a few hours we were unable to confirm to Ministers that the story was true. The luckless Lord Privy Seal had to tell the House of Commons that he did not know. Parliament exceptionally met on Saturday.

At a crowded Foreign Office Press Conference at twelve fifteen on Monday, it fell to me to announce that Lord Carrington had resigned. It was the saddest announcement I ever made. At home our elder son, Robert, home from university, put his hand on his mother's knee. "We'll be all right, Mum," he said. "Dad needs you." So Sue and I went to the wake together.

It was of course a quintessentially honourable resignation. Carrington was the responsible Secretary of State. You do not lose a colony by mistake. Someone had to go and he went. But there is more to it than that.

Why, after all, do Ministers resign? They resign because they fail to carry Cabinet. Not so. As the white paper subsequently made clear, twice in the previous six months Lord Carrington's Latin American policies had been approved by Cabinet. They resign because they fail to carry Parliament. Not so. In that terrible emergency debate on Saturday afternoon, it was Sir John Nott who lost control of the House of Commons. Lord Carrington mastered their Lordship's House with his usual consummate ease. I had of course been in the gallery at the Lords. My deputy had been in the Commons. So stark was the contrast that when we subsequently met in the Foreign Office courtyard I thought that the fuss was all over and he thought the government was about to fall. Thirdly, Ministers

249

resign because they lose the confidence of the Prime Minister. Not so. At least ostensibly, Mrs Thatcher tried to persuade him to stay.

The inwardness concerns the press which is why I was involved. On Sunday the press was calling for the blood of John Nott. On Monday it was calling for the blood of Peter Carrington. Why? The answer to that question is No 10 Downing Street. I make no complaint about that, you do not sacrifice your Secretary of State for Defence on the eve of a war. But it cost the government its ablest member. I sat in my office that weekend and watched the game move against my master. I asked him to bestir himself but quite properly he told me to back off. He took one look at the press on Monday and went to consult his closest political friend, Willie Whitelaw. When he came back the die was cast. He had to go. He resigned because he had concluded that he had become a liability to Mrs Thatcher's Government. He was no doubt right on Monday morning, but he would have been an asset again come Thursday. He was a great loss to the country, the government and the Foreign Office. He would have helped us to win that war by the confidence he had earned amongst his colleagues, not least in Washington. His successor, Francis Pym, was a good man but he could not have the same international authority.

The position of the Foreign Office Spokesman in wartime is different. The centre of gravity shifts across Whitehall to the Ministry of Defence. My role was to support Francis Pym in his efforts to sustain the loyalty of our friends and to neutralise the well meaning efforts of those who would mediate between opposites before the issue could be decided.

My MOD colleague, Brian Macdonald, became internationally famous for his taciturnity. Journalists began to draw comparisons between his low-key performance in time of crisis and the pyrotechnics with which I had tried to inspire and lead the press over Rhodesia. This notion is wrong on at least three grounds.

250

First, war changes the rules. What governments say in time of war affects the lives of British servicemen and the success or failure of military endeavour. This imposes discretion. The hunger for news is greater but it needs to be systematically denied.

Secondly, Brian's sepulchral voice was instantly recognisable. Within three days Buenos Aires was caught lying and Brian's gravelly tones were internationally recognised as the voice of truth. He said little. But what he said was believed. This was a priceless asset.

There was a third and different reason. At the beginning of the Falklands War Brian was told that they would have his guts for garters if he ever said anything that had not been approved in advance by the Chiefs of Staff and the Secretary of State. Necessarily this led to a ponderous presentation of verified fact. At the beginning of the Lancaster House Conference Lord Carrington sent for me. He wanted me to know that anything I said to the press he would defend in the House of Lords. Few Ministers would have had the courage and the selflessness to say this to an official. It gave me the confidence to think on my feet, to ask myself the question before the cameras, not just "what have I been authorised to say?" but "what would be the mind of Peter Carrington on this issue?" I was fortunate to serve such a chief at such a time.

There was a special meeting of the European Council in Paris attended by Heads of State and Government, Foreign Ministers and Finance Ministers. It was followed by a magnificent banquet at Versailles and a fireworks display. Mrs Thatcher decided that it would not be appropriate for her to be seen enjoying fireworks while her troops were at war in the Falklands. She and Francis Pym would leave after dinner, leaving Sir Geoffrey Howe, Chancellor of the Exchequer, to represent the UK. So our suitcases were taken to the Queen's Flight while we attended the dinner in black tie. At the end of the meal Jacques Chirac, President of France, asked us to remain in our places until *Messieurs, Mesdames les chef de delegation* had left the room. We stayed. I had been seated between the Mayor of

251

Paris and the President of the Bank of France. I had at least to be civil before making my escape. The Palace of Versailles is confusing. I emerged into the courtyard to see the Prime Minister's motorcade disappearing into the night. The same misfortune had befallen three other Foreign Office officials. We cadged a lift in a French police car and reached that airport just in time to see the Queen's Flight taking off – with our Prime Minister and our luggage. We returned miserably to our lodgings and slept in our underpants. In the morning we came down to breakfast in the only clothes we possessed. Geoffrey Howe thought we were the funniest thing he had ever seen. Later he sent us individual photographs of "four Foreign Office stuffed shirts". Heroic efforts by the administration of the British delegation booked us onto the first flight out of Charles de Gaulle. We were in Whitehall by mid-morning. It is I believe the only time that the Foreign Office News Conference has been conducted in evening dress.

A few weeks before the Falklands War Lord Carrington had summoned me again. "It says here," he said, "that you *want* to go back to Burma. Can that possibly be true?" I assured him that it was indeed true. He administered his famous red "C" and said, "Agreed, on two conditions. First you do not stay more than three years. Seductive little posts like that are the graveyard of promising careers. Second, that Iona and I can come to stay with you." So we went back to Burma. And in due course to our great delight Peter and Iona Carrington did indeed come to stay.

Chapter 10
Burma Again:
HMA Rangoon 1982-86

We returned to Burma in 1982 after nineteen years away. The country had been under military rule for twenty years. The first impression was that nothing had changed. As Nick reported at the time, the same whitewashed pagodas on every hilltop, the same smiling people, even the same old General, brooding in his mansion on the Inya Lake. We found the same potholes in the same places on the highway to Mandalay – and the same old ladies putting pebbles in the holes and pouring tar on top.

Of course this continuity was superficial. The Burmese people were poorer. Twenty years of tyranny had eroded their sense of fun, stifled enterprise and diminished hope. Some of the ethnic rebellions had been quashed; in 1963 there had been twenty-one, surely a world record. By 1982 only ten remained. Burma was a natural loner; the arc of mountains and the sea. At reduced levels of consumption she was still self-sufficient: she did not need and did not much want international relations. She was not yet the pariah that she was to become. But she was less involved with the outside world than under U Nu. There were only twelve international telephone lines. On the rare occasion when we had to telephone London, we would sometimes be greeted by a charming Burmese girl with the words, "I am very sorry. The rest of the world is engaged. Please try later."

British policy was still to maintain minimal relations with the thugs who ruled the country, against the day when the politics would permit wholehearted partnership to mutual advantage. Nick crusaded for Burma in Whitehall. Its strategic position and superb economic endowment meant that it was bound to be a valued trading partner in the end. There would be a time after Ne Win. Meanwhile, Burma mattered a little. We should do just enough by way of trade and aid to keep our foot in the door.

In the light of hindsight this policy was mistaken. In 1988 came Burma's "Prague Spring". For six weeks the people thought they were free. Then the army reasserted its authority, murdered several thousand student demonstrators in the streets with machine guns, and nothing was ever quite the same again. Nick's policy of business as usual was properly reversed. HMG disengaged from Burma and subsequent Ambassadors rarely spoke with the government to which they were accredited. One wonders what they were for. But in our time Nick was required to smile, to encourage, and to warn. The relationship was correct, stilted and constrained. There were memories of the colonial past and hopes for better things to come. Meanwhile, we were to grin and bear it.

As reported in Chapter 2, the embassy had a British staff of fifty in 1960 when we first came to Burma. In 1982 Nick had a staff of eight. (The present Ambassador has a staff of three.) But the Chancery building was the same old decaying five-storey office block on the waterfront near the Strand Hotel. The ground floor was occupied by the consulate and the British Council. The office proper was on the third floor. The rest was eerily empty, with the discarded furniture of decades stored in the attic where Mr Vice-Consul Fenton had once warned us about the dangers of Burmese food.

We had a vivid sense of homecoming. So many friends to meet again, so many remembered places. We even thought we spoke the language, in the belief that a foreign language was like riding a bicycle – once learned never forgotten. Nick blithely agreed to speak in public without adequate preparation. He had forgotten that since we were last in Burma we had spent three years in China, whose language is also monosyllabic and also tonal. Nick's speech was half in Burmese and half in Chinese – and he did not even notice. Back to school!

We remembered the fun we had had at the sailing club. Nick drove round. The same spectacular setting on a promontory in the Inya Lake. The same tall man behind the bar. "Ismael," said Nick, extending his hand, "do you remember me? We promised to come back and here we are. I have come to join the club."

"Oh, no, sir," said Ismael, his face long and solemn. "I'm afraid that will not be possible." Nick was dismayed. Things were even worse in Burma than he had imagined. "Would you come this way sir," continued Ismael. He led the way along the deck into the Commodore's office. Open on the desk was the membership book from 1960. There was Nick's signature acknowledging his membership. It had been carefully annotated "on leave for nineteen years". He could not join the club because he was already a member!

We brought a sail board with us. Charlie tried it out on his first holiday. He quickly got the hang of it and sped across the lake, straight for the forbidden inlet which led to the General's mansion. Anyone who sailed up that inlet would be shot. Soldiers in a punt were waving rifles. Charlie shouted over his shoulder, "Dad, how do I turn round?"

"Fall off," Nick shouted back. He fell off.

Julia aged nine crewed for Nick in a monsoon race. A tropical storm blew up. Boats capsized. Thinking that his daughter might be fearful, Nick ran for shelter behind an island. He need not have worried. Julia was dancing about on the foredeck. "Oh look, Daddy, he's sunk!" After twenty minutes the wind subsided as quickly as it had arrived. They emerged from cover to find that all the other competitors except one had capsized or retired. They sailed cautiously around the prescribed course and came second.

We celebrated Nick's fiftieth birthday at the club. We invited fifty friends and gave them an enormous brunch. There was a colourful Burmese band and dancers of indeterminate sex. In deference to Buddhist custom Nick ceremonially released fifty fish into the lake.

255

Nick discovered to his horror that the British staff of the embassy were flying to Bangkok at taxpayer's expense for dental treatment on the ground that Burmese dentistry was unacceptable. But there were three approved dental practices in Rangoon. And it was possible to arrange to see a dentist in Bangkok when it was our turn to carry the weekly diplomatic bag. He wrote to all staff warning that he would not approve travel to Bangkok for this purpose unless one of our approved dentists had certified that the work could not be done in Burma. Guess who was the next member of staff to have toothache! Nick took his pain to a Burmese dentist who extracted a tooth. He recommended a dental bridge, but did not have access to dental gold. Nick bought the gold in Bangkok on his next bag run and the dentist crafted and fitted the bridge. It served well for a decade. Years later a dentist in Dublin remarked that the bridge was the work of a brilliant dentist working with nineteenth century equipment.

Sue set off to visit friends. Most were living in the same compounds, older and poorer but delighted to welcome us back. The economy had been through hard times but had struggled on. Few buildings had changed, markets were identical, and men and women still smiled as they strolled in the streets in their beautiful simple *longyis*. Religious processions and ceremonies were still enjoyed with an exuberance rarely witnessed in the West.

The big change for us was to be living in Belmont, once the residence of the chairman of the Irrawaddy Flotilla Company, which in its day had run the largest inland water fleet in the world. We were a mite above our station. But Burma had a convenient law: foreigners could not own real estate. If however they happened already to own property at the date of this law, they could sell it only to the Burmese Government at the price they had paid for it (in 1947). Even HM Treasury agreed that this would pay the rent of a modest villa in the suburbs for only a few months. So we were prisoners in our golden cage. It was wonderfully situated for visitors, especially the money-strapped undergraduate friends of our children, being close to the centre of the city, within walking distance of the main markets, the railway, and the Sule and Shwedagon Pagodas. The lush garden kept out the noise of the city. It was filled with exotic insects, snakes, and birds as well as beautiful trees such as Flamboyant, Amherstia Nobilis, Indian Laburnam and many more. A tennis court, an orchid house and swimming pool added to our enjoyment every day. Most heart-warming was the welcome from the staff – "servants" they would call themselves – whom we thought of as rather indulgent uncles and aunts. We could not have been looked after better nor felt safer. Lingham, the Tamil butler, ex-Royal Navy, remembered us well and took Sue round the house and garden on her first morning, introducing her to each man or woman and their families who lived in simple quarters behind the house.

Later that morning Sue was horrified to see the huge wooden lift van containing most of the worldly goods of our predecessors, Gill and Charles Booth, being broken open by the staff. It had been stored in the garage during the monsoon because there had been no ships to take it on to them in their new post, Malta. Alas, no one had noticed that termites had invaded the crate. When everything was finally removed and spread out in the sunlight, to drive the ants away, the extent of the damage was all too evident. Everything organic had been eaten, wood, wool, leather, cotton, paper. Termites secrete a watery acidic liquid as they eat so everything removed from the crate was wet. The photos in albums had been washed clean. Not a single picture remained. Valuable books and carpets, which had survived several tropical monsoons were reduced to dust. The garden was now covered in all that was left of the Booths' family possessions and not a trace of a termite to be seen. After everything had been dried and repacked into the lift van it was sent off to the waiting ship. It was a horrible tale to tell Nick when he returned home for lunch. Wrongly, we decided to write and warn the Booths. It might prepare them for the shock. They wrote and warned the insurers to expect a massive claim. They in turn sent the claim to the embassy, arguing that the damage had been incurred on embassy premises so they had no responsibility. The Embassy Administration officer, as shocked as the rest of us, claimed he had never heard of termites so had never inspected the crate standing on the garage floor throughout the monsoon.

At one of the first receptions we attended at the Japanese Embassy, Sue noticed an elderly gentleman eyeing her with amusement. He came over to speak to her and challenged her to recognise him. It was he confessed a long time since they had met, nearly twenty years in fact. It dawned on her that this was Shorty, Sawbwa of Kentung, whom she had last seen being taken away from the Prome Road Nursing Home on a carrying chair by a dozen soldiers. He reported that he had been well treated. The worst suffering was uncertainty. They never knew when, if ever, they would be released.

For the rest of our four years in Rangoon we dined quietly on the anniversary of the 2 March coup, with Shorty and his artist wife Twee, and Uncle Monty Myint Thein, former Chief Justice of Burma, who had also been imprisoned along with the Shan princes and members of the elected government. Monty used to say that as Chief Justice he could never have approved an unconstitutional revolution, and in any case in law he would have become Acting President. "So they had to lock me up. They had no choice. In their shoes, I would have locked me up!" His only bitter complaint was that he was not allowed out for his beloved wife's funeral. She had been a lawyer and magistrate in democratic times and they were known to be deeply in love until the end.

Monty became a key figure in our lives. He was by any standards a remarkable man. Educated at Queens' College, Cambridge, he was Burma's first Ambassador to the UN and to China, and swiftly became Chief Justice. At the beginning of the Second World War he had been commissioned into the British army to help manage the retreat across the Chindwin River and over the mountains into India. At the border he turned back, buried his British uniform and set off for his home in Kalaw in the hills of the Shan State. Beside the river he encountered a young man puzzling over a paper that had been given to him by the Japanese. It was a list of the most wanted men in

258

Burma, and Monty's name was at the head of it. He tore it up. "It's just a laundry list," he said, "you don't need that." When in due course he reached his home he found it occupied by three Japanese doctors. He applied for, and was given, the job of mali (gardener) in his own garden and spent the war years living in his own servants' quarters. He records that the doctors were kind and considerate and nursed him through a bout of malaria. At the end of the war, when the British army was advancing up the hill, he furnished the doctors with letters of safe conduct in Shan, Burmese and English to ensure their safe escape across the border into Thailand (after the war they had a reunion). Then he dug up the bottles of Scotch and gin which he had carefully buried four years earlier, and prepared to welcome his former colleagues in appropriate style.

Monty became an unofficial teacher, philosopher and adviser to successive British Ambassadors. He knew everyone and everything about Burma and was a mine of information, of wisdom and of mischievous humour. When some foreigners had been kidnapped in the jungle by insurgents, he came to reassure us that he had made discreet contact with the leaders of the rebels who had assured him they would never kidnap a British diplomat. We surmised that the rebels knew the British would not pay. We have always agreed with this policy; the more ransoms are paid the more danger for us all. Monty heard that we were going trekking in Nepal and asked to call on Sue on a confidential matter. It was simply to advise her that, whatever the fashion, she must wear a skirt in the mountains, because wearing trousers she would be unable to relieve herself modestly on the mountainside. Monty asked us whether we planned to have any more children. He reckoned he did not have many years to live, and he would like to think he might be reborn into our family. What higher compliment could he ever pay us? He appointed to himself the duty of informing Nick whenever he learnt of the death of someone to whom the British Ambassador ought to pay appropriate respect. It is the custom to go immediately to the home of the deceased, where the neighbours will be busy cooking quantities of food, to sit amongst the bereaved beside the body in its coffin, to discuss the death, the dear departed and enjoy the food and

259

company. It was a time to remember, to praise and give thanks rather than to be sad.

When in due course we moved on to Ireland, Monty worried about the threats of the IRA. Having learned from the BBC World Service that there was a particular threat to Nick during a visit to Kerry, he went to the Shwedagon pagoda to offer prayers for our safety. His letter of concern made the world seem very small.

Uncle Monty was a rare personality, so affectionate and humble, unspoiled by the part he had played on the world stage and delighting for example in the two photos of himself with Chang Kai-shek and Mao Tse-tung after presenting his credentials to them in Nanking and Peking respectively in 1949. He displayed signed photos from Ho Chi Min and Nehru, yet his pride and joy was one of himself dancing with Princess Alexandra at the President's ball in 1961. He maintained to the end of his remarkable ninety-four years a lively correspondence with friends – real friends – in every continent and every political system. His knowledge was profound but worn lightly because his sense of humour twinkled irrepressibly. He wrote poetry and was able to explain the beauty of the Burmese harp and the inwardness of the rhyming rules of Burmese poetry. He loved company and gave parties in his modest little bungalow on Kaba Aye Pagoda Road well into his nineties, and kept in close touch with his "nephews and nieces" all over the world.

One of his "nieces" was Aung San Suu Kyi – now the leader of the democracy movement. Her mother was dear to Monty and he spent much time with her before she died. He told us that just before her funeral he had asked to be alone with her to say his own farewell. He was sure she was still a Christian at heart so he recited some prayers for her and sang a hymn before going back to the formalities. It's a lovely picture, an old Buddhist man whispering Christian prayers to comfort a dead lady. She had brought up her young children on her own after Aung San was assassinated in 1947, and served her country well as Ambassador to India for many years. So Suu was there in Rangoon for her last illness, death and funeral, and was swept into the maelstrom of Burmese politics by the traumatic events of 1988. After years of enforced isolation she stands firm against injustice, "The Lady" loved and revered by the Burmese people – all except the ones in power. We first met in New York at the UN where she was working in 1970. Then again in London with her "godparents" Paul and Pat Gore-Booth who had given the wedding party when she and Michael were married. So when Suu brought her children, Alexander and Kim, to visit their grandmother we naturally invited them for a meal and got to know them better. As a friend she is both merry and serene. One can send her silly birthday cards and yet remain slightly in awe of her.

Memories of remarkable Burmese friends crowd in upon us. U Thitila was a respected Buddhist monk who had been an air raid warden in London in the Second World War. Sue and he would discuss theology in his monastery. He once came to Belmont for breakfast and to preach a sermon. Daw Khin Myo Chit and her husband U Khin Maung Lat were giants in the worlds of literature and the democracy movement. U Bo Kay was an archaeologist who strove to maintain professional standards in Pagan in spite of thieves who plundered the museum and desecrated the shrines. We maintained contact with some old friends in spite of the constraints of their official position; U Thaw Kaung at the university library and his wife Daw Khin Than, Dr Pe Thein at the Ministry of Education and his wife Professor Daw Kyu Kyu Swe. U Sein Win, a glamorous film director in the 1960s, died of cancer in a monastery at the foot of Mandalay Hill. A dozen widows in Rangoon called themselves the "Golden Girls" and quietly got on with their lives in spite of the politics.

During our previous posting in Rangoon, Sue had sat on the Parochial Church Council of a little church in the suburbs. Now we were living near the Anglican cathedral it was natural for us to shift our regular churchgoing there. We arrived with some gifts from our home church and messages and memories of both our vicar and churchwarden in Kent. Those two men had come to us separately when they learned that we were to return to Burma. They had both been in Rangoon at the end of the war, involved in the release and care of allied prisoners of war. Both had attended the thanksgiving service for the POWs in Holy Trinity cathedral in 1945 when the only lighting was supplied by the headlights of a jeep at the back of the nave. The skeletal men had tried to stand erect but many had been carried out. The experience proved too much for their emaciated bodies. The vicar and the churchwarden told us separately that the horrors they witnessed were so terrible they had never been able to talk about it with anyone. The two men had been colleagues for years, but neither knew that the other had been present at that extraordinary service of thanksgiving. We introduced them to each other.

We were welcomed by the cathedral congregation – predominantly Burmese, Karen, Indian, with the occasional tourist or returning missionary. The scarlet robed choir sang from the English Hymnal and Sue was asked to help the younger members with their pronunciation – there are no final consonants in Burmese so these did not come naturally. But English was the lingua franca of the congregation and most services apart from the sermon were still conducted in it. After the coup in 1962 the Intelligence Bureau sent emissaries to sit in at services. They were astonished to discover that the church prayed for the junta. They needed it. We were able to raise the standard of the communion wine and to get religious books for the clergy from time to time. One of them asked for a copy of the New Testament in Greek with a dictionary and grammar. A bachelor then, he had been posted to the Chin Hills where he reckoned he might have time on his hands and wanted to try to translate the New Testament from the original Greek into Chin. It was a joy early on Sunday mornings to sit in the great cathedral. The fans whirred noisily and the sparrows flew in and out of the open windows and sounds of the market across the road filtered into the vaulted space. The vicar, David Than Lwin, lived with his family in a modest vicarage beyond the East End, surrounded by hibiscus and palm trees. Bare concrete floors were furnished with wooden chairs and tables and only a few photos and faded prints of religious places adorned the walls. The vicar's sweet wife had to work to feed her growing family – she was a nurse at the Rangoon General Hospital.

Conscious of their precarious position as a religious minority, the sturdy faith of those good people and their warmth and hospitality towards us was heart-warming and inspiring. Nick's position was neither here nor there. We felt loved.

Sue made a little pilgrimage to the sprawling, neglected Christian cemetery where we had attended the funeral of the wife of the British consul, who had died in childbirth in January 1962 just before our Rob was born. Twenty years on she tried to find Daphne's grave. Someone had heard of her intentions and cleared a space around the site. "Daphne Dugdale" and the dates were clear to see. But the rest of the area was jungle – complete with chattering monkeys. Sue sought help from other "Christian" embassies for the loan of their gardeners over several weekends. Youth groups from the cathedral and other churches in the city joined to help the clean-up. A beautiful park emerged, with wide paths, trees and shrubs, truly a charming garden where only chaos had reigned before. Many of the monuments had been torn apart by creepers and many were too far decayed to read, yet the calm and dignity of that crowded cemetery had been revealed, full perhaps of too much colonial history. The military requisitioned the whole area soon after our departure, giving little notice for the small Christian community to move or record the graves. It was "urgently required for military purposes". No such requirement materialised. The cemetery is jungle once again.

There was routine diplomacy in Alice-in-Wonderland. National holidays and state occasions were observed. Formal calls were paid. There were thirty-two foreign embassies. To the Burmese authorities we were an embarrassment. We might see and report things not intended for foreign consumption. Ambassadors who spoke Burmese were particularly suspect; we might listen to gossip in coffee houses or talk to peasants in paddy fields. So we entertained each other and exchanged rumours about the opaque nation to which we were accredited. Four members of the European community were represented in Rangoon – France, Germany, Italy and the UK. We got to know each other rather well. In a country like Burma EU solidarity was a reality. None of us had distinctive national interests

263

at stake. We shared what little we knew and co-operated as a matter of course.

There was a fire in Mandalay. The fire brigade demanded payment before they would put out a fire – the worse the fire, the higher the price. One third of the city was burned to the ground. A few people died. Many thousands were homeless and destitute. EU Ambassadors recommended to Brussels on humanitarian and political grounds substantial European relief aid. But there was a problem. EU aid could be given only on the request of the host government. The Burmese Government never asked for help. As it happened, the local EU presidency was held by Britain. Nick thrashed about looking for flexibility on both sides. Neither would budge. Nothing would induce the bureaucracy in Brussels to authorise aid without a formal request. Nothing would induce Burmese officials to ask. In despair Nick called on Foreign Minister U Chit Hlaing, an engaging Admiral with a sense of humour. He put the case starkly. People in Mandalay were desperate. The EU was ready and willing to help. But help without a Burmese request might be misconstrued as interference and neither party would want that. Could the Minister not at least say please? He offered a series of formulae. In vain. He promised that this interview would remain confidential, but if we did not succeed he could not vouch for what might be said to the press in Europe. The deadlock was absurd. It reflected no credit on either party. He was dismayed and exasperated. In these circumstances what would the Minister suggest? U Chit Hlaing rose from his chair and looked out of the window. With this back to Nick he spoke in rapid Burmese. There was a natural disaster in Mandalay. It was not the government's fault. The Revolutionary Government of the Union of Burma never asked for aid as a matter of principle. He could not depart from this principle. If, however, the European Union in its wisdom decided to provide assistance to the suffering people of Mandalay, the government would raise no objection and would provide practical co-operation. U Chit Hlaing for his part would be pleased. The Minister swung round to face his visitor and said in English, "Will that do?" Nick said that it would do. He took his leave. He reported that the Minister had expressed his pleasure and promised full co-operation. He filled in sixteen copies of an eight-page application form in French and sent it to Brussels. In due course the aid began to arrive.

The "principle" that the Burmese Government never asked for help was selectively applied. The Ministry of Health enquired whether the British Government could provide wheelchairs for injured soldiers and civilians. After some hesitation we agreed. Fifty wheelchairs arrived. The Finance Ministry asked us to pay 180% import duty before they could be cleared through customs. We referred them to the Ministry of Health who replied that they had no budget for this purpose. The Foreign Ministry formally demanded payment. We responded that the wheelchairs were a gift from the British people to the people of Burma. There was no charge. They cost nothing and 180% of nothing was nothing. Perhaps the wheelchairs are still in customs.

The British Deputy High Commissioner in Bombay was assassinated, apparently for Middle East reasons. This seemed to the Burmese authorities a little close to home. U Chit Hlaing summoned Nick and said that the Revolutionary Government had decided to place him under police protection. What could he say but, "Thank you, sir?" The next morning there appeared outside the residence a marked police jeep. Four constables with Second World War rifles sat in the back with a keen young lieutenant in front brandishing a pistol. The gates opened and the grey Daimler slid out into the traffic. The jeep did not move. So Nick and his driver got out, walked back to the escort and push-started the jeep. Wherever Nick went for the next two weeks, this little pantomime was repeated. If there had been any threat to his life it had certainly been magnified. The next time he met the Foreign Minister on a social occasion, he began, "Excuse me, Minister, do you think...?" U Chit Hlaing said "Yes". The police jeep was never seen again.

In our time – before 1988 – we sought every opportunity to meet the thugs in order to promote our residual interests and keep the door open for a more humane Burma in the future with a more civilised

265

relationship with the rest of the world. We discussed with the authorities issues arising at the United Nations, kept them informed of significant developments in the European Union and occasionally sought their support on British foreign policy initiatives. There were still a few commercial contracts to be won. Constructors John Brown were installing small gas turbines. One enterprising British businessman visited Burma nineteen times before he landed a contract for power distribution equipment. We sold a few second-hand ships. We maintained a modest programme of technical assistance including English language teaching, fisheries and prawn culture, even the care of elephants. Each of these required months of lobbying at ministerial level. But Ministers dared not be seen to be cultivating foreigners. So we assiduously attended public occasions in the hope of snatching a few words with one of them.

The Foreign Minister attended every National Day. He would sit on a sofa with the host Ambassador and exchange pleasantries. Other guests were permitted to greet him with the agreement of the embassy and the Chief of Protocol. The Queen's Birthday was a great occasion in our calendar. We chose to celebrate Her Majesty's real birthday in late April rather than the official birthday in June which was high monsoon. We invited 200 people to a grand reception in the garden. An early monsoon rain storm would have been a disaster. So the senior translator in Chancery would arrange for a pious monk to visit the residence before the party. For an hour he sat cross-legged on the veranda intoning Buddhist prayers before an enormous candle as a precaution against rain. It never rained. The modest cost of the monk and his candle was duly noted in the accounts as "rain insurance".

Another prized opportunity was an annual golf match between the Burmese leadership and the diplomatic corps on the Military Golf Course. Nick was no golfer, but that did not prevent him from being invited to the nineteenth hole at nine thirty in the morning. We drank whisky and swapped smutty stories with our hosts for two hours in exchange for the odd guarded conversation on matters of professional interest. The Minister of Defence was playing it cautiously with the Karens. The Minister of Agriculture was pleased with the harvest. The Minister of Planning and Finance thought things were going better than we did on economic reform. The Minister of Education did not want to talk about our English Language Project. Each slender morsel was bought by the consumption of a stiff whisky and an exchange of coarse yarns. Not Nick's scene at all, but the best opportunity of the year to meet them on their own ground and in relaxed circumstances – sometimes very relaxed circumstances. At least Nick was better off than his colleagues from Muslim countries; he had to pretend to be drinking heavily, they had to pretend not to be. On one occasion towards the end of our time, this charade on the nineteenth hole turned out to be critical.

Each April at the hottest time of year the entire Burmese population turned out onto the streets for the annual three-day water festival. Twenty years earlier it had been unrestrained mischief and delight – a bit like a Burmese version of trick or treat. Now it had been brought under state sponsorship to prevent it from getting out of hand. The diplomatic corps were formally invited by the Minister to attend a water throwing ceremony at the Foreign Ministry. Of course we attended. But afterwards we toured the capital in an embassy jeep loaded with tanks of water and stirrup pumps under a Burmese language banner proudly proclaiming us to be "The British Embassy Water Throwing Association".

Every Ambassador and his wife choose a style in which to do the job. We have always enjoyed entertaining. We loved extending hospitality to visiting VIPs or to backpackers, particularly friends of our children. We never forgot our home was on loan from the UK government and taxpayer, nor that one does business best with people one knows. In Burma we were blessed with such enthusiastic supporting staff so it was easy to throw all kinds of parties and stage events of every description. We found we needed help and persuaded the sister of Nick's godson, Jo Horwood, to spend her gap year as our social secretary in return for her fare, board and lodging with us and pocket money. She proved such an asset the government relented

267

the following year and we were able to employ Cathy locally. The Belmont staff positively grinned when we warned them we would have sixteen extra youngsters over the Christmas holidays. And we used them. They helped wrap more than a hundred little gifts for the "bran tub" which became another annual event. How else to provide presents for all the children in the servants' quarters which was in essence our village? They wrote and performed a pantomime for the annual Christmas party for the British community. It was joyful, and with the passing years increasingly vulgar. One year it began with Julia, aged nine, lamenting the shoddy toys she was given by Father Christmas:

Once in Chairman Ne Win's City
Stood a lonely little kid:
"How I wish my doll was pretty,
How I wish it had a head.
Father Christmas, please next year
Don't bring toys made in Korea."
Enter the wicked genie:
The baddy of this story
Is a very bad baddy
Of all the baddies that are in the world
The baddest baddy is he.
Baddy: *"I am the baddie from Korea.*
I can't stay now, I have diarrhoea"

In return we took our young guests to Mandalay by train in a private coach. (This sounds very grand but was in reality so grim our staff insisted on scrubbing out the coach and largely refurnishing it from the residence with everything from china to mattresses.) It had eight beds as well as a saloon and washing facilities. One group went ahead in our Land Rover – sometimes for short trips that plucky little car had twelve of us in it. The rest crammed into the train. On one such upcountry tour at Christmas time we were all staying in the new Thiripyitsaya Hotel in Pagan. We had gone to bed after seeing in the New Year and were woken by gales of laughter outside our window. Our kids were playing football with the hotel staff. On another occasion one of the boys' friends was posing us for a photo. We had just had a meal in a Chinese restaurant and were wearing Burmese dress. Neil was so absorbed in his camera he did not realise he had attracted a big crowd to watch. Then his *longyi* fell down and the whole area exploded in laughter.

Young Julia became an accomplished hostess, quick to hand round canapés at cocktail parties and to make polite conversation with visiting dignitaries. One day Sue and Julia returned home late for lunch. Lingham gravely reproached us and said he had shown the guests into the drawing room. Julia pushed her mother towards the stairs. "Hurry up and get changed while I look after them." She had no idea who the guests were, yet with natural grace she apologised for her parents who had been unavoidably detained; they would be here shortly. She was nine years old. The guests were charmed and we were forgiven.

Friends in the Shan State showed us generous hospitality whenever we went up into the hills; the writer Daw Mi Mi Khaing and her erudite husband Sao Sai Mong. The Sawbwa of Yaunghwe and wife Patricia gave a "picnic" for us at one of the festivals on Inle Lake – a fabulous meal with sixteen different dishes and a magnificent pile of fruit. Mi Mi Khaing should have been at the party but her astrologer had advised against the journey down the steep hill from Taunggyi, so naturally she stayed at home.

Sometimes the advice of astrologers was more positive. Sue organised Scottish Country Dance sessions weekly throughout the monsoon season leading up to the annual St. Andrew's Night party. With enthusiasts from the Burmese and foreign community we mustered about a hundred to pipe in the Haggis and all the other rituals before some energetic reels and strathspeys. After one such evening when the guests had gone home we turned wearily to go to bed. There, just below the bottom stair, lay an ornate diamond ring. Nick locked it in the safe in his study, confident that the owner would return for it next day. After three days we decided to phone around. The ring had an Oriental setting so probably belonged to a

Burmese friend. The couple who had danced most energetically were Ben and Matilda Ba Thein. Sue phoned Matilda. "Yes," she said, "it is mine. It was a gift from my mother. I knew you would phone." She explained that they had missed it before getting home but Ben had forbidden her to contact us lest she should disturb the household. If the ring had been found it would be perfectly safe. If it had not been found the servants might be blamed. But it was a precious ring of sentimental value as well as costly. In frustration Matilda turned to her astrologer for guidance. He assured her that the ring had been found and was safe. She would hear quite soon. "So I was expecting you to phone. I'll come and collect it now."

St. Andrew's Night was approaching and for once we had a real Scot to recite the Ode to the Haggis. But David Currie had only just arrived – a fisheries adviser – and his baggage was still in customs. He wanted to wear the "full fig" to do the honours. So Nick sent a formal diplomatic note to the Ministry of Foreign Affairs explaining the tribal customs of the Scots and stressing the importance to the Scottish nation that their rituals should be observed at the embassy. The response was immediate. The Ambassador and Mr Currie were invited to call on the Director General of Customs. We were conducted into a vast warehouse with mountains of goods awaiting clearance. When David's trunk was located he was allowed to extract only the kilt, sporran and skean dhu. He was presented with a receipt for "one man's skirt, one man's handbag and one kitchen knife". To his everlasting credit he signed. He recited the Ode perfectly.

Sue directed *Charley's Aunt* in honour of Uncle Monty's birthday. The electricity failed during the first Act. The cast carried on in the dark for a few minutes and then candles carried by the residence staff silently appeared in all corners till everything was well lit. By the second Act the normal electricity supply was restored. An unexpected joke brought the house down. A friend and colleague from the Indian Embassy was playing the uncle. His "son" thanked him for a generous cheque, and added, "You're a brick."

270

Sreeni replied in plummy tones, "A bit overbaked after all my years in India."

Our most ambitious show was *The Thwarting of Baron Bolligrew* with a cast of forty-five from thirteen different nationalities. The sewing group knitted chain mail for the knights, the bored ship's crew of a visiting British ship stuck in port turned up to paint the scenery, and laser swords were donated for the hero, David of kilt fame. He turned out to be a champion fencer and choreographed the fight with the wicked baron played by Sreeni. His beautiful wife was a classical Indian dancer and she took on the talking bird with grace and enthusiasm. Brian Knowles as the magician was supposed to reject his fee paid in chocolate coins, but he referred to the government's recent devaluation of all notes by tearing up "a demonetised bill". The audience loved it – it was topical pantomime. A Canadian carpentry teacher, David Eadie, built the stage with appropriated wood which was returned discreetly after the show. It all came together only on the first night. One final surprise was that the stage dragon, when it roared from its cave, belched real fire. One of the house sweepers had once been a circus fire-breather and after watching the rehearsals for weeks knew exactly where he was needed. After six nights playing to packed audiences we collapsed in a happy heap.

Sreeni and Leika, the Indian colleagues who had starred in *Baron Bolligrew*, were posted to Fiji. We wanted to give them a special farewell. We created a Liquid Theatre version of *This is your Life*, a theatrical experience we had once encountered in New York and reproduced in Peking and Kent. Basically, it is a dramatic production involving all the senses except sight. We chose the story of Sreeni's life from his birth and upbringing in India through his diplomatic postings in Moscow, New York, Burma and on to Fiji. The actors lead each guest in turn, blindfolded and barefoot, to experience these very different places in different bedrooms upstairs in the residence, through sound, smell, taste, and touch and by consuming tiny amounts of food and drink. The first, most important scene was a place to make the travellers feel secure, relaxed and happy. After

271

that, without exception, they loved every minute of the "play upon their senses".

A different kind of party we organised every year was for the children at the Blind School. We found willing volunteers to help. We devised tactile or audio versions of traditional party games, from musical chairs to obstacle races, including a treasure hunt all over the garden. Thirty or forty school-aged kids, blind but fearless, rushed around the garden with wild abandon, following distinctive sounds or feeling for hidden clues. There were a few collisions but no serious damage. The swimming pool was popular. Shivering with cold they insisted on staying in the water until the very last moment. We piled them into their bus, still wrapped in damp towels, and sent them off exhausted but wreathed in dazzling smiles.

True to his promise, Lord and Lady Carrington were early visitors. He was of course no longer Foreign Secretary and was not yet Secretary General of NATO. He was travelling incongruously as Chairman of GEC so we arranged a meeting with the elusive Minister of Industry 2 where for an hour they pretended to negotiate about an economic relationship between Burma and the company which both knew was never to be. Then we set out to show Burma to the Carringtons. In Taunggyi in the Shan mountains Peter expostulated about log fires in the tropics. In Mandalay he was told that it would take forty minutes to climb the holy Mandalay Hill. He said he would do it in half that time and astonished the locals by reaching the top in fifteen minutes with Susan panting in his wake. Nick was chivalrously escorting Iona at a more decorous pace. In Pagan we watched the sun set across the Irrawaddy from the top of the Thatbyinyu Temple. "This is outrageously beautiful," he complained, "why does not anyone know about it?"

Lord and Lady Romsey came to Burma for a belated honeymoon as the personal guests of General Ne Win, an invitation originally extended through Lord Mountbatten and postponed because of his assassination in 1979. To the consternation of Protocol Department, they brought with them as personal friends King Constantine of the

272

Hellenes and Queen Anne-Marie. All four guests were delightful and seemed to enjoy their VIP tour. For us it was an unusual opportunity to be for a few days on personal terms with the dictator of Burma. We found him much as we remembered him from Princess Alexandra's visit twenty years before, charming and amusing, vain and eccentric, cunning and ruthless. His original revolution had no doubt been based on a patriotic determination to prevent the fragmentation of the Union – but this had long since been overtaken by his resolve to remain in power at any cost to the people he governed. We were impressed by his ignorance of contemporary Burma and by the sycophancy of his personal staff. The conversation at dinner turned to inflation, which was rampant. Ne Win asked sharply what would be the cost in the market of the chicken we were eating. His aide quoted less than a quarter of the true price and glared at us to discourage contradiction. Ne Win grunted in satisfaction, "That's not too bad then," – and we went on to talk of other things.

General Ne Win would not come to the British Residence in our time. But when Princess Alexandra came back to Burma in 1980, Ne Win accepted an invitation to lunch at Belmont. We are indebted to our predecessors, Charles and Gill Booth, for the following story. During the Second World War the house had been the residence of the Japanese intelligence chief, Colonel Suzuki, who had been instrumental in persuading the Thirty Comrades to join the Japanese invasion of Burma and was the principal liaison man with Aung San and Ne Win. But the Burmese leadership soon discovered that "independence" under Dr Ba Maw was no independence at all. General Aung San sought audience with Colonal Suzuki to present a list of thirty demands.

Standing in the hall at Belmont after lunch in 1980, General Ne Win told the story of that interview which had taken place on that very spot. Suzuki had kept them waiting and then made a dramatic appearance on the half landing of the great teak staircase in full dress uniform. Suzuki was a small man. He paused on the bottom step and glared at his visitors. Aung San produced his petition. "What is this?" exclaimed Suzuki. Drawing his ceremonial sword he stabbed

273

the paper and threw it over his shoulder in a gesture of contempt. And that, said Ne Win to Alexandra in the hall of the British Residence, was the moment when Aung San decided to abandon the Japanese and join the British.

On the fortieth anniversary of the end of the Second World War the Ministry of Defence sent a planeload of veterans of the Fourteenth Army to visit the Commonwealth war graves in Burma, including five war widows two of whom had never been in an aeroplane in their lives. The party was led by the Secretary of State for Defence, Michael Heseltine in person, on an official visit – another charade because the two countries had no defence interest in common. At a formal meeting with Defence Minister General Kyaw Htin, the two men discussed nothing in particular for an hour. Then we set off to see Burma. Nick used the visit in a different context. It had always seemed absurd that he was supposed to cultivate relations with a military government without the advice of a resident Defence Attaché. He made his pitch – and on return to London Michael Heseltine duly despatched a colonel to Rangoon. He stayed for a few months. The argument was sound enough in theory. The problem in practice was that the Burmese authorities regarded foreign military representatives with the same suspicion as Burmese-speaking Ambassadors. They knew too much and were therefore never allowed to see anything interesting or talk to any military authority. In due course Colonel Bennett moved to Dhaka, where he was allowed to do his job and covered Burma by cross-accreditation and occasional visits.

Former Prime Minister Ted Heath came to Burma. We had an ancient grand piano in the residence and went to great lengths to get it tuned for him. The piano tuner spent the whole day tinkering. The Australian Ambassador had an electronic tuning device which he kindly brought round on the morning of Heath's arrival. As we arrived at Belmont from the airport Nick mentioned the piano. Mr Heath would be welcome to use it – but the monsoon tended to get to it a bit. Heath sat down and played seven notes. "Yes, it does," he said – and never touched the piano again. On his last day in Burma

274

Mr Heath went to the market and bought a simple, ancient, Burmese silver bowl. At our dinner in his honour that evening, he was incautious enough to boast about his purchase in the presence of the Director General of Archaeology, who was responsible for enforcing the Burmese prohibition of the export of ancient artefacts. The Director General took Nick aside to explain his embarrassment: there would be trouble at the customs. He suggested that we should send the bowl to his office early in the morning and he would see what he could do. We duly called. The Director General had the bowl on his desk as he offered us a cup of tea. "This should be in the National Museum," he said. He had prepared his certificate for the customs. It said in Burmese "This bowl is very beautiful and very old. But in the view of the Department of Archaeology it does not engage the provisions of section 3, subsection c of the Ancient Artefacts (Prohibition of Exports) Act of 1962". We presented this masterly certificate at the customs and Mr Heath left with his silver bowl.

A visit of a different kind was that of the Foreign Office Inspector, whose job was to examine embassies to ensure that they had the resources that they needed, and crucially not more than they needed, to do their job. The Inspector was Roger Westbrook, formerly Nick's deputy in News Department. We gave a dinner for him and his team, inviting Burmese friends who knew the embassy well and might be expected to convey a sympathetic view of our activities. Nick made a little speech – as was his custom – in both languages. In Burmese he urged his guests to tell the Inspector that we were overworked and underpaid. In English he told the Inspector that he had invited the other guests to tell him of all the fun we had in Burma. Roger did not miss a trick. He replied in Portuguese.

We invited all our living predecessors to celebrate Uncle Monty's eighty-fifth birthday. Three stalwarts came – Sir Richard Allen who had been our Ambassador in the 1960s, Lady Gore-Booth, widow of Sir Paul who had been Ambassador in the 1950s and subsequently Permanent Under Secretary, and Elizabeth Barraclough who had worked for Paul. It was a moving reunion. Monty came with us in a private coach on a regular Burmese train to his home town of Kalaw in the Shan State. More rejoicing.

The President of South Korea came on a state visit. The day before he arrived, his Ambassador in Rangoon appealed to Nick on the unexpected ground that he was an expert in cleaning carpets. There was a stain on the drawing room carpet and Ambassador Lee hoped to remove it before he entertained his President to dinner. On enquiry, Nick discovered that we did indeed have a carpet cleaner in the embassy with a man who could use it. He was despatched to the Korean Embassy. When the diplomatic corps paraded at the airport to receive the President, Ambassador Lee came across the tarmac to thank Nick for his help. Two days later while we were sailing on the Inya Lake there was a massive explosion at the nearby mausoleum to the national hero General Aung San. North Korean terrorists had tried to assassinate the President. But His Excellency was late because his wife had been shopping. The terrorists had mistaken the Ambassador's flag for that of the President. Ambassador Lee was dead. We mourned the death of a dear friend and colleague.

We spent as much time as possible on tour outside Rangoon, trying to gage the pulse of Burma behind the flummery of the capital city. There were still great swathes of the north and east of the country which were out of bounds for security reasons. But this left plenty of scope for travel. These exhilarating journeys often meant that we were out of touch with the embassy for up to three weeks. Nick left formal instructions with his Deputy that on no account was the embassy to pay ransom if we were kidnapped – and took a copy with him to show to any kidnapper. Seeing us off on one occasion, David and Sandra Smallman joked about our being kidnapped. "If you are," said Sandra, "I pity the kidnappers. Sue will make them all do Scottish reels in the jungle!"

We were often in Mandalay, still the cultural capital, where we had lived for our first year in Burma in 1960 and where we had many friends. We explored the holy hills of Sagaing and had incongruous theological conversations with learned monks in a monastery. We

276

took a boat to the ruins of the ancient capital Ava. We went back to Amarapura to see U Nyunt and his family and to gossip about old times. We drove north-west from Mandalay to Shwebo and Monywa on the banks of the Irrawaddy. On one occasion, about three miles from Monywa, a police sergeant jumped out of a bush and flagged us down. We feared trouble. But he saluted smartly and announced, "Sir, you are the Bangladesh Ambassador." Nick explained that he was indeed an Ambassador but not the Bangladesh Ambassador. Ambassador Keramat Ali was his friend. The sergeant was crestfallen. "Sir," he said, "are you *sure* you are not the Bangladesh Ambassador? I have been waiting in this bush for the Bangladesh Ambassador for three days." When we got to the Circuit House we found our Bangladesh colleague already in residence. At our earnest suggestion he went back to the bush to put his escort out of his misery.

Each year in November, Commonwealth Ambassadors used to go together by train to Moulmein in the south-east, and on to the Commonwealth War Grave at Thanbyuzayat, the Burmese end of the death railway, to pay their common tribute to the dead. One year Nick noticed a man on the hillside above the cemetery watching the proceedings through a telescope. He asked the Major in command of the security detachment who the observer might be. "Oh," replied the Major, "he is my opposite number in the KNDO, the chief of the local Karen insurgents. He normally holds this ground. But today in your honour, and by agreement with us, he has withdrawn so that we can bring you here in safety. When you have finished we will escort you back to Moulmein and he will reoccupy the cemetery. You see, the only thing that he and I agree about is that what you do here today is fit to be done."

Together with the French Ambassador, Yves Rodrigues, Nick flew to Bhamo where the Irrawaddy runs close to the China border. They hoped to learn a little about recent events in the north. They were met at the aircraft steps by the Chairman of the People's Council, who was of course the Major commanding the local garrison. "Welcome to Bhamo," he said, "this afternoon we shall

277

play golf." Nick responded that in that case it would be the first game of golf that he had ever played in his life. "Excellent," replied the Major, "then I shall win." – which in due course he did. Fortunately, Yves was a competent golfer and the diplomatic corps was not disgraced. At a meeting in the Major's office the two visitors asked leading questions about the political, economic and military situation. He parried them all. But he did let slip one point of interest. Pointing at the road on which we were standing he said proudly, "This is the famous Burma Road (which used to link India with China during the Second World War). You can go twelve miles that way and eight miles the other way. Beyond that the insurgents hold sway." In the evening we visited the Christian cemetery. Nick was examining the graves of British soldiers who had died in the aftermath of the conquest of Upper Burma in 1885. Yves was examining the graves of French bishops who had died in Burma one hundred years earlier. No wonder the British had to conquer Burma – to keep French influence out!

We visited Sittwe, the capital of Arakan on the eastern seaboard, and ventured upriver to Myohaung. The name means "Old City". We gazed at an image of the Buddha that claimed to have been carved in AD 250. The Circuit House was primitive. A typewritten notice in English announced that "European visitors may stay at the Circuit House at a charge of one rupee. Native servants may stay in the servants' quarters free of charge". It was signed "Andrew Dawlish, Deputy Commissioner, 1925".

By steamer from Rangoon we visited Mergui in the far south-east, a fishing harbour and provincial capital. From the deck of the steamer we saw a large bay full of the rotting hulks of vessels caught smuggling by the Burma navy. As at Bhamo, Nick tried leading questions on the Chairman of the People's Council. His response was direct: "My instructions are to receive you, not to answer your questions." We had aroused his suspicions by asking about water gypsies, the state of local crops and a cave full of the nests of rare birds. How did we know all this? We showed him the embassy copy of the colonial *Burma Gazeteer*. On the shelves of the residence library were a series of these admirable publications dated 1916 to 1921. The local pagoda boasted an immense sleeping Buddha, into which visitors could go through a tunnel. A notice over the entrance conveyed the invitation, "Enter between the holy legs into the divine intestines".

We went by steamer to Bassein in the south-west, and watched the sun set over the Irrawaddy Delta. We went in search of Naw Ohn Bwint who had been our sons' nanny twenty years before. The local Baptist minister knew her and promised to convey our little gifts. He showed us his simple church. A few minutes after we left the village he was arrested and interrogated by Military Intelligence. He must have known that this would happen when he welcomed us so warmly.

On our farewell tour of Burma in 1986, we ventured west of the Chindwin where foreigners were seldom seen. We came into a village square. The children crowded round the Range Rover, curious about the double cooling fan. Nick got out. *"Beka lathelay?"* they asked – the opening courtesy of a conversation, meaning literally "where do you come from?" Just for fun, Nick asked where they thought we came from and pointed to the flag on the car. Consternation.

"Japan? – oh, no, no, no... Germany?"

An old man stood in the shade leaning on a stick. He hobbled over, shaking his stick at the children exclaiming, "You don't know that flag? You should know that flag. That's the British flag. We'll be all right now they're back!" What does the British Ambassador say then?

Later that evening we arrived at the riverbank opposite Pagan in good time for the evening ferry. It had gone an hour early. The next boat was the following morning. By now we knew the drill in these situations. We got out, opened our books and settled down to wait. The villagers gathered and began to discuss what was to be done for

279

us. One family could offer us dinner, another had room in their house – but perhaps it was not grand enough? Just then a modern Zed-craft came in sight, the personal launch of the manager of the nearby fertiliser plant. The people crowded round and demanded that he take us to Pagan. He came up and greeted us and politely offered us the use of his boat, apologising that he had another engagement and could not escort us personally. For the first time we betrayed our knowledge of Burmese in thanking our would-be hosts for their hospitality and accepting the manager's gracious invitation. We crossed the river in style in the setting sun. Something always happens in Burma.

We went in search of the famous "Australian Road". Some years earlier General Ne Win had decided that for strategic reasons there should be a major highway down the west bank of the Irrawaddy from Monywa to Bassein. The Australians agreed to build it. The Burmese wanted to begin from the north and the Australians from the south. So they began in the middle. Then the two governments quarrelled over some clause in the aid agreement and work stopped. The result was a splendid four-lane highway running seventy-two kilometres from nowhere to nowhere. We drove from one end to the other. We met two other parties on the road. The first was the Foreign Minister U Chit Hlaing on official tour. The other was a group of twelve elephants whose drivers told us that they were from a nearby logging camp taking the elephants for a six-week holiday by the seaside. We were flagged down by the manager of the road project who insisted that we should take lunch with him and his family in their little bungalow on a hillside overlooking his road. As we arrived we heard the death screech of a chicken. An hour later chicken curry was served.

We visited Magwe on the Irrawaddy in central Burma and stayed at a guest house that had been little frequented. Sue availed herself of the flush loo. But it would not flush. At her third attempt, an angry snake came down the pipe from the cistern and stood up in the bowl, hissing defiance. Uncharacteristically, Sue stood on the bath and screamed. But Nick was listening to the BBC World Service and did not hear her cries. Eventually, the snake got bored and slid off down a hole in the floor. The watchman assured us that it was harmless.

Nick flew to Bangkok on the regular "bag run". On the return journey half the passengers were turfed off the scheduled Burma Airways flight because Brigadier Tin Oo, a senior member of the regime, was returning with his family from a shopping expedition. It was an amazing sight, the whole of the front half of the plane was stuffed with his booty. A fellow passenger was His Excellency the Ambassador of Nigeria (resident in Bangkok but cross-accredited in Rangoon) coming to Burma for the first time to present his credentials. His eyes were on stalks. Nick did his best to explain. A few weeks later Tin Oo was sacked, not for corruption but for advocating socialist equality. He was expelled from his palatial residence in Golden Valley in spite of his plea that his blind daughter would not be able to find her way about another home.

A new British Council lecturer arrived to join our English Language Programme. We shall call him Jonathan. He fell in love with one of his colleagues who had arrived a few months earlier. Then his Chinese wife arrived with their baby son to join her husband in post. An uneasy *ménage a trois* ensued. One night while Jonathan and his lover were having dinner in a restaurant, the house caught fire. His wife burned to death. The baby survived. The police arrested the cook, but he had no plausible motive and searching questioning revealed no evidence. They had to release him. Later they arrested Jonathan on suspicion of murdering his wife. It seemed more likely that she had committed suicide, mortified to find herself supplanted. These events shook the small British community to its foundations. Inevitably, the embassy became involved. Nick talked with both lecturers, separately and together, and with the Professor of English at the university. He had an uneasy meeting with the Deputy Minister of Education. All this was inconclusive. Nick had a consular duty to ensure that British citizens were fairly treated. He did not know that Jonathan was innocent. But he knew that he could not have a fair trial in Burma. The annual Diplomatic Golf Tournament had been arranged for the following week. Nick spoke on the

281

telephone to the Deputy Minister for Home Affairs. He suggested that this tragic affair was equally embarrassing for the Burmese and the British authorities. Perhaps the Minister would agree to discuss it entirely off-the-record on the nineteenth hole?

They sat together on a bench in the shade of a palm tree, sharing the inevitable whisky. Colonel Maung Nyunt was unusually keen to talk. He was indeed embarrassed. His police chief thought that Jonathan was guilty. His alibi depended on his lover. The fire had been started deliberately. The room had been doused with kerosene. Jonathan's bookshelves contained crime novels, including one about a man who had murdered his wife and set fire to the house. If the case came to court Jonathan would be convicted and sentenced to a long term of imprisonment. This would be bad for Anglo-Burmese relations and for Burma's reputation abroad. Did the Ambassador have any thoughts? Nick stressed that this was a matter for the Burmese authorities and courts. The British Government had no view. But he welcomed this unofficial discussion. On a personal basis he offered two comments on the reported views of the police chief. The evidence about the fire did not itself prove murder; it seemed to fit either murder or suicide. As for Jonathan's library there were a number of whodunnits on the shelves of the residence; this did not make the Ambassador a murderer. He suggested that neither he nor the Minister knew the truth, but he agreed that a trial would be embarrassing to both governments. He wondered whether a possible way forward might be for Jonathan to be expelled from Burma, without prejudice to the legal position. If the Burmese authorities were to follow that course HMG would make no public fuss. The Minister looked thoughtful and went into the clubhouse. A few days later Jonathan was expelled from Burma. He took his little family to Australia. As Nick drove home from the golf course he encountered at the edge of the military cantonment a platoon of some twenty marching soldiers, all amputees on crutches, under the command of a sergeant in a wheelchair. The human cost of civil war.

We took local leave in Nepal and went trekking in the Himalayas with Susan's brother Martin and his wife, climbing a small hill only

14,000 feet high in the magnificent arc of the Annapurna range. Near the top of this hill, Martin suddenly collapsed. The senior Sherpa diagnosed mountain sickness (wrongly as it turned out). We must descend at once. We came down 6,000 feet in a day and arrived in a village where we were not expected. We knew it was a feast day because everyone was drunk. We set up camp on the outskirts. The youngest Sherpa, Dorje, went into the village, had a dispute with a villager about the price of a chicken, struck at him with a stick, missed, and hit an innocent passer-by on the head. We were not the flavour of the month. That evening while we were eating dinner in the big blue tent one of the villagers came in, stood silently in one corner gazing at us with fixed expression, and left as silently as he had come. This was the Nepali equivalent of the Black Spot. The senior Sherpa said that the village had declared war on us. He asked us to go to bed at once. We crossed the field to our little tents and prepared for the night. Susan sat bolt upright clutching a carving knife. Nick implored her to put it away. She explained through clenched teeth that she would not use it as a weapon, but if they set fire to the tent she wanted to be able to cut our way out quickly.

We did not have long to wait. There was a cry of "Halbadaar" and the sound track of a B movie as the population of the village charged our encampment. The battle swayed this way and that, 200 drunken villagers against seven brave Sherpas, determined to defend us. But it was an unequal contest. The senior Sherpa came to our tent and called urgently, "Master come now, or they will kill Dorje." Nick put on his dressing gown and stumbled out into the night. Dorje had indeed been badly beaten. Nick was confronted by 200 angry and drunken villagers demanding satisfaction, without benefit of a common language. The village schoolmaster volunteered his services as interpreter – but he was as drunk as the rest and there was no way of knowing what he was saying. Nick expressed sorrow at the incident. He was sure that Dorje had meant no harm – it was an unfortunate accident. Britain and Nepal enjoyed excellent relations. He mentioned the long-standing service of the Gurkhas in the British army. We were all tired after a long day. Perhaps the best course would be to resume our discussion in the morning. He invited them to call again at seven in the morning. There was muttering and divided counsels. The schoolmaster said that they agreed to a morning discussion on one condition – Nick was to come into the village at once to see the victim of Dorje's murderous attack. They led him across the field, over a stone stile and along a track to a small mud built house with a flat roof, like pictures in a Sunday school Bible. He had to stoop to get through the door. The room was crowded. In the corner on a mattress, illuminated by a burning torch, lay a young man with a nasty head wound. Nick had his only inspiration of the evening. "This man needs medical attention," he said. "My wife is a nurse," (not strictly true – she was a biochemist – but she had been an auxiliary nurse in her university vacations and needs must when the devil rides). He went back to the tent and said, "Darling, it's your turn now." Susan drew her hair back into a bun, donned an apron and set off with our first aid kit in a black box with a red cross on it. The family clamoured for stitches. Sue was fearful of infection. She called for hot water and washed the wound. She poured in liberal quantities of antiseptic powder. She declared that he would be better in the morning. By the grace of God he was.

At seven o'clock sharp a deputation duly arrived at our camp led by the village headman, a charming old man who clearly regretted the whole incident as much as we did. We had set the stage for a Durbar, with Nick on a wooden throne and the petitioners sitting on the ground. Negotiations began. Sue offered to take another look at the wound. We offered to take the victim to hospital. None of this seemed to help. It began to dawn on us that what they were after was blood money. As soon as we mentioned this they brightened. We swiftly reached agreement on 250 rupees – about £5. Nick went to get his wallet. There was a sudden commotion. A much younger man ran up with a group of fierce-looking supporters. It transpired that he was the newly elected chairman of the Panchayati Raj – the local council. It was necessary for him to secure a better deal than the headman. So we agreed on an additional fifty rupees and began to pack up. Another commotion. Dorje came out of the tent, clutching his belly and doubled up in pain. His pantomime was convincing. Susan ran to him in distress and concern. But Nick had caught his grin and took the cue. "Three hundred rupees for your injured man; how much for mine?" We got fifty rupees off, gave 250 to the head man and got out of town. Dorje could not contain his delight that his deception had been so successful. Before we were even out of sight he was leaping and dancing in the road in a manner unbecoming an invalid.

An unexpected telegram arrived in Rangoon. Nick was invited to become Ambassador in Dublin. This was a real job. Our instinct was to jump at it. But there was a problem. Susan's sister Judy had lived in Ireland for many years. She had once said to Susan that she would never forgive her if we ever came to Dublin. She feared that the IRA would kidnap one of her four children. We had to consult her before we could accept. On the excuse of consulting the retiring Ambassador, we flew to Dublin and met Judy by private assignation in a seedy hotel in Bray. She had guessed. "Before you ask," she said, "the answer is 'yes'." We accepted the job and flew back to Rangoon to conclude our assignment.

Leaving Burma again was always going to be difficult. This time there would be no chance of being posted back to Rangoon. On our final evening we climbed the steps of the Shwedagon pagoda with heavy hearts to say farewell and strike the huge bell which superstition says guarantees return. The other tradition is to turn for a long last look at the Pagoda on the road out of town. There at the airport, friends and colleagues gathered and the Foreign Minister with his irrepressible grin arrived with an enormous harp as our farewell gift from Burma. We held it aloft before entering the aircraft, wondering how we would get it beyond Bangkok.

Chapter 11
Burma Revisited
1989-2015

Two years later came the disastrous events of 1988. Chairman Ne Win unexpectedly resigned. There was a heady interlude of apparent freedom before the army reimposed order by killing thousands of people in the streets with machine guns. In Dublin we received letters from Burmese friends recounting horrible events. A young man had been murdered by the army, another had joined the insurgents in the jungle, a girl had caught a stray bullet and lost her arm. There was nothing we could do. But we could go. Nick sent a telegram to his successor in Rangoon, Martin Morland, who had better things to do but nobly rose to the occasion and invited us to stay. We cancelled our engagements in Ireland and flew to Burma as a simple act of solidarity. Martin gave a party for us, fifty Burmese friends whom we had known for years. They were on different sides of the political divide, including former Prime Minister U Nu, his deputy U Kyaw Nyein and other old-style politicians, members of the new regime, and several leaders of the democracy movement including Aung San Suu Kyi herself. They could not talk to each other. But they came for us: we were in Burmese terms *than-nge-kyin* – we had been "young together". Martin scattered tables amongst the bushes in the garden and we moved among the guests enjoying nostalgic tales of the good old days.

Martin also lent us his car and driver (formerly our driver, Saw Po Thit). On the road outside Rangoon we stopped for petrol. Nick got out and talked to the pump attendant in Burmese. Walls have ears. So they discussed the weather. The attendant volunteered that it was OK in the cool season; it was not too bad in the monsoon but it got a bit hot in the hot season. Glancing furtively from side to side, he continued: "It was OK under the British, and not too bad under the parliamentary regime, but it does get a bit hot in the hot season."

Sue and Julia made two further return visits – in 1993 for Uncle Monty's ninety-third birthday, and again in 1999 during one of the interludes between Aung San Suu Kyi's periods of house arrest. She came to lunch. Sue had brought letters from Suu's family which she handed over, not knowing that one, from her husband Michael, revealed to her that his cancer was terminal – he was dying. Michael and Suu never saw each other again. The regime refused to let Michael come to say goodbye and Suu would not leave Burma because they would never let her return. After Sue got home to England she phoned Michael to report on Suu's wellbeing. "She seems very well, merry and full of fun. She enjoys the stupid things the Generals say about her and is interested in life outside her country – not a word about her perilous position." Sue did not know as she talked to Michael that he was so very ill. He died within weeks, allowed only a phone call to his wife by the Generals who hated her.

For a decade we argued about the wisdom and propriety of returning to Burma. Nick feared that his presence might in some way be misused by the regime to imply support. Sue said that he was being pompous. Aung San Suu Kyi had once said that foreigners should not come because it put dollars in the pockets of the Generals. That was enough for Nick. Sue said that we would not be going as tourists but to see old friends. When Suu had come to lunch in Rangoon she had asked where Nick was. Sue said that he had not come because Suu asked him not to. "I did not mean Nick." Subversive reply. By 2006 Sue had persuaded Nick that he should celebrate his seventieth birthday as he had his fiftieth by releasing fish into the lake in Rangoon. A warm invitation from the then Ambassador, Vicky Bowman, clinched it. We had a nostalgic time looking up old friends.

We were able to visit parts of Burma which had been off limits when we lived there. We went to Kyain Toung (Kentung) in the far

287

eastern Shan state and explored villages in the hills – three villages a mile apart, one Buddhist, one Christian, one animist; different in tribe, religion and language; disagreements about neighbouring rice fields had to be resolved in bad Burmese. In one village we noted a prosperous Baptist school – and a dilapidated government one. In the animist village the people were building a new house for their head man. We were invited to inspect the work in progress. We brought small gifts. A big drum hung at the entrance. Just in time we were warned that if we touched the drum we would have to sacrifice a pig.

In Myitkyina in the far northern Kachin State we sought out Bishop David Than Lwin, whom we had known as vicar of the cathedral in Rangoon twenty years before. He received us in full canonicals outside his cathedral and exclaimed, "I have been praying for this moment for eighteen years. Now you are here, you are addressing the Mother's Union in Burmese in five minutes." Nick did his best. We began to develop links between Myitkyina and our church in Kent.

The town seemed busy, with much Chinese influence. The local commander passed by, his jeep bristling with arms, followed by another with mounted machine gun. No one but us seemed to notice. A narrow boat with a long-tailed outboard motor took us noisily upriver to the fabled confluence, source of the mighty Irrawaddy. On the way we watched groups of men panning for gold in the river. We wept at the scarred hillside denuded of valuable forest. We climbed a headland for the view. A Catholic nun gave us hot water – too poor to buy tea leaves but she had delicious fresh grapefruit. The children sang songs. The government "clinic" was completely empty, as it had been since the official opening years ago. Round a table under the trees young men were planning the building of a new church to replace the tiny one they had outgrown. Almost all the little houses had crosses by the front door. On the way back our engine failed and we completed the journey in the close and intimate company of twelve pigs. Something always happens in Burma.

288

In Mandalay, we met up with Vicky, the Ambassador. We called on Daw Amah widow of the famous journalist *Ludu* U Hla with whom Nick had conducted a public correspondence in 1960. In those days Daw Amah had disapproved of our friendship with her husband; to a communist we were the hated imperialists. Now she showed Vicky the published correspondence from forty-five years earlier. We talked of her family's continuing brave struggle against the regime, so well known that our taxi driver dared not take us to her house.

Pagan had changed but still enchanted. The hotel was almost empty, but it covered our bed with flower petals. The massive new museum is a joke, far too big for the collection, with modern monstrosities beside ancient Buddha figures. It has a display with life-sized figures to illustrate how the ordinary folk lived in the twelfth century – the time of Pagan's greatness. It demonstrates all too clearly that the ordinary villager was better off then than he is now. A ride over Pagan in a hot air balloon at dawn was magical – a treat only available to rich foreigners. We gasped in awe at the thousands of pagodas built in happier more prosperous times. Seventy fish were duly released into the Inya Lake on Nick's birthday.

We visited Burma again in January 2011 with a group of twelve from our parish in Kent in support of the formal link between the parish and Bishop David's Diocese of Myitkyina, bordered by mountains, by India, by China and the rest of Myanmar. Kachins are a minority amongst Burmese. Christians are a minority amongst Buddhists. Anglicans are a minority amongst Christians. Anglican Christian Kachins face discrimination. They are poor and exploited. They are very far away. That is why we went. The most important thing about the visit was simply that it happened. We came to them in their isolation to affirm our fellowship with them in the Church. We were received everywhere with hospitality, generosity and rejoicing. It was a humbling experience.

We went back to the confluence then about to be drowned by the Myitsoun Dam, a massive hydro project to generate electricity – but only for China. The gold panning was now conducted on an industrial scale by a Chinese company which had bought the concession from the Generals. The last vestiges of the teak forest had been cut down for timber and had disappeared over the border.

We spent a week on a river steamer going south from Mandalay, revisiting the stupendous ancient capital at Pagan, the oil fields at Chauk, the pagoda at Magwe where Sue had once been frightened by a snake, the oldest golf course in Burma and the remains of the pre-Buddhist culture at Prome. We stopped at a village built on a sandbank, viable only in the dry season, where they took catch crops from the rich alluvial soil before fleeing the approaching monsoon. The real Burma was spread out before us. Our son Robert brought his family from his post in Brunei to Yangon to celebrate his birthday in the land of his birth. He released forty-nine fish. Granny and Grandpa were able to show his two sons where Daddy was born.

***

We had left Burma in 1986 with sadness. It had been our home for eight years. It is a beautiful country with the most charming people on earth, a distinctive language and culture and a unique unreality about it which captivates or repels foreigners. We were among the captives. Hinayana Buddhism is an essential ingredient. We never came to terms with its doctrine of the reincarnation of souls, the immutability of one's lot in life and consequent attitude of acquiescence in injustice. If a child was born blind that was because he had blinded someone in a previous existence. Susan was once told by a learned Buddhist scholar that she was certain to go to hell. She was a woman, which was a bad start, and in England as a magistrate she sent people to gaol, thus trespassing upon their space. All this seemed to us nonsense. But the practice of meditation, the sustained effort to escape from the tyranny of material things, produces an admirable courtesy and patience. The puzzle was to reconcile this gentleness and grace with the crude despotism of the Revolutionary

Government and its successors, the state law and Order Restoration Commission (SLORC) and State Peace and Development Council (SPDC) which have enslaved and impoverished the Burmese people since 1962. Burma must share the palm with North Korea, Zimbabwe, Somalia, Pol Pot's Kampuchea, as among the worst governments in the world.

In 2007 there were brave demonstrations in the streets. Once again they were ruthlessly suppressed. Commentators who should have known better spoke as if these demonstrations were the turning of the tide or the beginning of the end. They argued that the demonstrations were provoked by economic desperation, that they were led by monks (surely even the Colonels would not fire on monks?), or that modern electronic communications made it impossible to suppress an insurrection in secret. All this is true, but the power equation remained unchanged. Every mother wanted a son in the army and a foot on the gravy train. For half a century Burma was ruled by military thugs pretending to be socialists – an unattractive combination.

What should be the attitude of foreign governments to such regimes? In the old days we would have sent a gunboat. But we no longer have either the will or the power to compel change in a small country far away, and our gunboats are otherwise engaged. There remain two broad options. The first is to have nothing whatever to do with them. The second was the stance of HMG towards Burma in our time between the revolution of 1962 and the trauma of 1988; maintain relations on an active care-and-maintenance basis while seeking opportunities to nudge events in a constructive direction. This would mean working with the government and encouraging them to come to terms with the democracy movement. What we should not do is to pretend that we have influence where we have none, to maintain ineffective sanctions, to delude the suffering people into believing that we care, when manifestly we do not care enough. The United Nations demonstrated its impotence every time the representative of the Secretary General visited Rangoon. Amongst foreign governments, only China could deliver effective

291

change in Burma – and China had too much to gain from the status quo. India, Thailand and Japan could help – but all were preoccupied with Chinese influence and unwilling to take a stand. It behoved the rest of us to shut up. For the most part, that is what we did.

But at last there are signs of change. Since our time in Burma, that beautiful and courageous lady, Daw Aung San Suu Kyi has become leader of a democratic opposition. She won by a landslide the elections in 1990 which the Colonels were too incompetent to win and too complacent to rig. So they ignored the outcome. She has spent fifteen years under house arrest in her crumbling family home on the Inya Lake. Our taxi driver in Mandalay in 2006 had asked us whether we would see *The Lady.* We replied that we could not call on Aung San Suu Kyi on this visit because she was under house arrest. "But she is getting old," he said, "she will die, and then there is no hope for my country." A new constitution introduced in 2010 was carefully designed to preserve the "guiding rule" of the military in civilian guise. About 25% of parliamentary seats were reserved for serving military officers and a 75% majority was required for constitutional amendment. Some saw this as a window of opportunity. We saw it as a cruel charade. The following elections delivered a puppet parliament. But Aung San Suu Kyi was released from house arrest. We were able to see her in January 2011. She received us with her usual grace, charm and fortitude. She is a compelling figure, a hero of our time.

Against all the odds, the iceberg has begun to melt. Senior General Than Shwe, the brutal, corrupt and superstitious President, was replaced by General Thein Sein who, although he was Than Shwe's Prime Minister, seems to be a man of different stamp. Suu Kyi had private meetings with him. In by-elections in 2012 her political party, the National League for Democracy, won forty-three of the forty-four seats it contested. Suu Kyi took her seat as Leader of the Opposition. There is at last a free voice in that puppet parliament. She addressed the nation on state-controlled radio and television. Thousands of political prisoners were released, not all of them, but most of the key figures. The ban on public gatherings of

292

more than five people was lifted. Privately owned newspapers are once more permitted; one senior diplomat in Rangoon thinks that Burma may now have the freest press in South East Asia. The monstrous Myitsone Dam which we had seen at the confluence was suspended "in accordance with the wishes of the people". Since when have the wishes of the people counted in Myanmar? Suu Kyi is able to travel. The media report her activities. She has paid tumultuously successful visits to the United States and to Europe, including Norway to receive her Nobel Peace Prize. She addressed both Houses of Parliament in Westminster Hall and was seen doing so live on TV in Burma. The British Prime Minister and the President of the United States have visited Rangoon and met both her and the authorities. President Thein Sein has paid official visits to Canberra, Washington and London where encouragement for his reform programme was coupled with pressure on human rights, drawing the promise to release every last political prisoner by the end of 2013, a promise he did not quite fulfil. There is a rising tide of expectation in Burma.

But joy cannot be unconfined. There are grounds for scepticism. The first is an inescapable part of the end of tyranny. If you take the lid off a can of worms, you find worms – all the communal tension and latent hostility that military rule has suppressed for half a century. There are angry disputes about land tenure, about the Chinese exploitation of a copper mine near Monywa, communal riots in Meiktila in Central Burma and Lashio in the Northern Shan State. Army officers seize economic assets to feather their own nests before it is too late.

The fulcrum of this tension is in Rhakine State on the border with Bangladesh, where the Rohingya people – Muslims, long-term resident in Burma but never accepted as citizens – are feared, hated and persecuted by their gentle Buddhist neighbours. Around 200 people were killed in 2012. Some 100,000 are displaced, living in squalid refugee camps beyond the city boundaries of the state capital, Sittwe. Anti-Muslim sentiment is not new in Burma. An influx of Indians, many of them Muslim, followed the Raj into Burma in the

293

nineteenth and twentieth centuries. When we first came to Burma in 1960, much of the commerce and finance was run by Indians (and much of the rest by Chinese). Indigenous Burmans hated them for their commercial skills, and knowledge of the colonialists and their language. There were race riots in Rangoon in the 1930s. Ne Win's brutal expulsion of Indians won popular acclaim. More recently the military regime has clamped down on unrest of any kind. But democracy has revealed that the bigotry simmers still. A remarkable chauvinist monk, U Wirathu, stokes the flames from his monastery in Mandalay, whipping up Buddhist hysteria against the hated Muslims. Opportunistic opposition parties jump on the bandwagon. Jealous of the dominance of Aung San Suu Kyi's NLD, they take up Wirathu's proposal for a law to ban inter-faith marriage, exploiting and encouraging communal hatred to gain cheap popularity. There were dark-skinned Muslims in Rhakine State before the Burmese conquered it in 1784. They lived peaceably together for two centuries. Now they are persecuted for political advantage.

Early in 2015, there were new disturbances in Kokang District on the Chinese border in Northern Shan State. Phone Kyar Shin, an octogenarian warlord and long-time exile in China, re-emerged on 9 February and attacked army posts in Kokang. His motivation is financial rather than political – he has made a fortune in the past from gambling and narcotics. But his cause draws support from Kachin, Palaung and even Arakanese insurgent groups, possibly even from China. It will not help the peace process.

There is more trouble in the Kachin State in the far north. After seventeen years of ceasefire the Kachin Independence army lost patience in 2012, and the ethnic separatist civil war resumed. In spite of Thein Sein's public order to desist, Burmese commanders on the ground went after the rebels with helicopter gunships and jet aircraft, killing civilians, looting villages and burning churches. A foreign eyewitness reported: *The Burma army kill and maim unarmed civilians in their paddy fields or homes. A pregnant woman hid under a bed for two days; she heard an officer telling his soldiers, "If you*

see Kachins, just kill them." A grandmother was gang-raped for
three days.

As it happens, this Kachin State is the Anglican Diocese of
Myitkyina, with which our parish church in Kent has a formal link. It
was the object of our pilgrimage in 2011. Against this background,
our friend Bishop David Than Lwin journeyed in late 2012 to the
foothills of the Himalayas to dedicate a new church at Laizar on the
Chinese border. It was to him irrelevant that Laizar is a rebel
stronghold. This is not how it appeared to the Burmese authorities.
They told him not to go – so he went. He crossed into China to avoid
the fighting, then back into Burma to reach Laiza. He dedicated the
church in the face of threats from the army commander. Then he
received an ultimatum: get back to Myitkyina in two days or do not
return at all. He got back. He spent New Year 2013 at the Diocesan
Orphanage in Hopin, a small and supposedly secure town on the
railway line to Rangoon. Even there he could not sleep for gunfire
and explosions. Most Burmese hope that their long dark night is
ending. But gunfire in Hopin is also part of the picture. Nick paid his
last visit to Myitkyina in November 2014 in connection with the
parish link. Twenty-eight people were killed in fighting on the eve of
his arrival, which caused some local consternation.

The endemic problems that beset U Nu when we came to Burma
in 1960 have not gone away; racial and religious tensions, economic
inequality, resentment of foreigners, ethnic minority insurrections.
Suu Kyi is wildly popular. The burden of expectation on those
slender shoulders is overwhelming. But she cannot resolve these
problems by herself. She is not a good delegator; her lieutenants in
the National League for Democracy lack her unique authority and
skill, and she needs to watch her back.

There have been false dawns before. Power remains with the
military. Democratic MPs are a tiny minority; 43 out of 626. Suu Kyi
says herself that she has a mountain to climb before Burma can be
free. The military pressures on General Thein Sein are enormous. His
colleagues fear retribution if they lose power. Aung San Suu Kyi has

conspicuously not endorsed attacks on the military for abuses of human rights in Kachin State and Arakan. In an interview for BBC Radio 4's *Desert Island Discs* in 2013 she was asked about this. She replied: *If I were to take sides it could create more animosity between the two factions. Security and the rule of law are more important.* In the same interview she explained her sympathy for the Burma army which had kept her under house arrest, threatened her life and committed wholesale abuses of human rights: *I am a friend of the army. People criticise me now for being their poster girl. But my father was the father of the army and the soldiers were his sons, they are part of my family. I don't like everything that they have done, but if you love somebody I think you love her or him in spite of, not because of.*

Militant liberals overseas find this perversely forgiving. Richard Lloyd-Parry in *The Times* asked whether she was "*Saint or Sell-out?*" The doyen of Burma-watchers, Professor Josef Silverstein, writing in *The New York Times* under the headline *A Shining Star Loses Her Lustre* pronounced that she was "*making herself irrelevant*". The suspicion gains ground that this beautiful, gracious and iconic figure is selling her birthright for a mess of potage – compromising the future of her people to gain power for herself.

We believe this to be nonsense. She has never been the kind of all-or-nothing human rights democrat approved by Amnesty International and the Burma Campaign. She well knows that in Burmese conditions the army must retain a special role in the state, and without this assurance the army would simply hold on to power, and neither Aung San Suu Kyi or the outside world would be able to stop them.

President Thein Sein told *Time* magazine in 2013 that "we are in the midst of an unprecedented period of transition, from military to democratic government, from armed conflict to peace, from a centralised economy to a new market-oriented economy." To Johns Hopkins University in Washington he confessed that much work remained to be done. "I know how people yearn for democracy. We

296

must forge a new inclusive national identity, end all forms of discrimination, banish inter-communal violence and bring perpetrators to justice." The reality is not quite like that. But at least he talks the talk. This is the miracle for which Burma's friends abroad have waited. It may indeed be the basis of Suu Kyi's accommodation with Thein Sein. She has morphed from an icon into a politician. She has found the courage to engage with a nasty military regime and to make compromises to secure practical advances for real people. She must surely be given the time and the benefit of every doubt. The idealists should not rush to judgement. They should consider how this extraordinary transformation of Burma first began. The catalyst was Suu Kyi's private dialogue with Thein Sein, without which it would never have happened. We may never know what passed in those private meetings. One may speculate that she promised amnesty for past misdeeds in exchange for Thein Sein's support in developing freedom for Burma. If so, which of us outside the country has the right to condemn her? Would her people be better off if she had elected to stand aside from the political bear pit and burnish her halo in splendid isolation? Is reconciliation not better than vengeance – not just in moral terms but for the future stability of a nation?

In 2015 there are two processes. A Commission of the *Pyithu Hluttaw*, the Burmese Parliament, under the chairmanship of the Speaker and with the active participation of Aung San Suu Kyi, has been working through 300 draft amendments to the 2010 "Guided Democracy" constitution, out of 30,000 suggestions submitted by the public. Very few have been approved. The key issue is Article 59F of the Constitution, which debars from executive office anyone whose spouse or children owe allegiance to a foreign power. This of course disqualifies Suu Kyi from standing for President because her late husband, Michael Aris, was British and her two sons hold British passports. The negotiations seem to founder on this point. She must remove this constitutional obstacle; the Generals are determined to maintain it. It seems unlikely that this crucial issue can be resolved.

In parallel, a ceasefire is in place with thirteen ethnic minority rebellions. The government meets regularly with representatives of these minorities to discuss "autonomy". But what is autonomy? The declared objective is to develop a "federal state". But what is federal? – autonomous regions delegating defined powers to a Union, or an all-powerful central government throwing scraps to the regions? The overwhelming preponderance of Burma proper in size, population and wealth would make a genuinely federal solution difficult even with goodwill. And goodwill is in short supply. There is deep disagreement. Progress is slow. The outcome of these two negotiations will determine the future of Burma. There is a long history of failed constitutional settlements. There is danger of backlash from the Generals if Thein Sein makes enough concessions to satisfy the democrats.

Suu Kyi for her part has begun to warn the West not to take political reform in Burma for granted. "A bit of healthy scepticism would be good," she said to Martin Woollacott of *The Guardian* on 6 April. "Too many of our Western friends are too optimistic about the democratisation process here." She insisted on the need both for serious talks on the transition to democracy and for constitutional reform – Article 59F and the *virtual military veto over constitutional amendment*. If not, she did not exclude the possibility that she might boycott the election. There may yet be serious trouble ahead. The elections have now been called for 8 November 2015. The NLD will contest them. General Thein Sein says he will not stand again for President.

In July we heard for the first time from Senior General Min Aung Hlaing, Commander in Chief of the army of Myanmar and a key figure behind the scenes. He made four significant points:
- He and the army would respect the outcome of the elections *provided they are free and fair – which they will be.* Make of that what you will.
- A return to full democracy would have to wait until peace had been negotiated with all insurgent groups – "perhaps five or ten years," he said. One fears it might be longer.

298

- Meanwhile the political parties would have to play by the rules of the army's "disciplined democracy". There was no threat to ignore or annul the elections as in 1990, but equally no promise to reduce the military grip on political life. He seems to be saying that the children can go on playing in the playground while the grown-ups get on with the job.
- Asked whether he would stand for President, he did not say no. "The duty of a soldier is to serve the country in whatever role."

In August, the Speaker of the Lower House of Parliament, former General Shwe Mann, was abruptly purged from his role as chairman of the military dominated party, the Union Solidarity and Development Party. A few days later Aung San Suu Kyi announced that she would form an alliance with Shwe Mann. She told Parliament that his dismissal revealed who was the ally and who the enemy; she would work with the ally. The plot thickens.

The situation of the Burmese people is incomparably better than it was three years ago. But perhaps they should not be looking for a further dramatic breakthrough in November 2015. *The Economist* has prophesied a "Circle of Disgruntlement". The outcome seems likely to disappoint everyone. The army and its cronies will see their majority reduced, renewed proof of their unpopularity and the illegitimacy of their power. The ethnic minority parties will secure minimal representation and no federal solution. They will be tempted to go back to war. Aung San Suu Kyi's National League for Democracy will be frustrated by the constitutional mathematics, cheated of victory and unable to form a government – "a thumping victory without the thump". Suu is disbarred from the presidency and it is the President who appoints the Prime Minister. The President himself is chosen by an electoral college made up of both houses of Parliament which meets in February 2016. They must choose from three candidates, one nominated by each House and the third, of course, by the army. The two losers become Vice-Presidents. The NLD has no obvious candidate apart from Suu Kyi so they may have to back an outsider – conceivably Speaker Shwe Mann – while Suu contents herself with a lesser role, perhaps his old post of Speaker.

Thus the election may not be the happy culmination of a peaceful evolution to democracy, but the harbinger of acute political uncertainty and unpredictable horse-trading. In this case the circle of disgruntlement will include a fourth group, foreign democracies who have been swift to dismantle sanctions and welcome into the democratic fold a nation which is not yet democratic.

The situation remains uncertain. Democracy is possible, but it is not inevitable. It is hard for comfortable democrats abroad to imagine the promotion of democratic values in Burmese conditions. Yet that is the task to which Aung San Suu Kyi has set her hand and we must wish her well. It stretches the imagination to suppose that the army can concede genuine democracy – or that Suu can settle for less. But this is the best opportunity that Burma is likely to get. We begin to dare to hope for Burma.

Chapter 12
Ireland:
HMA Dublin 1986-91

We had honeymooned in Ireland in 1959. We remembered the charm, the beauty and the poverty. Children played barefoot on the streets of North Dublin. Cafes on the highway asked for payment in advance so that they could send a ragged child out to buy the ingredients. The slow-thinking Irishman was the butt of smug English jokes.

Thirty years later the picture was transformed. Ireland was no less beautiful, its people no less charming, but the land of saints and scholars, of poverty and poetry, was beginning to emerge into the harsh light of the European Union. This did not happen overnight. Ireland was still dominated by a conservative Catholic theology. The political system – proportional representation in multi-member constituencies – concentrated the attention of politicians on the parish pump and away from the national interest. Ireland remained hypersensitive to anything which might impugn its nationhood. But in general Irish society was becoming more like the European norm. Irishmen were wealthier and more self-confident. The Celtic Tiger cub was growing stronger.

This was good news for Britain. The East-West relationship between Britain and Ireland was already good. We had much in common; we owned each other's companies and bought each other's products, we shared two cultures – English and Gaelic – and laughed at the same jokes. In spite of the experience of the centuries (or perhaps because of it) we were never truly foreigners to each other. A million Irishmen lived and worked in Britain. About a quarter of a million residents of the Republic were entitled to UK citizenship. But the relationship was complex and paradoxical. We were condemned to partnership by geography – we must share these islands, and by history – all those 800 years that no Irishman forgets and no Englishman remembers. Irishmen north and south of the border shared an astonishing mutual ignorance. The disparity in size was inescapable. Irish attention to Britain was constant and obsessive. British attention to Ireland was fitful and occasional. We knew each other well, loved each other dearly and misunderstood each other almost all the time. The new Ambassador found himself a temporary custodian of a relationship so ancient and intimate, so elusive and volatile, that no one outside these islands could properly understand it. It was special, distrustful, incestuous. We needed to make it more ordinary.

Early in our time, Nick was pinned to the wall on a social occasion by a distressingly nubile young lady who lectured him about the sins of his government. It was some minutes before he discovered that she was talking about Oliver Cromwell. She was perfectly serious. In vain did he protest that Cromwell did awful things in England too. This was not just Irish resentment of English arrogance and exploitation. It was "The Irish Question" – the political identity and constitutional future of Northern Ireland. To British minds partition was a fact, the issue was the democratic will of the people of Northern Ireland. To many Irish minds partition was a festering wound; the democratic will of the people of Ireland had been gerrymandered to produce a permanent Protestant/Unionist majority in the six counties.

Against this background the job was clear: to build on the East-West relationship between Britain and Ireland – solid economic interests, partnership in the European Union, mutual delight – so as to make it possible for the two governments to address *together* the problems which history had laid at their door. We needed to nurture our neighbourliness so that we could address our ancient antagonisms.

302

A good start had been made in 1985 with the signature by Margaret Thatcher and Dr Garret Fitzgerald of the Anglo-Irish Agreement, in which for the first time the Irish Government recognised that the future of Northern Ireland was a matter for the people of Northern Ireland, committed itself to co-operation against terrorism and to support devolution. At the same time the agreement recognised that the Republic had a legitimate interest in British decisions on Northern Ireland. It was detested by Unionists and by Sinn Fein alike. Its practical implementation was full of pitfalls which occupied time and effort on both sides. But it marked a decisive shift. It also meant that Nick spent much of his time on Northern Ireland matters, was often in Belfast and London on the business of the Northern Ireland Office and had at least as close a relationship with successive Secretaries of State for Northern Ireland, Tom King and Peter Brooke, as he had with Sir Geoffrey Howe at the Foreign Office.

For our first three months in Dublin the Irish Taoiseach (Prime Minister) was Garret Fitzgerald, academic economist turned politician, Irish patriot without anti-British instincts, architect of the Anglo-Irish Agreement and a man of international stature. He readily agreed to receive Nick's first call but insisted that the formal meeting be followed by an informal dinner at his home. Garret knew that he would lose the forthcoming elections and was determined to stamp the new Ambassador's Irish thinking with the imprint of Fitzgerald and Fine Gael. He talked almost without intermission for three hours in his characteristic rapid delivery, mixing anecdote with analysis, expounding the Irish attitude to Britain and distinguishing the "blarney and bluster" from "elements of the Irish soul". We did not have to agree with all of it, but for a new boy it was pure gold. His wife, Joan, was by then confined to a wheelchair but had not lost her sense of mischief. When Nick bowed to greet her, she seized his bow tie to expose its elastic and exclaimed, "The *British* Ambassador with a fake tie! Whatever next?"

Garret's coalition duly collapsed, Dick Spring's Labour Ministers resigned from the Cabinet and a general election was called for 17

February 1987. The outcome was a hung parliament. Charles J Haughey was elected Taoiseach by eighty-two votes to eighty-two on the casting vote of the Speaker. Haughey was a more difficult interlocuteur than Fitzgerald. He was shifty and secretive – for good reason: he was subsequently shown to be a crook. He was also an Irish Republican by both instinct and expedient. He harboured constitutional reservations about the Anglo-Irish Agreement, against which he had campaigned in the election. It required an amendment to the Irish constitution to remove the claim to sovereignty over the north. In the teeth of the Irish doctrine of neutrality, it required co-operation on the ground between the security forces of Britain and Ireland. It required Irish acquiescence in devolved government in Northern Ireland, which meant Republicans sharing power with Unionists. Most sensitive of all, it required the extradition of Irish terrorists to face British justice in which Haughey had no confidence. The Justice Minister, Gerry Collins, told Nick that in British courts men were innocent until proved Irish.

Nick was publicly denounced by the Spokesman for the Irish Government for exceeding diplomatic norms on the ground that he had been talking to opposition politicians about extradition. The Danish Ambassador put it well at a meeting of the twelve EU Ambassadors at which the Secretary for Foreign Affairs, Noel Dorr, represented Ireland: "We diplomats serve in two kinds of country – democratic countries where we can talk to the opposition, and totalitarian countries where we can't. Mr Dorr, which is the Republic of Ireland?" The Foreign Minister summoned Nick to ask him to forget the incident. He taught him a new Hibernianism. It was, it seemed, "codology". Ireland was full of this kind of trap for the unwary. The Ambassador's job was changing. Garret had signed the agreement on behalf of the Government of Ireland but his signature conveyed the assent of only half the Irish nation. We now had to make it stick with the other half.

There was another constraint on security co-operation. Ireland was not a member of NATO. Neutrality was a legacy of de Valera's refusal to go to war against Nazi Germany in order to demonstrate that Ireland was a distinct and sovereign Republic, not to be taken for granted. In British eyes this was irrelevant to the attitude a democracy should take towards terrorism. But neutrality was deeply ingrained in Ireland. The Irish army was never allowed to engage. The Garda Siochana – the Irish police force – operated under ground rules which limited cross-border co-operation. The anodyne Single European Act was controversial in Ireland because some saw it as a contravention of neutrality.

Haughey took three early decisions to consolidate his fragile hold on power. He adopted his predecessor's economic policies; the notorious spendthrift became an apostle of fiscal rectitude, thus establishing a national consensus in support of retrenchment. He campaigned for full-hearted Irish participation in the European community so that the greatest possible share of resources would be dispensed from the centre in the interests of the periphery. Thirdly, he accepted the Anglo-Irish Agreement. Haughey took these decisions because he was a realist – but he remained an instinctive Republican. He continued to nurse his constitutional reservations about the agreement, about devolution in Northern Ireland, about extradition, about the impact of the Single European Act. He would not condemn Sinn Fein from which his own party Fianna Fail had sprung, or co-operate fully with us against cross-border terrorism.

The ambiguity towards terrorism was briefly resolved by three incidents in 1987. A Dublin dentist was kidnapped by a terrorist who eluded the security forces for six weeks. The ship *Eksund* was seized by the French authorities with a cargo of arms from Libya for the IRA. Then an IRA bomb killed eleven people at a Remembrance Day parade in Enniskillen. The world was moved by Mr Gordon Wilson's public forgiveness for his daughter's death live on the early morning radio. All Ireland wept. The Taoiseach and his Cabinet attended the memorial service in St Patrick's Cathedral. The Lord Mayor of Dublin opened a book of condolence at the Mansion House and personally carried it to Enniskillen to present it to her colleague. In his message to the Prime Minister, Haughey declared that all the security forces in the island must combine to bring the perpetrators to

305

justice. Irish Ministers began to speak of the wickedness of the IRA. Padraig Flynn, as green a Republican as any in the Cabinet, quoted Arthur Miller: "This is a sharp time, now, a precise time. We no longer live in the dusty afternoon when evil mixed itself with good and befuddled the world".

But within weeks Nick was reporting to London in a formal despatch entitled "Litany of Horrors". The British Attorney General announced that there would be no further prosecutions in the "Stalker Sampson affair". The Court of Appeal rejected the second appeal of the Birmingham Six. Irish Ministers declared that the British Government was refusing to honour Irish legal requirements on extradition. The British Home Secretary announced that the Prevention of Terrorism Act (PTA) was to be made permanent. A Catholic youth was shot dead by a British soldier as he crossed the border at Auchnacloy. A British soldier was reinstated in his regiment after serving three and a half years of a life sentence for murdering a civilian in Northern Ireland. The PTA was used against an Irish visitor to London about whom the Irish Deputy Prime Minister had made formal representations. Three unarmed Irish terrorists were shot dead in Gibraltar. The Taoiseach demanded to know whether the British Government was trying to destabilise his administration. A major Irish paper pronounced the Anglo-Irish Agreement "dead". A series of unconnected events had brought us from harmony to full crisis in six weeks from a standing start.

The point of the despatch was not to complain about the decisions themselves – although if the Irish dimension had been considered at the time some of them might have been more tactfully expressed. In spite of the provisions of the Anglo-Irish Agreement, the Irish had not been informed of any of them. As seen from Dublin, London had barely noticed what the Irish saw as a major crisis. Anglo-Irish relations were notoriously volatile, but this difference in perception was potentially dangerous. The report was written on 21 March 1988 to alert London to these dangers. It had a mixed reception. When it reached the Prime Minister, Nick was summoned to Downing Street. He spent an uncomfortable hour with Mrs Thatcher. She was shocked that our perceptions were so different. She had nothing but contempt for Mr Haughey who pretended to support the agreement while working to undermine it. There was zero co-operation with the Irish. Nick suggested that it was his duty to "tell it like it is" in explaining Irish views to British Ministers. When he talked to the Irish he talked her language. We needed Irish co-operation to achieve our security and political objectives. We should engage their co-operation by explaining ourselves to them. The Prime Minister agreed that Ambassadors should report honestly and that we should work harder to explain difficult decisions to the Irish. But she instructed Nick to tell Mr Haughey in words of one syllable what she thought of him; the acid test was their performance on security co-operation. She rose. The interview was over. Nick half expected to be sacked. She hissed in his ear, "Go back to Ireland where you belong." She meant it kindly. A few weeks later Nick was offered a knighthood. He never knew whether this was coincidence.

A few days later he called on the Taoiseach to carry out Mrs Thatcher's instructions. He appealed for full-hearted co-operation on the ground against terrorism, and a clear acknowledgement of the principle of consent. He stressed how deeply Mrs Thatcher's personal confidence had been shaken. Haughey commented that personal confidence, once destroyed, could not be restored. Nick said that was a counsel of despair. Haughey retorted that the Irish had lived with despair for 800 years.

There was only the one time Sue was really worried – scared stiff in fact. Nick had planned to go to Dublin Airport to greet some VIP (a "visiting fireman")from London. The bodies of the "Gibraltar Three" were arriving at the same time and the route to the airport was festooned with black flags. The IRA could be expected there in force. Sue begged Nick not to go. He replied that he wasn't going to let the IRA dictate his movements. So he went. Waiting at Glencairn Sue got a call from the guards at the gate. Was she expecting visitors? They had not been notified. Who were they? From the embassy. Send them down. Sue watched as two senior colleagues with solemn faces disembarked at the front door. Nick's deputy and

307

the next most senior diplomat. If anything had happened to Nick, it was these two men who would come to tell her. Her guts melted. There is no other way to express the feeling when you know you have become a widow. Very slowly she walked to the front door, rehearsing in her mind the right things to say. But she heard the butler say, "Please wait here till the Ambassador gets back." They had come to see Nick. He was alive. Sue tried not to shout for joy but to receive these good friends quietly. It transpired that a parcel bomb destined for the embassy had exploded in the post office. No wonder everyone was looking grim. But should the staff be sent home? Nick would deal with that when he got home. Meanwhile, fear banished, Sue would do anything anyone wanted.

One result of these events in the spring of 1988 was the establishment in London of an "Iceberg watch" to ensure that dangerous issues were identified in advance. Another was "Nick's Diner", an informal gathering of the two Cabinet Secretaries and the most senior officials on both sides who met twice a year, usually over dinner at our home, to chew the fat and alert each other of issues which were likely to cause grief. This was the stuff of our professional life in Dublin. Most of it was happy and constructive. But volatility and passion lurked just below the surface.

"Nick's Diner" met at Glencairn, the baronial mansion on the southern outskirts of Dublin which served as the British Ambassador's residence. We used to say that we lived in a mediaeval castle built by an American gangster in 1905. The gangster in question was Boss Croker, an Irish-American Tammany Hall chief who retired with his ill-gotten gains to his native Dublin, bought the modest Georgian home of a retired judge and turned it into the extravagant folly which we knew and loved, complete with battlements and tower. He built it to re-establish his respectability in Edwardian Dublin – and failed. So he built stables and bred racehorses. His famous horse, Orby, won the English and the Irish Derby in 1907 and instantly re-established his respectability on both sides of the water. Croker became a local celebrity. He married a Red Indian princess. He became Lord Mayor of Dublin. When he died in

1925 he had himself embalmed and laid in a mausoleum on an island in a small lake just outside our front door. The O'Brien family bought the house in 1939. They dug him up and moved him up the hill to Kilgobbin Churchyard, where Susan cultivated roses around his grave in memory of our distinguished predecessor. What the O'Briens did not notice was that from the mausoleum to the churchyard the house stood in the direct line of sight. We had only one piece of furniture which dated from the boss's era, a magnificent grandfather clock which stood in the hall and which struck every hour on the hour precisely what hour it pleased. It became clear to us that the boss lived in that clock... And when the moon rides high... That at least was the story we told to dinner guests who would not go home. We gathered them in the hall at a few minutes to one and waited for the clock to strike. It might strike six or thirteen. It never let us down by striking the right time. And when our guests had stopped laughing they found themselves out in the garden looking for their cars.

The Glencairn grounds were extensive. Seven acres near the house were cultivated as a garden and used for entertaining. Beyond was The Glen with three big ponds connected by small waterfalls and some magnificent trees. Outside the high wire security fence, a further twenty-seven acres of fields were used by a local farmer. As soon as we collected the keys to leave the inner sanctum the minders were mobilised, but near the house it was considered safe to play tennis or croquet or build snowmen.

Susan decided to make changes. With encouragement from London, trees along the drive were felled to remove the dense barrier of foliage. A tall hedge of alternate green and copper beech trees, planted to keep the world at bay, were thinned to open up wide views of the countryside and to the sea beyond. The lime walk was pollarded. More than fifty tons of timber was taken away. Daylight, breathing space, a welcoming driveway instead of the rabbit hole down which we had been hiding. Money was even found to restore the conservatory – the last remaining from the acres of glass which had once provided "the boss" with exotic fruit and flowers. The

309

clearance of the Glen was a family job during the children's holidays, and a retired British farmer in the area supervised the overall maintenance and provided logs for the fires in winter. The only notable feature outside the wire was the grave of the racehorse, Orby, and her daughters. Once when Nick and Sue were inspecting them three locals came over to warn them that it was a dangerous place to explore. "There are men up at the house with machine guns. Honest!" Our minders kept their faces straight.

Glencairn Golf was introduced to us by a predecessor, Sir John Peck, who still lived in Dublin, and for whom we had the privilege and delight of giving a wedding breakfast. The game entailed hitting a tennis ball from the furthest bedroom down the corridor, across the landing, down the magnificent mahogany staircase, across the hall and down another passage to the library. The players took turns using whatever "weapon" they chose so long as it was not normally used for sport. Fire tongs, kitchen equipment or gardening tools were fine but not a tennis racket, croquet mallet or cricket bat. If you broke anything you were out. Sue's nephews and niece, who frequently visited us, became experts. We loved celebrating their birthdays in front of a huge fire in the library, followed by silly games depending on the weather. Having youngsters around helped remove stuffiness from the residence.

Our social secretary, Olive, had a little office just inside the front door. She never tired of telling us how she loved her job. She dealt with the invitations, keeping an index of guests' addresses and records of their visits. She attended the big events. She welcomed guests with enthusiasm and introduced them to us as necessary. Annoyingly she and the butler were often bickering. One time Sue swept in and declared that if they did not stop it they would both have to go! She claims she only lost her temper with staff three times and it was always over an argument between two staff members. These rare outbursts had the desired effect and we never sacked anyone – except for the cook in Mandalay when he tried to murder the houseboy. His own wife told us we had to do it.

310

Michael, the butler, particularly enjoyed visits from Sue's sister and family and usually loaded up their car with logs before they went home. He had been in the army before this job. He was proud of his work and had very high standards. The glass and silver sparkled and were laid out with military precision. His favourite event was the Christmas party for the children at the Sunshine Home. These kids had serious disabilities and deformities and were completely dependent. Every week Sue would go down the road to help prepare them for a "swim" in a warm therapy pool. It was fun for them because they had more freedom of movement in the water. At Glencairn we gave them their favourite food, attempted a few simple games and sang familiar carols. Each child collected a small gift from the tree and the decorated house gave them plenty of new things to look at. Michael was gentle, competent and cheerful, radiating happiness.

His deputy Mahmoud, originally from Algeria and married to a member of the embassy staff, lived in the lodge by the gate. Much too intelligent for the job, he gave it his all, proved an invaluable member of the household and succeeded Michael as butler when we left Ireland. He once discussed Ishigaro's novel *Remains of the Day*, marvelling at the Japanese author's ability to understand the workings of a big country house, let alone the sensitivities of the butler who worked in it.

We inherited a wonderful cook, Sarah, a tower of strength. She was not a trained chef but she was a "natural" and full of enthusiasm. She had said she would only stay on a year – to settle us in – but in the end stayed the five years till we left. She said she loved the variety; a drinks party for 200, a picnic to take to the races, a formal dinner for twenty, a brunch for 500, tea for war veterans or a children's party. And in between she was free to experiment on us. Her political sympathies surfaced in subtle signs. A soup made from Jerusalem artichokes appeared on the menu as "Palestine Soup". Her amiable black Labrador, Thomson – "big, black and beautiful, like his namesake" – came for walks with us and picnics in the Wicklow Hills. Elizabeth ably assisted Sarah and cooked for the staff so that in

311

all our five years there Sue never had to cook one meal – in such a huge state of the art kitchen she would have been a bit lost!

Glencairn's extensive gardens were maintained by three gentlemen aged eighty-six, seventy-six and sixty-one. Leo was so deaf that it was impossible to give him instructions. He went on cultivating the acre of walled kitchen garden as he had done for the past sixty-one years. We persuaded him to retire. His deputy then gratefully hung up his boots as he had felt that he could not go before his boss. In their places we employed two young women, Jane and Kate, recent graduates of Horticultural College. Both the atmosphere and the appearance of the gardens improved. They grew herbs and rare vegetables for Sarah and bountiful flowers for the house. Michael, the young groundsman, sixty-one, stayed on. The chickens had the run of a little orchard and laid eggs all year round because the security lights fooled them into thinking it was permanent summer.

Christopher, the footman, an elegant gentleman, had officially retired but he lived alone and had a standing invitation to lunch in the staff room. He skilfully arranged the flowers around the house. He helped out whenever we were short staffed. He showed Sarah how to turn down the guest beds "so that the ladies don't have to bend their legs when they get in." He kept an eye on upstairs where Helen and Marie were in charge of the cleaning and laundry when Annie, in her nineties, had been persuaded to fold up her duster.

Despite the long hours and late nights it was a cheerful establishment. Dinners usually went on into the small hours and some of our official guests were difficult to please even when sober. Because the staff put on such a good show they sometimes gave the impression they were there 24/7 as in the East. Nick and Sue would find shoes outside the guest room doors at night, so they had to stay up to polish them or press the suit hanging on the bathroom door.

Glencairn had been "modernised" when acquired by HMG in the fifties. The nude statues on the newel posts of the main stairs were

312

removed, and stained glass, painted ceilings, old-fashioned baths and ornate radiators were carefully concealed. Happily fashions were changing and Sue was able to reverse these changes revealing many of the idiosyncrasies of Boss Croker's home – notably the stained glass ceiling of the hall portraying the legend of the birds, and the painted ceiling of the morning room with every bird that was known to exist in Japan. It stirred her into writing a guide to the house. An offer to print it from a publisher of guides to many of Dublin's public buildings was withdrawn on the reasonable grounds that few of the public had access. We were saddened to learn that the Labour Government of 1997 had ordained the sale of Glencairn. It was sold to a developer who packed many new homes onto the surrounding land but preserved the house and garden. It proved impossible to find suitable alternative accommodation for the Ambassador, so it had to be bought back at considerable cost to the taxpayer. At the time of writing the Ambassador still lives there.

We were privileged to live in such a "palace". It was a valuable diplomatic tool as well as a fun place to live and entertain. Dinners were used for discussion and debate and were of course planned carefully. The current tensions between the two governments set the agenda. We tried to ensure that each gathering was politically balanced and professionally diverse. Sometimes we feared that we had overdone the diversity and that our guests would soon be at each other's throats. It usually turned out that they had been at school together and were delighted to see each other.

In every post Sue had tried to study the local language. So in Ireland it was obvious that she should have a go at Irish. The first tentative steps were taken at Gael-Linn in Merrion Square, a "total immersion course" taught without the use of English. Lesson One involved asking names, saying "Hello" and making introductions. Lesson Two was in an imaginary pub where we learned how to order a Guinness. Lesson Three was about brawling – which followed naturally from Lesson Two. Sue tried to keep a low profile for reasons of discretion. She registered under her maiden name and answered such questions as "What brings you to Ireland?" with "My

313

husband's business". The only time a little anxiety was expressed by "security" was when Sue joined the party at the end of the course which was held in an Irish-speaking Republican "club", a well-known rendezvous for the IRA. A fellow student shared a joke with Sue one night as they strode briskly round the square for a breath of air halfway through the evening's lesson. The teacher was strongly anti-clerical. His young student was himself a priest. He told Sue in confidence how amused he was by the invective hurled at the priesthood. Sue did not tell him she was also enjoying the anti-British rhetoric.

The language revealed something of Irish culture. Only a religious people with time to spare could follow the greeting "God be with you" with the reply "God and Mary be with you" followed by "and Patrick, and Bridget..." and so on, adding all the local saints. The toasts in Irish in the pub were also instructive. "May you die in Ireland!" for example, and "May you always have a wet mouth!"

Then Sue engaged a teacher for private lessons. After some months he chose to teach her a few phrases "in case she should ever have to speak in public". She learned them off pat. Coming down for a reception in Glencairn one evening she was surprised to discover all the expected "agriculturalists" were speaking Irish. Everyone was grinning from ear to ear, including her teacher who was not on the guest list. Speeches were made. Sue and three friends who were also learning Irish were presented with a Fainne – literally a ring. Wearing such a pin indicated that you wished to converse in Irish. So Sue was called on to speak. All her recently acquired public phrases were strung together. What a trick to play on her!

Later she became more confident, after time spent in the Irish-speaking parts of the south-west with these three friends from Dublin – her "Gang of Four". She was even interviewed on TV and radio in Irish and began to get fan mail. Irish speakers in Northern Ireland (some of whom wrote in not very good Irish) were pleased that the Republican appropriation of the language had been challenged. It had not been her intention in trying to learn it, but Sue's attempt to master the native tongue pleased a surprising number of people.

One summer when the "Gang of Four" were staying in different guesthouses in the Dingle Gaeltacht, Sue was shopping in an Irish-speaking gift shop. An English woman came in and immediately the language changed. After she left the shopkeeper turned to Sue and said in Irish, "Don't you find it surprising that the British are still coming over here to holiday after the way we treat them?" It was hard to reply in English let alone Irish. The "we" implied her alias had not been rumbled.

We paid our first official visit to Cork, second city of the Republic, and home of an Irish culture distinctive even in Ireland. We called on the Lord Mayor, local Members of Parliament, the president of the university college, the Harbour Master, leaders of industry and commerce, arts and sciences. On the third evening we gave a little dinner in an excellent restaurant to thank those who had received us so kindly. The guest of honour was Peter Barry, who had been Foreign Minister under Garret Fitzgerald. He made a graceful speech. At one point he mentioned Ireland's "appointment with destiny" the following day, a reference to the referendum on the Single European Act. This enraged Senator John A Murphy, a notable opponent of Irish membership of the European Union. He interrupted, banging the table, protesting about Barry's introduction of partisan themes. We had been thinking that our little diplomatic foray into Republican Cork had been going rather well – and here it was collapsing about our ears. The soft-spoken president of the university college saved the day. "Mr Ambassador," he said, "this is the time when we sing Irish songs." His wife sang a haunting Gaelic melody. Before long John A Murphy was singing Irish songs and we all went home in good humour.

Police protection was a feature of our lives in Ireland. It was not agreeable because it robbed life of spontaneity. But it was necessary. A predecessor, Christopher Ewart-Biggs, had been assassinated by the IRA in 1976, and Lord Mountbatten in 1979. We were obliged to

315

take security seriously. The Office was a fortress. Glencairn was heavily protected. We travelled in an armoured Jaguar so heavy that it often scraped the tarmac leaving a trail of sparks. An armed police escort followed us wherever we went, sometimes in the most incongruous places. And if we got out for a walk in the Wicklow Hills they came too with their machine guns. It rather changed the atmosphere of a picnic. For five years we were never alone except in bed. This theme will arise from time to time in the course of our story. But it did not dominate our lives. You cannot live in the constant expectation of assassination. We learned to plan our movements so as to accommodate police requirements and then to ignore them. One saving grace was that the restrictions applied to Nick alone. It was a joint decision of the two governments that Sue was either safe or expendable. She could jump into our little car and go out whenever she wanted. Only if Nick went with her did we need to mobilise the Gardai.

We went to stay with Irish friends in Sneem in County Kerry. Our host took us by trawler on a rough day to visit Skellig St Michael, a dramatic outcrop of rock eight miles off the coast where there was a spectacular lighthouse and an eighth century beehive monastery. The parish priest came too to participate in an interdenominational service in the monastery. Father Murphy had been priest at Sneem for twenty-five years. He had visited Skellig his first year but had been so seasick that he never went back. He thought that it was time to try again. The poor man was sick before we left the harbour. He installed himself on the lee side of the boat, solicitous for his neighbours. He would be smiling as the boat heeled in the wind and his head disappeared beneath the waves. He was still smiling when he came up again. Somehow he climbed the 284 steps cut into the living rock by monks so long ago, and struggled through his part in the service. Then we went down again. There was a place where the steps took a right angle turn to the left. Ahead was the wild Atlantic 200 feet below. Father Murphy went straight on. One of our minders seized him by the arm and put him back on the path, undoubtedly saving his life. Father Murphy did not notice. On the way back to Sneem another minder stood amidships holding a rope and apparently chanting a psalm. Then we heard what he was saying. "I can't be sick on duty. I can't be sick on duty."

We returned to Sneem two years later. On the eve of our departure the Deputy Commissioner of the Garda Siochana asked to see Nick urgently late at night. He was sorry to report that our travel plans had fallen into the hands of "subversives". He was embarrassed because the plans had in fact been leaked to the IRA by a disaffected police sergeant. Nick asked whether the police were advising us to cancel the visit. "Oh no, sir, if you go it is our business to keep you safe." We went. When we arrived the entire mountain was covered with policemen. The Chief Superintendent, no less, who was in charge of the operation asked us to stay at home the following morning.

There was a busload of young men at the entrance to the cul-de-sac. They claimed to be foresters come to check the forest at the head of the lane. "But, sir, there is no forest at the head of the lane."

Half an hour later the Chief Superintendent came back. The corners of his mouth were twitching. "It's all right, you can go out now." They were real foresters but they were in the wrong county. When we got back to Dublin the front page of the Irish Republican newspaper *An Phoblacht* carried a photograph of Nick taken through the telescopic sight of a rifle under the headline "We let Fenn go". Nick was besieged by journalists demanding to know whether he had confidence in Irish security. He had of course the fullest confidence.

We were made very welcome at Lansdowne Road, the home of Irish rugby. In soccer, Northern Ireland and the Republic field separate teams. In rugby the island plays as one. Since Nick was, in a sense, the Ambassador of half the Irish team to the other half, it seemed appropriate that we should attend international matches. But the delicate question arose – for which team should we cheer? We consulted Garret Fitzgerald, himself a keen rugby fan who never missed a match. The solution exploited the fact that Susan is partly Scottish. When Scotland came to Lansdowne Road she should cheer

317

for them. Nick would cheer for England when they were playing. In all other circumstances we cheered for Ireland. That way one of us was always cheering for Ireland and both of us got to support our own teams. The story was often told of the time during The Troubles when France and Scotland declined to play in Ireland. But England came – and had the grace to lose. At the dinner that evening the English captain made a short speech which has never been forgotten in Ireland. "We may not be much cop at rugby, but at least we show up."

The representation of Northern Ireland in the Republic gave rise to another perk. The British Ambassador had a standing invitation to the Commissioners of Irish Lights, the voluntary body responsible for the maintenance of lighthouses throughout the island of Ireland. Once a year the Commissioners went on a tour of inspection in their flagship the *Granuaille*. In the eighteenth century, we were told, they had been offered the choice between a free uniform and a free lunch. They chose the lunch and had been eating it ever since. Certainly their Lordships the Commissioners lived on that ship like kings with fine food and wine. After dinner the Admiral would ask the captain the position of the vessel. The captain would send for the bosun who gave precise co-ordinates, so that the Admiral knew which Head of State to toast. One year Nick went with them from Cork to Limerick, visiting en route twelve of the most magnificent lighthouses in the world: Kinsale, Galley, Fastnet, Mizzen, Bull Rock, Skellig, Blasket etc. We lived well, but when we arrived at a lighthouse the Commissioners were instantly professional. We went ashore by bouncing dinghy, by breeches buoy or by crane operated from the rocks. We walked to the lighthouse, examined the light for technical faults, interviewed the lighthouse keeper and inspected his living quarters. We witnessed the end of a noble profession. Within five years the last lights were automated. Some of the keepers had followed their fathers and grandfathers in the job and could imagine no other way of life.

We attended the launch of a new lifeboat at Howth, just north of Dublin. An English Duke, President of the RNLI in the UK, was invited to launch it. Sue discovered that she was underdressed. Then about twenty dignitaries were invited on board to look around. Sue's flat shoes and trouser suit were suddenly appropriate. Without warning the ship put to sea. A demonstration "rescue" had been laid on and we were stuck on board for another hour and a half. No mobile phones in those days. Many missed appointments. A priest missed the wedding he had agreed to conduct. The Lord Mayor of Dublin, Bertie Ahern, later Taoiseach, thought our discomfort a rare joke.

The Gardai implored us not to bring a boat to Ireland. They would have been obliged to provide it with a permanent guard. At Dun Laoghaire there were three yacht clubs in a row, the Royal St George, the Royal Irish and the National – popularly known as the nobs, the snobs and the yobs – but no one would tell us which was which. We joined the Royal Irish. Nick became a regular crew member for an Irish judge. This required that the Police Marine Service should inspect the boat. When the judge took his boat out of the water for the winter he found that the bottom had been adorned with games of noughts and crosses.

Nick's cousin Jonathan brought his boat from Devon to circumnavigate Ireland. We joined the crew from Westport to Galway, around Connemara. We had negotiated with the Gardai that they need not actually have a presence on board. It would be sufficient for them to follow us by car, so long as Nick reported progress by short wave radio. One evening we arrived at Innisbofin, a romantic little island harbour with a ruined Oliver Cromwell fort and a straggle of white painted cottages up the hill from the quayside. We ghosted in on the dying wind, dropped the anchor and furled the sails and enjoyed our first gin and tonic of the evening. No one in Innisbofin had a clue who we were. Then there put out from the jetty a red painted dinghy rowed by two gentlemen in city suits who were plainly not accustomed to the sea. They made their erratic course across the harbour and came alongside. One of them stood up in the dinghy and saluted. Then everyone knew who we were. When

319

we went ashore to Mrs Day's pub, we were courteously welcomed, "Good evening, Your Excellency."

Each year the great and the good would gather at summer schools on the west coast – informal conferences organised by enthusiasts in a wide range of literary, artistic and political subjects. We were soon addicts. Sometimes Nick was invited to speak. Sue and Julia enjoyed classes in Irish step dancing. Small gatherings in pubs and halls – especially pubs – were the most interesting. Government Ministers and opposition politicians rubbed shoulders with students and academics, journalists and poets. We were in a pub meeting in La Hinch until long past closing time and the doors had been locked. We followed our minders out through the kitchen, down the garden path and over the wall. The London columnist, Peterborough, in *The Telegraph*, reported the story back to front – that we had asked the guards to break *into* a pub after closing time. When we complained we were assured by our Irish friends that they preferred the fiction, so we let it stand. Another fictitious story in the press concerned the commotion we had caused by arriving at the Galway races in a green helicopter. The helicopter had in fact transported the Minister of Finance, one Albert Reynolds. Sue protested loudly, in the hearing of an Irish tycoon, that she had never even *been* in a helicopter. This prompted an invitation to dinner, including transport by his private helicopter, to meet the writer Graham Greene.

One "summer school" on "The Year of the French" took place in Ballina, a stronghold of Republicanism. Again our daughter came with us and had an unexpected experience of local feelings. She and Sue were waiting in the hotel lobby for Nick's impromptu press conference to end. The manager asked a favour. "I am besieged by townsfolk who want to shake your hand and welcome you to Ballina. Would you ever have a word with them now?" So they stood at the hotel entrance as people lined up to shake their hands and thank us for coming to Ballina. "This is our first visit from a British Ambassador and we welcome you most warmly. You are safe here."

At the same time Nick was greeted by the local Fianna Fail TD (Member of the Dail – the Irish parliament). They shook hands. The politician smiled for the cameras and said through clenched teeth, "Welcome to Ballina, Ambassador. Never come again. This has just cost me sixty votes." It was the precision that impressed.

On our first visit to Bunratty Castle near Limerick, Nick was collared by the director. "We need your help, Ambassador. The period chosen to 'dress' the model village is just before the First World War. We need a wall map for the school room, one in which most of the world is coloured pink. We cannot find one in all Ireland." It took nearly eighteen months to locate one. It is still there.

In our five years we visited most of the famous tourist sites including Blarney Castle to kiss the Blarney Stone. Nick's father had done it properly years earlier, when there had been nothing to stop him falling head first from the top of the castle keep. He was dismissive of the new safety net which destroys the challenge – and its effectiveness?

We stayed in a charming coastal village called Schull, from the Irish for Mary's School, and yes, pronounced "skull". The local IRA made a costly mistake. They blew up a prominent transmitter on the hilltop above the harbour thinking they would be disrupting NATO communications. All local televisions ceased to work. The IRA were not the flavour of the month. Our security was tightened. The local commander shared a joke with our minders. He said his small son had noticed the unusual police activity. "Who is it for, Dad? It can't be Reagan or Thatcher, there are no patrolling aircraft or ships in the bay. I guess it must be Ian Paisley."

We tried to find somewhere for a snack lunch. There seemed to be several houses selling Guinness but they were all closed. One minder opened the door of an unprepossessing establishment. Seconds later he shot out firmly shutting the door behind him. "Holy Mother of God, you're not going in there!" An IRA coven? No, it was full of cigarette smoke.

On a nostalgic return to the scene of our honeymoon we found Mrs. O'Connor's guest house flourishing. Her son had extended the cottage but changed little – "at the request of our regular English visitors." We incautiously mentioned that we had been before in 1959. At once the old Visitors' Book was produced – and there was Nick's signature – "N M Fenn". But as always we were travelling under false names and had to disown the signature. We were in an active Republican area of Kerry and the police presence was not welcome. But we were assured of a warm welcome if we came back on our own.

Visiting an old friend who lived near Bantry we were horrified to learn how intrusive had been the Garda preparations for our visit. There had been at least one man at her house for forty-eight hours before we were due. Mary just said, "I am glad they are looking after you."

"But," Nick expostulated, "surely none of your friends would want to murder me?"

"Perhaps not, but I do not know anyone in these parts who would not shelter your murderer."

The Irish Minister for Food invited us to inaugurate the First Irish International Food Fair at Kinsale on the reasonable grounds that our countrymen ate more Irish food than the Irish. It was a truly memorable weekend; speeches of course, and dinners, lunches, teas and receptions, Irish hospitality at its most overwhelming. We staggered up to bed for a few hours, but were summoned down again by the Minister early next morning to accompany him on a parade around the streets to pipe bands and an obligatory tasting of the delicacies proffered by every stall. To escape the forced feeding Nick grabbed an old-fashioned delivery bicycle and cycled off with minders in hot pursuit. We stopped the car on the drive home to telephone Glencairn. We would need no supper, nor any other food for a couple of days. Ambassadors need stamina in Ireland.

322

The annual Wexford Opera Festival was a different kind of feast. You do not need to be an opera buff. The intimate theatre is crowded with men in black tie and women in their finest dresses, eager to see the little known operas performed by little known soloists. The choir is mostly local townsfolk, yet the standard is remarkably high. Then all day there are musical offerings all around the town for a fellowship of regulars. It's like a large old-fashioned house party. The Murphy's stout and oysters are as much a part of the celebrations as the opera. Bernard Levin captures the spirit of the occasion with his account of the disaster which struck one year. He tells of the whole cast sliding off the steeply raked stage into the orchestra pit. The stage floor of smooth, white plastic, to represent marble, was made sticky to help the cast get a grip. Alas, a cleaner noticed the stickiness and helpfully washed it off.

All year round Dublin offered a bewildering choice of visual arts, concerts, exhibitions and theatre. We were frequent clients of The Abbey and The Gate. Sporting culture was provided in horse racing and rugby. We learned to take the sporting tips from our minders with a pinch of salt.

The British Council opened in Dublin and brought some quality British culture to Ireland. The stops were pulled out for Dublin's year as European City of Culture. We saw three excellent productions of *Hamlet* in one year alone. In spite of apprehension in London, the council's activities were widely welcomed. Only the greenest Republicans smelled cultural imperialism.

A Maori exhibition came to Dublin for which national warriors had been flown halfway round the world to perform rites respecting their ancestors. The crowd of guests, academics and diplomats, sceptical at first, were moved by the reverence of the sounds and movements taking place in the dark in the centre of Dublin. There was an exhibition of Himalayan Tankhas inaugurated by the Dalai Lama himself in the Chester Beatty Library. This superb building houses an eclectic collection brought to Dublin by the great man himself when he discovered that the temperature and humidity in

323

Dublin vary less over the year than in any other city. In the same gallery we witnessed the then Crown Prince of Japan open an exhibition of a newly restored copy of the worlds "first novel" written by a Japanese court lady in the fifteenth century.

One of the delights of life in Ireland was a series of concerts under the title "Music in Great Country Houses". There are many such houses in the Dublin area, some open to the public on a regular basis, others only for special events like these. They were always agreeable evenings, the company stimulating, the setting romantically decayed, the chamber music of high quality.

Once we had settled in we allowed ourselves to invite to Glencairn representatives of the old Anglo-Irish Ascendancy and to accept invitations to their homes. We might hesitate in the winter because our hosts could not afford to heat their mansions properly. Many layers of clothing recommended. On arrival one was ushered into a grand reception room where guests were huddled round the blazing hearth. We would sprint along icy corridors to the dining room, hoping for a lucky place at table near the fire. The food was always excellent and the conversation enjoyable. Drink was generous. Inner warmth and bonhomie compensated for numb fingers and toes.

Not all castles were equally cold. We spent many weekends in considerable splendour as guests of the "old families". All had fascinating histories to tell and most were experts and enthusiasts in fields as diverse as botany and pop music. Nick was asked by the Earl of Rosse, Brendan Parsons, to open an exhibition in Birr Castle about one of his ancestors and he invited us to stay the weekend. Before his father died, our host had run the UN aid programme in Bangladesh so we found we had friends and experiences in common. Although reluctant to give up UN work to run the family estates, he had thrown his energy into making a success of his newly inherited responsibilities. He started a small museum in the stables, invited the international coach and horses races to use the estate, promoted concerts and worked hard to restore the castle. He developed a

324

famous collection of magnolia specimens and planted a meadow of beautiful fritillaries. An ancestor had been a well-known plant breeder and there is a lovely peony called the "Countess of Rosse". His wife is a talented painter. Her luminous, sensitive watercolours enrich the walls of their home. Brendan enjoyed telling how, years earlier, the family had hurriedly redecorated the chief guest room to welcome Princess Margaret after her engagement to Lord Snowden, and the new wallpaper had peeled off and fallen on top of her during the night.

While we were in Ireland the last of the Talbots died, bringing to an end a family who had lived in Malahide Castle, just north of Dublin, since the Norman invasion. We often took visitors to see the castle and to wonder at the family portrait hanging in the mediaeval hall, portraying fourteen members of the family before they set out together for the Battle of the Boyne. Not one of them survived the day. Lord Dunsany and his charming wife were wise and kind living in quiet retirement. Lord Longford, despite his years, was still active in the House of Lords in London. The Knight of Glin had a castle home beyond Limerick where he and his wife enjoyed entertaining, and he busied himself with the Georgian Society. In Dublin this lively body ensured that the Georgian heritage and architecture is valued and preserved. There were many more who kindly welcomed us into their homes and worked hard for their country outside or on the edge of politics. Lord Killanin served on the International Olympic Committee. Sir Alfred and Clementine Beit had a fine art collection of international fame. He gave it to the National Gallery in Dublin. But alas, it was stolen from their home. We were glad to be able to enjoy company such as theirs whenever this could be done without offending political sensitivities.

In Dublin we admired the work of Lutyens, including the monumental war memorial garden built to honour the Irish dead of the First World War. He had also restored Lord Revelstoke's island and designed a guest house by the jetty. We sailed there one weekend. The Garda boat sent to protect us was driven onto a sandbank and we had to pull them off before paying our call on his

325

Lordship and his wallabies. It's a small and now comfortable castle set in a park surrounded by a high stone wall – to keep the wallabies from escaping.

Fresh from Burma, we naturally took an interest in the Burma Star Association of veterans from the Burma campaign of the Second World War. These splendid old soldiers would entertain us in their clubhouse and we invited them back to Glencairn. Sue arranged a slide show of pictures of Burma. They were indignant that she had included not a single picture of a "chinthe" (mythical lion, symbol of the Chindits, who now guard pagodas all over Burma). Sue had to arrange a second slide show composed exclusively of chinthes.

Mr O'Sullivan was probably the best dentist in Ireland. He was noted for his strong Republican views. He would fill Nick's mouth with his professional ironmongery and then say something quite outrageous when the Ambassador could only grunt in protest. Nick once spent five hours in his chair when root canal treatment went wrong. It was not the pain that was memorable, but the frustration of interrupted dialogue.

A British Ambassador in Ireland is, whether he likes it or not, a kind of Irish grandee. He is invited to Irish occasions from which other foreigners are excluded. He is welcome in Irish homes, the decaying mansions of the Anglo-Irish aristocracy, the modern homes of successful Irish businessmen, the cottages of ordinary folk, centres of Irish learning, music, drama, painting, even to the Member's Bar at the Irish Parliament. He is invited to make friends with those who see his nation as their enemy. He has unexpected opportunities to say and do healing things. There is almost never time to seek instructions. In these circumstances the diplomatic instinct is to say and do nothing – which would render him grade one useless. So he makes it up as he goes along. He ventures out onto his high wire clutching his whisky and soda, knowing that if he gets it wrong people will die, and if he gets it right fewer people will die.

Colleagues, particular EU colleagues, were incredulous. How did it come about that the representative of the ancient enemy, the hated oppressor, had an access in this society that was denied to them? They knew little of the intensity and complexity of the Anglo-Irish relationship and nothing about the high wire act. But they knew that wherever they went in Ireland the British Ambassador was there before them. And they found it galling. Nick had to pretend that he spent his time, as they did, consulting and negotiating on the business of the European Union which was more professionally and effectively done in Brussels.

In most diplomatic capitals the Ambassador who has been longest in post becomes the doyen of the diplomatic corps, with certain professional roles to discharge between the host country and the corps as a whole. In Ireland, and in certain other Catholic countries, the doyen is always the Papal Nuncio, the representative of the Vatican. We served under two Nuncios. Archbishop Allibrandi had been nineteen years in Dublin when we arrived. He knew Ireland well and saw it narrowly through Catholic eyes. His political views were indistinguishable from those of Sinn Fein. Nick, as the representative of the head of a schismatic church and a colonial oppressor, had nothing to commend him. The only policy was to be elaborately courteous in public and have as little as possible to do with the doyen. His successor was the former Archbishop of Malta. He had been educated in Britain, came to Ireland from Pakistan and held the UK in high regard. He considered that the Nunciature had been too devious and too tolerant of terrorism. There could hardly have been a starker contrast. He endeared himself to us by accepting our invitation to attend the annual Remembrance Day service which his predecessor had always ignored. This created a minor sensation. The press besieged the cathedral demanding to know why he had attended. His answer was straightforward: "Why ever not?" Alas, this caused such an outcry among Irish nationalists that he never came again.

The US Ambassador, Margaret Heckler, had been Secretary of Health in Ronald Reagan's Cabinet and had been sent to Dublin because of her strongly pro-Irish views. Nick embarked upon a one-man crusade to persuade her that the United Kingdom was a valued ally of her government and that terrorism was the enemy of democracy. After diplomatic occasions, Nick took to calling at the American residence on his way home. Sometimes they talked long into the night. Margaret Heckler was an attractive widow. They learned to be more circumspect. Her successor was a charming elderly gentleman whose younger brother had been US Ambassador in Dublin some twenty years earlier. We all went to Northern Ireland for the installation of the new Cardinal Archbishop of Armagh as Primate of All Ireland. It was cold and foggy. As we emerged from our cars, Robert Gates said, "Gee, Nick, it's grand to see you here in little old England." Then, seeing the dismay he went on, "Oh shucks, I've got it wrong again."

Two EU colleagues were unfortunate enough to die in post in Dublin. When the Italian died all EU Embassies except the British put their flags at half mast as a sign of mourning and respect. British diplomatic flags fly at half mast only on the express command of the Queen. Nick sought dispensation but did not get it. So he took the flag down altogether. A few weeks later the French Ambassador fell off his horse when out hunting. This time Nick half masted the flag without seeking instructions.

There was a good deal of public diplomacy including after-dinner speeches, newspaper interviews, radio and television. At times of crisis Nick would try to project a calm and sympathetic English voice, commending British policies which were unwelcome to the audience. In quieter times we could just be ourselves, showing that we did not have horns and tails. Nick gave a full half-hour interview on *Hanley's People*. We appeared together on the *Pat Kenny Show*. Sue made her husband proud by becoming the first wife of a British Ambassador ever to be interviewed on Irish television in the Irish language. At a Rotary Club dinner Nick was tipped off that among the guests was a certain John Murray, founder of Murray's Car Hire, from whom we had hired our car on honeymoon thirty years earlier. So he told the story. We had driven the car onto Inch Beach and it

328

had been overtaken by the tide and buried. The delicate question had arisen with Mr Murray whether this was an act of God or the act of a damn fool. After a careful correspondence Mr Murray had declared that he had had no idea that we were on honeymoon. He hoped that we would accept as a belated wedding present the waiver of the debt. Nick understood that Mr Murray was in the audience. If he would care to come to the rostrum he would like to thank him personally. The old man came forward, tears streaming down his face, and we hugged for the cameras.

The annual Horse Show at the Royal Dublin Society was an occasion for the Ambassadors of competing nations, in morning coat and top hat, to lunch with the President of Ireland and to parade with the teams. Nick rather enjoyed this flummery, and the British team sometimes excelled.

We attended the premiere showing of a famous Irish film along with President Paddy Hillery. There was an emotive extradition case at the time. An anti-British demonstration was mounted as we emerged from the show. "Fenn out!" they shouted, "Fenn out!" The President of Ireland said quietly, "Nick, I think they're here for you," and got into his car.

In 1990 President Hillery had run his full term and elections were in train for his successor. The Fianna Fail candidate was Brian Lenihan, Deputy Prime Minister and the most popular politician in Ireland. He would have made a genial President in the traditional mould. He took time out from campaigning to attend the inauguration of a new museum dedicated to the memory of Michael Collins, famous from the independence movement and the civil war. When Nick asked him how things were going he said that he was home and dry, "provided that I can keep my fat mouth shut for another two weeks." Two nights later he was caught telling full frontal lies on television and lost on the second ballot. The candidate of Fine Gail was a latecomer and a northerner. This opened the door to the astonishing success of Mary Robinson. Ireland's chauvinist and conservative society elected a woman and a militant liberal. She

329

said that she would respond to the cry of the poor, promote Irish culture, represent the seventy million Irish diaspora, make Ireland the conscience of the international community and extend the hand of love to both communities in Northern Ireland. "I am of Ireland: come dance with me in Ireland." Irish presidents have minimal powers. But Mary Robinson was a symbol. She stood for integrity in public life, for state above party, for an end to the tribal politics of the civil war, for a new pluralist Ireland, open tolerant, inclusive. Nick commented to London that she had begun a process "which in time will make this country a happier place and a less angular neighbour."

We received a succession of high-level visits. Secretaries of State for Northern Ireland came either bilaterally or for meetings of the Inter Governmental council under the Anglo-Irish Agreement. Tom King had not been involved in the negotiation of the agreement and did not much like it. He soldiered loyally through the meetings. Peter Brooke conveyed a quite different impression. On his first visit the television cameras showed him climbing out of his car outside the Foreign Ministry to shake hands with Gerry Collins, his Irish colleague. It looked for all the world as though he were extending his hand to the Irish nation. "Hello," he said, "I'm Peter Brooke," though everyone in Ireland knew who he was.

Each Minister in the Northern Ireland Office came to consult Irish colleagues about their areas of particular responsibility. Co-operation was possible and necessary on ordinary matters, well beyond the security agenda which caused so much angst. Nicholas Scott came to consult the Irish about the success of their National Lottery. Neil Kinnock, then leader of the Labour Party, came to watch Wales play Ireland for the wooden spoon of the Five Nations Cup. Margaret Thatcher came for the European council in Dublin Castle. Just as we were leaving the Princess Royal came for a horse show, the first member of the royal family to visit in our time, foreshadowing, we hoped, the success of the Queen's visit in 2011.

Family in Ireland is specially valued. Susan's sister Judy lived just south of Dublin and had been uneasy about our posting (Chapter

330

10). But she felt that her four children were missing out having no relatives at hand (their father is from Glasgow). We rejoiced in being only a couple of miles down the road from each other. For our part we benefited from having real family close by to share picnics, Christmas and birthdays, and to escape from diplomatic restraints. We had rumbustious times at Glencairn when we could forget being "Excellencies" and enjoy being Uncle Nick and Auntie Sue. Sue would return their visits alone, lest Nick's escort should attract unwelcome attention amongst the neighbours.

One fine day Sue drove north with Judy and Julia across the border to the beautiful Mountains of Mourne. They had a delightful and uneventful day until the journey home. Sister Judy asked to stop in Newry, the border town, to phone her children to warn them she would be late. Sue parked the car to view the river, leaving the keys in the car. Julia locked and slammed the door. It took nearly two hours to get anyone to unlock it. In the meantime they had to lurk around the car, right in the middle of the dangerous town centre, watching several groups of young squaddies patrolling in their "foursome ballet" with guns at the ready. A reluctant mechanic from a nearby garage eventually released the catch and they hastened to the border crossing. The soldiers who checked us through looked mere schoolboys. On reaching home Sue turned on the radio. Three soldiers on duty at the Newry border crossing had been blown up by the IRA.

We had known Christopher and Jane Ewart-Biggs from the time of our posting to Algiers in 1967. They had preceded us there and gave us a useful briefing. So it was natural to ask Jane to stay with us in Glencairn on her many visits to Dublin in connection with the prize she had established in memory of her husband. Sometimes she said she would stay with us but always backed out. Christopher's assassination had taken place in 1976 a few yards from the entrance to Glencairn. On one occasion, when we still thought she was coming, we noticed with horror that the show house for a new housing estate opposite the residence had been labelled "The Ambassador", exactly by the spot where the bomb had been hidden.

331

Our urgent appeals to the estate agents were heard and understood. But Jane could not face coming back.

In Dublin the St. Patrick's Day Parade was more civilised than in New York. One tired of everything being turned green. Green beer should not taste horrible for a little added colouring but it did. Local characters and celebrities took part in the parade down O'Connel Street. The owner of the biggest supermarket chain, Fergal Quinn, walked beside his big float giving away free samples with panache. We joined the rest of the diplomatic corps on a viewing stand opposite the post office to share the fun. It was embarrassing to be summoned and singled out to sit beside the Lord Mayor, but one could hardly decline so we enjoyed it.

We were invited by the Catholic Archbishop of Dublin to attend a requiem Mass at the pro-cathedral after the Hillsborough disaster in England. Scores of Liverpool fans had been crushed to death or badly injured. It was a terrible tragedy but we were surprised that the church in Ireland should react in this way. We had forgotten the long association between Liverpool and the Republic. When we reached the cathedral we found it and the streets outside crowded with mourners. Inside it was a sea of red and white, the club's colours. During the service souvenirs and trophies were carried up to the altar, a moving tribute and for us a useful lesson.

Nick was under police protection wherever he went. In the Republic security was provided by the Irish police, the Garda Siochana; in Northern Ireland by the Royal Ulster Constabulary, the RUC; and in England by the Special Branch of the Metropolitan Police, the Met. He often had to be in Belfast. It was a two-hour drive. But neither the Garda nor the RUC would escort him to the border. The Garda turned back a mile south of the border; the RUC picked him up a mile north of it – so that for the most dangerous two miles in Ireland he had no protection at all. It became clear that his driver was scared by this anomaly. He foolishly reported it to London in an effort to get the practice changed. The result was that he was forbidden to drive across the border at all. The alternatives were not encouraging. There was a train. But the Garda disembarked at Dundalk and the RUC boarded at Newry; same lacuna. There was no direct air link between Dublin and Belfast. A light aircraft plied between Dublin and Londonderry – but Derry was a long way from Belfast. In the end he found himself taking the scheduled flight from Dublin to Douglas Isle of Man and a connecting flight from Douglas to Belfast City.

We were enjoined to take a few days "security breather" in England six times a year. The Garda would escort us in our own car onto the ferry at Dun Laoghaire. We were met by the Met at Holyhead and asked to drive fast by devious routes to the Holyhead police station where the number plates were changed. Irish plates were thought to be too obtrusive. Thence we could drive to Applecroft, our home in Kent.

But Applecroft too was turned into a fortress. There was bulletproof double glazing on the windows, with anti-bomb blast net curtains inside, security lights, bulletproof doors and an emergency telephone to the local police station. Two features struck us particularly. If anyone poured petrol through the letter box it would be guided by an internal pipe back onto the shoes of the intruder. And there was a lock on the fuel tank. When we came to refill the tank we mislaid the key. The tanker driver rose to the challenge. He unscrewed the air valve and filled the tank from the other end! These elaborate measures have at last paid off. Applecroft still enjoys a local reputation as Fort Knox. We are not troubled by burglars.

One day our son and his fiancée were staying in the house while we were in Ireland. Glancing out of the window one morning Robert saw two men hiding in the bushes across the field in front of the house, pointing now and then at Applecroft. He telephoned the emergency number, woke his fiancée and they climbed over the back fence to take refuge with the neighbours. The police arrived in force. The roads were blocked and the village was cordoned off. In a couple of hours it emerged that the two suspicious characters were plain clothes policemen from the Met. Knowing that we were not in residence, they were scouting around to see from which vantage point a terrorist could approach Applecroft undetected.

Security cast a shadow even over church on Sunday. We were not to establish a pattern so we would choose at the last moment which church to attend. In Dublin it was often St Patrick's Cathedral or our local Church of Ireland church in Tullow. On tour we took pot luck. It might be a vast empty Church of Ireland cathedral where, with our minders, we doubled the congregation. Perhaps the Church of Ireland should give its crumbling ancient churches to the Catholics who would be better able to maintain the national Christian heritage. Weekly Mass was still required of the Catholic population, though "going to Mass" was already a social ritual. We smiled at the crowd of men lurking outside church doors gossiping till the final Amen when they made a dash for the pub. On Saturday afternoons there were big notices outside the churches, "Mass 5.30. Counts for Sunday".

St Patrick's, the National Cathedral of Ireland, is worth mention because of its ancient incongruities. A special stall with the royal coat of arms carved on the back is set aside for the use of "The Viceroy". The British Ambassador is expected to sit in this pew unless the President of Ireland is present, in which case the President sits in the Viceroy's pew and the British Ambassador sits behind him. A British Ambassador in Ireland is conscious that he represents, not just the Queen and her government, but also the Supreme Governor of the Church of England. The Dean would walk in procession before the pew, pause and bow to the secular power. The Ambassador would gravely return the courtesy. In our time the Dean was the saintly and jovial Victor Griffin, a leading spirit in moves towards peace and reconciliation. At the annual Service of Remembrance around 11 November he honoured the dead in the traditional way despite regular hysterical demonstrations against the wearing of the poppy. Nick could never take seriously the passionate antagonism that was aroused by this symbolic flower. He would say to the press, "This is not a Protestant poppy. It is not a British Poppy.

334

It commemorates the dead of two world wars – British and Irish alike."

The Queen's birthday party was of course our National Day. It was also an occasion to demonstrate that Her Majesty the Queen was not a partisan figure, but the Head of State of Ireland's closest neighbour and friend, and that she took no position as between the Irish factions. Nick introduced a practice which is commonplace in some capitals but was new in Ireland. Towards the end of the reception he would call the assembly to order and propose, "Your Excellencies, my lords, ladies and gentlemen, the Queen."

At the QBP in 1990, this time-honoured phrase was quickly echoed by an unmistakeable Irish Republican voice: "The Queen, God Bless Her."

Slightly surprised and rather pleased Nick ploughed on. "Your Excellencies, my lords, ladies and gentlemen, the President."

Same Republican voice: "The President, God help him." It was of course Senator John A Murphy. Progress, of a sort!

When we arrived in Ireland in 1986 we had set ourselves objectives: to make Anglo-Irish relations more ordinary, to build on the East-West relationship so that the two governments could address together the north-south problem left over by history. By the time we left in 1991 some progress had been made – not principally by the embassy in Dublin but by the Northern Ireland political parties and the Northern Ireland Office. As this chapter has shown, progress could not be made in Belfast without keeping Dublin on board. Within a few years the Good Friday agreement would transform Northern Ireland, bringing in time Dr Ian Paisley and Mr Martin McGuinness together in government. Such a notion still seemed like a fairy tale in 1991. It was nevertheless the policy of the British Government to make it possible. Now that it has happened there can be no turning back. There are dissident Irish nationalists still and sporadic terrorist violence will continue for some years. But Ireland

335

will not go back to war. Neither community would follow its leaders if they tried. The way is open to a stronger, more prosperous Ireland, north and south, and a fuller partnership between the UK and the Republic. It was an excitement and a privilege to be part of that endeavour for five years. At last we are beginning to be ordinary.

The Chief Clerk (Head of the Administration of the FCO) came to Dublin in 1990. Nick had five more years to serve and we were beginning to ask ourselves "what next?" Our diverse experience did not fit us for any of the great traditional embassies such as Washington, Paris, Berlin, Moscow. Possibly Peking? Possibly UK Permanent Representative at the United Nations in New York? Perhaps even Hong Kong? The Chief Clerk had a suggestion. What about New Delhi? Nick consulted Sue. We both thought it was the natural answer. Why had we not thought of that before? We had Asian experience in Burma and China. And after Burma and Ireland we were becoming experts in post-colonial trauma. We accepted.

Before we left we wanted to give a small party for the Gardai who had kept us alive over the past five years. We invited them to bring their wives so that we could show them some slides of what we had been up to together. "Oh no, sir," they objected, "we tell our wives how difficult and stressful it is to travel with you. The pictures will show us having fun." But they relented and they came. They presented us with a table lamp in Waterford Glass.

On the morning of 16 August we took the eight forty-five ferry from Dun Laoghaire. Our minders waved us off from the quayside. We waved back. Then we fell into each other's arms. We had loved Ireland. We felt that we had made some small contribution to the improvement both in the Republic and in Northern Ireland. We were sad to leave. But the dominant emotion was relief. After five years it was good not to be Her Majesty's Ambassador in Dublin, not to be under police protection, and not to be under the pressure of wrestling with one of the great unsolved problems. New unsolved problems awaited us on the other side of the world.

Chapter 13
INDIA:
British High Commissioner,
New Delhi 1991–96

India is an exciting country. Our first impressions on arrival in 1991 were of size, diversity and vigour, a fabulous culture confronting formidable problems.

The starting point is the scale of the enterprise. Mercator does not do it justice; larger than the European Union with three times the population. From the mountains and jungles of the neglected north-east to the salt flat deserts of the Rann of Kachchh; from the Himalayan ramparts to the palm fringed shores of Kerala, all the legendary diversity of India is true. The Indian-ness of India is easy to recognise but difficult to define.

There are problems built to scale:

• Poverty – a quarter of a billion people in a state of absolute poverty, more than the whole of Africa and Latin America combined – and a larger middle class than the United States of America. India lives in a village; 75% of its people are villagers. Urban squalor shocks the tourist. More intractable is the unrelenting, grinding, caste-bound poverty of the countryside.

• Second, population – too many Indians, 932 million according to the population clock outside the All-India Institute of Medical Science when we were in Delhi. It increased during our five years by more than the total population of the United Kingdom. It exceeds a billion now and will overtake China by 2025 to become the most populous nation on earth.

- Illiteracy and disease. Of these teeming millions, 50% are illiterate and 5% are crippled or blind – equivalent to the population of England on crutches.

In his address to the nation on Republic Day 1996, President Shankar Dayal Sharma identified the "four great evils" which beset the body politic in India: "communalism, casteism, criminalisation and corruption".

- Communalism. India is 80% Hindu. It is tempting for the leaders of Hindu nationalist parties to exploit religion for political purposes. But India is also the second largest Muslim state in the world, and its 120 million Muslims cannot indefinitely be treated as second-class citizens. As Gandhi and Nehru saw, India is a secular state or it is nothing.

- Casteism. The same is true of caste, the rigid social hierarchy which so baffles foreigners. Politicians who come to power on the votes of one caste must govern in the face of the hostility of others. The political awakening of the lower castes and their exploitation by politicians is a crucial development of recent years.

- Criminalisation. It is commonplace for members of Legislative Assemblies to have criminal records. Politicians boast of the private armies with which they mobilise their votes. The first two acts of a government of one northern state were to repeal the laws against cheating in examinations and against banditry in the state.

- Corruption. We in Britain wring our hands over sleaze and MPs' expenses. Rightly so. But we do not begin to understand how the systematic exploitation of public office for private gain gnaws at the vitals of the body politic. Politicians are corrupt because it is impossible to be elected without breaking the law.

Against the awesome problems must be set the glories of India: the resilience, authority and integrity of the Supreme Court; the activism and determination of the Chief Election Commissioner and the Indian Commission for Human Rights; the contempt of ordinary

338

Indians for corrupt politicians – in spite of widespread cynicism, politicians still fear exposure. The army abhors politics; isolated in its cantonments, loyal to its professional ethos, heterogeneous in recruitment, and preoccupied with its military duties. There will not be a *coup d'etat* in India.

The saving grace is Indian society – tolerant, secular and exuberantly free. The visitor cannot escape the clash of opinions, the strident individuality, the fiercely independent press. Every Indian has his nostrum from which every other Indian dissents. Indian elections need one million polling booths, two million policemen, five million election officials and 750 million voters. Democracy on such a scale is a wonder of the world. Nor is this just the Westminster pattern adopted by choice in 1947. That provides the form. The underlying reality is 2000 years older – Aryan rather than Semitic – in the habit of village elders to settle their differences by interminable discussion. That is the secret of India's unity in diversity and the main ground for confidence in her future.

Since independence India and Britain had enjoyed an ambivalent relationship. After forty years we had not fully escaped from the Raj, nostalgia on the one hand and resentment on the other – a lousy basis for friendship. On the Indian side there was a weight of anti-colonial sentiment and an infinite capacity to blame the British for all the ills of India. On the British side there were assumptions about India that were formed in other times and a tendency to patronise. Yet we had always been friends – or so we told each other. Our long association had given us things in common which we valued – habits of thought and language, parliamentary democracy and the rule of law – culture, cricket and the Commonwealth. But this distant and respectful friendship was tempered by radically different views of the world – NATO and the Non-Aligned Movement – and by frankly scratchy bilateral relations. Then three things happened. The end of the Cold War cut India adrift from her moorings. Uneasy in the presence of a single superpower, India identified the European Union as a possible counterweight, and within the Union she found Britain more intelligible than the others. Then Indian economic reform made India more interesting to Britain. And British economic recovery made Britain more interesting to India. Here were the seeds of something new.

We arrived at a time of turbulence. A few months earlier the new Congress government of Narasimha Rao had faced an economic crisis brought about by inertia and vested interests, by economic mismanagement, political instability, the impact on oil prices of the first Gulf War, the disappearance of the Soviet Union and the collapse of international confidence. The discreet help of the Bank of England during the critical days was not publicly acknowledged but was privately valued. Mr Narasimha Rao was the world's most implausible revolutionary. Instinctively a cautious man, the crisis impelled him to overturn forty years of Nehruvian socialism and open the Indian economy to the outside world. As he said at the time, you don't shilly shally with disaster. This was a test of the fortitude of the Indian leadership, an opportunity to escape from the shackles of post-Imperial dogma. By the same token, it was an opportunity for Britain to escape from its Indian doghouse. The question was whether these opportunities were real or illusory; was the new India fact or fiction?

The British Foreign Secretary, Douglas Hurd, was to visit India six weeks after our arrival to make his own assessment of the economic reforms and to consider with Indian Ministers what sort of relationship between the United Kingdom and India might be appropriate in the new environment. He wanted advice. Nick was instructed to "understand India" quickly and to submit his initial assessment as a contribution to the briefing for the visit. This plunged him into a frenetic round of ministerial calls, diplomatic consultations and urgent discussions with colleagues. His tentative conclusion, submitted to London on 6 January 1992, was that this huge endeavour faced formidable obstacles, that the governing elite was committed to it and that progress was likely, if only because there was no viable alternative. He advised Mr Hurd to congratulate India on the progress of reform, to offer continued British support and to explain our concerns within the framework of economic solidarity.

In the event Douglas Hurd went further. He reviewed the traditional relationship with his Indian colleague and pronounced it inadequate. In its place they instituted a "structured dialogue" under which we should consult each other about all manner of things. He declared at his press conference that "our instincts and our interests begin to run together". This was perhaps not yet quite true, but it set objectives for his new High Commissioner. Douglas Hurd gave us a glimpse of a world in which we could escape from the rancour of post-colonial politics into a mutually profitable economic partnership, where frank discussion on sensitive issues would be normal instead of offensive; Kashmir, Punjab, nuclear matters and human rights. Our job for the following four years would be to make a reality of this vision. Nick's predecessors were summoned to the South Block (Foreign Ministry) to be spanked. Nick was summoned to be consulted. It was different. We were lucky.

A very early call was on Dr Manmohan Singh, then Minister for Finance and now Prime Minister of India. He was a charming Sikh, with a dazzling academic reputation as a socialist economist. He had been brought in to manage the crisis. After the usual courtesies Nick said that he had been reading some of the Minister's published works. The reaction was immediate. "You are accusing me of being a socialist."

"Minister, the word did not cross my lips."

Manmohan Singh leaned forward. "I'll tell you," he said, "I was a socialist. I am a socialist. Anyone with responsibility for a nation with so much poverty must be a socialist. But, High Commissioner, it does not work!" Nick wanted to hug him. The central argument of Indian politics over the next decade, and the central feature of our time there, was whether if you wanted to help the poor of the earth the best way was protection, or whether you had first to generate the resources.

341

It seemed that India in 1991 presented a political and economic opportunity. Perhaps we might rediscover each other. This was the challenge. We shall revert to these matters towards the end of this chapter. First we record our perceptions of India.

The superficial impression of New Delhi was not of new beginnings but of splendid continuity. We admired the India Gate, the Rajpath and the magnificent Lutyens buildings on Government Hill. The presentation of credentials is staged with fine Imperial panache. Nick arrived with the Indian Chief of Protocol in an open coach drawn by four horses. Dressed in morning coat and top hat he inspected an immaculate guard of honour, mounted the grand ceremonial staircase of Rashtrapati Bhavan – residence of the President of India and former palace of the Viceroy – walked in procession down the vaulted corridors until, under the great central dome, he met a kindly old gentleman, exchanged the texts of unspoken ceremonial speeches, delivered his credentials from Her Majesty the Queen and the letters of recall of his predecessor, adjourned to the drawing room where he presented Susan and his senior staff, and had a cup of tea.

The same splendour was displayed on Republic Day in January and at Beating the Retreat on the Rajpath; motionless camels outlined against the setting sun and the incongruous strains of "Abide With Me" from the carillon. All over India we would be greeted by mini guards of honour – formal gestures of friendship and respect. We learned to take them for granted until once at Orchha, an ancient ruined city in central India, Nick made to inspect the guard and was called to order by the lieutenant in charge. "The City of Orchha is under the protection of the God Ram, sir. Only Ram inspects guards of honour in Orchha." He might have told us that before.

The British diplomatic presence in India matched the size of the continent. Together with its three subordinate posts, New Delhi was our second largest diplomatic mission in the world (a long way behind Washington). Nick had a total staff of over 1,000, most of

342

them of course Indians but including over a hundred British. The scale of everything was awesome. But perforce we settled in quickly. No doubt this owed something to our experience as Head of Mission in Rangoon and Dublin – but also to the pressure of events. Our first house guest arrived on the same plane as we did, closely followed by the Secretary of State and then the Prince and Princess of Wales. We had no time to ease ourselves in slowly. We hit the ground running.

The High Commission residence in New Delhi is a magnificent mansion set in spacious gardens in the government quarter, designed as it happens not by Lutyens but by his great rival Baker. It was still known as "2KG" (2 King George's Avenue – now more properly 2 Rajaji Marg). It had been planned as a family home for the then Secretary of the Government of India. We met elderly citizens who remembered playing in the garden with the children of the family before independence. Some British politicians thought it too grand for a civil servant. Our non-British diplomatic colleagues, who mostly lived in purpose-built residences, designed to impress rather than be lived in, were vocally jealous. It was a joy to live there and to be able to entertain hundreds of official houseguests. The staff worked hard to keep the house efficient and welcoming, despite their awesome uniforms with high cockades on their turbans. They were all professionals with high standards and discreet demeanour taking pride in what they did. They told us at the end of our posting that they knew from the start that we would work well together. Sue had shown such patience waiting for the flag to unfurl before taking a first photograph. She had had no idea anyone was watching.

A crucial member of the staff of every Head of Mission is the Social Secretary. Our Nalini was inherited from predecessors. She knew everyone in Delhi and was full of wise advice. Daughter of the famous Field Marshal Cariappa, she came from Coorg in South-Central India where the people look like Greek gods and the women wear a distinctive style of sari in the most brilliant coloured silks. Her immediate colleague was the Comptroller, Delia Macmillan, who ran the house for us. She supervised the rest of the staff and kept an eye on the fabric. She was British but had lived in India many

343

years and understood the culture and how to source the loveliest furnishings for the house. Her taste was impeccable.

The impressive "major domo" Kucheru had served a succession of High Commissioners as Head Bearer. He saw his place as one pace behind Nick's shoulder and wanted to be present on all occasions. He hated the electric bell we introduced at table so that, on the rare occasions we ate alone, he took to lurking just outside the door instead. He was crestfallen if Sue went upstairs for a cardigan instead of asking him to fetch it. He sorted all our laundry putting clean items away every evening, polished our shoes, supervised the mending. Oh, how we missed him when we came to leave India! He was in day-to-day charge of the rest of the residence staff; three other bearers who ferried drinks and waited at table, the cooks, the laundryman, and the sweepers who did the cleaning. For the first years we had two chefs from the Baruha tribe in Bangladesh who are famed for their culinary skills. But when one of them retired he found he was bored so made himself available most days. There were three full-time gardeners (malis) who also did most of the flower arranging around the house and regularly won prizes at the Delhi Flower Show.

When our son brought his family to visit us with his three-month old twin sons we borrowed a highly recommended "nanny" from a family who were on leave. "Vimy" was a great success and we decided to take her on the staff permanently when her current employers were posted elsewhere. It did not seem such a revolutionary notion. We had employed women in other residences, and Vimy liked the idea. The rest of the staff were horrified at the prospect of a female colleague and at first conspired against her. Sue explained to Kucheru that visiting ladies might feel easier with a woman looking after their bedrooms, especially if they were not feeling well. After a month Sue asked Vimy whether she was being treated with proper respect. She replied that her only problem was to get a pass onto the compound for her servant.

We came to know our two drivers, Imtiaz and Daleep, rather well. India is a large place and we spent a lot of time in the car with them. Both were excellent and enthusiastic about looking after and driving the cars. They knew Delhi and much of India well. Imtiaz confessed to Sue when he got her across India two hours early for a train, that he could not allow any other car to be in front of him. Daleep was a wonderful guide for visitors and happy to make huge efforts to show them the sights and help with their shopping. But he was not a clock watcher and would occasionally bring them home late for their next engagement.

The compound was guarded by charming Gurkhas who were smart and smiley and made us feel secure. Morning and evening they climbed onto the roof to keep the Union flag flying. In doing so they must have seen miniature peepul trees taking root in the gutters and crevasses, but they would not touch so holy a tree. Sue took on the job of weeding the roof from time to time.

She was offered a chance to redecorate the house. She decided it all looked fine. A little shabbiness made the place more like a home and less like a hotel. Available funds should be spent on the garden. It is a big garden with beautiful lawns, trees and flower beds. But the swimming pool dominated the view from the terrace, and lunch guests were treated to scenes of daughter Julia and friends disporting themselves in the water. Sue wanted to interrupt this spectacle with Lutyens-style design and features. The story was later circulated that she had redesigned the garden in order to put on Shakespeare plays. Not true. Shakespeare became possible because of the design, but was not the reason for it. Another myth had been born. In fact there were three drama productions in the garden in our time, *Charley's Aunt, The Importance of Being Earnest* and *A Midsummer Night's Dream.* Indian members of the audience knew the Wilde and Shakespeare by heart and complained that Sue had cut some of their favourite lines.

The garden is famous for its birds. There were plenty to keep us busy just learning their names. One of Nick's illustrious

345

predecessors, Malcolm Macdonald, helped us identify species with his beautiful little book *Birds in my Indian Garden*. Peacocks flew in from next door and a kingfisher came to explore the new pools and fountains. We never spotted a golden oriole, but warblers, barbets and sun birds were many and varied. Sadly, the hawks decimated the white doves, vulnerable on their spacious dovecot. Magnificent grey hornbills nested close to our bedroom window, weaver birds joined us for breakfast, babblers squabbled in the shrubberies and parakeets squawked loudly from tree to tree. The vultures were a nuisance because of the bits and pieces of dead animals they dropped all over the garden. One dropped a smelly message near Secretary of State Douglas Hurd as he read his briefs by the swimming pool. A mongoose scuttled round the borders assuring us freedom from snakes. But we were plagued by monkeys. From time to time a troop of langurs would be despatched from the military barracks next door to invade the garden, swing through the trees and destroy everything in its path. Notices in the guest rooms warned visitors to keep the windows closed against them and we had regularly to repair the television aerial, although it was swathed in barbed wire. Baboons liked to sit on the roof and throw things down on us. Sue once interrupted a rehearsal of her current play to borrow the Comptroller's airgun and take potshots at them. For a nasty moment the cast feared she was making a point about their acting. She prided herself on being quite a good shot and often pelted monkeys and vultures in an attempt to drive them off. But they would just shrug and move off, returning all too soon. Perhaps they had poor memories; airgun pellets were not painful enough. Both monkeys and vultures are protected species so we had to endure them.

The main gates of the residence had once been elegant railings but now had fixed sheets of steel to stop bullets. In the monsoon they also stopped the flood waters. Several feet of water around the BHC Office Compound prompted the Administration Office to send us some sandbags. As our gate opened to admit the lorry a tidal wave of muddy water swept across the forecourt, through the front door and across the main reception rooms. The carpets shrank away from the walls. Suction machines removed most of the water but the smell lingered for months.

One wing of the residence was often full of "backpackers", friends of our children and young adventurers from the family. The youngsters were usually sensible. Only one ignored advice and had a bad time in Kashmir. He was forced to swim for his life from a houseboat and found himself in a bus which was ambushed and fired on. Tummy bugs and dehydration were the chief worries.

Pantomimes during the Christmas holidays were staged in the Amenities Hall in the club in the High Commission compound. Sue helped with costumes and make-up and bags of enthusiasm. Our first Christmas we were invited as guests to the UK staff party. Each department produced a sketch based on life and characters within the office – close to home and vulgar. Nick and Sue decided that his "office" should also contribute a sketch in subsequent years. One was based on Mrs.Thatcher and "The Indo-British Partnership Initiative"; one on a recent inspection with digs at every department, and one with digs at ourselves on our plans for retirement.

There was also a Christmas Day tradition involving the trial of the High Commissioner for some alleged misdemeanour. One year it was a complaint that the swimming pool was out of action for too long while being rebuilt. After a "trial" by King Neptune (the Naval Adviser), Nick was punished by immersion in the fountain outside the main entrance. Having learnt from his first experience, Nick explained the scenario to his Indian bodyguards the following year and asked them to pretend to prevent it. They were a bit too realistic. The "pirates" sent by King Neptune to grab the High Commissioner were surprised to be pushed away with real rifles.

Shortly after our arrival, the Defence Adviser, Brigadier Percival, was leaving on retirement. His colleagues laid on a spectacular Indian farewell, culminating in a ceremonial ride around the compound perched on the howda of a richly caparisoned elephant. Nick was invited to "take the salute" on the steps of the office

347

building. He appeared at the appointed time, acknowledged the Brigadier's salutation, and advanced to greet the elephant. It thrust his trunk between his legs, swung him over his shoulder to deposit him neatly beside the Brigadier, and bore them away to the plaudits of the crowd.

All these high jinks took place in the BHC compound, a virtual mini UK. As well as the Chancery offices and barracks for the Gurkhas who protected us, there was a hospital with UK doctor and local nursing staff, a shop for imported goods, a club and bar, a squash court, tennis courts and a swimming pool. Monthly Christian services were held in the Amenities Hall and a bookshop stocked a range of books, cards and gifts. Homes for most of the staff were located here in a mix of detached houses, flats and a couple of delightful courtyard communities, all set in landscaped gardens and surrounded by high walls. The chief complaint of those who lived there was the noise from an adjacent hotel where fashionable weddings were held night after night during the cold season. The real danger of the compound was that it was too successful in recreating mini Britain in India. Why come all the way to India if you never leave the British compound?

A distinctive feature of Delhi hospitality was that the meal was served very late. Drinks were provided for hours – usually whisky for men and sherbets or juice for ladies. At last the hostess would appear, apologise charmingly for the delay and invite us in to the usual buffet. Food was consumed hurriedly and everyone went home. We learned to fit in a couple of receptions before a dinner party. However, for our own dinners, we would start on time, linger over the meal with discussion, political debate and occasionally short speeches. We all adjourned for coffee and a nightcap. Most guests understood our odd British timing. Some may have suspected that we were trying to economise on whisky.

Weddings in India are extravagant and colourful as well as noisy and the ceremonies go on for about a week. Indian families put on a magnificent show in all their finest clothes and dazzling jewellery. It was worth attending just to marvel at the silks and embroidery, the gold and pearls. A step into Bollywood.

One Delhi wedding which sticks in the memory was the marriage of the daughter of friends of ours and the son of a British politician. The bride's parents had insisted that the wedding ceremony be translated from Sanskrit into English so that all the guests could understand it. The bride, a lively lass with a high-powered job in Geneva, swallowed hard before promising to take her husband's buffalo to water. Then she refused point blank when required to adopt all his beliefs and opinions. Stalemate. The marriage could not go ahead. Eventually, with all her fingers extravagantly crossed, she promised and the ceremony proceeded. But afterwards Indian matrons began to complain. They had unwittingly given the same undertakings in Sanskrit at their own marriages years ago, but now were horrified to discover what they had promised.

There was an outbreak of bubonic plague in India. Heads of Mission were briefed by the representative of the World Health Organisation. Thanks to the advances of medical science the plague, which had wrought such havoc in the Middle Ages, was now an easily controllable fever. We should take care over personal hygiene and report to a doctor the first signs of fever or headache when simple drugs would cure us in a day or two. Nick passed on this advice to his colleagues. It tallied precisely with the advice of the High Commission doctor. Most East European and Third World embassies closed their doors and headed for the airport. Western Missions continued business as usual. The press of course did their best to whip up hysteria. The *Daily Mirror* published a front page photograph of an Air India airliner on the tarmac at Heathrow under the banner headline "Plague Plane". Not a single member of the British High Commission left his post. None caught a cold.

Sue always had a go at the language of every country we served in. She managed to pass the first level of the FCO Hindi exam and enjoyed writing the beautiful script. But it was discouraging to find, as we travelled further from the centre, that Hindi was less and less

349

useful. In South India and the North Eastern "Seven Sisters" on the other side of Bangladesh, it was deemed almost an insult to use anything but English. Only in the so-called "cow belt" of the middle Gangetic plain was it the first language. English really is an Indian language. The other languages, which vary from state to state are spoken by millions and read too. There are innumerable newspapers printed in these languages and thriving literatures. A pity so many, especially women, are still not able to read at all. Mind you, one can be too clever. Sue almost made a fool of herself one morning when Kucheru brought her a copy of a Hindi newspaper with her bed tea. She was able to read the headlines which announced that the Indian Prime Minister had resigned. The English language papers reported no such thing. A few discreet phone calls confirmed the suspicion that the city of Lucknow had a tradition of April Fool's pranks. It was April the first and a Lucknow newspaper.

The President of India, Shankar Dayal Sharma, was a noted Hindi scholar but he delivered his inauguration address in English. He was barracked by a backbench MP demanding that he speak in "the national language". The President responded in Hindi, "I will address the nation in Hindi when my brethren in the south ask me to do so." He completed his speech in English, and then delivered it all over again in Hindi.

Sue spent a lot of time working with splendid Indian charities. Her instinct was to roll up her sleeves and scrub floors, but she found that this was not what they wanted from her. They had plenty of manual labour. They wanted high profile visits on their special days for fundraising or prize-giving. She was persuaded that she was more useful bringing in the cameras. So much of our contact with charities around the country was at arm's length. Just occasionally we were allowed to contribute ourselves. One good lunch party for wealthy women at 2KG raised enough money to refurbish an old people's home. At least we experienced the range and variety of projects which were addressing the problems, however daunting. A few examples:

• Mobile Creches provides care and nursing facilities for babies and nursing mothers on building sites where most of the heavy manual work is done by women.

• Child Relief and You (CRY) co-ordinates fundraising and training for children's workers across the board.

• Amar Jyoti works with disabled and deprived children together, with amazing results.

• The Delhi Commonwealth Women's Association operates an impressive hospital with imaginative outreach into some of Delhi's worst slums.

• There are literally hundreds of heart-warming efforts by middle-class women and retired military officers to improve the lot of the poor and disadvantaged.

• The major international organisations are busy as well and we visited many projects run by Oxfam, Christian Aid, Save the Children Fund and Sightsavers International.

• The British aid programme was our largest in the world. We used to build power stations – but this was better done by the private sector. In our day the programme concentrated on primary health care in Orissa, slum development in the big cities and primary education in Andra Pradesh. These allowed us to witness devoted work at the grass roots level.

All this activity left an impression of how much was being done and also how much still needs to be done. Moreover, through our encounters we were privileged to get to know many remarkable human beings all over India.

One Indian friend is a cancer survivor. She has built a team of others who support patients on first diagnosis. The patient's first encounter outside the consulting room is with someone who can say, "I have had cancer, and look at me." This goes a little way to reassure those who hear the diagnosis simply as a death knell. Sue's friend also lectures to women's groups on self-examination for breast cancer, a major advance in public awareness. Other medical friends talk to similar groups about AIDS. Promiscuity is denied by most Indians. A woman asked, "How can I persuade my elderly husband to wear a condom when I am long past child bearing?"

351

A man with a sexually transmitted disease was asked why he went to prostitutes. "I have a wife who is an excellent cook, but I also like to eat out."

There were dozens of Burmese refugees in Delhi – many with dramatic stories to tell of their escape from Myanmar. Sue helped to arrange English classes for the students and sourced funds from *Prospect Burma* for them to learn computer skills and tailoring. The UNHCR gave most of them a small monthly allowance which they pooled. A sympathetic Indian politician lent them premises behind his official residence just round the corner from 2KG where a young Burmese artist had his studio surrounded by political posters. When we left India we gave them a collection of Burmese artefacts – to remind them of home, or to sell if they could. At our farewell party in 1996, the Burmese refugee community agreed to cook Burmese food – for themselves as well as other guests – and we set them up beside the swimming pool. They cannot often afford to drink alcohol and by the end of the evening several had overindulged. But they just smiled even more broadly and giggled happily as they stayed on and helped clear up the garden. They knew the staff and kitchen set-up because one of the events we staged for them was at Thingyan (Water Festival) when they turned up with all their children. They spent a lot of time in the swimming pool with water pistols and plastic buckets to throw water over everyone. They cooked delicious Burmese food. In the afternoon they gave us a performance of Burmese dancing, singing and comedy. It was moving to witness their wit and good humour so far from home.

Sue enjoyed helping distribute "Juggi Jumpers" woollen pullovers knitted in England by WI members for slum children at the start of winter. The wife of the British Council Director, Robina Arbuthnott, sacrificed much of her house to sorting bags of woollens carried out free by British Airways. The jumpers were knitted to a distinctive highly coloured pattern to deter selling on. Once sorted into sizes, with a few discarded as unwearable by any shaped infant, we set off into the Juggis (slums). Police were on standby to deter a riot as

352

children came forward to collect a sweater of approximately the right size. All were eager to don the stripes and return to their parents smiling coyly. The parents would whip the jerseys off the children and send them back for another one. It was all done in good spirits but there was such a demand for these awful garments a stampede was always possible.

There was no lack of culture in Delhi. We attended lectures, concerts, debates and book launches at the India International Centre. The British Council's branches and libraries all over India ran excellent cultural programmes as did other embassies and foreign institutes. We were privileged to meet outstanding Indian actors, painters, architects, dancers, musicians, and writers. One of our favourite haunts was the Crafts Museum. Every month or so different craftsmen could be watched in the demonstration area working with materials brought from their part of India. It was a great place for buying presents. The residence garden began to fill with large clay horses, a beautiful carved Rajasthani dovecot, enormous pots and clay birdbaths, most of which had to be left behind.

The impression of continuity was strengthened by the presence of stayers-on. Bob and Anne Wright presided over the British community in Calcutta and demanded the presence of the High Commissioner to present the Queen Mother's Cup to the winner of the annual horse race. Martin Howard had once been Naval Adviser at the High Commission, then the representative in India of Rolls Royce. He and his wife Annie run a small farm and a splendid B & B south of Delhi and founded the village school.

One unsung privilege of being British High Commissioner in India was to conduct, on behalf of Her Majesty the Queen, investitures for the recipients of British honours who could not conveniently travel to London to receive them. Dressed in the full regalia of a Knight Commander of the Most Distinguished Order of St Michael and St George, one presented the insignia of MBE, sometimes OBE, to people who really deserved them – who had served Britain and India for decades – aid workers and the founders

353

of charities, retired soldiers and poets, long-serving members of the High Commission staff. These were humbling and rewarding occasions. One such was Nalini Cariappa, social secretary to successive High Commissioners. Another was Dora Scarlett.

Dora worked in the villages of Tamil Nadu for fifty years or so. She was over eighty and her health was causing anxiety among her friends. We were delighted to meet her and impressed by what she had achieved. She had been a communist in her youth but was disabused by the Soviet invasion of Hungary in 1956. She moved to India to work for the eradication first of leprosy then of TB. She was now working with village elders and others to improve the lot of women both by education and political empowerment. We readily recommended this formidable lady for an honour. The Deputy High Commissioner in Madras was able to conduct the investiture before she died.

We took Douglas Hurd's instruction to "understand India" as a licence to travel relentlessly to see for ourselves the depth and diversity of the continent in which we worked. Nick claims to be the only person of any nationality to have made a public speech in the English language in every one of India's states (then twenty-five, now twenty-eight). The twin joys of our time in India were the friends we made and the places we visited. It is difficult not to sound like a travel brochure in describing it. Sue wrote detailed journals after all our tours which would be tedious to reproduce here. The alternative is a tiny sketch of some of the more remarkable places and incidents along the way.

Our first travels outside Delhi were to the three Deputy High Commissions in Bombay, Madras and Calcutta (since renamed Mumbai, Chennai and Kolkotta). Built on a narrow isthmus, sticking out into the Arabian Sea and sheltering its superb natural harbour, Bombay is the capital of the State of Maharashtra and the commercial and financial capital of India. We called on the Governor (M A Alexander, wise adviser to successive Indian Prime Ministers), the Chief Minister, the Leader of the Opposition and the leader of

Shiv Sena – disturbing, fanatical Hindu nationalist, Bal Thakeray; on the Governor of the Reserve Bank of India; on leaders of industry and commerce, both Indian and British. Nick spoke at conferences and seminars. Together with the Deputy High Commissioner and his wife, we walked on the splendid sandy beach, dined with tycoons in their sumptuous apartments and visited the appalling slums. In Bombay, more than any other city in India, opulence and penury live side by side. We often came back to Bombay in the following five years to escort British Ministers and promote business opportunities. The city was attacked by Muslim terrorists in 1993. The Stock Exchange was bombed out of its mind on Friday evening and opened for business as usual on Monday morning, and the price of shares went up. That is the way to react to terrorism everywhere and always.

Madras (now Chennai) has a less frenetic atmosphere. Built on a swamp at the mouth of a river and strung out along a superb straight beach where the rolling waves of the Bay of Bengal beat upon the Coromandel Coast, Madras has something of the feel of a seaside resort. It is also the capital of Tamil Nadu, the commercial centre for Southern India and therefore the seat of a British Deputy High Commissioner. Tamil Nadu is the centre of Tamil culture in India and of its characteristically flamboyant Hinduism, famously displayed in the great temple at Madurai. It is a desperately poor state with subsistence fisheries along the coast and subsistence farming in the hinterland. Heroic charities seek to raise living standards and human rights, to ensure the participation in India's democracy of the lower castes and tribes, the excluded Dalits, the villagers and, above all, women.

We visited Kanniyakumari at the southern tip of India to see a British Government fisheries project. Traditionally the men would go out in their dugout canoes and catch the fish overnight and the women would carry them to market in baskets. But the ice would melt in the heat of the day, the fish would drip onto their saris and they would stink of fish so that they were not allowed onto the buses and had to walk, so the fish would deteriorate and fetch a lower

355

price. A simple device was to replace the baskets with aluminium which did not leak. They invited the High Commissioner to carry on his head one of their new aluminium baskets, with predictably disastrous results.

The Chief Minister in our time was the redoubtable lady Jayalalitha, dubbed the Tamil Margaret Thatcher. She was always courteous to us, but she treated her Cabinet and state assembly as vassals and terrified the officials of the Union Government in Delhi with whom she crusaded for the interests of her distant state. Returning in triumph from one such encounter in Delhi, she was met at the airport by her entire Cabinet who prostrated themselves on the tarmac before her. She walked right over them.

The former French colony of Pondicherry is an enclave in Tamil Nadu, famous for its ashram founded by Sri Aurobindo Ghosh and largely funded by his devoted French disciple known as the Mother. We stayed with the French Consul General in his elegant mansion overlooking the ocean, drank excellent French wine and did our best with diplomatic French. The Government of France spends a great deal of money to provide free French language education for all citizens of the territory. We woke to the sound of the sea and opened the shutters to see a typically French garden leading down to the shore where tall palm trees framed the vivid blue sea and sky. Beneath the windows a servant was filling a crate of drinking water bottles from the garden tap. Later we met the British families of the new city of Auroville in one of their comfortable homes. It was designed for people of all races, religions and politics to live together in co-operation. The individuals we met were enthusiastic, intelligent and qualified. They had recently learned to their dismay that their children, though travelling on British passports, would have to compete as foreigners for university places in the UK and pay overseas fees. One of them volunteered to show us round the leafy campus and the spherical meditation centre. Idealism in practice. We wished them well.

The River Cauvery rises in Karnataka and flows across Tamil Nadu into the sea near Madras. Both states are in desperate need of water. A bitter dispute arose between them on the distribution of the Cauvery waters. There are many such disputes all over the world. We were briefed one morning by Jayalalitha, flew to Bangalore at lunchtime and were briefed the same evening by the then Chief Minister of Karnataka, Mr Bangarappa. They might have been discussing different rivers on different planets.

A later Chief Minister of Karnataka, the socialist politician Deve Gowda (later briefly Prime Minister of India) encountered Nick for the first time on a public platform in the state capital, Bangalore. He paused in the middle of his speech and declared, "High Commissioner, do not screw me." It transpired that he knew we lived in Delhi whose policies he conceived as being driven by Washington and regarded us as representatives of the Centre. It was Delhi that was not to screw Mr Deve Gowda, not London.

The other state of the extreme south is Kerala, spectacularly different again. Palm fringed shores, lagoons and backwaters, steep mountains to tea and coffee plantations, it is a tourist paradise with a thriving port at Cochin. It is only 50% Hindu, 25% Muslim, 25% Christian – and 100% literate. You see them on street corners looking over each other's shoulders to read the local newspaper. Tradition has it that the Apostle St Thomas preached at Thiruvananthapuram and founded the Ma Thoma Church when we British were still running about in blue paint. Until recently it had been under communist rule, but was now held precariously for Congress.

We spent a long weekend in a cabin by the beach on the idyllic Indian Ocean islands of Lakshadweep off the coast of Kerala. We were hospitably received by the local collector and enjoyed with him an excellent sea-food supper. He did not seem to have much else to do.

One tour of the south sticks in our memory. Ten cities, ten speeches in ten days. By the end of it Nick collapsed, speechless, feverish and miserable. Sue had to make his speech to the undergraduates at Mangalore in his place. She was able to visit Breek's School where her Uncle Eric Willy, had been a well-loved headmaster for many years. His wife Aunt Dorothy was remembered with affection at Lushington Hall the boarding house where she had presided. Mount Hermon is relatively new and provides boarding education for the children of expats who live all over Asia. It still offers a fundamentalist version of the Christian Gospel. The kids seemed happy. At tea some old boys who remembered the Willy family joined with us to recall "the good old days". We were also taken to visit the extraordinary Toda people who have just about been rescued from extinction. They worship the buffalo, their women have long ringlets even in old age and their distinctive weaving uses only black, red and white threads. A couple of young women have managed to bring the advantages of modern life to the dwindling group, progress in health and education is at last being made and a people who cut themselves off from the outside world are thriving.

In Coorg we stayed in Madikeri in the home of the Cariappa family with the jungle all around. The piercing call of the Whistling Schoolboy woke us each morning. Nalini, our social secretary for our first two years, had by then retired to her roots. She took us to visit her father, the revered Field Marshal Cariappa who was pleased to see we had brought a large bottle of whisky for him. He was the first Indian Commander in Chief of their huge army, and still an imposing figure in his nineties.

Goa has a special fascination. The old city has impressive Roman Catholic basilicas on the square of a quiet little "Portuguese" town. The Chief Minister invited us to tea with his English wife in their charming and modest suburban home. The Governor by contrast is housed in a magnificent residence on a promontory overlooking the harbour. Sue foolishly admired the terracotta animals on the balustrade, and four were delivered to the hotel next morning.

Andhra Pradesh is the sprawling south-central state with its capital in the ancient Muslim city of Hyderabad where much history is gathered. In our day the Congress government was defeated by a Telegu nationalist party. In Delhi there were dire predictions of disaster. In the event Mr Naidhu ran a remarkably tight ship, restored the state's finances, raised the living standards of the poor and began to attract foreign investment to Hyderabad which was second only to Bangalore in bringing "Silicon Valley" to India. In Vijayawada we visited a British charity for street children which ensured that each child learned a practical skill to earn a living – cloth printing or agriculture.

The last of the Deputy High Commissions was at the other end of India in the former Imperial capital of Calcutta (Kolkotta) where the Raj was visible and nostalgia tempting. Raj Bhavan, former residence of the Viceroy and now the home of the Governor of West Bengal, the red brick Writers Building, headquarters of the state government, the cathedral, the Victoria Memorial. But a strange thing has happened. Stand under the dome of the memorial and watch the faces of the crowd gazing at the statue of the young Queen Victoria. No hatred or resentment against imperialism. This is their Queen. Queen Victoria has become a Bengali princess.

The Chief Minister was the veteran communist leader Jyoti Bassu, an English country gentleman in Bengali dress, who talked to us elegantly about Shakespeare and Glyndebourne, about cricket at Lords or racing at Ascot, evading our questions about the politics of the Communist Party of West Bengal. Calcutta was once the prosperous capital of British India. Under communist management since independence it had fallen behind and was now a shadow of its former splendour. But it still has high aspirations which we tried to help them fulfil. Linda Chalker, Minister for Overseas Development, came to Calcutta in 1995. She was the first Minister we have known to conduct a press conference on a municipal garbage dump or to discuss sexual health with prostitutes in the red light district.

A young British banker, Tim Grandage, was so struck by the plight of street children in Calcutta that he resigned his bank commission and founded a superb little charity, Future Hope, which coaxed these cruelly abandoned children into his reproduction of a British boarding school and taught them rugby as well as formal education and useful modern technical skills. Nothing was too good for his large "family".

In the mountains near Kalimpong in West Bengal we visited Dr Graham's Homes, a boarding school, originally for orphans, founded by a redoubtable Scottish Presbyterian in 1901. Its pupils included the children of Himalayan royalty and street children from the slums of Calcutta. They were all treated the same. There was a wide curriculum, but all pupils learned two things well. The first was the English language. The second was integrity. With these two qualifications they could get a job anywhere in India. Friends there advised us to move the Headquarters of the High Commission to Kalimpong close to the Chinese border, where monthly visits could be made to Calcutta and twice a year to Delhi.

Uttar Pradesh was then the largest state in the Union (it has since been sub-divided into three). If it had been an independent state it would have been the sixth most populous nation on earth. There was a strong Muslim community in the capital, Lucknow, but the state was under the control of the Bharatiya Janata (Hindu nationalist) Party. Communal tension was rising in a small town, Ayodhya, where a famous mosque had been built in Moghul times (allegedly and plausibly) on the site of an earlier Hindu temple dedicated to Ram. Hindu nationalists wanted to dismantle the mosque and build a new temple. We visited Lucknow and called on the BJP Chief Minister Mr Kalyam Singh in May 1992, six months before the disaster which struck India on 6 December. (An angry Hindu mob, under openly political leadership, stormed the mosque and provoked communal riots all over India.) Kalyam Singh readily agreed to our request to visit Ayodhya and ensured that we were received there by staunch Hindu nationalists. The local Muslim leadership were confident that the Supreme Court would find in their favour, but if by

360

some mischance it found against them they were in the last analysis loyal citizens of a secular state and would obey the law. The Hindu leadership said that they would obey the court because it would find in their favour, but in the last analysis the god Ram was above the law. To the press we said nothing except that we had come to learn. This did not prevent a critical commentary in *The Pioneer* under the headline "What does the Viceroy think he is doing?" British High Commissioners have to be cautious in India.

We went white-water rafting in the upper reaches of the Ganges. We drifted slowly down the holy waters at Varanasi. We presented a minibus to a primary school. Nick was asked to sit down after the first sentence of his speech because the garlands had arrived. We were belatedly honoured with so many garlands that we could not see over the top. Sue visited women's groups organised by SEWA, an NGO involved in empowering rural women and giving them skills to make money for their families. The traditional chikan work, a cross between *broiderie anglaise* and white on white applique work, sells well all over India and for export. The women in these programmes were doing well financially but worried that the next generation would not bother to learn the skills.

In the hills of Uttar Pradesh near Dehra Dun was a model English public school, a boys' boarding school called The Doon. We visited twice for Speech Day. We might have been in Sussex. Once we coincided with the visit of the Dalai Lama who gave an excellent accessible talk to the boys. One holiday a school party of boys and staff went white-water rafting on a tributary of the Indus which had never been rafted before. The daughter of the master in charge wanted to go, so our daughter Julia went too to keep her company. It was an adventurous undertaking which nearly came to grief before eventually emerging triumphant. On a different visit Julia and another young lady accepted a dare to jump off a suspension bridge some seventy-five feet above the Ganges. Julia could not sit down for a week.

The neighbouring state of Bihar was a disaster area, a byword for corruption and poverty. If you walked down the street of the capital city, Patna, you were dodging sewers, and admiring the ingenious ways in which the citizens had installed illegal connections to the electricity supply. In consequence no one paid for their power, the state electricity board was bankrupt and there was no longer any electricity to steal.

The Chief Minister was Laloo Prasad Yadav, ebullient maverick who presided for years over the collapse of governance in Bihar. He told us that he would be the next Prime Minister of India. Perish the thought. He was colourful, eccentric, cunning and uncouth. A diplomatic colleague had recently called on him and enquired after his upbringing. Laloo took off his sandals and put his feet on the table: "You see, High Commissioner, no toenails. All trodden off by buffalo." He allowed his sons to ride their motorbikes through the wards of the main hospital. They had displaced the staff to live in the doctors' quarters.

We went to Orissa to look at the British Primary Health Care project and to commend the decision of our compatriot, Lord Swraj Paul, to establish a steel plant north of Cuttack near Bhubaneshwar. The wily Chief Minister, Mr Biju Patnaik, had bussed in an enormous crowd of 110,000 to celebrate his success in attracting this substantial British investment. Nick knew that he would not be understood by such a multitude – but Mr Patnaik rose to the occasion and offered his services as interpreter. Nick made his standard "investment" speech. Biju Patnaik translated vigorously. By the wild enthusiasm of the reaction we suspect that he was making some quite different speech.

Beyond the four Deputy High Commissions in Delhi, Bombay, Madras and Calcutta and the trade development office in Bangalore, all over India there were "Consular Correspondents", resident British citizens who were always available to help their compatriots, usually young compatriots, who got into trouble in their area. One story bears repeating because it was unusual. The daughter of Irish friends of ours was travelling in India and they had lost contact. Perhaps she was in residence in an ashram. Her parents had not heard from her for months. The Irish Embassy in Delhi was tiny and did not have the resources to make enquiries. In desperation, the parents telephoned Susan who contacted the consular correspondent. Within two hours the wayward and penitent girl was on the phone to her parents in Dublin. No fuss. No fee. But a family reassured.

Since we lived on the doorstep of Rajasthan we frequently accompanied friends and family round the Golden Triangle of Agra, Fatipur Sikhri, Jaipur and back to Delhi. There was no escape from the tourist crowds at any time of year but it was still worthwhile. The Taj Mahal, graceful tribute of the Maharaja to his wife, enchants equally at dawn and by moonlight. Perhaps a cow pulls an ancient lawnmower and then eats the cuttings; a wife at a family picnic applies henna to her centre parting – sign of her married status; bored Western youths are struck dumb by the magical white tomb that greets them as they come through the archway. Sue was just out of the picture for the iconic portrait of Diana, Princess of Wales, in 1992.

When son Robert brought his first wife Michelle to visit from New York we decided the only way to show them the romantic India was a week on the "Maharaja's Train". Nights in great comfort on board and each day a new wonder to enjoy.

We drove out to the edge of the Rajasthani desert with friends to spend a night in the splendidly restored palace of Neemrana. Gazing out through the dust and smoke of the evening fires of the village to watch a golden sunset is an enduring memory. Sue took her friend and former colleague, Carolyn Macginnis, there to begin a quick tour of the Shekhavati district where the walls of the villages are covered with the most beautiful and amusing paintings already fading with neglect. The Marwari merchant families were patrons of the arts as well as financial advisers to many Maharajas. It is said much of the decoration on inner walls was simply to amuse their womenfolk who were not allowed to go out. That trip is memorable for the disaster

363

we met in Bikaneer. The hotel had never heard of us. Our arrival coincided with the popular camel fair at Pushkar and hotels for miles around were bursting. Daleep, ever resourceful, persuaded the hostel for Indian civil servants to give us a room. It was not quite the filthiest room we ever saw, but trays of dirty dishes and uneaten food encouraged us to leave as soon as possible next morning.

On a tour of Gujarat we stayed with an ancient Maharaja. His barns were filled with vintage Rolls Royces and the reception rooms with stuffed animals. The carpets crunched as we made our way into dinner on layers of plaster from the ceiling. Over the meal the family quarrelled about serving us alcohol, forbidden in the state. The women had been brought from their seclusion in the Zenana. They were as elegant, sophisticated and polished as any actress in a Noel Coward play. The food, mock Western laced with more ceiling plaster, was barely edible. We were put up in the nearby visitors' palace, unchanged since 1920.

In another city of Gujarat we held a reception for British passport holders. We met Mr and Mrs Patel, Mr and Mrs Patel, Mr and Mrs Patel, on and on all evening. They were all delightful.

From there we explored Katchchh guided by the exemplary Collector of Bujh. Passionate about his patch, he took us on a tour of the Banni villages and introduced us to the women, magnificent in their brilliant dresses, sitting like a bed of flowers outside their round whitewashed homes. They gossiped happily and worked away at colourful embroidery and mirror work to sell. He described his job. "Last week I was organising drought relief, today I am bringing in helicopters to rescue the people from floods. Such is the life of the Collector of Bujh." We fell in love with him, his family and his district. His books are beautiful.

In Madhya Pradesh the Chief Minister educated us in the mysteries of government and elections. He was a model of old-fashioned courtesy, clarity of exposition and love for his state. It was refreshing to meet civil servants and politicians who loved their work and seemed to have contempt for the corruption and venality surrounding them. Others were such obvious rogues one almost forgave them.

At Bhopal Eye Hospital we were told again about the appalling tragedy which overtook the city and surroundings in 1984. The explosion at the Union Carbide factory has blighted the city ever since. There was no progress in securing compensation for the thousands who suffered. In Khanha Park we stayed at Kipling Camp and enjoyed swimming in the river with Tara, a young elephant. We rose early to look for tiger. The park in the misty dawn was enchanting – and we did hear a tiger munching his kill in bushes beside the track.

We enjoyed the romance of the vast ruined palaces of Mandu. The white dome of the Buddhist temple at Sanchi thrilled us with its exquisite ancient sculptures, the work of ivory carvers. Orchha was fun with an intriguing history – if one believes it. The fort and palaces of Gwalior had something of everything, enormous chandeliers, towering fortress walls and a charming little chapel where we picnicked.

Further south we stayed as guests of a fertiliser factory in order to have time to explore Hampi. There is too much to see properly and more is being discovered every year. The lazy little Tungabhadra river slides among the ruined temples and palaces. The Queen's Bathing Palace, a vast water tank and images, and innumerable temples reminded us a little of Pagan in Burma.

The tiny Himalayan Kingdom of Sikkim could not be missed. Two trees planted in the Botanical Garden in Gangtok commemorate our visit. The monasteries are perched on shoulders of mountains, secluded and spectacular. The buildings in the capital have two legs on terra firma and the others on long stilts above precipitous valleys. It was better not to think about it.

From Sikkim to Darjeeling there were two routes, one long and sensible, the other short and crazy. We took the latter. The bridge had few planks left so Imtiaz crossed it at full speed with his eyes shut, reciting the Koran. The steep, single track upwards was only wide enough for jeeps but we raced up all the hairpin bends. The police waiting for us at the hotel were worried. They could not believe we had come up the hill on such a road. Darjeeling boasts a wonderful old-style hotel named the Windamere (sic). We were warmly welcomed by the elderly proprietor, Madame Tendafla. There are coal fires in the bedrooms and compulsory six-course dinners. There is a notice on the toilet: "Will clients please note that this water closet has been serving mankind since the year 1926". And on the dressing table: "If you lose a button, call for Kimche: there will be no charge: she sews for love".

The crossing from West Bengal to the "Seven Sister" states the other side of Bangladesh was dangerous. Inner Line passes are still required. It is another country. They feel neglected. We enjoyed tea estates in Assam where wild elephants do much damage. Burma Oil was first produced here at Digboy. It still is.

The Chief Minister welcomed us to Itanagar, capital of Arunachal Pradesh. "This is a dry state because the Brahmins in Delhi think we tribals cannot hold our liquor. High Commissioner, will you join me in a Scotch?" He gave a party for us and dressed us all in local costume. We had to sample rival rice wines made by the wives of each of his Ministers, and to judge which was the best.

At Imphal in Manipur we noticed the signpost to Mandalay and had a weird sense of homecoming. Local tradition claims that the game of polo originated in Manipur. They presented us with a polo stick. The head is at an acute angle to the handle so the players can hook each other's sticks during play. It is displayed in our Kent oast house beside another trophy, a Naga spear.

Mizoram is one hundred per cent Christian and one hundred per cent literate. They told us that they were celebrating the centenary of

366

the Gospel. Oh yes, one hundred years since the arrival in Aizawl of the Rev Wilfred Jones. They were all Welsh Presbyterians with accents to prove it. They had arranged in our honour a concert of local music. It began with the Halleluia Chorus. The villages are strung along parallel ridges where bananas grow in abundance. The deep valleys are full of malarial swamps so no one lives there. There were similarities with Burma here too, in architecture and dress. Many refugees arrive across the border.

We could not drive to Agartala, capital of Tripura, because of unspecified bandits on the road. We flew in a tiny Cessna plane. The culture there seems entirely Indian. The shrines beside the road under holy banyan trees, the food, the dress, the language – all far removed from the rest of the Seven Sisters. We were taken to a model farm from where we looked west and down onto a train chuffing along in Bangladesh.

So to Meghalaya, the "Scotland" of India, to a hotel which might have been in Darjeeling with brass bedsteads reflecting the flames of an open fire, and lovely pine trees, green grass, lakes and flowering shrubs. We did not manage to visit "the wettest place in the world" where a fine mist falls when it is not pouring with rain. It was not a huge disappointment. The daily flight to the rest of the world had been delayed in Calcutta. If we did not catch it we would have been stranded. It emphasised the isolation of these distant states. The train down in the valley takes days to reach West Bengal.

In Kohima, capital of Nagaland, they prepared separate programmes for the High Commissioner and his ladies. It provided for Julia, aged seventeen, to address a gathering of 1,400 schoolgirls. Without a moment for thought or preparation, Sue counselled Julia to tell the girls why she was there and her plans for the future. It was enough. Sue was equally caught out. Doors were thrown open in the Naga Hospital to reveal the entire staff assembled to hear her speech. One does one's best. Nick's challenge was different. They gave a tea party for us in the Old City of Kohima. A gentleman with hornbill feathers in his hair made a speech denouncing our government for betraying the Nagas to the Indians in 1947. Then another gentleman with feathers in his hair made a speech denouncing us for not denouncing our government for betraying the Nagas to the Indians in 1947. Nick had to reply. He said that it was fifty years too late to address a representative of his government on such a question. It was a matter for the elected government of the Republic of India. As for armed resistance, the speakers may have heard that we had a problem with terrorism in Northern Ireland, they could hardly expect a representative of the British Government to countenance rebellion. And by the way, he had brought 250 books from the British council for presentation to their library. Everyone applauded, enjoyed the tea and we all went home. But the headline in the *Nagaland Banner* the following morning was "Great Britain, great betrayal". You cannot win them all.

A year later we returned to commemorate the fiftieth anniversary of the Battle of Kohima in 1944 when the might of Imperial Japan had confronted the might of Imperial India across the Deputy Commissioner's tennis court and slaughtered each other in their thousands. It was a turning point of the Second World War – now almost forgotten. The outcome was that Japan did not invade India. Down the shoulder of the mountain from the tennis court is the Commonwealth War Grave Cemetery, with the famous inscription at the bottom: "Stranger tell them of us and say, For their tomorrow we gave our today". The Ministry of Defence flew out two planeloads of veterans of the battle, including several widows who were confronted with their husbands' graves after fifty years. Pretty emotional stuff. We climbed the hill slowly because every rock and every palm tree had a story to tell and the veterans would tell it. The Naga veterans came down from the mountains with their British campaign medals on their tunics and embraced their comrades in arms after half a century. Then we stood to attention for the Last Post.

After the ceremony, Nick and his reluctant Defence Adviser slipped away to lay a wreath also at the Japanese War Memorial. We invited the veterans to come with us, but none of them would. We may have caused offence. Perhaps it was too soon. But there must

368

come a time to address the future as well as the past. When Nick sent a photograph of this to his Japanese colleague in Delhi, Ambassador Yamada wept.

The same thought inspired a change we tried to make to the commemoration of Remembrance Day at the Commonwealth War Grave Cemetery in Delhi. In 1947 the new Government of India – perhaps foreseeing future sensitivities – left the organisation of Remembrance Day in the hands of the British High Commissioner. The tradition we inherited was that we invited the wartime allies and Commonwealth High Commissioners and of course the Government of India. So the Russians and the Chinese came, but the Germans, Italians, Spanish, Portuguese and Japanese did not. This seemed to us a bit odd in modern terms. So Nick took soundings. The Foreign and Commonwealth Office said this was a matter exclusively for the High Commissioner in Delhi. The Government of India declined to offer advice. The Dutch Ambassador said that if we invited the Germans, he would not come. The Australian High Commissioner said that if we invited the Japanese he would not be allowed by his government to come. One of his colleagues had been sacked the previous year for attending such a ceremony. So we said nothing and let the anachronistic arrangement stand for another two years. Then, in our last year, when the two colleagues in question had moved on, we changed it without consulting anyone. We invited the entire diplomatic corps. The Dean, His Excellency the Ambassador of Senegal in his fine white robes, presented a single wreath with great *élan* on behalf of us all, and everyone went home happy.

The Andaman and Nicobar Islands lie in the Indian Ocean closer to Burma, Thailand or Malaysia than to India, a two-hour flight from either Calcutta or Madras, but are part of the Republic of India. They are memorable for several different reasons:

- The capital, Port Blair, lies at the southern end of South Andaman Island. Just offshore is Ross Island which was the British Naval Headquarters before the Second World War. It was abandoned in face of the advancing Japanese and never reoccupied. So the

369

jungle took over. It lifted the Officers' Mess and the Presbyterian Church some yards off the ground before the buildings crumbled – and now only the roots of the plants outline the shape of the Church, the Mess and other public buildings raised high against the sky.

•   The colonial authorities used the Andamans as a place of exile for political prisoners. We were taken to see the notorious Cellular Gaol – Kalapani – and shown a partisan *son et lumiere.* Quite good for a British representative to come to terms also with this part of our common heritage. Then we discovered that the most notorious Governor of the gaol had been an Irishman and were able to claim that he was nothing to do with us.

•   The islands are known as mini-India because the tribes and religions live together without communal tension. They intermarry. We were told that their grandfathers had been interned, and when they were released they were so enchanted by the islands that they decided to stay.

•   Two of the islands are still inhabited by naked, negroid, Stone Age savages who do not know how to make fire. If you land on their beach they shoot you with poisoned arrows, so on the whole people do not land on their beach. Once a year the Department of Anthropology and Archaeology come in a fast speedboat, leap onto the beach, leave behind a large box of goodies and jump back on board. The natives watch the 747s going overhead. What do they make of them? And what does the Republic of India do with these of its citizens?

•   The islands are the only part of India that is administered by the Indian navy. The Admiral invited us to picnic from his launch on another island which he swore was uninhabited. Nick was snorkelling in the shallows and was slightly irritated to be tapped on the shoulder. It was a naval rating, up to his knees in the sea, holding a silver salver. "I thought you might like a cold beer, sir."

Nick went to Punjab to see the Golden Temple in Amritsar, the holiest of Sikh shrines. In those days there was a Sikh insurrection in Punjab and a very tough Chief Minister in the state capital, Chandigarh, the late Mr Beant Singh, and an even tougher Chief of Police Mr KPS Gill. Their policy for the Punjab consisted of two

370

elements: security and development. Not a word about reconciliation, not in their vocabulary. A two-dimensional policy is bound to fail, we thought. Two years later we called on them again and had to congratulate them on the signal success of this policy. Who thinks of the Punjab in India as a problem now? The tough guys won.

The border with Pakistan is at Wagga between Amritsar and Lahore. There is impeccable competitive drill as the flags are raised at dawn and lowered at dusk. The two military detachments march towards each other, scowling fiercely, and when they are about one foot apart they about turn and march away again. We discovered that only forty-two people a day cross that border. Two great Asian neighbours stand with their backs to each other. The striking cultural identity of Lahore and Agra made more poignant the things said to us in Islamabad by Pakistanis recalling their happy childhoods in Lucknow or Hyderabad.

Nick visited Islamabad at the invitation of the High Commissioner there, Sir Nicholas Barrington. We each had to report different stories to London. We were both determined that, whatever the tensions between India and Pakistan, the two of us would not fall out over them. We were professionals serving the same government. Nicholas knew a great deal about the tribes of Afghanistan and northern Pakistan. He took Nick to Peshawar and to the market there; the vegetable stall, the hardware stall, the AK47 stall. We went up the Khyber Pass and stood on the top looking down into Afghanistan. Nick understood some of the difficulties faced by any government in Islamabad.

Special mention must be made of Bhutan, a Buddhist Himalayan kingdom of stunning natural beauty lying north of Calcutta between Sikkim and Arunachel Pradesh. We have no diplomatic relations, but the British and Bhutanese representatives in Delhi are appointed by the two governments as the channel for communication between them. When Nick first called on the Ambassador of Bhutan he asked, innocent like, how it came about that two countries with such excellent friendship did not enjoy diplomatic relations. The

371

Ambassador replied, "Some time ago the foreign relations of His Majesty the King of Bhutan were conducted on His Majesty's behalf by a certain great power. That great power advised His Majesty never to have diplomatic relations with Great Powers. His Majesty has accepted that advice." The original advice was of course tendered by British India to prevent the accreditation in Thimpu of a Chinese Ambassador. The role has been inherited by India, who maintains the advice for the same reason. But Bhutan can hardly pick and choose between permanent members of the Security Council. So no British Embassy in Thimpu either. The only foreign powers represented there are India, which has an immense gubernatorial embassy, and Bangladesh. The King of Bhutan makes up for this by inviting each successive British High Commissioner in India to visit Bhutan as his personal guest. It is the best way to go.

We flew into Paro, the only airport in the kingdom, and on by car to Thimpu. It is another world. Narrow fertile valleys between towering mountains, everyone dressed in national costume, all buildings conforming to the national standard and tiny villages huddled beneath enormous stone dzongs (temples and administrative centres). We stayed in great comfort in a royal guest house and were shown the principal sights by a member of the King's household. We called successively on the Minister for Foreign Affairs, who was charming and urbane, the Minister for Education (because HMG was building a new Secondary School at Paro) and the Minister for Trade. Nick asked him how he should reply if a British businessman in Delhi enquired how he should pursue trade with Bhutan. The Minister's response put an end to the conversation. "High Commissioner, you have not understood. I am the Minister for Trade. That means that my job is to *prevent* trade between the Kingdom of Bhutan and other countries."

A year earlier, HM The King had suddenly decreed that, with effect from the following September, all instruction in schools in Bhutan should be in the medium of the English language. Panic in the Department of Education. Our predecessor had put them in touch with Voluntary Service Overseas and thirty-two young British teachers were teaching the teachers all over Bhutan. We attended their annual conference in Thimpu. One young lady had taken four days to get to the capital – three days walking in the forests and one day in a jeep. All of them seemed to be enjoying their unusual lives. The programme to teach in English began on time.

The highlight of our visit was our call on the King. He had been brought home early from his school in Surrey to inherit the throne of a mediaeval mountain kingdom and was trying to bring it into the twentieth century in the space of a generation. Not an easy task. He had invented a parliament but everyone wanted to vote for the King. He received us warmly and an audience which was scheduled to last twenty minutes went on for an hour and a half. He seemed to value an interlocutor who, though elaborately respectful, was not a sycophant, would tender honest opinions and even on occasion express disagreement.

At the end of our stay we invited our new Bhutanese friends to a party at the government guest house. We had brought a case of whisky with us. But we were advised that, good Buddhists though they were, the Bhutanese drank brandy. Excellent cognac was available at the royal shop – at a price. Since we had no diplomatic relations we were not spared the punitive import duty. The party was a huge success, and it consumed our entertainment allowance for the following three months.

There was only one significant international issue involving Bhutan in our time – immigration from Nepal, another Buddhist Himalayan kingdom to the west, separated from Bhutan only by the tiny Indian state of Sikkim. We remembered the time when Bhutan had joined the United Nations in 1971. The organisation had been discussing the question of micro states. There was a proposal (now long abandoned) that to qualify for membership of the UN a state should have a minimum population of 1 million. So the King of Bhutan declared his population to be 1.2 million – and no one knew enough to contradict him. Then they had a census and discovered that the population was only 800,000. Ten years later another census

373

reported that the population was indeed 1.2 million, but it had grown not by Bhutanese reproduction but almost entirely by immigration from overpopulated Nepal. One third of the population were Nepali – a clear majority in the three southern counties. There was fear that Bhutan's distinctive culture would be overwhelmed. In response the King decreed that everyone resident in Bhutan at the date of his decree was a Bhutanese citizen, and would be issued with a certificate of citizenship to prove it. At the same time the borders were closed. Any further immigration was illegal. Still they came. A few years later a Royal Commission was established to tour the southern counties. There were 200,000 Nepali peasants who had failed to produce Bhutanese certificates of citizenship and were expelled with some brutality. They took refuge in UN Refugee camps in south-eastern Nepal. There were demonstrations in the streets of Kathmandu, and Nepal complained bitterly to the UN that Bhutan was infringing the human rights of its people. Bhutan replied that like any other sovereign state it had the right to determine and enforce its own citizenship laws, and to protect its unique culture from being swamped. The stand-off continues to this day.

Outside Thimpu there was almost no electricity in Bhutan, but a multitude of torrential mountain streams. The obvious answer was hydro, but Bhutan did not want big dams and hydro-electric power stations. India by contrast was energy hungry. The King negotiated with an Indian company to manufacture and install a hundred mini-hydros – steel cylinders that looked like torpedoes. Dropped into mountain streams, these cylinders generated modest quantities of electricity. Within a year, even the remotest village in the kingdom had at least one light bulb. They called it "The King's Light". The Indians also built one large conventional hydro-electric station on the road near the border town of Phuntsholing. Some of the electricity generated here was diverted to India to pay for the torpedoes. India got power: Bhutan got free electricity.

On a later visit to Bhutan we were accompanied by a remarkable young lady. Nicola Naylor was an aromatherapist. She came to India to meet the gurus of her craft in Southern India – Bombay and Pune,

374

Madras and Pondicherry. When she had finished her professional journey she set off alone backpacking around South India – Cochin, Coimbatore, Mysore, Bangalore. This may not seem unusual until we explain that Nicola is totally blind. An Indian friend telephoned us from Coorg to ask if we would meet her off the plane and put her up for a few days in Delhi. She wanted to go trekking in the Himalayas. We tried to dissuade her. We took her white-water rafting in the Ganges instead and she came with us to Bhutan. Then she went trekking anyway.

This last visit to the kingdom was overshadowed by the British hostage crisis in Kashmir (see below). Nick came briefly to pay valedictory calls in Thimpu, but he flew in separately from Calcutta and returned to Delhi as soon as he decently could. Sue and Nicola drove in from Darjeeling across bandit country with a driver from the Deputy High Commission. Once down from the hills the drive is mostly through tea gardens and looks peaceful. But it has to cross the bandit lands where Bodo gangs press their political demands with bombs and kidnappings. It was here that the Land Rover Discovery broke down. The driver coaxed it into a village as the daylight faded. Sue and Nicola held torches to light the engine as a young lad took over the repairs. Across the street heavy goods vehicles were forming protective squares to sit out the hours of darkness. As sentries took up positions on the lorries we paid and thanked the lad for his efforts and slowly drove out into a pitch-dark no man's land. It was a tense couple of hours before we finally pulled into the courtyard of the hotel at Phuntsholing on the Bhutan-Indian border. There had been frantic telephone calls with Delhi, but now, near midnight, a reassuring call was possible. We had arrived. All was well.

The King's staff had organised a wonderful farewell trip right across the country, staying at royal guest houses in "fairy tale" locations. They were disappointed by Nick's decision to leave. So Sue and Nicola willingly volunteered to go on alone. Early rains had washed away many roads, and after an unplanned overnight stop at a guest house at Tongsa, Nicola and Sue were given a privileged tour of the magnificent monastery there. The novice tutor cradled a formidable cat-o'-nine-tails. Then in order to continue the journey the two of them had to clamber across a landslide which had destroyed a hundred metres of the road. Nicola was carried over piggyback by our guide. We journeyed on to Bumtang in a locally hired pick-up truck (in the company of a monk who silently climbed aboard) and waited for the Land Rover to catch us up. The welcoming royal guest house was decorated in vibrant reds, yellows and oranges. As we walked down the village street that evening the local chief, Dzongda or District Commissioner, came to meet us. He had been clearing out the pool which fed the hydro-electric generator which was temporarily blocked with mud. He had invited voluntary labour from each house. If they wanted any more electricity they must send someone to help with the cleaning. He was confident all would be well. Sure enough, one after another the lights came on as we strolled down the single street. He took us to the local shop-cum-wine bar where we drank the local apple juice and bought some cheese and honey. The guest house had lights and heaters on when we returned. It was wonderfully comfortable and quite enchanting. The next day was planned by the Dzongpa who came everywhere with us – a diligent and charming host. After a long day visiting all the monasteries and other sights we found a stone bath prepared for us beside the river. Stars shone brightly on the rushing water as we soaked in deep wooden troughs filled with water at just the perfect temperature. There is a partition at one end of the trough with several holes allowing the water to circulate freely throughout. Stones heated in a fire on the shore, when immersed in the water at the end of the bath, seem to keep the water at a perfect temperature almost indefinitely. Only growling stomachs persuaded us to dress and go inside for supper. Next day Anthony the driver managed to catch up with us, none the worse for the adventure. Sadly we left the Bumtang valley early next morning for a ten-hour drive to Tashigang. The roads were terrifying and spectacularly beautiful, taxing Suc's vocabulary to describe them for Nicola. We stopped at another royal guest house at Mongar to eat our picnic facing green valleys and snow-capped mountains, just like a holiday postcard from Switzerland. Our last night was spent in a guest house that was just as colourful as all the others, and we were spoiled with diligent attention and another huge meal.

On our final day we visited a school for blind children (very old-fashioned according to Nicola) and a textile museum where samples of all the thousands of traditional weaving patterns are preserved. At the border town of Jonkar the Indian army had been instructed to look after us and we enjoyed more comfort and privilege. We even had our own batman for the evening. Brigadier and Mrs. Ranjit could not have been better hosts in their spacious bungalow overlooking the plains of Assam.

The final drive was again through bandit country. Our Land Rover was escorted at speed all the way to Guwahati, capital of Assam. We stopped only once when the pilot-jeep's radiator started to boil and water from a stream was used to top it up. This extraordinary journey was one of the happiest and most frightening of Sue's experience. What a pity Nick had to miss it and Nicola could not see it.

A feature of our life in India was the large number of official visitors, which multiplied as the Indo-British relationship prospered. Our residence with its incomparable staff was busy almost every day with a lunch, a dinner or a reception, and had resident house guests more often than not keeping Nalini's successor, Nita Singh, very busy. In our last full year, 1995, there were thirty-six official visitors, including sixteen Ministers, four members of the royal family, former Prime Minister Baroness Thatcher, former Speaker of the House of Commons Baroness Boothroyd, the Lord Mayor of London and the Archbishop of Canterbury. A few visits will convey the flavour.

We had been in post for only three months when TRH The Prince and Princess of Wales came on an official visit. Their marriage was already under strain, but both performed superbly in public. Those who knew of this visit only from the British press would know three things about it: that he sent Princess Diana to the Taj Mahal alone when a decade earlier he had promised to bring his bride, that when he tried to kiss her on the polo field at Jaipur he missed because she turned her head away at the last moment, and when she had her marvellous day with Mother Teresa's people in Calcutta he did not bother but went trekking in Nepal. All these things are true. But they omit fifty public engagements, alone and together, in six Indian states in five days, each one of them a wow. The Indian press, sceptical in advance, reported the visit with mounting incredulity as a great success. The British press was interested only in the signs of tension between them. Indian newspapers began to pick up the reporting from London and to replay it, wondering if they had been taken for a ride. But by the end of the visit they had learned to ignore the prurient sensationalism of their British colleagues and to report straightforwardly what they saw and heard – the heir to the British throne and his beautiful wife touring India, admiring what they saw, speaking sensibly in measured tones about the Indo-British relationship and enjoying themselves. One up for India.

There was one intrinsic oddity. The Prince and Princess of Wales were instantly recognised all over the world. Almost no one in India knew the new High Commissioner and his lady. Of course we had to give a splendid reception for the royal couple, although we hardly knew our own staff, let alone our guests. So we corralled the guests in designated groups in a huge tent with a route amongst them marked with garlands of marigolds. There was one group for diplomats, another for Indian royals, a big group of British business people and expats, another of journalists, of Indian politicians, of NGO representatives, of musicians and authors, academics and so on. Nick led Prince Charles clockwise round the guests and Sue led Princess Diana anti-clockwise. Members of staff were stationed at each pen. We presented them and they in turn presented selected members of their group. It was an outrageous way to treat a guest and a few objected to being herded. But TRH of course charmed everyone and they were able to meet a real cross-section of Delhi society. During the reception a group of Rajasthani musicians played soothing music. From there we moved on to dinner with the Prime Minister in his freezing, foggy garden. The reception was hard work for all concerned, yet, in the end, seemed to be enjoyed by staff and guests alike. We did not fluff our introductions because we had to remember the names only of our own staff.

The Princess Royal came to Ladakh for Save the Children Fund of which she is President. She knew more about the Leh Nutrition Project than the Ladakhis knew. When you fly into Leh at 10,000 feet you are advised to spend twenty-four hours flat on your back to adjust to the altitude. Tell that to the Princess Royal. She is not that kind of gal. She went straight into her programme with her High Commissioner panting in her wake. We drank yak's milk rancid butter tea out of silver goblets with the Queen Mother of Ladakh and her newly crowned son. We camped at a place called Gya at 14,000 feet. We had little tents. Princess Anne had a royal pavilion from the Field of the Cloth of Gold with a reception room, a bedroom and a bathroom – with hot and cold running water thanks to a guy halfway up the mountain with an oil drum full of water and a fire beneath it in case HRH should want to wash her hands. That's hospitality. The next day she was greeted at a nomad encampment at 17,000 feet by a hundred horsemen with white scarves of greeting in their hands and grins from ear to ear as they galloped beside her Land Rover. They were expressing their gratitude to the princess for installing their new water pipe which enabled them to maintain their high grazing for two more months each year.

Princess Alexandra came to India as Patron of Sightsavers International. There are fifteen million blind people in India, 75% of them can be cured. That is eleven million miracles waiting to happen at £20 a throw. Alexandra toured the country opening eye hospitals, watching cataract operations, visiting projects, making speeches. With some trepidation she also ventured into some of the more exuberant temples in South India. She gave valuable support to her excellent cause.

Michael Howard came as Secretary of State for the Environment to develop an international environment initiative with his Indian colleague. The Indian Minister gave a private dinner at his home

379

with his telephone on the table, explaining to Mr Howard that he was orchestrating a political *coup d'etat* against the Indian Prime Minister, Mr Narasimha Rao. The coup failed, but it led to the resignation of a senior Cabinet Minister, Mr Arjun Singh.

We had come to India in 1991 with the notion that the economic crisis presented a political and economic opportunity. After forty years of professed friendship and mutual exasperation, perhaps this was a chance to rediscover each other. The idea was simply expressed by a visiting British Minister: "An Indian is the only person on earth who can buy from a Scot and sell to a Jew and still make a profit." If we could only get out from the shadow of the Raj and into a sensible economic partnership, all sorts of things might become possible that had not been possible before.

The opportunity depended crucially upon Indian economic reform. This enterprise faced formidable obstacles such as political instinct, bureaucratic lethargy, industrial vested interests, public sector unemployment, inflation, poverty, population and corruption. That it succeeded was due to the courage of two men, Prime Minister Narasimha Rao and Finance Minister Manmohan Singh, to the intellectual tenacity of a few senior civil servants, to India's innate entrepreneurial spirit and above all to the gravity of the catastrophe that provoked it and the fact that there was no viable alternative. Good progress was already made in our time. The licence Raj dismantled, the rupee convertible, foreign investment welcome, the economy opened to the outside world. There was still a massive agenda but the die was cast. The year 1991 had proved to be a watershed and the reforms were irreversible.

Indians began to claim that there was an ideological consensus in favour of reform. In May 1995 Ken Clarke as Chancellor of the Exchequer toured India in pursuit of this elusive consensus. He talked to the Congress Government at the Centre, to the BJP Government of Rajasthan, to the communist Government of West Bengal, to the Shiv Sena Government of Maharashtra, and to the Janata Dal Government of Karnataka – all the legendary diversity of

India spread out before him. He concluded that there was no ideological consensus. But there was something better – a common economic imperative. It was already in India's interest to pursue the reform programme as vigorously as political constraints would allow. So the opportunity did exist. Could we grasp it?

In January 1992, Douglas Hurd and Madhavsinh Solanki had set up a "structured dialogue" under which we had been consulting each other ever since. On the basis of this dialogue we had developed by the time we left India a partnership in the defence of democracy against terrorist attack with an Extradition Treaty and a Confiscation of Assets agreement to prove it. We had environment and forestry initiatives which enabled British and Indian delegations at international conferences to identify the common interest from amongst divergent trends. We had a Defence Consultative Group, to promote our mutual understanding in defence matters, to encourage interaction between our armed forces and to enhance co-operation on defence procurement, equipment and research – defence with the Indians! The British Council continued its distinguished work on education, culture and development. We had a Development Co-operation Office in Delhi and the largest British aid programme in the world, much more intelligently targeted than before, on education, health, social welfare, justice. We had agreements on research, industrial development and technology transfer. All this in the space of four years.

But the heart of the matter was the Indo-British Partnership Initiative, launched by the two Prime Ministers when John Major was in Delhi as India's Chief Guest on Republic Day in January 1993 – itself an astonishing tribute to a relationship transformed. He came with seventeen tycoons and together they worked out a partnership to enhance trade, investment and technology transfer, to banish mutual misconceptions, and to spread the gospel from the large companies to small and medium enterprises, and from the metropolitan cities to the states and smaller towns. The results were dramatic. Visible trade increased by 70% in three years in both directions to a total of £3 billion in 1996. British investment

381

approvals in India increased five-fold in the first year and doubled again in the second year – ten-fold in two years and perhaps fifteen-fold in three years. New Joint Ventures totalled 172 in year one, 193 in year two and 158 in the first nine months of year three – that is 523 in the first 1,000 days, more than one every other day. In November 1993 Douglas Hurd and Dr Manmohan Singh inaugurated Indo-British Week in Bombay with 300 British businessmen. One billion pounds worth of contracts were signed on board the Royal Yacht *Britannia* in a single day – in the days when we had a Royal Yacht *Britannia*. A year later, Richard Needham, Minister for Trade, brought eighty-five businessmen on *Concorde* – in the days when we had a Concorde. The initiative gave place over time to an enduring Indo-British Partnership which transformed the attitude of each country to the other. Prime Minister Major defined this change in a speech in Bombay in 1996. We had banished the ghosts of an empire that nobody mourned, rejecting both nostalgia and resentment, and building instead a modern partnership between sovereign democracies. We could properly cherish our common heritage but build upon it something new, no longer based upon the shifting sands of sentiment but on the sound rock of mutual interest. We had been paid for five years to make that dream come true. It was a peculiar privilege for us to serve in India at such a time.

HM The Queen was to visit India and Pakistan on the fiftieth anniversary of their independence (and of partition) in 1997. Nick's last despatch forecast that this would be a huge success and recommended that we should set aside our inhibitions and celebrate with India the achievements of her first fifty years. Diplomats should never count chickens. The visit was a disaster. The single-handed achievement of the late Robin Cook who made a speech *in Islamabad* criticising India for her human rights record and her policy in Kashmir just before the Queen came to India. Mr Cook did not understand India. He came to power nursing his idea of "an ethical dimension" to foreign policy. Nick had called on him in London the previous summer and commended to him the success of current British policies towards India. "You don't understand, High Commissioner, there is going to be a change. Relations with India are a matter of human rights." Nick acknowledged that human rights in India were dreadful – but it was one of the areas where progress was being made. "It depends," he concluded, "on what you want to achieve. If you want to strike a posture that is easy, but it will be directly counter-productive, raising Indian hackles and undermining our Indian allies who are beginning to improve matters. If on the other hand you want actually to improve human rights, you start with the economics and come to human rights through the confidence you establish..."

"No, no, no," he said. "I can't play that game. Straightforward stuff, me." Robin Cook's straightforward stuff set back the cause of human rights in India and the Indo-British Partnership by perhaps a decade.

(As we write in 2010, a new British Prime Minister, David Cameron, visits India with a business delegation trying once again to banish the ghosts of the Raj and to build an economic partnership. In an uncanny echo of Robin Cook in Islamabad, he criticises Pakistan from India. We seem to have short memories.)

As we left in 1996 there was a lively debate in India about her role in the world. She had come to accept the dominance in certain fields of the single superpower but did not like it. Her foreign policy was more assertive. She demanded permanent membership of the Security Council. She denounced the unequal Non-Proliferation Treaty. She did not know how to improve her ragged relations with her neighbours, nor how to address the underlying problem that she seemed to them so big. Until the intervention of Mr Cook she continued to court the United Kingdom as a valuable economic partner and the most intelligible member of the European Union. The rivalry between the two Asian giants, India and China, weighs heavily on Indian diplomacy. It should weigh heavily on the rest of us. At the time of writing China is ahead on points. The outcome may depend upon internal developments in China, whether they can indefinitely sustain their superb balancing act of a capitalist economy with a totalitarian polity. The likelihood must be that economics will

383

win in China and that therefore China will become the second superpower. But if politics wins in China we would put our money on Indian freedom.

The indefinite and unconditional extension of the Non-Proliferation Treaty in 1995 was a shock to the Indian establishment. Indian acquiescence in a complete test ban treaty became conditional upon a parallel programme for complete nuclear disarmament. Siren voices in Delhi demanded that India declare herself a nuclear weapon state. Nick tried in his farewell calls to warn against this step. In vain. Prime Minister Narasimha Rao told him that if India were to resist the domestic pressure to go nuclear, she would need clearer evidence that the nuclear weapon states were serious about nuclear disarmament. He asked Mr Major to help. India has of course since gone nuclear and provoked the Government of Pakistan to follow suit. As we feared this has diminished Indian security. With conventional weapons India was the dominant power in the sub-continent, but now that India and Pakistan, as well as China, have nuclear weapons, India has become one player amongst others. South Asia has become less safe and less stable. But it is not plausible for the UK to preach to India on a matter of this kind. It cuts no ice.

The other critical issue was Kashmir. Relations between India and Pakistan were very bad (and have since got worse under the impact of terrorist attacks in India with Pakistani support). In pursuit of Douglas Hurd's three points we sought to encourage bilateral talks, an end to cross-border support for militants and a genuine political process in Kashmir. Some key political prisoners were released in 1994. There was some progress on Human Rights in 1995: a National Human Rights Commission, an agreement with the International Committee of the Red Cross and a new policy of transparency. But attempts to launch a political process were repeatedly frustrated. Narasimha Rao assured us that a full measure of autonomy would be on the table "anything short of *azadi*" (independence). The problem was that no government of India could contemplate the secession of Kashmir on ground of its religion, but no Government of Pakistan could settle for less. Successive

384

governments of India had so trampled on Kashmiri sensitivities that attempts to mount a political process within the Indian union met with violent opposition from militant groups, financed and armed from Pakistan. This is one of those insoluble international issues to which everyone knows the ultimate answer – a more generous dialogue with the Kashmiri leadership, elections conducted under international supervision, and autonomy within the Indian union. It is just a question of how much blood must still be shed before we get there.

Towards the end of our time Nick went to Srinagar, capital of Kashmir, on instructions, to explore the prospects for the implementation of our three points on the future of Kashmir. He called on the Governor and the Chief Minister – and on a series of militant leaders, some of them in secret, all of them viscerally opposed to Indian rule in the valley. They seemed to have no remedy to offer but endless, fruitless terrorism. Nick went to Baramulla, a small town with a great deal of insurgent activity, and made a public speech to 200 citizens, no doubt carefully vetted by Indian Intelligence, shortly after the burning of the Charar-e-Sharief shrine when passions were inflamed. As he left a peasant plucked him by the sleeve. "High Commissioner, we are simple folk. We don't understand about India. We don't understand about Pakistan. But we are ground between the upper and the nether millstones (eloquent gesture confirming the interpreter). Will the High Commissioner please ask them to stop?"

Our last great disappointment in the diplomatic service was failure to secure the release of hostages in terrorist hands in Kashmir. Ten trekkers were kidnapped in July 1995 by a group called Al Faran, created for the purpose by the Pakistan based militant Islamic group Harkat-ul-Ansar. The four women were swiftly released. A Norwegian was brutally beheaded. One of the Americans escaped. The other four were held captive, two British, one German and a second American. The representatives in Delhi of the four governments – Britain, Germany, Norway and the United States – quickly established a consultative relationship with the Indians, at first to restrain Indian enthusiasm for a dramatic rescue which would have precipitated murder, and later to co-ordinate our policies and actions. The safety of the hostages the primary objective; no substantive concessions to terrorists; no ransom, no release of prisoners. That left negotiation and diplomatic pressure. A representative of the British High Commissioner set up a dangerous office in Srinagar and established working relations with the militant groups. Colleagues in Muslim missions around the world made representations. The High Commission staff was augmented by specialist representatives of the army, the intelligence services and the police. The Indians made contact with the kidnappers and talked to them each evening from one Kashmiri mountain top to the next. Their special forces circled. We made contact ourselves and talked to them in Delhi and in Srinagar, encouraging them to see that the courageous, honourable and compassionate thing to do was to let their captives go. The pride of the terrorists would not let them settle for nothing; the Urdu word is *zid*, honour, arrogance, obstinacy. So we tried to devise a way in which they could feel that they had achieved something without substantive concessions. A few days before we left India, Nick was probably the last to speak on the telephone with the terrorist leader. He talked up the international credit which they would earn by generosity, but had to say that the British Government would pay no price. We now believe that they were murdered shortly thereafter. Nick cannot regret the line he took – but he will carry their deaths on his conscience as long as he lives.

The wives and girlfriends of the four hostages stayed in the British High Commission compound for nine months. On the first evening Nick welcomed them, promised that the High Commission would do everything in its power to secure their men's release, but explained the British Government would not pay ransom. To do so would place every British citizen in India at risk. Throughout their long ordeal these four very different women never once asked us to pay. That showed courage of a high order.

Margaret Thatcher, former Prime Minister, and former Speaker, Betty Boothroyd, on separate visits to India both visited them, encouraged them and congratulated them on their fortitude.

For nine months the British High Commission subordinated other policy objectives to this single challenge. It is impossible to guess what this cost the taxpayer. All four tourists had been warned by their respective consulates not to go trekking in Kashmir. The warnings were dismissed as bureaucracy. Why do intelligent adults behave so irresponsibly?

We left India in February 1996. We made a series of farewell tours in India, and valedictory calls on Indian Ministers and diplomatic colleagues. Nick made many speeches. We attended innumerable parties. We were showered with gifts in the authentic Indian manner. Our colleagues in the High Commission gave us an extraordinary send-off in the compound, ending with the senior staff physically towing us off the premises in a carriage normally drawn by horses while we stood with a whip to prevent backsliding. The most memorable of our eleven postings drew to a close.

Chapter 14
Envoi

We were expelled from India for committing the crime of being sixty years old. We did not want to go. India was approaching a critical general election. We knew all the candidates. Our successors knew none of them. It was not their fault; they had not arrived. It was an extraordinary moment to change horses. But there was no appeal against the ultimate tribunal of old age.

Nick knew that protest would be useless. As a junior Private Secretary in the 1960s he had drafted letters rejecting eloquent appeals from distinguished Ambassadors who explained why their continued presence in post was indispensable for the conduct of Anglo-Ruritanian relations. So he telegraphed the Foreign Office, explaining that in these unusual circumstances he proposed to leave India on his sixtieth birthday. The reply was immediate. *No objection. But if you miss the plane we will not pay your fare.* We thought they were joking, but we caught the plane.

Three weeks later Nick was in a crowded underground train in London. A lady got on who was very black, very beautiful, and very pregnant. Without any process of rational thought he got up and offered her his seat. Her reply was eloquent, *No shit, fuck off, you sexy bastard.* Nick collapsed into his seat to the sniggers of other passengers. He reflected first that he must look older than he thought. Then it dawned on him that his country had changed while he had been abroad. He did not understand the culture which he thought he had been representing overseas for thirty-seven years.

Our resentment was quite misplaced. Compulsory retirement at sixty made possible a rewarding post-retirement life. Nick became Chief Executive and then Chairman of Marie Curie Cancer Care, a

Trustee of Sightsavers International and Guide Dogs for the Blind, Joint Chairman of British-Irish Encounter, Governor of the Jawaharlal Nehru Memorial Trust and of his old school, Honorary Fellow of his old College, Vice President of The Leprosy Mission, Patron of the Indian charity Arpana, of the Marden Heritage Centre and the local charities Catriona Hargreaves Charitable Trust and Safe Anaesthesia Worldwide, Churchwarden of St Michael and All Angels Parish Church, Marden. Sue became a Justice of the Peace and a Governor of Bethany School. We have travelled extensively. We enjoyed things which, five or ten years later we would not have attempted.

Compulsory retirement also made possible the writing of this book. Our son gave us a mug with the legend: *The older I get the better I was.* We thought we had better get on with it.

CHAPTER 15
Reflections

It may be appropriate to end this little book with some reflections on the diplomatic life we shared for thirty-seven years. We need to be clear about the role of an Ambassador – and by extension any other diplomat. What is an Ambassador for? And what is he not for?

The role of a diplomat

Sir Henry Woton, seventeenth century Ambassador to the Court of the Prince of Orange, wrote in the visitor's book of his colleague the British Ambassador in Rome, "An Ambassador is an honest man sent to lie abroad for his country". It is of course a three-fold pun. It can mean to lodge abroad, or to tell lies abroad, or to sleep around abroad – not entirely unknown in the annals of diplomacy. For this third meaning he was sacked by his humourless monarch, James I. Too late. He had already bequeathed to his profession that reputation for mendacity from which it has suffered ever since. There are innumerable definitions. The eleven year old daughter of a colleague of ours once told her teacher that a diplomat was a mat, laid down between two countries so that both sides can wipe their feet on it. Sometimes it has felt like that. Most definitions stress the art of elegant untruth. A diplomat "can tell you to go to hell in such a way that you look forward to the journey". He "can do and say the nastiest things in the nicest possible way". Our own favourite is from Lester Pearson, Foreign Minister of Canada in the 1960s: "Diplomacy is letting someone else have my way".

Our experience, however, is that the essence of diplomacy is the opposite of its popular image. An Ambassador may on occasion have to be economical with the truth. But fundamentally he must "tell it like it is". He must never mislead governments into thinking that things are better than they are. When he is given an unwelcome

390

message, he must deliver it straight, without fear or gloss (Chapter 11). Obvious illustrations from our time include the Falklands. General Galtieri would never have invaded the islands if he had had the slightest idea that in response Margaret Thatcher would mobilise the largest armada of modern times to throw him out. And Iraq (first time round – Desert Storm). Saddam Hussein would never have invaded Kuwait if the United States Ambassador in Baghdad on the eve of the war had managed fully to convey her instructions and told him bluntly what would be the consequences of invasion. When diplomacy fails war tends to follow.

The first function of an Ambassador is the one that everyone knows – representational. The British Ambassador represents Her Majesty the Queen, Her Majesty's Government and the United Kingdom in, say, Ruritania. This is a public role – state occasions, social functions, speeches. Hence the image of the handsome man, greying at the temples, sipping his Martini as the sun sets behind the palm tree, exchanging platitudes or secrets with the wife of the President. Princess Alexandra returning from tea with the President of Burma in 1961, "My God, what one does eat for Queen and country!" The Ambassador must be omnivorous – sea slugs in China, sheep's testicles in Algeria, yak's butter tea in Ladakh. He must enjoy his food and drink and be seen to appreciate the exciting things that are set before him. He must be a bit of a glutton, perhaps even a bit of a soak.

Secondly, he must speak up for Britain, in the traditional sense of the herald. The suspicion that diplomats go native is true in one sense, but utterly false in the sense in which it is intended. It is his core function to be British, even to the point of caricature. He must of course do as he is told by the British Government, even when he disagrees with it. He must convey messages from British Ministers to their Ruritanian colleagues. He must act on instructions, sometimes anticipate, even invent, instructions; he must be faithful to the *mind* of his Ministers, not only what they say but what they *mean*. To this end he meets Ruritanian Ministers, officials, opposition leaders, tycoons, trades unionists, journalists, academics, commending

391

everywhere the notion that the British Government is right on all issues, that British society is perfect in all respects, that British industry is the most valued commercial partner – in short, that Britain deserves gold when in his heart he knows that she deserves only silver. He will not always succeed. But the more he is known and trusted in Ruritania, the nearer he will come to success.

Thirdly, he must interpret Ruritania to Britain. He must be a spy. He must report the views of the government of the day, but also other currents of opinion, including the military. He must understand the culture. He must assess, explain, project, prophesy. If he is doing his job the British Government will never be taken by surprise, and British decisions about Ruritania will be taken on the basis of accurate and not inaccurate information.

Then and now
These three roles are enduring. But the world in which Ambassadors work has changed dramatically in our time and since. When we began in the aftermath of Empire the baddies in the world were the Brits, and our most trenchant critics were the Americans – they brought the British to their knees and effectively expelled Anthony Eden from Downing Street in 1956 because of Suez. We became perforce expert in post-colonial trauma; in Burma and Algeria, at the UN, in Zimbabwe, Ireland and India. Now the baddies are the ugly Americans because of their power and wealth, sometimes also because of their arrogance and ignorance. The image is somewhat improved by President Obama. But the demonisation of the USA has gone too far. We should not forget how badly we behaved when we were top nation, nor the natural insularity of a continent – one third of Americans have never seen the sea, the impact on the American psyche of 9/11, the historical symbolism of the Statue of Liberty, the traditional welcome to all comers, the generosity, hospitality and freedom of American culture. And we should not forget either where British interests lie. Whatever view you take of Afghanistan and Iraq, British Prime Ministers are right to put at the top of their foreign policy agenda the need to retain the confidence and friendship of the most powerful nation on earth. And

this is fully compatible with the vigorous defence of distinctive British interests and with active participation in the European Union.

Secondly, the demonisation of Islam is also a dangerous aberration. There are problems – Afghanistan, Iraq, Taliban, Al Qaeda, Axis of Evil. But the enemy is not religion, it is fanaticism, of which alas, Christians and Hindus, Jews and even Buddhists are also capable. Our Christian culture, multi-cultural society and secular liberties are precious. They need to be cherished, not discarded, in the face of terrorist attack. We declare ourselves to be fanatical anti-fanatics.

Thirdly, no purpose is served by apologising for the past, for slavery, for empire, for war. We may wish that things had been otherwise. We may understand, sympathise, regret. But the pre-emptive cringe is neither a graceful nor a useful posture. The Irish complain about Oliver Cromwell, the Indians about partition, the Nagas about the Indians – they are tilting at windmills that have long since vanished. The apportionment of blame is a function for historians. The beginning of wisdom is to ask the question, how did we get into this mess? But the statesman and the diplomat will also ask how do we get out of it? Where do we go from here? How can we build a better world starting where we are?

A peaceful world is possible
For our part, we believe that a more peaceful world is possible. There is no clash of interests – over water, territory, resources, hegemony – that is not rationally capable of peaceful and humane solution. But it is difficult for all of us consistently to behave rationally. Dictators need diplomatic "victories" to keep their people quiet. Democrats are vulnerable to populist pressures. Professionals are often busy with detail and may miss the wood for the trees. Peace, though logically possible, often seems out of reach. The spectre of disaster stalks the world and the price of peace really is eternal vigilance. We have lived on the edge of disaster in Burma, in Zimbabwe, in Ireland, in Kashmir. There are also Sudan, Korea, Cyprus and Iran. Most dangerous of all is the Middle East because of

393

oil, and because it is composed of two colossal historic injustices: the injustice done to the Jews, first by the Romans and then by generations of Europeans, culminating in the horrors of the Nazi gas chambers, and the injustice done to the Palestinians, first by the Balfour Declaration and then by Israel and the indifference of the world. There is no easy way. But progress can be made. Professional diplomats cannot deliver their domestic public opinion to support painful compromise. That is the job of politicians. But professionals can nudge the process forward – as in our time in Rhodesia, in Northern Ireland, in the Indo-British Partnership Initiative. We outlined in Chapter 12 the shape of a possible settlement in Kashmir. In the same way everyone knows the shape of an eventual settlement in the Middle East. And in Ireland it is happening before our eyes. No issue is beyond the imagination of man to resolve.

In this increasingly complex world, Ambassadors are more and not less necessary. Modern technology indeed makes it possible and necessary for those who carry responsibility for the peace of the world to be in direct communication with each other. But there are nearly 200 sovereign states and dozens of dangerous issues on the boil at any one time, and others which may not be dangerous may be seen to injure the national interest and rightly occupy the attention of Ministers. It is fanciful to suppose that Ministers can do it all by telephone or by flying visits. Livingstone Merchant put it well in 1964, "The priceless asset of the diplomat is that he is *there.*" There is no substitute for the patient cultivation of friendship, access, trust over years, against the day when we may need to ask a favour, strike a bargain or explain a painful truth. Nor can even the closest of neighbours do without embassies amongst themselves. The Scandinavian countries tried it, and after three years their embassies were back. The Australians tried to replace their professional diplomats with "citizens". It fell apart under the impact of the earthquake in Peking.

But Ambassadors need to understand that they are of no importance in themselves. Diplomacy is the most self-important profession in the world. The French can say it better than we can, *folie de grandeur; deformation professionelle.* Ambassadors are of value *only* if they speak for governments, facilitate communication between them, and tender confidential advice in the knowledge that it will remain confidential. The Governments of India and Ireland were not interested in the views of Nick Fenn, only in the views of HMG.

Much has been written about the qualities necessary for successful diplomacy. We may perhaps ignore the view of Hume Wrong, "a good head for liquor and an infinite capacity for producing polite guff on any subject at a moment's notice." Baron Silverdruys is often quoted, "sharp discernment, sound judgement, studied opinion, firm convictions and a humble bearing." We have commented on the need for humility. Our list would be rather different: first, integrity – an Ambassador must be trusted by both sides; second, loyalty – both sides must know whom he serves; third, imagination – to see the fleeting opportunity as it passes by; fourth, clarity of thought and expression, to assess developments and convince his audience; fifth, courage – courage to confront powerful Ministers and not to flinch in the face of physical danger (Chapter 11). Diplomacy is an increasingly dangerous business and the Ambassador must not be deflected by fear. Finally, a capacity for hard work and long hours, sometimes at the expense of family and other loyalties.

The Ambassador is, first and always, a servant.

Open government is bad government

Diplomacy demands discretion. International relations cannot flourish unless public agreements can be privately arrived at. Premature publicity arouses populist pressures which destroy the possibility of progress. This flies in the face of current fashion for open government. But confidentiality is indispensable to good governance, and also to democracy. So far from being a bastion of our liberties, the Freedom of Information Act was a disaster for democracy.

Time was when policy was declared in Parliament by elected Ministers and scrutinised by elected Parliamentarians – not aired in advance on the *Today* programme. The advice tendered by unelected officials was not a legitimate matter for enquiry. Open that advice to public scrutiny and you turn first-class public servants into second-class politicians. We are not good at it. The danger is obvious, officials no longer tender advice exclusively in the public interest, they shade the advice against the possibility of leak or publication. And this corrodes democracy. Advice can be exploited for electoral advantage. Intelligence reports can be published to influence public opinion in the approach to a war. A Prime Minister can ask about a candidate for senior office – "Is he one of us?" All these in different ways undermine the integrity of the public service and diminish the trust on which our system rests.

In the 1980s a middle ranking official in the Ministry of Defence made himself briefly the darling of the chattering classes by shopping his Minister and sending to *The Guardian* a secret memorandum on the sinking of the *Belgrano* in the Falklands War. Whistle-blowing or disloyalty? Who elected Clive Ponting? By what right did he overrule his elected Minister? Upon what democratic principle can this be justified?

We have reported (Chapter 2) the confidential memorandum about the dictator of Burma that Nick wrote for his Ambassador under the protection of the fifty year rule. Then the rule was changed to thirty years so that things written by public servants could be published while they were still in service. Qualitative change. That memorandum became legally accessible to public scrutiny while Nick was still in service. If it had been published while he was Ambassador in Rangoon and while Ne Win was still in power, he would have been rendered useless to his government. (By the grace of God we had left Burma before the thirty years expired.) There is no great public interest that would be affected by withholding such material. Why make it public? Simply silly. Officials must be allowed to tender dispassionate advice without fear of publication.

The alternative is to drive controversial discussion off the public record and behind the arras – and that is not sensible either.

There are two corollaries of this view. First, retired Ambassadors should shut up. The mobilisation of former Excellencies in public to support or oppose current issues does not improve the policies at which it is directed. Its effect is to damage the confidence of current Ministers in their successors. By the same token, diplomatic memoirs are often superficial or disloyal. That is why this book has been so long in gestation, and why we have tried so hard to convey flavour without betraying confidence.

Secondly, democratically elected governments must tell their people the truth. We no longer believe our governments. It can be done. In our own small way we have done it (Chapters 5 and 9). In six years as a government press officer Nick never told a lie. He rarely told the whole truth either. But journalists understand reticence in the national interest, or to protect the lives of agents or the grief of widows. We have treasured a T-shirt presented to Nick by the press corps after the Zimbabwe settlement. It says on one side "Of course I know" and on the other "but I'm not telling". Public reticence is a dying art – and democracy is the poorer for it.

Diplomatic families
One of the greatest attractions of the diplomatic service – and one of its most intractable problems – is the nomadic lifestyle and its impact upon families. We have been fortunate. As a Research Assistant at Birkbeck College Susan was earning twice Nick's Foreign Office salary when we were posted to Mandalay in 1960. It did not occur to either of us that she should not give up a fascinating research project which subsequently won its leader the Nobel Prize in order to come with him (Chapter 1). Both of us were eager for the excitement and challenge of strange lives in foreign cultures. Nick has kept Sue briefed on his job – if only so that she could exploit opportunities at receptions and with her neighbours at diplomatic dinners. Sue has shared family and domestic concerns as a matter of course. We have travelled together in the countries of our assignment

– two heads are always better then one. Sue has made a point of learning the language wherever we went, and she was the first wife of a British Ambassador in Ireland ever to be interviewed on Irish television in the Irish language. For us it has been a partnership from beginning to end. We have done it together. Our different perceptions have enriched us both. They have enriched this book.

Some colleagues have been less fortunate. And it has become more difficult. Our culture has changed. Both partners in a marriage now expect to work. But sometimes the chosen career of the diplomatic spouse cannot easily be pursued in the country where the diplomat is posted. It is no longer obvious that a spouse will "pay, pack and follow". Our advice would be to give it a whirl, try the diplomatic life overseas to find out whether it can work for you. If not, consider the priorities. If necessary, leave the service. Marriage is more important than a job, however fascinating.

The Office has made great efforts to respond to the changing culture and to make things easier for wives, for female diplomats, and for married couples both of whom are diplomats. Time out to raise families, joint postings and job sharing are all now part of the system. We take comfort from the recent appointment of an Ambassador to Country X, and the simultaneous appointment of his wife as Ambassador in the adjacent Country Y, resident with her husband in Country X. There have been appointments of husband and wife as joint Ambassadors holding office by rotation. The issues can be made less angular by imagination and care, but they cannot be eliminated. They spring not from diplomacy but from the nomadic nature of the profession and the requirement that a member of the service can at least in principle be required to serve anywhere on earth at short notice, without reference to school terms or the impact on a partner's work.

An Ambassador and his wife are inescapably "celebrities" in the country where they work. It goes with the job. In post we discovered to our dismay that the same is true of their children. The whole family is in the spotlight. If diplomatic children behave badly in

398

public this will reflect badly on the reputation of "British children" everywhere, rather as dull food at diplomatic residences will convey the impression that "British food" is boring. Unfair, but that is the way it is. We hope we did not do too badly, but it was sometimes a strain. Charlie declared early on that he could never be a diplomat because you have to invite into your home not only strangers but people you dislike. (We made a note to be more careful in future about how we talked about our guests!)

The education of children is another thorny issue. It is relatively easy while they are small, but as soon as they get to school age a decision is required on whether to keep the family together or to send them to boarding school in England. Some parents cannot bear to be parted from their children for a whole term at a time; others value the international experience, cosmopolitan culture and linguistic skills which go with education in post, and accept that this imposes on their offspring new friends and new teachers, a different education system in a different language every three or four years. An example is recorded in Chapter 7. For our part we wanted our children to have a coherent education in whatever language or culture – and in practice that meant boarding school in England. We were lucky. They thrived. And the joyful reunions on the tarmac of strange airfields at the end of every term made up for the awfulness of parting at the end of every holiday. Separation drove the family closer together. Not all diplomatic families had that fortunate experience.

A parallel issue arises with elderly parents. In Peking, when Mao had died and the Embassy was working flat out, Nick did not know for three weeks that his father had suddenly gone blind (Chapter 7). His mother thought he did not care.

British diplomats and their families get more support from their government than their colleagues in most comparable Foreign Services. On first arrival in post for example, the family will be met at the airport, escorted to their accommodation which will have been cleaned from top to bottom, with overnight supplies in the fridge and flowers on the table. Someone will call in the morning to show them the way to the embassy, the local sights, the shops, the schools, the medical and dental facilities and so on. They will be invited out to lunch and entertained generously in the early weeks until they have found their feet. A French colleague will take a taxi from the airport to his hotel and then start looking for a flat.

The Service

The Service we joined in 1959 may have been a mite stuffy, overdressed and punctilious. It had time for scholarship and eccentricity. It was also dedicated, confident and loyal. The service we left in 1996 was still dedicated and loyal, but it was overstretched, under-resourced and uncertain. We were not sure that Ministers deserved the loyalty they still enjoyed. We saw the rot set in in the 1960s. Harold Wilson's Government did not trust the civil service after thirteen years of Conservative rule. They sought to cut it down to size. Successive administrations have continued the process, partly to contain expenditure and partly because of the politics of envy. In the early 1970s, the Central Policy Review staff even recommended that we should choose to have a second-rate diplomatic service appropriate to a second-class power. Mercifully, the government of the day rejected this recommendation on the ground that a second-class power had more need of its diplomats, not less.

At the time of writing, when we are trying to climb out of the hole left by recession, this will sound like special pleading for the Foreign Office. It is not so intended. Of course no department can be immune from national austerity. But we make four points:

- In the context of government expenditure as whole, the diplomatic service costs peanuts.
- HM Treasury decrees that cuts must be made in sterling. Much of FCO expenditure is incurred in foreign currency. When the pound depreciates, the impact of the cuts is amplified.
- No cuts should take effect unless Ministers have approved not just the cuts but their consequences. It is silly to close embassies

(and disproportionately expensive to reopen them) until Ministers have decided that this is the appropriate outcome of their decisions.

• It is for Ministers to determine the kind of public service they think the British people need. But further substantive cuts require commensurate cuts in functions. Ministers must stand up in the House and say that the answer to that question is that I do not know and I do not propose to find out.

If we do not want the second-rate service envisaged by the CPRS, we hope that we shall defend the first-class one we have while we still have it.

Like other branches of government, the diplomatic service is subject to an endless series of reviews. As we left India, we were caught between the rival jurisdictions of the Under Secretary's Command, the Top Management Round and the Inspectorate. There was a Fundamental Expenditure Review, a Senior Management Review, A Private Finance Initiative, Resource Accounting, a Review of Allowances, the Harris Scrutiny, the Future of the Estate and much else besides. No doubt each of these will have served some purpose useful in some part of the public service. But we were in danger of spending so much time examining how we do things that we had no time left to do them.

For us the ultimate abomination was the drive to privatise the civil service, encouraging bright youngsters to opt out in mid-career and opt in again, having learned the magic of the City. The avowed purpose was to make the Service more like a business, and therefore it was assumed more efficient. But it is not a business, it is a Service. Following city practice, we are now paying unnecessary bonuses to competent staff instead of paying them properly in the first place. We seem to be deliberately destroying the public service, with its own ethos and career structure, its own disciplines and rewards. One day we shall wake up and find that it has gone. And it will take a couple of generations to recreate it.

Diplomacy is fun

401

The purpose of this book as set out in the Introduction is to portray what fun diplomacy is. Our last reflection is that it is indeed fun. Few other professions would have enabled us to travel the world in the service of our country, not just to visit but to live in foreign cultures, to begin to understand how people think if they think in Burmese or Irish or Hindi. And each new posting was not only a new country but also a new job, promoting British interests, supporting British commerce, protecting British citizens, projecting British ideas. Few professions would have enabled us to meet every day interesting and sometimes powerful people, to rub shoulders with royalty and political leaders, with tycoons and academics, with the unsung heroes who devote their lives to the service of suffering humanity around the world, and with ordinary folk in their natural habitat, pursuing their ordinary lives in ways which to us are exotic. Yes, diplomacy is fun.

But it is a little more than that. Diplomats collectively – the *diplomatic corps* – are potentially an instrument for peace. They know each other well. They trust each other – or they know better than to trust each other. They understand the other fellow's point of view – that besetting sin of the Foreign Office for which the Baroness Thatcher never forgave us. One of the delights of the profession is the occasional opportunity to take informal soundings, to float implausible notions, to seek new ways to circumnavigate a roadblock. And we do this with professional colleagues in the service of other governments.

Our elder son, aged five (now himself a senior diplomat), was playing in the back garden with his friends, watched by his mother from the kitchen window (Chapter 3). The conversation turned to their daddy's occupation. Julian's daddy made houses. Johnnie's daddy made jam. What did Robin's daddy make? Long pause. Then Rob threw back his fair hair in a gesture of defiance and declared, "My daddy makes peace." We'll buy that.

27540117R00223

Printed in Great Britain
by Amazon